UNRAVELLING SOCIAL POLICY

Unravelling Social Policy

Theory, Analysis, and Political Action Towards Social Equality

Fifth Edition, Revised and Enlarged
DAVID G. GIL

SCHENKMAN BOOKS, INC.
Rochester, Vermont

Copyright © 1973, 1976, 1981, 1990, 1992

SCHENKMAN BOOKS, INC.
118 Main Street
Rochester, Vermont 05767

Printed in the United States of America

Library of Congress Cataloging in Publication Data

Gil, David G.
   Unravelling social policy: theory, analysis, and political action
   towards social equality / David G. Gil.—5th ed., rev. and enl.
   p. cm.
   Includes bibliographical references.

   1. United States—Social policy. 2. Social policy. I. Title.
   HN65G515 1992
   361.6" 1" 0973--dc20 91-33357 CIP

ISBN 0-87047-056-6
ISBN 0-87047-057-4 (pbk.)

To Eva,
Gideon and Lisa,
Daniel, Deborah, and Michael

Contents

**TECHNICAL APPENDIX: AN ILLUSTRATION OF
SOCIAL POLICY ANALYSIS AND DEVELOPMENT**

**LEGAL APPENDIX: THE UNREMUNERATED
WORK ACT OF 1991 (H.R. 3625)**   405

LIST OF CHARTS AND TABLES

Foreword

This fifth edition of David Gil's widely used book *Unravelling Social Policy* brings the book up to date and adds significant new comment in several important matters. It carries on the important contributions of the author in four earlier editions. There are two new essays and some material has been revised.

Of particular interest to scholars and practitioners in the social policy arenas should be Gil's linkage of social policy with human biology and the history of mankind. This analysis provides a framework and background of social policy seldom mentioned in the numerous books on social policy which have appeared in the last two decades.

This new addition is timely. The decade of the 1990s will witness increasing activity in the policy-making arenas (legislative, executive, and judicial) as we begin to tackle the myriad of problems which remain unsolved—child abuse, the homeless, family disorganization, crime and juvenile delinquency, drug abuse, housing shortages for poor and low income families, millions still living in poverty, the fragmented health and medical system with millions denied access to medical care—these are merely indicative of the "unfinished business" of our society.

As we seek solutions to our many serious problems, our leaders and those involved in establishing social policies for our society need to understand better the forces and processes which establish or change social policies, to predict the consequences of social policies, and to establish goals for the "good society" toward which social policies should lead us.

In spite of the worldwide interest in this issue, there has been little systematic analysis of social policy or even agreement as to its definition. In this volume David Gil attempts such analysis and definition. He develops a model against which a specific social policy might be analyzed and assessed.

Readers of this book may disagree with many of Gil's observations and comments and even with his basic goals centering around his concept of equality and egalitarianism. But his simple formulation of a model and a methodology of analysis of social policies is a significant step forward in the attempts to develop a more scientific approach to the study of social policy.

Social policies, which determine a country's programs and services in such matters as income distribution, employment, education, health services, housing, and levels of living (to mention only a few) are too important in the lives of all people to be left to chance or as a response to individual or group interests without objective analysis. What are the basic goals of our society, or rather, what are the goals which we should strive for in our society? How does any specific policy relate to these goals? These are fundamental questions which do not receive enough attention in today's political arenas.

As a former official in the Federal Government, I have seen major social programs established on the basis of the conviction of a single important official or a single case brought to the attention of a member of Congress, or on the basis of pressure from a small special interest group, without any in-depth analyses or consideration of ultimate consequences. As a result, the "unintended consequences" of such action make lively case histories for academic studies.

A semantic or definitional stumbling block in analyzing social policy has been the fact that many students of social policy relate the very term to a "desirable" or "good" goal or activity. This distorts attempts at objective analyses. Totalitarian governments may have well-established and accepted social policies which would not be considered "desirable" or "good" in a democratic society. The model proposed herein has a neutral quality, making it useful for analyses of any social policy. Likewise, it is useful whether considering "holistic" or overall social policies or whether it is used to analyze "piecemeal engineering" proposals—the latter being the more likely and numerous in today's complicated society.

Dr. Gil's model and methodology is an attempt at some rational and systematic appraisal of social policies. It will undoubtedly be improved upon in the years to come. Its contribution lies in its innovative proposals upon which a more sophisticated scientific analysis of social policy can be built. It is, therefore, an important and significant step forward in our efforts to develop more effective ways of assessing and predicting the results of proposals in the social policy arena.

Charles I. Schottland

Charles I. Schottland, former Professor of Law and Social Welfare and former President, Brandeis University; former United States Commissioner of Social Security; President of the National Senior Citizens Law Center

Preface to the Fifth Edition

Publication of a fifth edition of *Unravelling Social Policy* is a source of mixed feelings: satisfaction that interest in this work has not abated almost two decades after its initial publication, and regrets at its shortcomings.

Authors are not necessarily done with a work when they submit it for publication. This was certainly so with this book, each edition of which reflected further stages of my studies of social policies and social change. My understanding of these issues has deepened with time through study of emerging social conditions, writing, teaching, and living; and new insights had to be integrated into theoretical formulations and concrete illustrations.

Part One reflects my current thinking on a theory of social policy and on a method for analyzing and developing policies: I trace the sources of social policies to biological evolution, intrinsic and perceived human needs and interests, and selected aspects of the human condition in nature. I also clarify the dynamics of social values and consciousness in relation to social policies and social change. The framework for analysis and development of social policies has been revised to correspond to these theoretical insights. A detailed illustration of policy analysis and development is included in this edition as a methodological Technical Appendix, rather than as part of the text.

A Legal Appendix contains a Bill filed in 1991 in the U.S. House of Representatives by Congresswoman Barbara-Rose Collins of Michigan, *The Unremunerated Work Act of 1991 (H.R. 3625)*. If enacted, this legislation would implement aspects of the Parents' Wages Policy discussed in this book since its first edition in 1973, and analyzed in the First Appendix of this edition.

Part Two, Political Action Toward Social Equality, has not been changed in substance since the first edition, but certain changes in language seemed necessary. Language changes were also made throughout the work, for one cannot write on social equality and human liberation in language shaped by a history of domination.

xiii

Part Three contains a set of essays, written since the original publication of this work, to demonstrate the application of my theoretical and value perspectives to important policy issues. The present edition includes two new essays. The final essay traces links between my experiences in Europe prior to and during World War II, and my subsequent search for insights into the roots and dynamics of violence, injustice and war.

Acknowledgments

Research for this book was conducted within the Social Policy Study Program at the Florence Heller Graduate School for Advanced Studies in Social Welfare, Brandeis University. The Social Policy Study Program is supported by the Office of Child Development of the U.S. Department of Health, Education, and Welfare under Research Grant No. PR-288-1. The generous assistance of the Office of Child Development is gratefully acknowledged herewith.

I wish to thank Dr. Charles P. Gershenson, Director of Research of the Office of Child Development, for his encouragement throughout the stages of this study; Ms. Ann Orlov, Editor for the Behavioral Sciences at Harvard University Press, for suggesting the writing of this book; Charles I. Schottland, President of Brandeis University, and my colleagues at the Heller School, especially Professors Roland Warren, Pamela Roby, Carol Brown, Michael Brower, Barry Friedman, and Leonard Hausman, whose critical comments and counsel helped clarify my thinking; Professor Richard M. Titmuss of the London School of Economics, Professor Peter Townsend of the University of Essex, and Dean Alvin L. Schorr of New York University, whose pioneering studies of social policies inspired my own explorations in this field. I also owe special thanks to my research associates, Robert Colbourne and Uri Davis, and to these students in my Seminar at the Heller School: Sheldon Gelman, Brin Hawkins, Janet Poppendieck, Bruce Lagay, Jesse McClure, Ann McInvale, Malcolm Morrison, and Arthur Naparstek. Their challenging questions and comments contributed immensely to the development of my own thinking on matters of social policy.

Thanks are also due to Mrs. Virginia Normann for her patience, understanding and skill in preparing the manuscript, and to my wife, Eva, for her patience and understanding in listening to, commenting on and improving my work.

D.G.G .
1971

Students, colleagues, and friends who contributed to my studies of social policies and social change since the publication of the first edition in 1973 are too numerous to be acknowledged by name and I thank them anonymously. I can, however, thank Eva, my wife and intellectual partner for constructive critique of my evolving ideas and writings. And I want to express special thanks to Sandra Henao for thoughtful assistance in preparing the manuscript of the revised edition, to Susan Kashanski for preparing the index, to Robin Dutcher-Bayer for editing it skillfully, and to Kathryn Miles for seeing it through production.

D.G.G.
1992

Introduction

Social policy issues are constant items on the public agenda of the United States on local, state, and national levels. In spite of this widespread public concern with matters of social policy, however, our society lacks a comprehensive and internally consistent system of social policies, one that would be conducive to the realization of the inherent human potential of all its members. The United States is not at all unique in this respect. Social policy questions are, and have been, objects of public concern in every known human society throughout evolution, but comprehensive, and truly satisfactory solutions to these questions have usually eluded people's grasp.

One frequently identified obstacle to the development of a comprehensive and consistent social policy system in this and other countries is the fragmented, parochial, and incremental approach pursued by various self-serving groups in the "social marketplace" in efforts to change conditions which they consider undesirable in terms of their perceived interests. Some social scientists suggest that this tendency to fragmentation, parochialism, and incrementalism in the development of social policies is an intrinsic aspect of democracy in a complex and pluralistic society, and that it therefore could not be eliminated entirely, although its scope could be reduced. Other scholars reject such a narrow conception of democracy and of human potential.

A second, perhaps more fundamental, obstacle to the development of a coherent social policy system is hardly ever mentioned. This obstacle is the curious lack of clarity and agreement as to what social policy actually is, and what its domains and functions are within society. Correlatively, there is also insufficient comprehension of the nature of the processes through which social policy systems operate, of interactions among these processes, and of their consequences for the quality and circumstances of life in society, and for human relations and experience.

This book attempts to tackle both these obstacles on theoretical, methodological, philosophical, and political levels. As for the latter obstacle, which is essentially on the level of theory and method, this study develops and illustrates the use of a conceptual model of social policies and a framework for systematic analysis and development of such policies. Concerning the former obstacle, which is philosophical and political in nature, the study explores implications of the proposed conceptual model of social policies for an alternative approach to political action aimed at structural social change toward an egalitarian, humanistic social order.

The conceptual model of social policies and the analytic framework constitute a theoretical base and a method, respectively, for facilitating insights into the dynamics and consequences of past, extant, and newly generated social policies, and of the political processes within which these policies evolve. The model and framework should, therefore, enable governmental and other formal and informal societal units to engage in analysis and development of social policies in a more effective manner than is possible at present, and to design more comprehensive and internally less inconsistent systems of social policies.

Social policy analysis is, of course, carried on constantly by many individuals and groups, within and outside governmental agencies. However, those who engage currently in such analyses lack a systematic and comprehensive approach which is widely accepted for the purpose. Existing approaches to social policy analysis differ along several dimensions. First, they differ in the definition of the concept "social policy." Many analysts proceed in their work without clarifying the meaning of this concept, while others define it in vague terms. Analytic approaches differ in the nature and scope of the questions and foci examined in the analysis of specific social policies and their consequences, and also in the skills, scholarly competence, and resources of the analysts themselves. Finally, analysts differ in overt and covert value premises. Different combinations along these dimensions yield a large number of analytic approaches and it is therefore not surprising that social policy analyses, and predictions derived from such analyses, tend to vary widely. In view of this current state of the "art" of social policy analysis, it seems highly desirable to develop a more systematic approach which should lead to similar factual conclusions when employed by different analysts in the analysis of the same policy, irrespective of their individual value orientations.

It should be emphasized, however, right at the outset, that the approach to social policy analysis and development presented in this book is not meant to produce "automated solutions" to policy issues faced by decision-makers in and outside the government, or to relieve them of the responsibility to weigh against value premises or political considerations factual conclusions reached by means of the proposed approach. Social policy analysis is not expected to provide definite answers to moral and value dilemmas. An effective analytic approach should, however, enable analysts to identify aspects of social policy issues which require moral and value choices, and to distinguish these from other aspects which can be decided on the basis of factual information.

Designing new and more adequate social policies and gaining insights into their dynamics and consequences with the aid of the conceptual model and the analytic framework constitute, however, only first, albeit essential, steps toward comprehensive, internally consistent, and humanly satisfying systems of social policies. Understanding must be followed by consistent political action if significant social changes suggested by systematic policy analysis are ever to become social realities. Policy analysis and development lead thus, willy-nilly, to questions concerning strategies of political action for social change. To explore these crucial questions the focus of the book shifts in Part Two from theoretical and methodological considerations of the conceptual model and the analytic framework, to a philosophical inquiry into implications of that model for political action toward structural social change. This inquiry is a logical necessity if one is interested not merely in gaining knowledge about the dynamics and consequences of various social policies, but in applying this knowledge to the active promotion of changes in the extant social policy system. Clearly, also, a valid conceptual model of social policies constitutes an excellent source for such an inquiry into strategies for political action, since the model's function is to unravel the "mystery" of social policies by identifying their processes, and the forces and conditions which can bring about variations in the established patterns of these processes.

More specifically, the book's outline is as follows. Part One presents a theory and method for analysis and development of social policies. The first chapter surveys prevailing thinking about social policy among leading writers on this subject. The second chapter articulates a theory and conceptual model of social policies. In the third chapter a framework for systematic policy analysis and development is derived from the conceptual model and the use of this framework is explicated.

In Part Two, conclusions are drawn from the theoretical insights implicit in the conceptual model of social policies for political action toward an egalitarian, humanistic social order. Part Three contains several essays on social policy issues which incorporate the theoretical perspectives developed in the book. The Technical Appendix is concerned with the application of the proposed theory and method. This section illustrates the use of the framework in the analysis of one specific policy proposal, "Universal Mothers' Wages and Children's Allowances," and in the development of two alternative social policies, "Selective Mothers' Wages and Children's Allowances," and "Parent's Wages."

A second appendix presents a Bill, filed in the U.S. Congress in 1991, The Unremunerated Work Act of 1991 (H.R. 3625). If and when enacted, this legislation would implement an aspect of the Parents' Wages policy discussed in this book in 1973. It would mandate inclusion in the GNP of the estimated aggregate of unremunerated work performed by women and men in our society. Such acknowledgement in the GNP is but one step toward eventually compensating individuals who perform such unremunerated work.

Social scientists are not, nor should they attempt to be, without value commitments of their own. Try as they may to keep personal values separate from scholarly work, they are not likely to succeed in these efforts. It seems, therefore, important for social scientists to clearly state their individual value orientations in areas relevant to the scholarly pursuit at hand.

I am firmly committed to social policies which promote the fundamental values enunciated in 1776 in the Declaration of Independence of the United States of America, namely, " ... that all men are created equal, that they are endowed by their Creator with certain unalienable Rights, that among these are Life, Liberty and the pursuit of Happiness..." These values, it would seem, can be realized for all members of a society only when its social policies equalize their rights and opportunities. Equality of rights and opportunities in this context is not to be understood in a narrow, mechanical-quantitative sense, but in accordance with the profound and eloquent exposition by the British philosopher and social scientist R. H. Tawney in his treatise, *Equality*,[1] and George Bernard Shaw's recently discovered lost essays, *The Road to Equality*.[2] Briefly, social equality is one feasible organizing principle for shaping the quality of life and the circumstances of living of individuals and groups in society, as well as for structuring all human relations. The principle of social equality derives from a central value premise according to which every individual and every social group are of equal intrinsic worth and, hence, are entitled to equal civil, political, social, and economic liberties, rights, and treatment, as well as subject to equal constraints. Implicit in this central value premise is the notion that all individuals should have the right to freely actualize their inherent human potential; to lead as fulfilling a life as possible within the reality of, and in harmony with, the natural environment; and to be free of exploitation, alienation, and oppression, subject only to the general limitation that any individual's and group's rights to freedom and self-actualization must never interfere with the identical rights of all other individuals and groups.

Social equality as conceived here seems predicated upon a social order involving rationally planned and appropriately balanced, collective development, utilization, and preservation of all natural resources; equal access (for all individuals and groups) to work and social roles within the totality of tasks to be performed by society; and equal distribution of rights to available material and symbolic, life-sustaining and life-enhancing goods and services. It should be reemphasized, though, that social equality aims at actualization of individual differences in innate potentialities, not at monotonous uniformity. This is not meant to be realized by dividing all available resources into identical parts for distribution to every member of society, but rather through distributive and allocative systems based on thoughtful and flexible consideration of individual differences and needs. Obviously then, a social order based on egalitarian value premises will differ radically from one based on the alternative principle of "social inequality." In the latter model, individuals and groups *are thought* to differ in their intrinsic worth and, hence, to be entitled to use as much of the available goods and services as they can gain control over through competition with, and exploitation of, other individuals and groups, and through exploitation of the natural environment.

The value commitments sketched above are likely to be sensed throughout this book, especially in the selection and discussion of substantive illustrations such as the Mothers' Wages policy, and in the exploration of implications of the conceptual model of social policies for political action. However, the proposed conceptual model and the framework for social policy analysis can be utilized by scholars and analysts irrespective of their personal value premises. This is as it should be: analytic tools should conform to criteria of scientific objectivity, but the analysts should maintain their human and social characteristics and responsibilities.

NOTES

1. R.H. Tawney, *Equality*(London: George Allen and Unwin Ltd., 1964). With a new introduction by Richard M. Titmuss—First   published in 1931.

2. Bernard Shaw, *The Road to Equality: Ten Unpublished Lectures and Essays*, 1884-1918 (Boston: Beacon Press, 1971)

Theory and Method of
Social Policy Analysis and Development

1
Emerging Views of Social Policy

Students who examine the literature on social policy in order to discern the meaning of this widely used concept soon realize that it lacks a commonly accepted definition. Social scientists and policy analysts differ in their views concerning the domains of social policy and the processes through which social policies operate.

Many writers on social policy seem to assume that the concept is self-explanatory, that it conveys the same meaning to every reader, and that it therefore requires no definition. Thus, some of the most perceptive analysts of social policy in the United States have used the term social policy in the titles and throughout the text of important books without ever specifying its meaning. Illustrations of the tendency to avoid the issue of definition are Alvin Schorr's *Explorations in Social Policy*,[1] S.M. Miller and Frank Riessman's *Social Class and Social Policy*[2] and Miller and Pamela Roby's *The Future of Inequality*.[3] These books reflect their authors' comprehensive view of social policy which goes far beyond conventional social welfare policies and programs. They seem to consider as core functions of social policy the reduction of social inequalities through redistribution of claims, and access, to resources, rights, and social opportunities. Yet, these authors choose not to develop a definition of the central focus of their inquiries. Similarly, the editors and authors of an important journal, *Social Policy*, though using the concept as title of their publication, refrain from defining it.[4] Editorial comment and articles in *Social Policy* reveal an implied definition akin to that reflected in the foregoing books.

Many other authors seem equally reluctant to define social policy in precise terms. Thus T. H. Marshall, a sociologist at the University of London, opened his book, *Social Policy*, with the statement: "Social Policy is not a technical term with an exact meaning"[5]; and Howard E. Freeman and Clarence C. Sherwood, both sociologists in the United States, express an identical view: "Social policy is a lay term, not a technical one, and like most such terms it defies simple definition."[6]

Martin Rein, a prolific writer on social policy issues in the United States, declares in a collection of his papers: "... no formal definitions are attempted here," and cites the authority of Gunnar Myrdal for avoiding the definitional task of "terms such as economics, sociology, or psychology."[7]

However, in spite of their view that the concept of social policy cannot, or need not, be defined, these latter authors, and many others on both sides of the Atlantic, have struggled to define it in abstract and generally valid terms, and have suggested a wide range of explicit or implicit definitions. Thus, Freeman and Sherwood develop a four-layer definition of social policy as a philosophical concept, a product, a process, and a framework for action, respectively:

At least four different uses or definitions can be distinguished, however:

1. Social policy as a philosophical concept. In an abstract sense, social policy is the principle whereby the members of large organizations and political entities collectively seek enduring solutions to the problems that affect them—almost the opposite, that is, of rugged individualism.

2. Social policy as a product. Viewed as a product, social policy consists of the conclusions reached by persons concerned with the betterment of community conditions and social life, and with the amelioration of deviance and social disorganization. Often the product is a document—what the British call a "white paper"— which lays out the intended policy for an organization or political unit.

3. Social policy as a process. Here, social policy is the fundamental process by which enduring organizations maintain an element of stability and at the same time seek to improve conditions for their members. Existing social policies are usually never fully developed; they are continually modified in the face of changing conditions and values.

4. Social policy as a framework for action. As a framework for action, social policy is both product and process. It assumes the availability of a well-delineated policy which is to be implemented within the context of potential changes in the values, structure, and conditions of the group affected.[8]

Rein answered his own question "What is Social Policy?" with a series of progressively more comprehensive definitions, starting with:

> Social policy can be regarded as the study of history, politics, philosophy, sociology, and economics of the social services. The definition of the term "social services" involves a stubborn ambiguity. The definition should, at least, be broad enough to encompass services such as education, medical care, cash transfers, housing, and social work.[9]

Rein subsequently expanded his foregoing initial formulation and adopted the more comprehensive orientation reflected in the writings of Richard M. Titmuss, a leading British social policy theorist and analyst.[10] Here is Rein's expanded definition:

> Accordingly it is not the social services alone, but the social purposes and consequences of agricultural, economic, manpower, fiscal, physical development, and social welfare policies that form the subject matter of social policy.[11]

One further definition suggested by Rein is:

> ... to define social policy as planning for social externalities, redistribution, and the equitable distribution of social benefits, especially social services.[12]

Eveline M. Burns, a major analyst of social policy in the United States since the early thirties, viewed social policy as:

> ... the organized efforts of society to meet identifiable personal needs of, or social problems presented by, groups or individuals.[13]

Charles I. Schottland, another leader in social policy development in the United States, and a former Commissioner of Social Security, suggested the following broad and general definition:

> A social policy is a statement of social goal and strategy, or a settled course of action dealing with the relations of people with each other, the mutual relations of people with their government, the relations of governments with each other, including legal enactments, judicial decisions, administrative decisions, and mores.[14]

Schottland's views on social policy are similar to the following definition in a pamphlet on social policy goals issued by the National Association of Social Workers:

> Public Social Policy... consists of those laws, policies, and practices of government that affect the social relationships of individuals and their relationship to the society of which they are a part. [15]

Kenneth E. Boulding, an economist with a long-standing interest in social policy, offered the following formulation in a paper in which he attempted to draw a dividing line between economic and social policy:

> ...it is the objective of social policy to build the identity of a person around some community with which he is associated....social policy is that which is centered in those institutions that create integration and discourage alienation. [16]

In turning to the views on social policy of British social scientists and policy analysts one finds as broad a range as in the United States. T.H. Marshall, whose doubts concerning the feasibility of defining social policy in precise terms have been quoted earlier, was nevertheless quite ready to commit himself to a specific formulation. He stated that social policy:

> ...is taken to refer to the policy of governments with regard to action having a direct impact on the welfare of the citizens, by providing them with services or income. The central core consists, therefore, of social insurance, public (or national) assistance, the health and welfare services, and housing policy. [17]

Richard Titmuss, whose influence has been noted in Rein's work, presented a more comprehensive view of social policy than Marshall, his colleague at the University of London. Titmuss considered "the direct public provision of services in kind (e.g., education and medical care) and the direct payment of benefits (e.g., retirement and family allowances)" as the "iceberg phenomena of social welfare," and "fiscal welfare and occupational welfare" as "the indirect or submerged parts of the iceberg of social policy." [18] Titmuss' incisive analysis of the foregoing "three components of social policy," the familiar, overt one, and the less familiar, covert ones, is reflected in the following excerpts from a lecture on "The Role of Redistribution in Social Policy" which he delivered in 1964 to the staff of the Social Security Administration of the U.S. Department of Health, Education, and Welfare:

All three categories of social policy have a great deal in common in terms of redistribution. They are all concerned with changing the individual and family pattern of current and future claims on resources set by the market, set by the possession of accumulated past rights, and set by the allocations made by Government to provide for national defense and other non-market sectors. Social welfare changes the pattern of claims by, for instance, directly providing in kind education or mental hospital care either free or at less than the market cost. Fiscal welfare changes the pattern of claims by taking less in tax (and thus increasing net disposable income) when a taxpayer's child is born, when its education is prolonged, when men have ex-wives to maintain, when taxpayers reach a specified age, and so on. An individual's pattern of claims on resources is today greatly varied through fiscal welfare policy by his or her change in circumstances, family responsibilities and opportunities available (and taken) for prolonged education, home ownership...and so on ...Occupational welfare, provided by virtue of employment status, achievement and record, may take the form of social security provisions in cash or in kind. Such provisions are legally approved by Government and, as in the case of fiscal welfare, they may be seen as alternatives to extensions in social welfare. Their cost falls in large measure on the whole population. It is thus, like social welfare and fiscal welfare, a major redistributive mechanism.....A substantial part of these occupational welfare benefits can be interpreted—again like fiscal welfare— as social policy recognition of dependencies; the long dependencies of old age, childhood and widowhood, and such short-term dependencies as sickness and the loss of job rights.[19]

Peter Townsend, a sociologist at the University of Essex, seemed to be working on the development of universal definitions and conceptions of social policy. His approach, a continuation of Titmuss' penetrating analysis, is illustrated by the following excerpt:

We must define social policy not just as the strategy of development of the social services as defined by government but as the underlying as well as the professed rationale for institutionalized control of present and future social development. Included would be measures adopted and organized by government but also by industry, voluntary associations, professions and other bodies to meet specifically social objectives, the achievement of social equality or justice, the redistribution of wealth, the adjustment of income to meet the needs of dependency, equality for women, equality for people of different race or religion and so on. It would include employer welfare and fiscal benefits as well as the formally defined public social services. This definition is very wide but something like it seems to me to be inescapable if we are to keep before ourselves the new as well as the old inequalites.[20]

A. Macbeath of The Queen's University in Belfast seems to have come closest to developing a comprehensive, abstract, and universal conception of social policy. According to him:

Social policies are concerned with the right ordering of the network of relationships between men and women who live together in societies, or with the principles which should govern the activities of individuals and groups so far as they affect the lives and interests of other people.[21]

The final definition to be quoted in this brief and selective survey of emerging views on social policy is by Father J. A. Ponsioen of the International Institute of Social Studies in The Hague, Netherlands. In an essay entitled "General Theory of Social Welfare Policy" Ponsioen examined the "semantics" of social welfare policy. After defining "policy" as

a continuous and deliberate activity aimed at a remote purpose or ideal which becomes realized progressively according to circumstances, possibilities, resistance, stimulating forces and counter-forces

he suggested the following, strongly value-oriented definition of social policy:

as a policy which aims at a continual reform of society in order to eliminate weaknesses of individuals or groups in that society. In its progressive realization it assists the weak people, prevents weaknesses, and constructs or ameliorates good situations.[22]

SUMMARY

The foregoing excerpts from writings of social theorists, policy analysts, and social welfare program administrators in the United States and overseas reveal a growing trend toward comprehensive formulations of the concept social policy. While agreement on a universally valid concept of social policies, their common domains, functions, and general processes has not been achieved, the essential elements and the broad outlines of such a concept can already be discerned in the literature. Several dilemmas can, however, be identified in current thinking about social policies. Many authors tend to equate social policies with the social services or the policies that shape social welfare programs. While such a conception of social policy may be useful for administrative and legislative purposes, it seems unsatisfactory from the perspective of social theory, mainly because it is dysfunctionally narrow and because the terms social services and social welfare have themselves not been clearly defined. Their use in the definition of social policies thus merely substitutes one vague notion for another. It may be noted in this context that current views of social welfare services range from a narrow conception according to which these services aim to ameliorate needs and problems of individuals and groups which result from temporary shortcomings of a supposedly self-regulating, free-enterprise economy; to a comprehensive conception, according to which these services comprise a broad array of societal provisions including education, vocational training, health-care, housing, income maintenance, personal social services, treatment of delinquents, recreation, etc. Harold L. Wilensky and Charles N. Lebeaux, who examined this issue several decades ago, referred to these two conceptions of social welfare as "the residual and the institutional."[23]

Irrespective of whether authors subscribe to a narrow or a comprehensive conception of social welfare they tend to consider economic issues as a separate policy domain, apart from social policies. This seems to be an arbitrary distinction with untoward consequences for the development of social as well as economic policies. Implied in this conceptual separation of economic issues from social policies is a view of the economy (and of economic development and growth) as ends in their own rights, rather than as means for the attainment of social ends.

Implied in it is also the hypothesis, or rather the illusion, that constant growth of the Gross National Product (GNP) will result, automatically, in the gradual disappearance of poverty and of poverty-related social problems. Furthermore, viewing social policies as apart from economic policies deprives social policy development of its most potent tools, and consigns to social policies the function of dealing merely in a reactive and ameliorative fashion with the fallout problems of economic policies.

Equating social policies with social welfare services and programs leads also to a fragmentary, "categorical" approach to the analysis and development of social policies. In such an approach, specific social policies are conceived of as societal responses to specific social needs or problems (such as income insufficiency, child neglect and abuse, poor health and education, substandard housing, delinquency, etc.) rather than as elements of a comprehensive system of social policies, all of which, through their combined effects, shape the overall quality of life in a society, the living conditions of its members, and their relations to one another and to society as a whole. As a consequence of this categorical, fragmented conception of social policies, their underlying common domains and dynamics are usually disregarded, as is the fact that the very needs and problems which specific policies are expected to resolve are themselves the consequences of extant and earlier social policies. It should be stressed in this context that a comprehensive conception of social policies reveals them to be the dynamic source of all social problems, for these problems are rooted in the fabric of a society which in turn derives from, and is constantly maintained by, its system of social policies. Social policies are, therefore, not merely potential solutions of social problems but are also their powerful underlying causes.

It seems appropriate to end this review of current thinking about social policies with the observation that several leading authors on the subject have already cut the umbilical cord which, for too long, had linked the conception of social policies to the social services. In doing so, these authors have extricated themselves from the web of theoretical and practical difficulties inherent in this linkage. The quest for a universally valid concept of social policies seems thus to have entered a theoretically, more promising stage. The continuation of this quest is the subject of the next chapter.

NOTES

1. Alvin L. Schorr, *Exploration in Social Policy* (New York: Basic Books, Inc., 1968).

2. S. M. Miller and Frank Riessman, *Social Class and Social Policy* (New York: Basic Books, Inc., 1968).

3. S. M. Miller and Pamela Roby,*The Future of Inequality* (New York: Basic Books, Inc., 1979).

4. Frank Riessman, ed., *Social Policy* (published six times a year by Social Policy Corporation, New York, NY. (First issue May/June 1970).

5. T.H. Marshall, *Social Policy* (London: Hutchinson University Press, 1965), p. 7.

6 Howard E. Freeman and Clarence C. Sherwood, *Social Research and Social Policy* (Englewood Cliffs, N. J.: Prentice-Hall, Inc., 1970), p. 2.

7. Martin Rein, *Social Policy: Issues of Choice and Change* (New York: Random House, Inc., 1970), p. 3.

8. Freeman and Sherwood, *Social Research and Social Policy,* 1970, p. 2. By permission of Prentice-Hall, Inc., Englewood Cliffs, New Jersey.

9. Rein, *Social Policy: Issues of Choice and Change,* p. 4.

10. Richard M. Titmuss, *Problems of Social Policy* (London: His Majesty's Stationery Office, 1950). Richard M. Titmuss, *Essays on the Welfare State* (Boston: Beacon Press, 1969). First published 1958. Richard M. Titmuss, *Income Distribution and Social Change* (London: George Allen and Unwin, Ltd., 1962). Richard M. Titmuss, *Commitment to Welfare* (New York: Pantheon Books, 1969). Richard M. Titmuss, *The Gift Relationship* (New York: Pantheon Books, 1971).

11. Rein, *Social Policy: Issues of Choice and Change,* p. 4.

12. Rein, *Social Policy: Issues of Choice and Change,* p. 5.

13.   Eveline M. Burns, "Social Policy: The Stepchild of the Curriculum" in *Proceedings, Ninth Annual Program Meeting, Council on Social Work Education* (New York: Council on Social Work Education, 1961).

14.   Charles I. Schottland, personal communication.

15.   National Association of Social Workers, *Goals of Public Social Policy* (New York: National Association of Social Workers, 1963).

16.   Kenneth E. Boulding, "Boundaries of Social Policy," *Social Work*, Vol. 12, No. 1, (January 1967): p. 3-11.

17.   Marshall, *Social Policy*, p. 7.

18.   Titmuss, *Commitment to Welfare*, p. 192.

19.   Titmuss, *Commitment to Welfare*, p. 192-193.

20.   Peter Townsend, "Strategies in Meeting Poverty" (paper presented at the International Conference on Family Poverty and Social Policy, Manchester, England, September 20, 1969).

21.   A. Macbeath, *Can Social Policies be Rationally Tested?* (L. T. Hobhouse Memorial Trust Lecture No. 27, King's College London, 2 May 1957. London: Oxford University Press, 1957).

22.   J.A. Ponsioen, "General Theory of Social Welfare Policy" in J.A. Ponsioen, ed., *Social Welfare Policy—Contributions to Theory* (The Hague, The Netherlands: Mounton & Company, Publishers: 1962). Volume III, Series Maior, Publications of the Institute of Social Studies, p. 18.

23.   Harold L. Wilensky and Charles N. Lebeaux, *Industrial Society and Social Welfare* (New York: Russell Sage Foundation, 1958), p. 134-40.

2

Toward A Theory Of Social Policy

INTRODUCTION

Social policies and processes of policy development can be identified in all human societies since the evolutionary emergence of the species, several hundred thousand years ago. Social policies may be understood as rules—formal and informal, past, present, and future—for the ways of life which different groups of people evolve in pursuit of survival in particular natural environments. The drive to survive by satisfying innate, as well as socially shaped needs, seems, therefore, to be the motivating source for policy development. Entire systems of social policies, and the social orders they maintain, reflect responses of different human groups to the needs experienced and perceived by them, and to the existential imperatives inherent in the human condition.

Social policies and social orders emerged through the trials, errors, and choices of people struggling to master survival in contexts of real and perceived scarcities, real and perceived threats to existence, and ignorance concerning nature, human nature, the universe, and relations among these. Social policies resulted from efforts to create order out of chaos and to transcend the species' initial random behavior and ruleless condition. Social policies originated in people's actions and in their relations to one another and to their environments. Those which were perceived as compatible with survival needs were repeated routinely, and thus became institutionalized. Once people perceived specific practices as conducive to the satisfaction of their needs, the rules implicit in these practices came to guide subsequent behaviors; to shape the circumstances and quality of people's lives, and their relations to one another and to their environments.[1]

ASPECTS OF THE HUMAN CONDITION RELEVANT
TO SOCIAL POLICIES

To unravel the sources and dynamics of social policy evolution, certain characteristics of the human condition should be noted.

1. Humans share with other species biological drives to survive, develop, and propagate. They will unfold their innate potential spontaneously when living in natural and socially shaped environments in which they can satisfy their basic needs.

2. Humans are by nature social beings. Their infants are not viable in isolation from adult care for several years, and they become fully human only through relations and interactions with members of a particular group which shares a common way of life. While noting the social nature of humans, one should note also that every human being is unique in genetic, physical, psychological, experiential, and historic terms. These aspects of the human condition—the social nature of the species, and the individuality of people—involve potential tension. Different cultures reflect different perspectives and ideologies concerning these aspects. In some societies, people have evolved balanced, integrative, and harmonious perspectives, while in others, they have come to emphasize mainly one aspect and to nearly disregard the other. Social policies and ways of life of different societies reflect these variations.

3. Human survival is greatly facilitated by biologically evolved capacities for consciousness and mental processes of thought, abstraction, memory, reflection, imagination, language, and communication. These capacities, and their organic base in the brain, evolved along with declines in the specificity of genetic determination of human behavior and ways of life.

   In genetic terms, humans have evolved into one of the least programmed species. This does not mean that human life is not genetically circumscribed. It merely means that except for instincts and reflexes, human genes do not determine and transmit between generations specific behaviors and patterns of life, as the genes of other species do to a far greater extent. Rather, human genes determine behavioral ranges and limits within which people must make choices in order to develop ways of life conducive to their survival. As a consequence of the paucity of genetic specifications and the extended immaturity of offspring noted above, human groups survive only when they succeed to create relatively stable, viable patterns of life, including systems of care and socialization for their young.

The particular ways of life of human groups, and the policies which guide and maintain them, are thus not ordained by biology, nor by superhuman forces. Rather, humans themselves are the shapers, transmitters, and changers of the ways of life which emerge from the responses of different groups, in different places and times, to the existential imperative to complement genetic transmission with societal processes. This imperative is reflected throughout history in the ubiquity of cultural and political processes focused on maintaining or transforming previously established ways of life and social policies.

4. The evolutionary shift from genetic determination of ways of life toward genetic openness and social shaping of these ways, has important consequences for the human species in terms of opportunities and risks. On the one hand, humans are able to adapt to diverse and changing environmental conditions all over, and even beyond, the globe: at different times and places they have created ways of life conducive to the fulfillment of everyone's basic needs. On the other hand, the lack of ways of life tested and selected by biological evolution implies the possibility of choosing and perpetuating ways which are inadequate or less than optimal, for survival, development, and the fulfillment of basic human needs. Such imperfect choices were especially likely under the conditions in which human groups took their early steps toward creating social orders and social policies. These early conditions involved pervasive ignorance of life, nature, human nature, and the universe; limited technological capacity and skills; and a deep sense of insecurity due to precarious

circumstances of life. Under these conditions people tended to preserve and transmit to their children in authoritarian fashion ways of life evolved by trial and error (provided these ways seemed minimally adequate) and they came to fear and resist changes in them.Yet, in spite of these conservative tendencies which seem inherent in biological, social, and psychological aspects of the human condition, the ways of life and social policies of human groups have usually undergone changes, mostly gradually and incrementally, but at times at accelerated rates and in a revolutionary manner. These reformist and revolutionary processes reflect equally strong tendencies which also seem inherent in the human condition: pursuit of development and fulfillment of innate potential and enhancement of the quality of life, through individual and collective action propelled by critical consciousness.

5. To be viable, ways of life must bridge, through thought and organized action, gaps between people's basic needs and resources in their natural and social environments. The better the fit between needs and resources, the better are the conditions for individual and social development. When societies fail to generate and transmit minimally adequate ways of life, they cease to exist. Humans tend to survive, however, even when their ways of life are far from optimal. Yet, imperfect ways will inevitably be reflected in underdevelopment of innate human capacities, and in diverse physical, emotional, and social ills and problems.

BASIC HUMAN NEEDS

The source of energy which has propelled people throughout history to evolve and maintain or modify their ways of life is the innate drive to survive and develop, and to establish conditions suited to fulfillment of basic needs. In this sense, the evolution of social orders and social policies is motivated by basic human needs—a crucial constituent of the human condition. Knowledge concerning human needs is imperfect. However, fulfillment of the following set of interrelated needs seems necessary for healthy growth and development:[2]

—*biological-material needs*: stable provision of biological necessities; sexual satisfaction; and regular access to life-sustaining and enhancing goods and services, the types, quantity, and quality of which vary among different cultures and over time;

—*social-psychological needs:* stable, meaningful social relations and a sense of belonging to a community, involving mutual respect, acceptance, affirmation, care and love, and opportunities for self-discovery and for the emergence of a positive sense of identity;

—*productive-creative needs*: meaningful participation, in accordance with one's innate capacities and stage of development, in the productive activities of one's community and society;

— *security needs:* a sense of trust and security emerging from the experience of steady fulfillment of biological-material, social-psychological, and productive-creative needs;

— *self-actualization needs:* becoming what one is innately capable of becoming through creative productivity and self-expression;

—*spiritual needs:* discovering and giving meaning and coherence to one's existence in relation to people, nature, and the world, along known, unknown, and ultimately unknowable dimensions;

This set of related, basic needs is not based on mere speculation and theorizing, but reflects known and observable aspects of the human condition in nature. *Biological-material needs* reflect essential aspects of the life process. No living being is ever self-contained, but must continuously interact with its environment, to exchange energy and materials, and assure a flow of life-sustaining and enhancing resources and processes. *Social-psychological needs* reflect the essentially social nature of the human species which is due largely to the nearly total dependence of infants on material and emotional support from mature caretakers. *Productive-creative needs* reflect the existential imperative for human work as a basis for life. This involves productive interactions with other humans and the environment to generate a steady flow of necessary material goods. These needs also reflect the social nature of the species in that productive activities involve cooperation within and across generations, reaching back to the dawn of human history. *Security needs* reflect the existential anxiety which all conscious beings experience, as well as the reality of ever-present, relative scarcity of life-sustaining goods. *Self-actualization needs* reflect a spontaneous tendency of all living beings in nature, from single cells to complex organisms, to unfold and express their innate potential. And *spiritual needs* for meaning and coherence in one's existence which are inherent in the capacity for consciousness, reflect a universal tendency of humans to search for answers and insights when confronting the incomprehensible phenomena of life and death, origins and destination, and time and space.

BASIC HUMAN NEEDS, REAL HUMAN INTEREST AND SOCIAL POLICIES

The interrelated, basic needs of people, which seem intrinsic to the human condition, tend to change their forms of expression over time, in different societal contexts. Their substance and dynamics are, however, constant and universal. Human survival, development, and physical, emotional, and social health and well-being depend always on an adequate level of fulfillment of these basic needs. Such fulfillment can, therefore, be understood as the *real, objective interest* of people anywhere and anytime, regardless of their subjective perceptions of needs and interests (which may or may not include fulfillment of these basic needs).

People's subjective perceptions of needs and interests result not only from becoming conscious of their innate, basic needs, but also from socialization in particular societies with unique ways of life and socially constructed definitions of needs and interests. People's actual perceptions of needs and interests may, therefore, correspond to, overlap with, substitute for, or conflict with their basic needs and real interests. When perceived needs and interests do not overlap sufficiently with people's basic needs and interests, socially defined substitutes (e.g. material wealth) may be realized, while basic needs (e.g. meaningful human relations) remain unfulfilled. Sociologists have used the notion of "false consciousness" to refer to perceptions of needs and interests, which do not include people's basic needs and real interests.[3]

Whether people correctly perceive their basic needs and real interests, and can actually satisfy them in everyday life, depends on their natural environment and on their ways of life and social policies. Since individual and collective efforts to satisfy these needs have always been the source of energy and motivating force behind the evolution and transformations of ways of life and social policies, *an appropriate criterion for evaluating any way of life and social policy system should be the extent to which people can actually fulfill their basic needs.*

Basic needs will seek expression and fulfillment, whether or not people are conscious of them, for the life energy underlying these needs does not disappear when perceptions concerning them change. When the realization of basic needs is thwarted consistently, beyond a level of tolerance, by a society's way of life and social policies, constructive developmental energy tends to be blocked and transformed into destructive energy, which may be expressed in destructive or self-destructive behaviors and attitudes. In other words, when constructive developmental tendencies are "violated" by a society's ways of life and social policies, emotional and social ills and problems ensue. Societies whose policies inhibit the realization of people's basic needs may, therefore, be considered "structurally violent." Such societies tend to induce reactive "counter violence" from individuals and social classes whose development has been thwarted, against themselves or other individuals and social classes. Societies will usually respond to such reactive violence with "repressive violence"—a seemingly interminable vicious cycle, which can be reversed only when structural violence ceases, and people can fulfill their basic needs as a result of fundamental changes in ways of life and social policies.

When people's basic needs can be realized in a society, people tend to develop spontaneously, normally and healthily in accordance with their innate capacities. In contrast to "structurally violent" societies, societies whose ways of life and social policies are conducive to the realization of people's basic needs may be considered "structurally nonviolent."

To sum up, the presence of physical and mental ills and social problems suggests that prevailing social policies may obstruct and violate individual and social development by thwarting the realization of basic human needs and real interests, even though perceived needs and interests may be realizable for many people. To overcome and prevent such ills and problems, prevailing social policies would have to be transformed into alternative policies, conducive to the fulfillment of basic human needs and real human interests.

Fragmentary adjustments of policies may relieve symptoms of ills and problems, but are unlikely to assure the fulfillment of basic needs and real interests. Such relief may be appropriate as emergency measures to reduce human suffering, but must not be confused with fundamental solutions of a society's ills and problems.

A CONCEPTUAL MODEL OF SOCIAL POLICIES

The above discussion of the human condition and of human needs and interests reveals the essential elements of a conceptual model of social policies. Models are representations of selected aspects of social reality, the purpose of which is to facilitate understanding of the structure and dynamics of the phenomena they represent.

A model of social policies should identify the key variables of all social policies, facilitate analysis of specific social policies and policy systems and their consequences, and aid in development of alternative policies and policy systems. A model of social policies is based on the premise that all social policies, in spite of differences in substance, objectives, and scope, deal directly or indirectly with the same domains, and operate through the same processes of societal existence. Thus, policies dealing with such diverse issues as agriculture, trade, and industry; work and conservation; health, education, and economic security; housing and transportation and taxation; are assumed to affect underlying common domains, and to involve underlying common processes. A model of social policies should identify these domains and processes and should reveal relations among them.

A corollary of the foregoing premise is that the social policies of a society are not independent of, but interact with, each other, and constitute a comprehensive system. It is this entire system, rather than any specific social policy, which through its aggregate effects, shapes the common domains of all social policies. However, while discrete social policies are elements of a comprehensive system, they are not necessarily consistent with each other. On the contrary, inconsistency among different policies of social policy systems is to be expected because of conflicts of interests among groups and classes in internally fragmented societies, which underlie the evolution of social policies.

Several concepts require clarification before presenting the variables of social policies:

a. *Societies* are groups of interdependent human beings (individuals, families, or households) who pursue life together in particular locations over which they exercise a degree of collective control. The boundariesof societies in membership and territory tend to be flexible.

Members of societies share a way of life which evolved over time through the interactions of people in pursuit of survival and enhancement of the quality of life. Members also share a common history and a sense of belonging to a distinguishable human group and they are perceived in that way by others. These perceptions and self-perceptions are important aspects of people's sense of identity. However, the sense of belonging and identity is not necessarily uniform, but tends to vary among subgroups and classes when societies are internally divided.

The viability of societies, in biological and cultural terms, requires development of systems of resource management, production, distribution, socialization, and governance, in order to assure survival needs of members, though not necessarily of all members. Economic self-sufficiency is not required, however, when trade with other societies can fill gaps in necessaries.

In the course of growing up, people internalize into consciousness concrete and abstract aspects of their society's ways of life. The resulting shared consciousness enables them to interact with, and relate to, one another in meaningful ways. However, not everyone internalizes the same elements of the established ways of life, as differences in consciousness tend to emerge between groups and classes in divided societies.

While societies are usually organized to assure biological and cultural continuity, they tend to undergo, over time, manifold changes in ways of life, membership, and boundaries.

b. *Social policies* are guidelines for behavior, evolved through societal processes, which specify and maintain or transform the structures, relations, values, and dynamics of a society's particular way of life. While established social policies are results of societal processes throughout history, individuals and groups may develop and promote alternative policies to those in force in a society, and participate thus actively in the process of ongoing policy evolution.

Specific social policies focus on particular domains of social life. However, because of manifold links and interactions among various domains of a society's way of life, discrete policies will affect, indirectly, domains beyond the ones with which they are primarily concerned.

All social policies, in force at a time in a society, constitute its *system of social policies* and shape its way of life through their combined effects and interactions. Policies, in contemporary societies, tend to be codified in formal legal instruments. However, such codification has not been an essential aspect of social policies throughout many stages of human evolution.

c. *Social institutions* are clusters of discrete social policies, which shape major aspects of social life, such as management of resources, work and production, exchange and distribution, governance and legitimation, and reproduction, socialization, and social control.

Operating Variables of Social Policies

The review of the human condition led to the conclusion that societies must devise, maintain, and transmit between generations, relatively stable ways of life, and that social policies serve as the medium for this maintenance and transmission. They are specifications, abstracted from these ways of life, as well as guidelines for their reproduction or transformation. Designing a conceptual model of social policies requires the translation of the concept, "ways of life," into concrete institutional systems or processes, and to identify the ones which seem essential to the viability of societies. The following interrelated institutional systems or processes seem to meet this test:

—Human life depends on regular exchange of materials and energy with natural and social environments. Societies must, therefore, devise and maintain *systems for the development, management, and conservation of natural and human-created resources.*

—To undertake the development, management, and conservation of resources, and to transform them into life-sustaining and life-enhancing goods and services suited to human use, societies must devise and maintain *systems of work and production.*

—To facilitate access to, and use of, life-sustaining and life- enhancing goods and services, and social, civil, and political rights and responsibilities, societies must devise and maintain *systems of exchange and distribution.*

—To facilitate making of choices, and implementing decisions concerning the design, maintenance, and operation of their institutional systems, societies must devise and maintain *systems of governance and legitimation.*

—To assure biological and social continuity, prepare people to participate in the institutional systems of their societies, and assure effective participation, societies must devise and maintain *systems of reproduction, socialization, and social control.*

While these institutional systems are listed here separately and sequentially, they do not function in real life apart from one another. Rather, they are dimensions of a unified process of social life, although they are conceptually distinct. Each institutional system interacts with the others and depends on them. All are equally important, as societies would not remain viable should one of these systems cease to function.

Together, these institutional systems constitute the essential dimensions of the ways of life and policy systems of societies. Hence, they are the underlying, real foci of all social policies, regardless of the manifest content of specific policies. These systems are, therefore, the operating variables of the conceptual model of social policies. Variations of these systems and interactions among them generate the specific contents, objectives, and scope of different social policies.

Outcome Variables of Social Policies

To complete the conceptual model, the outcome variables of ways of life, which constitute the common domains of social policies, are identified below:

—circumstances of living of individuals, groups, and classes;
—power of individuals, groups, and classes;
—nature and quality of intrasocietal human relations among individuals, groups, and classes;
—overall quality of life.

These conceptually distinct outcome variables do not exist in isolation from one another, but affect one another. They are shaped by the combined effects of the operating variables, and, in turn, influence the operating variables.

DEFINITION OF SOCIAL POLICIES

Having identified the outcome variables of ways of life as the common domains of social policies, and the essential institutional systems or processes of ways of life as their operating variables, a formal definition of social policies can now be presented:

Social policies are guiding principles for ways of life, motivated by basic and perceived human needs. They were derived by people from the structures, dynamics, and values of their ways of life, and they serve to maintain or change these ways. Social policies tend to, but need not, be codified in formal legal instruments. All extant social policies of a given society at a given time, constitute an interrelated, yet not necessarily internally consistent, system of social policies.

Social policies operate through the following essential institutional processes and their manifold interactions:

a. development, management, and conservation of natural and human created resources;
b. organization of work and production of life-sustaining and life-enhancing, concrete and non-concrete, goods and services;
c. exchange and distribution of life-sustaining and life-enhancing goods and services, and of social, civil, and political rights and responsibilities;
d. governance and legitimation;

e. reproduction, socialization, and social control;
Through the operations and interactions of these essential institutional
processes, social policies shape the following linked outcome variables
of ways of life:
  a. circumstances of living of individuals, groups, and classes;
  b. power of individuals, groups, and classes;
  c. nature and quality of human relations among individuals, groups,
    and classes;
  d. overall quality of life.

Chart #2.1(p. 26) presents all the variables of the conceptual model of
social policies along with their dynamic sources (basic and perceived
human needs) and a suggested criterion for policy evaluation (the extent
to which human needs can be met).

COMMENTS ON OPERATING AND OUTCOME VARIABLES OF SOCIAL POLICIES

Resources which people use for survival and for developing ways of life
consist of three distinct, though related, types:

  a. matter and energy from and beyond the earth in their natural,
    untouched state, in live and lifeless, and renewable and nonrenew-
    able forms. Land, minerals, water and air; vegetation and wildlife;
    and light, heat, and other radiation belong to this type of resources.
  b. physical, intellectual, emotional, and spiritual capacities of people,
    living now and in the past, anywhere on earth.
  c. concrete and abstract, live and lifeless products of past and present
    human work and creativity. These products are results of interac-
    tions and combinations of a and b above, of natural matter and
    energy, human capacities, and earlier products of human work.
    Lifeless artifacts; domesticated and cultivated, live products; knowl-
    edge, skills, and ideas discovered and created by people belong to
    this type of resources.

  Key policy issues concerning resources, which every human group
must settle in some manner, are: Who should control the development,

management, and conservation of resources? How, toward what ends, in whose interest, and under what conditions should this control be exercised? The variability of historic, current, and potential future policies concerning resources is reflected in such systems as tribal communalism, monarchic-feudalism, mercantilism, free enterprise capitalism, monopoly capitalism, centralized state-socialism, decentralized democratic socialism, and producers cooperatives. Each of these policy systems has

---

CHART #2.1 CONCEPTUAL MODEL OF SOCIAL POLICIES

DYNAMIC SOURCES OF SOCIAL LIFE AND SOCIAL POLICIES
Basic and Perceived Human Needs

    a. biological-material
    b. social-psychological
    c. productive-creative
    d. security
    e. self-actualization
    f. spiritual

INSTITUTIONAL SYSTEMS OR PROCESSES	OUTCOMES OF INSTITUTIONAL SYSTEMS OR PROCESSES
a. development, management, and conservation of natural and human-created resources	a. circumstances of living of individuals, groups, and classes
b. organization of work and production	b. power of individuals, groups, and classes.
c. exchange and distribution of goods, services, rights and responsibilities	c. nature and quality of human relations among individuals, groups, and classes
d. governance and legitimation	d. overall quality of life
e. reproduction, socialization, and social control	

CRITERION FOR EVALUATING POLICIES
Extent to which basic and perceived needs can be met

Note: Variables of the model interact with one another in multiple ways, rather than in a linear manner.

different consequences for individual and social development, social power and human relations, conditions of living, and the overall quality of life.

Work may be defined as activities by which people pursue their abiding interest in meeting innate and perceived needs. It involves use of human energy and capacities in varying combinations with resources from the natural and social environments, in processes oriented toward survival and the enrichment of life.

Work is an essential aspect of the development of material and nonmaterial goods and services, and of knowledge concerning nature, human life, and social realities. Work has biological, psychological, social, economic, political, and cultural sources, functions, and consequences. It facilitates biological and social existence and affects its quality. It can serve as a medium for the discovery and use of people's creative and productive potential. It provides opportunities for people to find and actualize themselves, and to achieve a sense of identity. It is a medium for people to interact with and relate to one another, and to their community, society, and natural environment. Work is essential for the evolution of social institutions which, in turn, define the meaning and shape the particular organization and design of work. Work is the human ingredient of all wealth, and a major factor of individual and social development and well-being.

Since work always involves the use of resources, it depends on access to resources. Obstacles to such access tend, therefore, to reduce the efficiency and effectiveness of human work and productivity.

Human work is understood best when it is conceived of as transgenerational, collective processes, rather than as discrete, individual acts. For any moment of human work depends, directly or indirectly, on countless preceding and concurrent moments of work by other people.[4]

Major policy issues concerning work and production which all societies must resolve in some manner include the following:

—In view of innate and perceived needs of people, which material and nonmaterial goods and services should be produced, in what quantities and quality, in whose interest, and in what order of priority?

—How should work be defined: which activities should be considered work, and which should be excluded from a society's work system, subject to what criteria?

—How, and by what criteria, should the aggregate of work, required for necessary production, be divided among members of a society? Who should do what work, on what terms, and how much work should people do? How should society make sure that all necessary work will actually be done?

—How much choice should people have concerning the type and amount of work they do? Should the ranges of choice vary for different groups of people, and if so, what criteria should be used to identify the groups?

—How should people prepare for work during different stages of life?

—How should people be motivated to work, to perform their work efficiently, and to achieve high levels of quality in their work?

—How should efficient use of limited human and other resources be assured? And how should the natural environment be protected and conserved?

—How should work be designed, and what criteria should be considered in its design? Should the needs, development, and well-being of workers be included among these criteria?

—What is the value of work, and by what criteria should the value of different types of work be determined?

—Who should control and manage work and production: should workers themselves control and manage their work, or should other groups or classes do so?

The above list of policy issues concerning the organization, design, and definition of work and production is not meant to be exhaustive, but to indicate major issues. Many links between work and resources are implied in the list, since policies concerning work depend on, and affect, policies concerning control and management of resources. The variability of policies concerning work and production parallels, therefore, the variability of policies concerning the management and control of resources noted above. Major patterns concerning the organization of work and production include: tribal-communal work systems; independently managed farming, crafts, and "professions"; slavery and serfdom; craft-guilds; wage-labor under capitalism and centralized socialism; and self-managed worker-cooperatives. As noted in relation to the patterns of resource control, different patterns of work and production vary in consequences for the conditions and quality of life, and for social power, human relations and development.

Rights to use and appropriate natural resources and shares of the material and nonmaterial goods and services produced in a society are always established through societal processes. Such rights are distributed among a society's members in accordance with values and social policies developed for that purpose.

The widespread notion of "natural" human rights reflects wishful thinking, for in real social situations, people can usually not exercise any rights which have not been acknowledged and established by their society. People can, of course, act to promote changes in prevailing definitions of rights. However, until such redefinitions are accepted, proposed rights can not be exercised in a legitimate manner.

While rights are social constructs rather than natural phenomena, basic human needs are rooted in nature. However, people can satisfy their nature-rooted needs from resources produced in society only when distributive policies acknowledge their rights to do so.

What is valid concerning the distribution of rights to natural resources and material goods and services is valid also concerning social, civil, and political rights and responsibilities. People can exercise these rights and responsibilities only when social policies define and acknowledge them—for everyone, or for specified groups.

Societies use different techniques for distributing rights to individuals and groups: rewards, entitlements, and constraints. Rewards are rights distributed in exchange for performance of work, such as wages, fringe-benefits, work-based pensions, titles, and social prestige. Entitlements are rights distributed to people by virtue of belonging to a society or to a specified social group. Thus all citizens may be entitled to the vote, free speech, health care, and education; children may be entitled to school meals and children's allowances; and veterans to pensions. Constraints may be viewed as negative rewards or negative entitlements, since they limit the rights distributed to individuals and social groups. One should note in this context that rights in society can never be unlimited. Zoning laws which limit the rights of land owners; taxation which defines limits on income, wealth, and wealth transmission; and fines, jail terms, and other forms of penalties, are illustrations of constraints.

Rights can be distributed directly, in kind, such as land, public education and health services, or indirectly in the form of money, through market mechanisms or government income transfers. Money is a " right equivalent" which can be transformed with relative ease, at the owner's discretion, into a broad range of goods and services. Rights, in the form of money, can also be saved for future claims to goods and services, and transferred to others through gifts and inheritance. Income and savings expressed in units of money are rough measures of levels of rights of individuals and groups in modern societies.

Money can also be understood as rights to, or claims on, other people's work, since the goods and services for which it is exchanged are products of work. Hence, earning money means earning rights to the work of others in exchange for one's own work. An important policy issue concerning this exchange is whether the money one earns commands a similar or different quantity of work from the quantity one performed to earn it.

Whether societies distribute rights through entitlements, rewards, or constraints; in kind or through money; they must settle policy issues such as the following, in order to establish explicit or implicit criteria for the distribution of all kinds of rights:

—Who, and what groups or classes, should receive what share of the aggregate material and nonmaterial resources and products of society? On what terms should they receive their shares?

—To what extent should distributions be based on socially acknowledged needs of people, and to what extent on their individual contributions to the aggregate social product?

—When distributions of rights are in the form of rewards for work, should all types of work be considered equal in value and command, therefore, equal rewards, or should different types of work be accorded different value and command different levels of rewards? How should such difference be determined?

—Should gender, age, and health status affect the distribution of rights, and if so, in what ways and to what extent?

—Should factors such as race, national origin, sexual orientation, religion, and political perspectives affect the distribution of rights? How, and to what extent?

—The distribution of rights in societies can be understood as direct or indirect exchanges of work contained in different products, since distributions depend always on the aggregate social product and the organization and division of work behind that product. Implicit in these links between distribution, exchange, products, and work is the question: What should be the terms of exchange? Should it be fair, balanced, and free of overt and covert coercion, or unbalanced, exploitive, and coercive? How should the value of work and products, and the fairness and balance of exchanges be established? And how is the presence or absence of coercion to be judged?

Governance and legitimation are processes by which people make, implement, and validate societal choices and decisions concerning the essential institutional systems of resource management, organization of work and production, and exchange and distribution of goods, services and all kinds of rights. Governance and legitimation may have been relatively simple processes in small, homogeneous communities without significant internal social divisions and conflicts of interests, and with ample opportunities for achieving consensus through face to face communications. In large societies, on the other hand, which are usually divided internally and permeated by conflicts of interests among different social groups and classes, governance and legitimation tend to be complex processes involving overt and covert coercion.

Major policy issues which all societies must settle concerning governance and legitimation and which, in modern societies, tend to be dealt with and codified in formal constitutions, include the following:

—Who should participate in governance and legitimation?

—In what manner, and by what criteria, should individuals be selected to undertake various tasks of governance and legitimation?

—How should processes of governance and legitimation operate?
—Should there be a set of goals to guide the processes of governance and legitimation? If so, what should these goals be?
—Whose interests should be considered and satisfied by processes of governance and legitimation?

Reproduction, socialization, and *social control* assure biological and societal survival and continuity of human groups. Major policy issues concerning biological reproduction include:
—What size is appropriate for a population in relation to a society's natural and human-created resources?
—What size is appropriate for subunits of society, such as households and families?
—What practices are appropriate concerning relations between males and females, contraception, abortion, and infanticide?
—Who should be involved in making decisions concerning the above issues affecting biological reproduction?

Socialization prepares members of societies for participation in established ways of life, as well as for their transformation. It begins at birth and continues throughout life. It is linked to all the institutional systems of societies, and is carried out by families and households; schools, and settings of worship and ritual; media of communication; processes of exchange and distribution of goods, services, and rights; settings of work and production; settings of art, recreation, and entertainment; and processes of governance and legitimation. Major policy issues concerning socialization include:

—Who should be responsible for different aspects and stages of socialization?
—How should these aspects and stages be integrated and supported with resources?
—How, and by whom, should decisions be made concerning goals and priorities of socialization?
—What criteria should be used for access to different channels of

socialization leading to different life-paths and roles in societies divided into social and occupational classes?

Social control involves processes of coercive enforcement of conformity to behaviors expected in accordance with established ways of life. It is used with individuals and groups who fail to respond in socially expected ways to normal processes of socialization, or who refuse to conform to established patterns for individual or political-ideological reasons. Policy issues concerning the use of social control include:

—What situations are to be dealt with by social control measures, and what should be the goals of using processes of social control?
—What measures of social control are appropriate for different situations in which the use of control and coercion is considered valid?
—What procedures are to be followed when coercive measures of social control are to be used?
—What are the rights of individuals and groups subjected to coercive measures of social control?
—What are the responsibilities and rights of the agents of social control?
—In whose interest should measures of social control be used?

Circumstances of living of individuals, groups, and classes in any society are largely a function of what resources they control, what work they perform, what goods and services they can claim and what rights they can exercise, what shares they have in governance processes, and what kind of socialization they experience. In short, people's social conditions are results of the combined effects of the particular manner in which the essential institutional systems of their society operate. People's circumstances of living are, of course, also affected by chance events and by their genetic makeup, their physical and psychological attributes, their innate capacities, and their health. However, while these individual variables are important for the unique life paths of people, the social reality of groups and classes is understood best as outcomes of the operating variables of social policies.

Power in society, of individuals, groups and classes is

> The ability ... to carry out ... wishes and policies, and to control,
> manipulate or influence the behavior of others, whether they wish to
> cooperate or not. The agent who possesses power has resources to
> force his (sic) will on others.[5]

Implicit in this definition is that power is neither an independent
variable, nor an innate attribute of individuals, but a result of the
combined effects of the major institutional systems of resource management, work organization, rights distribution, governance, and socialization, in the same way these systems influence other circumstances of
living. Power is actually an aspect of people's circumstances of living.
However, because of the crucial importance of the distribution of power
for social life and societal evolution, it seems valid to identify it as a
special variable among the outcomes of social policies. Like all the
outcome variables, power, in turn, also affects the operating variables in
a continuous process of policy evolution.

Power is not only the ability to influence and control others, as
suggested in the above definition, but also the ability to resist control by
others. It is always relative to the power of other individuals, groups, and
classes, and is best understood as a relationship among possessors of
different levels of power, resulting from society's distributive policies.

Finally, like all circumstances of living, the power of individuals is
also related to their personal attributes and to chance events. Yet, for
understanding the social dynamics of the power of groups and classes,
individual attributes and chance events seem less important than the
influence of the operating variables of social policies.[6]

Nature and quality of relations among people in society, like their
circumstances of living and relative power, are also affected by personal
factors and chance events. However, if one examines societal dynamics
and tendencies of human relations, rather than relationships among
specific individuals, one is likely to find that the operating variables of
social policies are the main influences on (and the best predictors of)
intrasocietal relations among individuals, groups, and classes. The
reason for this seems to be that people are more likely to associate, to feel
more comfortable, and to behave more spontaneously with people who

do not hold power over them, and with whom they share circumstances of living and important interests, than with people who do hold power over them, live in markedly different circumstances, and with whom they do not share important interests. Hence, relations of people in society will usually reflect (and grow out of) their circumstances of living and relative power, rather than their personal characteristics.

Overall quality of life, the final outcome variable of social policies, may be easily comprehended by common sense. Precise definition and measurement are difficult, however, as this concept involves not only objective characteristics, but also subjective perceptions and judgments. The quality of life is a multidimensional phenomenon reflective of the circumstances of living of all members of a society. It may be represented by biological, demographic, ecological, psychological, social, cultural, economic, and political indicators, to the extent that such indicators are available.[7] Measurements on these dimensions have to be supplemented by indicators of subjective perceptions and judgments derived from periodic studies of representative population samples. It does seem clear, however, that objective as well as subjective aspects of the quality of life are influenced by policies concerning management and conservation of resources; organization of work and production; distribution of goods, services and rights; processes of governance; and reproduction, socialization, and social control.

VARIABILITY OF SOCIAL POLICIES AND SOCIAL CHANGE

The essential institutional processes discussed above as the operating variables of social policies—resource management, organization of work and production, distribution of rights, governance, and socialization—vary widely in substance, objectives, and scope among different societies in different environments. They vary also over time in the same society as a result of demographic, ecological, political, cultural, and technological changes.

Each discrete social policy guides the behavior of people with respect to certain aspects of one or several institutional processes or operational variables, in order to attain particular results on the outcome variables—circumstances of living, power, social relations, and quality of life. To illustrate, the Social Security Act of the United States specifies terms concerning retirement of workers from employment and entitlements to work-related pensions and medical care. The policy thus guides behaviors concerning organization of work (retirement); distribution of rights (work-linked pensions and medical care); management of resources (creation of the social security trust fund from payroll taxes and disbursements from the fund); governance and legitimation (operation of the Social Security Administration in accordance with laws, regulations, and judicial decisions); and socialization (public information, education, and counseling concerning the provisions of the Social Security Act). The Social Security policy was designed to affect, directly, the circumstance of living and relative power of people prior to and following retirement, and, indirectly, their social relations and the overall quality of life in the United States.

The range of variability of the institutional processes or operating variables of social policies is virtually unlimited, and so is the range of variability of the outcome variables. Using again the Social Security Act as illustration, it has been amended many times since it was enacted in 1935. Each amendment, be it minor or major, has modified behaviors concerning work, rights, resources, governance, and socialization. Each has caused different, intended outcomes for circumstances of living and social power, as well as for social relations among individuals and classes, and for the quality of life. Each change has also resulted in unintended outcomes.

Specific social policies imply specific modes of operation of one or several basic institutional processes, and specific interactions among them. Changes of social policies and of entire systems of social policies involve corresponding changes of institutional processes and of the interactions among them. Desired modifications in circumstances of living, social power, social relations, and quality of life can consequently be achieved in a society by means of appropriate modifications of operating variables of social policies. This proposition is fundamental for social policy analysis and development. For implied in it is a frequently disregarded corollary, according to which, *significant changes in social power and social relations and in the circumstances and quality of life can occur only when a society introduces significant modifications in the way it manages resources, organizes work and production, exchanges and distributes rights and responsibilities, governs its public affairs, and organizes socialization processes for its members.* Social policies which involve no real modifications of these essential institutional processes, or merely slight modifications, can therefore not be expected to bring about significant changes on the outcome variables. By examining proposed changes in social policies in terms of expected effects on basic institutional processes or operating variables, one can determine whether they would yield real and significant changes, or merely superficial and insignificant ones—new variations on old, status quo themes. To illustrate, the circumstances of living and the relative social power of poor people, and their relations to other social classes could not change significantly by policy modifications involving merely cost of living increases in the minimum wage and in assistance payments to recipients of public welfare. To achieve significant changes of the circumstances of living, power, and social relations of poor people, policies would have to *modify their relative shares* of resources, work, goods, services and rights, governance, and socialization.

SOCIAL POLICIES AND SOCIAL PROBLEMS

"Social problems" which individuals, groups, and classes perceive concerning living conditions, relative power, relations with others, and the overall quality of life, are intended or unintended outcomes of prevailing institutional processes. While new social policies can be designed to solve perceived social problems, past and current social policies are the actual causes of the problems. Understanding social policies as causes and also as potential solutions of perceived social problems provides a theoretical base for the proposition that real solutions of social problems require thorough modifications of the social policies and the institutional processes which cause them. Such thorough modifications can be designed to eliminate and prevent the problems, rather than merely ameliorate their impact in an ad hoc fashion.

The futility, noted above, of cost of living adjustments of the minimum wage and of public assistance rates as antipoverty policies, illustrates the importance of tracing social problems to underlying social policies, in order to attack them at their sources. Poverty is widely considered to be a social problem. Its causes include social policies which result in lopsided, concentrated control over resources, and unequal access to work, goods, services, and rights. The inevitable outcomes of these policies are widespread deprivation in circumstances of living, and powerlessness. Cost of living adjustments can not, nor are they intended to, overcome the systemic roots of poverty. They can only protect people against more severe poverty. Eliminating and preventing poverty would require policies designed to overcome the lopsided control over resources and the unequal access to work, goods, services, and rights.

SOCIAL POLICIES AND ECONOMIC POLICIES

In accordance with the model of social policies presented above, economic policies, which shape the management of resources, the organization of work and production, and the exchange and distribution of goods and services are not a separate policy domain, but an integral aspect of social policies. Economic policies are, however, frequently separated conceptually from social policies. Such a separation leads to a view of economic activities as disassociated from human needs, social values, and social purpose. Moreover, the separation inhibits development of effective social policies, since it leaves policy planners without important operational variables to influence the circumstances and quality of life, relative social power, and social relations. Finally, the separation reduces social policies conceptually to a residual function, focused mainly on victims of economic policies. Many social scientists and journalists tend to accept this conceptual separation, although it lacks a sound theoretical rationale.

The separation of economic from social policies emerged gradually, over several centuries, along with the development of capitalist economic institutions, and seems to have reinforced these institutions and their ideology.[8] As a consequence, economic policies and activities came to be regarded widely not as means toward social ends, but as ends in themselves, subject to supposedly self-evident, "natural" laws. Economic growth, measured by increases of the GNP, is now widely accepted as desirable, regardless of the type, quality, and social significance of the goods and services included in the GNP (or excluded from it, e.g. parental child care), without much concern for the extent to which the distribution of goods and services meets the basic needs of people, and with little allowance for hidden costs and "dis-benefits" which are often unintended by-products of economic activities.[9]

The conceptual division between economic and social policies is also reflected in the notion of "rational economic human," according to which people are by nature selfish and motivated primarily to maximize their perceived material interests. This notion permeates the classic theory of capitalist economics. It underlies Adam Smith's assumption that the public good tends to emerge automatically, as if propelled by an "invisible hand," when people pursue their material interests, selfishly and competitively, in "free" markets, subject to minimal governmental interventions and controls, and undistorted by monopolistic tendencies.[10] These expectations concerning the spontaneous emergence of the public good have not been realized, although government action to promote the public good has usually been restrained in capitalist societies due to the teachings of Smith and his disciples. Avoiding market "imperfections" has, however, proved unattainable, with or without governmental interventions, as monopolistic tendencies seem intrinsic to competitive dynamics.

HUMAN NATURE AND SOCIAL POLICIES

How valid is the assumption that attitudes and behaviors of "economic human" are inevitable manifestations of human nature? This is an important issue for social policy theory, since nature-determined attitudes and behaviors of people limit the variability of social policies. Attitudes and behaviors which are inevitable by nature, can not be eliminated by social policies, nor can social policies induce attitudes and behaviors beyond the range of human capacities.

The assumption that selfish and competitive pursuit of material interests is an inevitable expression of human nature seems open to question although it is widely taken for granted. This assumption accords with a general tendency of people to perceive and justify the dominant patterns of their way of life as inevitable expressions of human nature. In perceiving their attitudes and behaviors as compelled by nature, people disregard that these attitudes and behaviors emerged as survival-maintaining and life-enhancing adaptations to human-evolved societal institutions, and that they are guided by social policies which reflect and reproduce the established institutional dynamics.

Attitudes and behaviors in social situations are, indeed, rooted in human nature in the sense of nature-determined possibilities, but not in the sense of nature-determined inevitability. Alternative attitudes and behaviors are usually possible, and are being and have been practiced in other places, times, and conditions by people who evolved different institutional systems and social values and policies reflecting and reproducing different ways of life. Human nature is always broader than the attitudes and behaviors dominant in a particular society. Each way of life is thus merely a selection from a wide range of possible attitudes and behaviors all of which are alternative manifestations of human nature.

People in many societies at different times, and in different situations, have indeed acted selfishly and competitively in pursuit of perceived material interests and they have related violently, cruelly, and destructively toward other individuals, classes, and peoples in order to dominate and exploit them for material gain. There is, however, also ample evidence throughout history, that people have acted and related towards others cooperatively, caringly, and lovingly, and that human attitudes and behaviors can be motivated by non-material, social, and philosophical ends.[11] These latter tendencies are, therefore, within the range of human nature, in the same way as capacities for selfishness, competitiveness, violence, and destructiveness in pursuit of material ends.

Which of the natural capacities of people are actualized at different times and places, and in different social relations and circumstances, seems to depend on the historic and contemporary institutional context in which they live, and their prior experiences and socialization. It seems, therefore, valid to conclude that while attitudes and behaviors ranging from extreme selfishness and materialism to cooperation, social concern, and mutualism are definitely part of human nature, their expression is never an inevitable biological function, but is always socially, culturally, and situationally conditioned, and guided by prevailing social policies and values.

Related to the above discussion of the effects of human nature on social policies, is the question whether the usual linkage between the organization of work and the distribution of rights is determined by human nature and therefore fixed forever, or whether it is subject to change. Policy changes concerning this linkage would be reflected in varying degrees of interdependence between these operating variables of social policies, ranging from nearly complete dependence to nearly complete independence between them.

Differences of work roles among members of a society are a usual aspect of the organization of work, once division of work has emerged in the course of societal evolution. However, inequalities of rights are, logically, not an inevitable consequence of differences in work roles. Many societies have, however, adopted inequalities of rights as a taken-for-granted corollary of the division of work, and have institutionalized inequality of rewards for different roles in the work system. This tendency is reflected in a high correlation between different types of work and different levels of rights. It is, of course, feasible, from a theoretical point of view, to distribute rights equally among all members of a society by means of universal entitlements, irrespective of the different tasks they perform. Such an approach to rights distribution would be reflected in independence between levels of rights and types of work. Obviously, any intermediate level of linkage between these operational variables of social policies is theoretically possible, and can be designed in social reality.

The relatively high correlation between the organization of work and the distribution of rights, which is a dominant tendency among contemporary societies (including several postcapitalist ones), is usually justified by reference to incentives and human motivation. It is widely assumed that in order to recruit people for diverse work roles in society, they must be attracted through differential incentives built into the reward system. While this may be a correct description of prevailing attitudes and behaviors, it does not reveal their sources and dynamics, nor does it answer the question whether this response pattern is biologically determined, and thus the only possible behavioral mode.

Some comments seem necessary here concerning human motivation, because of the importance of this issue for a theory of social policy and for the proposition that the linkage between work organization and rights distribution is subject to significant variability as a major avenue for changes in social policy. Human motivation seems to be a function of biologically given factors and socially learned tendencies. The relative importance of these two sets of factors is not known, but there seems to be little question that learned tendencies affect human motivation. These considerations suggest that existing patterns of motivation and of responses to incentives reflect existing patterns of socialization, and that variations in socialization patterns could produce, over time, variations in motivational attitudes and patterns of response. Accordingly, the patterns of human motivation used to justify inequalities in the distribution of rights in prevailing social orders do not seem fixed by nature, but seem open to change by means of variations in processes of socialization. The view that people are guided inevitably by the profit motive is, therefore, not necessarily a correct indication of the social, psychological, and cultural potential of humankind.

One further comment concerning human nature and social policy seems necessary, which is that self-orientation is not the same as selfishness. Self-orientation is rooted in the biological drive to survive and unfold innate capacities. Humans share this nature-determined drive with all living beings and pursue life, development, and well-being as an inevitable expression of their nature. This pursuit need not be competitively directed against others, need not involve disregard for the developmental needs of others, and need not involve manipulation, exploitation, and destruction of others, to advance perceived self-interests. Self-orientation need not take the form of "selfishness," which is only one particular mode of expression of self-orientation. There are alternative modes to express self-orientation, some of which involve regard for, and commitment to, the developmental needs of every individual, and avoidance of manipulative, exploitative, and destructive attitudes and practices toward others. Such alternative modes affirm everyone's individuality, in contradistinction to individualism which affirms merely one's self.

Orientation toward survival and development of others is not an inevitable human tendency, except, perhaps, in parent-child relations. However, people have a natural capacity to acquire and express such an orientation, in the same way as they have a natural capacity to acquire and express selfish and individualistic attitudes and behaviors.

The actual manner in which people tend to express self-orientation depends largely on the dominant tendencies and the internal logic of the way of life into which they were socialized, and the social policies which reflect and maintain it. Social policies do not induce people to be self-oriented, nor can they prevent them from pursuing this nature-determined orientation. However, social policies are the medium which shapes the manner in which people tend to express their self-orientation: competitively, selfishly and individualistically, or cooperatively and in a manner involving concerns for everyone's needs, and affirmation of everyone's individuality.

CONSCIOUSNESS, SYMBOLIC UNIVERSE, AND SOCIAL POLICIES

Consciousness is a mental faculty by which people become aware of, and can reflect about themselves, their natural and social environments, and relations between selves and environment. Consciousness emerges from active engagement with one's world, rather than from passive absorption of it. It involves internalization of a socially constructed reality—adaptation to it, and integration into it—as well as reflection about and imagining alternatives to this reality as a basis for reconstructing it. People tend to form in their consciousness images of their societies' concrete ways of life and of the social policies which maintain them, as a result of experiencing, observing, and participating in these ways of life and social policies. Sociologists have referred to these images in people's consciousness as "symbolic universe."[12]

Internalization into consciousness of aspects of the symbolic universe concerning one's social position, social class, and entire society, enables people to think, act, and relate in accordance with societal expectations and prevailing social policies. As they do so, guided by their consciousness, their behavior, in turn, reinforces their consciousness of the prevailing symbolic universe, and their capacity to participate appropriately in the concrete ways of life. In short, participation in established ways of life and social policies shapes one's consciousness of them, which facilitates further participation and reinforcement of consciousness—a lifelong process of interaction of behavior and consciousness.

The symbolic universe which individuals form in their consciousness reflects reality as constructed by a particular society in the course of its unique history. It does not reflect objective reality which is probably unknowable, as all knowledge emerges through societal processes, and is affected by them. The versions of the symbolic universe in the consciousness of different individuals in the same society tend to vary. People, especially in complex, internally divided societies, differ in social conditions and social class position, as well as in individual history, biology, and characteristics. All these dimensions affect the emergence of individual consciousness. As a result, the consciousness of different individuals in the same society will overlap, but will also differ. People's ability to communicate and interact effectively will be affected by the extent of overlap and difference in their individual consciousness. The consciousness and symbolic universe of people from different classes within societies and from different societies may differ markedly, which can cause difficulties in communications and interactions. Because of this, immigrants are likely to feel disoriented in a new society until they internalize into their consciousness major aspects of that society's symbolic universe.

Failure to develop a symbolic universe in one's consciousness which corresponds roughly with that of people with whom one lives—the cause of that failure may be organic, social, psychological, or political-philosophical—may interfere with an individual's ability to function in social situations and relations. Such individuals may be considered and treated as deviants, when their behavior does not conform to what is considered normal in their society, but reflects a unique, individual consciousness and symbolic universe.

The consciousness of people reflects their subjective perceptions of socially constructed reality, and serves as a frame of reference for individual thoughts and actions in everyday life. In accordance with the internal logic of individual consciousness, human behavior is always "rational," i.e. oriented towards the goals of individual actors, and makes sense to them at the time they engage in it, given their perceptions and feelings. Subjectively rational behavior may, however, seem irrational to others whose consciousness, perceptions and frames of reference differ from those of the individuals whose behavior they observe. It may also seem irrational to the individuals themselves, when their perceptions, feelings, and frame of reference change with time. For "rational" behavior is always relative to a specific consciousness.

It follows from these comments that social life always proceeds simultaneously on two interacting and interdependent levels, neither of which can function without the other: the level of concrete behavior, and the level of consciousness of individual members of society. People can not act unless their consciousness is engaged in their actions, and their actions are prefigured in their consciousness. For action and thought, or body and mind, are always a living unity, rather than separate domains.

In the course of societal evolution, ways of life and their images in people's consciousness emerged simultaneously; as people acted in pursuit of survival, their actions were prefigured and reflected in their consciousness. Once the images of actions, and reflections on them, became parts of people's consciousness, they facilitated repetition, routinization, and institutionalization of the actions as elements of ways of life and social policies. Analogous to the emergence of consciousness in the evolution of the human species, the consciousness of children also emerges as they interact with their social and physical environments, and participate in specific ways of life. Consciousness, on any level, emerges always in an active mode of living.

Consciousness serves usually as a medium for individual adaptation to established ways of life, and hence as a force for societal continuity. However, it can also evolve into "critical consciousness" and serve as a medium for critical reflection, and as a source for innovation of ways of life and social policies based on alternative perceptions of needs and interests. Such transformations of consciousness can be communicated to others, and can lead to collective actions aimed at social and cultural transformations.

The capacities of people for critical consciousness and for initiating social change are not actualized easily, however. Major obstacles to their actualization are that critical consciousness can emerge only gradually as children mature, but that the critical use of consciousness is usually not encouraged in the course of socialization. Critical consciousness is least developed during infancy and childhood—crucial stages of socialization during which children experience strong pressures for adaptation to established ways of life. Moreover, socialization of children occurs under conditions of physical, emotional, social, and economic dependence on adults who dispense rewards and sanctions, and are perceived as all-powerful. These circumstances reduce opportunities for the emergence of critical consciousness, and enhance opportunities for consciousness to serve societal continuity. They are, therefore, important sources of the prevalence of conservative tendencies in social evolution, rooted in the very societal dynamics and physical aspects of the relationship of children to adults. Other sources of conservative tendencies were noted above in comments on the human condition.[13]

One further aspect of consciousness which strengthens conservative tendencies is that children experience and come to perceive established ways of life as "objective reality," to be taken for granted as valid and permanent—a force demanding submission and resisting challenge. The human origin of prevailing ways of life is thus obscured, and gods, heroes, and superhuman ancestors are credited with "creating" them. Having developed such a consciousness of socially constructed reality while growing up, people are poorly prepared to critically examine established institutional systems and social policies, and to become involved in movements for comprehensive social change, even when their basic needs can not be met. Instead, they tend to view particular problems which affect them as isolated fragments, and to seek issue-specific, incremental solutions, which leave established ways of life and social policy systems essentially unchanged.

MAJOR THEMES OF CONSCIOUSNESS

Several major themes can usually be discerned in the consciousness of individuals and in the symbolic universe of societies:

- —images of the established way of life, its institutional systems and social policies, its customs and traditions, and of prevailing circumstances of living, relative social power, and social relations;
- —systems of ideas, beliefs, and meanings: interpretations of nature, human nature, and the universe; life and death; origins and destinations; time and space; the known, unknown, and unknowable; relations among these notions and between them and concrete ways

of life, institutional systems, and social policies;
—perceptions of individual and collective needs and interests—the sources of internal logic and rationality of ways of life, and of individual motivations, attitudes, values, and behaviors;
—social values and personal values; value dimensions relevant to social policies;
—ideology: description, interpretation, justification, validation, and reinforcement of the established way of life, social policies, and socially constructed reality;
—critical consciousness: reflections, questions, and challenges concerning the established way of life, social policies, and socially constructed reality; alternative visions.

These themes of consciousness can be distinguished conceptually, but should be understood as a unified mental process involving several related and interacting dimensions.

Images of Ways of Life and Conventional Wisdom

The first theme is an abstract equivalent of concrete aspects of social life as perceived by individuals. It is a road map of the social landscape in which one is expected to move, act, and relate. Without such a map, people would feel disoriented and incapable of appropriate involvement in social life.

The second theme is a depository of variable scope of "conventional wisdom" and of insights and assumptions concerning essentially incomprehensible phenomena and processes which humans always confront, and which they interpret and reinterpret, motivated by their "spiritual needs." This theme contains also notions concerning reciprocal links between these insights and assumptions and actual human behaviors, institutional systems, and social policies.

Basic and Perceived Needs and Interests

The core of the third theme is awareness of biologically rooted, basic human needs, and of corresponding, real human interests in the pursuit and satisfaction of these needs.[14] However, superimposed upon this awareness are often perceptions of socially redefined needs and of corresponding, redefined human interests in pursuit and fulfillment of these socially shaped needs. Depending on the scope and intensity of the superimposed perceptions, the awareness of basic needs and real interests may be partially repressed, i.e., displaced from consciousness into subconsciousness and unconsciousness.[15] Such changes in awareness and perceptions result from socialization in internally divided societies, when dominant classes, by virtue of their hegemony over systems of ideas, are able to induce most people to perceive their needs and interests in ways compatible with the needs and interests of powerful social elites.[16]

In addition to awareness of basic needs and interests and perceptions of socially shaped ones, the third theme also involves awareness of individual motivation to act in accordance with basic and perceived needs and interests. Finally, the third theme of consciousness involves the notion of collective needs and interests, which can be illustrated by concepts such as "national interest" and "national security." Such concepts have a strong emotional appeal which tends to inhibit reflection and reasoned analysis of their actual meaning. Collective needs and interests refer undoubtedly to individual needs and interests shared by some collectivity. What is usually not specified, however, is who belongs to that collectivity. In subtle ways, the impression is conveyed that the needs and interests of every member of society are included.

In small, classless societies, the needs and interests of every member may indeed be included in, and represented by, collective needs and interests. However, in large societies, divided internally into social classes, "collective needs and interests" are defined by dominant classes in accordance with their needs and interests. Yet, the emotional appeal of terms such as "national interests" and "national security" tends to mobilize support from dominated classes for social policies and societal practices which are potentially damaging to their own needs and interests. Many wars, fought mainly in the interest of social elites of large, divided societies, illustrate the readiness of dominated classes to serve, suffer, and die for a "national interest" which may not include their individual needs and interests.

Social Values and Personal Values

The next theme of consciousness concerns social and personal values. The origin and evolution of values are similar to those of social policies, since values are actually a special type of social policies. They differ from other social policies in their importance for the maintenance and transformation of ways of life, their level of abstraction, and the extent to which their human origin tends to be forgotten and denied, and projected onto gods and supernatural powers.

Social values are guidelines which people evolved in the course of societal evolution, in order to differentiate behaviors whose outcomes they "valued," and which they therefore considered proper and worthy of repetition, from behaviors whose outcomes they disliked and did "not value," and which they therefore considered improper and not worthy of repetition. In other words, values are behavioral rules to distinguish "good" actions from "evil" ones, and to ensure repetition of "good" actions, and avoidance of "evil" ones.

The yardstick or frame of reference for what is "good" and "valued," and what is "evil" and "not valued," are the real and perceived needs and interests of those who judge or "evaluate" behaviors. Accordingly, social values are always rooted in needs and interests, basic, real, and/or perceived. Behind every social value, one can, therefore, discern certain interests, and value analysis should explore whose interests are to be served by given values.

Social values can represent everyone's needs and interests, such as respect for and the preservation of everyone's life, or the needs and interests of particular social groups or classes, such as preservation of privileged conditions for males, members of the white race, and owners of property.

In the course of history, dominant social groups succeeded to coerce and induce dominated groups to internalize and accept as valid social values (and social policies shaped by these values) which served the perceived needs and interests of the dominant groups, but affected adversely the needs and interests of dominated groups. Women have internalized values assuring male privilege, and propertyless classes have internalized values assuring the sanctity of property, regardless of its sources. Even members of nonwhite races have, at times, internalized values assuring the privileged conditions of the white race.

The internalization of social values serving the needs and interests of dominant social groups seems to have been achieved initially through coercive measures. However, coercion was gradually complemented, and often replaced, by processes of socialization and social control rooted in, and aided by, organized religion, mythology, and ideology. These systems of ideas, which were developed by priesthoods and cultural-ideological elites, associated usually with dominant social classes, denied the human origin of values, and projected their origin onto gods and spirits, whom they endowed with imaginary powers to inflict severe sanctions for non-submission to established social values.[17]

It is remarkable that dominated social classes who submit to, and accept the validity of, social values which adversely affect their needs and interests, while serving the needs and interests of dominant classes, are usually much larger in numbers than the latter. By virtue of their numbers, they actually have potential power to transform social institutions and policies in ways conducive to the satisfaction of their needs and interests. However, they are unlikely to act together toward fundamental changes of ways of life and social policies in accordance with their needs and interests unless they reject in their consciousness the validity of social values which uphold the privileged conditions of dominant social classes.[18]

In short, social values may be understood as fundamental social policies which, when internalized into the consciousness of most members of a society, tend to shape and constrain the malleability of existing and future institutional systems and social policies, as well as the actions and thoughts of people.

While most people will usually internalize into their consciousness the dominant values of their society, there are nevertheless also sets of "personal" values in everyone's consciousness, which may differ significantly from overtly professed social values, and which may influence their behavior in everyday life. When personal values are in conflict with accepted social values, contradictions are likely to become manifest in people's behaviors. The prevalence of antisocial and criminal behavior, as well as acts of principled civil disobedience and conscientious objection, all of which do not conform to dominant social values and established social policies, illustrate this possibility.

Value Dimensions Relevant to Social Policies

When studying relations between social values and the ways of life and social policies of societies, one should be concerned mainly with value dimensions which exert a decisive influence over essential institutional processes or operating variables of social policies. These value dimensions include:

—equality vs. inequality
—liberty vs. domination, exploitation, and oppression
—self-orientation and individuality vs. selfishness and individualism
—life affirmation vs. disregard for life
—collectivity-orientation and mutualism vs. disregard for community
—cooperation vs. competition

The ways of life of societies invariably reflect their dominant positions concerning these interrelated value dimensions, and it is, therefore, possible to discern these positions by examining established social policies. These dominant value positions influence the process of policy development: they will be reflected in proposals for new policies, and they will constrain the range of possible changes in existing policies. Significant shifts in policy systems simply can not occur unless they are preceded by significant shifts in people's consciousness with regard to positions on these value dimensions. Links between these value dimensions and social policies are reflected in the fact that societies whose members consider inequalities in circumstances of living and power as "natural" stress selfishness, individualism and competition; practice domination and exploitation; and will preserve through social policies inequalities concerning work and production, management of resources, and distribution of goods, services and social, civil, and political rights. On the other hand, societies whose members are truly committed to the notion that all humans are intrinsically of equal worth stress individuality, cooperation, and mutualism; affirm life and liberty; reject domination and exploitation; and will evolve social policies which assure to everyone equal rights and responsibilities concerning work and production, management of resources, and distribution of goods, services and rights.

Some comments concerning these value dimensions seem indicated. The dimension of equality vs. inequality concerns, perhaps, the most fundamental issue of all social organization: should all people be considered and treated as equals in intrinsic worth and rights, in spite of manifold differences among them, or should some be considered and treated as more worthy than others and, therefore, be entitled to privileged conditions?

Social equality, it should be stressed, is a philosophical, not a mathematical notion.[19] Hence, it does not imply dividing everything into equal shares among all people, nor does it require monotonous sameness in life styles. Rather it means that everyone should be equally entitled to realize the basic human needs and interests discussed above, within the limits of available resources, in order to actualize one's unique individuality and become what one is innately capable of becoming, without interfering with the identical rights of others.[20] Marx's pithy phrase, " from each according to one's capacity, to each according to one's needs," is, perhaps, the clearest formulation of the philosophical meaning of social equality.

Another aspect concerning social equality, which should be noted, is that a society can be organized along egalitarian or inegalitarian lines. It can not become "more" or "less" equal as is often suggested in political discourse, for there simply are no degrees of equality. There are, however, degrees of inequality, and a society can become "less" or "more" unequal. When people advocate "more equality," they are merely proposing a lesser degree of inequalities, but not equality.

The dimension liberty vs. domination involves also fundamental issues of social life: should all people be self-directing subjects, free to pursue their needs and interests, or should some people be dominated and coerced to satisfy the needs and interests of others, whose liberty involves rights to dominate and exploit the former? Put differently, does liberty imply rights for some to dominate, coerce, and exploit others, and to deny others rights to the same exercise of liberty?

The contradictions implicit in these questions can be resolved conceptually, when one realizes that liberty in a society can never be absolute, in the sense of acting as one pleases regardless of consequences for the liberty of others. Even an absolute monarch in a hierarchically organized society is unlikely to exercise such uninhibited, absolute liberty. In real life, liberty is never absolute, unless one lives alone, in total isolation.

The proper question concerning the dimension liberty vs. domination should not be, therefore, whether people should pursue the fiction of absolute liberty, but what types of limits on absolute liberty are likely to yield the highest possible level of liberty for all people. The answer to this question seems to be that the highest level of liberty for all, and for society as a whole, can be attained when constraints on everyone's liberty are roughly equal. This conclusion differs from the widespread view that moving toward an egalitarian society inevitably causes reductions or even loss of liberty. This simplistic view seems valid only when liberty is conceived of as unrestrained rights to pursue one's needs and interests regardless of consequences for the liberty of others.

Closely linked to the dimension liberty vs. domination is the issue of governance: should it be a real democracy (i.e. self-rule "of the people, by the people, for the people,") with every individual having equal power and rights, or should it be some alternative model, involving rule over people by powerful elites, castes or classes, acting in their own interests, and exploiting the majority of people? Equal liberty for all seems only possible under real, comprehensive democracy. All forms of domination and exploitation imply essentially nondemocratic forms of governance, regardless of appearances, such as elections and political parties. People who are truly free would never choose voluntarily to be dominated and exploited. Therefore, whenever domination and exploitation are present in a society, no real democracy exists, regardless of the labels those in power use to describe their mode of governance .

The value dimension self-orientation and individuality vs. selfishness and individualism has been discussed above in comments on human nature.[21] The essential point concerning this dimension is that self-orientation and individuality are expressions of a basic human tendency rooted in nature, while selfishness and individualism are socially shaped expressions of this tendency, involving readiness to disregard and negate the need for self-orientation and individuality of others. Individualism and individuality, and selfishness and self-orientation are often equated in popular discourse. This causes confusion and inhibits understanding of actual social reality.

The value dimension life-affirmation vs. disregard for life concerns a fundamental, philosophical issue which underlies all other value dimensions: should people act consciously in ways conducive to the preservation of life, their own and that of others, or should they pursue their own existence in ways which disregard or undermine the existence of other people? Moreover, should they act in ways that protect nature around them, and conserve the basis of all life, or in ways that exploit and destroy the environment, in the interest of shortsighted gains. In short, should people view themselves as integrated into nature and the life process of all species, or should they view themselves as masters over nature, entitled to use and abuse it.[22]

The next dimension, collectivity-orientation and mutualism vs. disregard for community, concerns an issue people have struggled with throughout history: the tension between social and individual aspects of the human condition.[23] Can people develop and thrive by acting on their own, in lone pursuit of their needs and interests, or is individual development and fulfillment more likely to be realized in a communal context, when the development of each individual is facilitated by, and contributes to, the development of other members of society.

Humankind seems now at a critical stage—a time of conflict and transformation in social philosophy and practice. For many millennia, individuals lived submerged in communal formations. Then, during the Middle Ages, emphasis on the individual emerged gradually as a liberating idea and force, often negating the nurturing context of community. Over the past two centuries, people seem to be groping towards a synthesis of these apparently antithetical tendencies. A search is in progress for social formations conducive to individual development and fulfillment in harmony with local and global community, and with the natural environment. Humankind is living through a significant, revolutionary phase, although consciousness of this revolution in values is not widespread.

The final value dimension, cooperation vs. competition, addresses practical implications of the philosophical dilemma concerning the tension between community and individual: should people cooperate in building life, or should they compete in pursuit of survival and well-being? Does competition motivate people to ever higher levels of creativity and productivity, as is widely assumed, or does cooperation facilitate a better climate for creative and productive behavior? These questions can be answered only in relation to the entire social and cultural context in which they arise. In some situations cooperation seems appropriate, while in others competition may lead to better results. In still other situations, various combinations of competition and cooperation may be appropriate. Hence, choices concerning this value dimension depend on broader choices concerning the way of life people "value," the policy "outcomes" they desire for themselves and their society, and which value positions are most likely to result in the policy outcomes they desire.

Ideology

Next among the major themes of consciousness are the ideologies of society, dominant as well as alternative ones. The following quote from a dictionary of sociology clarifies the meaning of this concept: Ideology is,

> a system of interdependent ideas (beliefs, traditions, principles, and myths) held by a social group or society, which reflects, rationalizes, and defends its particular social, moral, religious, political, and economic institutional interests and commitments. Ideologies serve as logical and philosophical justifications for a group's patterns of behavior, as well as its attitudes, goals, and general life situation. The ideology of any population involves an interpretation (and usually a repudiation) of alternative ideological frames of reference. The elements of an ideology tend to be accepted as truth or dogma rather than as tentative philosophical or theoretical formulations, despite the fact that ideologies are modified in accordance with sociocultural changes.
> ... The concept was given great prominence in the writings of Karl Marx, who defined it as a system of ostensibly logical ideas that in

reality are a justification for the vested interests of a particular social class, the most dominant ideology in a society being that of the ruling class. Karl Mannheim used the term to refer to ideas that are distorted by the historical and social setting of individuals and groups.[24]

Ideologies, like other themes of consciousness, are products of collective human actions and thoughts throughout societal evolution. Notions, which were gradually elaborated into internally logical systems of ideas, were formed simultaneously, and in constant interaction, with the development and institutionalization of ways of life. Ideologies interpreted, justified, and reinforced ways of life as they emerged and were reproduced and stabilized, regardless of differences in institutional orders (egalitarian, cooperative, communal societies, slave holding city-states and empires, feudal societies, capitalist nation-states, or imperialistic global systems). Ideologies became a potent force toward relative stability of social order, and came to reflect the interests of individuals and classes who supported the status quo from which they benefited objectively and subjectively.

With the passage of time, as societies grew in size and became fragmented into dominant and dominated classes, and as institutional patterns and ideological systems became more complex, the origins of the patterns and ideologies in collective human actions and reflections were gradually forgotten. Along with this collective amnesia, extra-human forces (in the form of human-created gods), came to be perceived as creators of life and as originators of social patterns and ideologies. This projection from humans onto infallible, all-mighty, super-human agents greatly enhanced the influence of ideologies over the everyday behavior and consciousness of people. For, henceforth, to question ideological premises involved an inconceivable challenge to the gods and their absolute truth and power. Social sanctions for such challenges were usually swift and extreme. These projections and sanctions were certainly compatible with the perceived interests of dominant social classes, whose very dominance and privileged circumstances were justified and legitimated by prevailing ideologies.

As the ways of life which ideologies reflect underwent evolutionary and, at times, revolutionary transformations in the course of history, so did ideologies. However, in spite of constant interactions between institutional patterns and ideologies, the correspondence between these concrete and abstract dimensions of social life is usually not a perfect one. Rather, there are often time lags between changes in practice and changes in ideologies, and there are also contradictions between them, so much so that some students of society have viewed these dimensions as separate domains: the world of action and human relations, and the world of ideas.

The more complex and fragmented societies became in the course of change and development, the more difficult grew the task of creating illusions of inclusive societal interests, and the less successful became the process of ideological integration and indoctrination. Real and perceived conflicts of interests among age-groups, sexes, families, clans, tribes, races, religions, castes, and social classes within politically unified societies gave rise to variations on major ideological themes, to internal contradictions, and to the emergence of counter ideologies.

Dominant, privileged social classes have usually held hegemonic roles in the development and dissemination of ideologies. Most people tend, therefore, to internalize ideologies which are disseminated by (and compatible mainly with the interests of) social elites, but potentially damaging to their own real interests. Unless people encounter and internalize alternative ideologies, conducive to their own needs and interests, or somehow develop such alternative ideologies together with others with whom they share life experiences and social conditions, they are likely to support in consciousness and actions, ways of life and social policies which inhibit their development and affect adversely their well-being.

Critical Consciousness

The final major theme inheres in the human capacity for critical reflection. This can result in critical consciousness, the Achilles' heel of all established social orders, and a necessary, though not sufficient, precursor of all social change. Critical consciousness can initiate counter-themes to each major theme of consciousness. It can question and challenge internalized images of the established way of life, its institutional systems and social policies and their outcomes, and the customs and traditions inherent in the way of life. It can reflect on, and transcend, conventional wisdom, insights, and assumptions concerning nature, human nature, and the universe. It can distinguish between real human needs and interests, and socially shaped, perceived needs and interests. It can unravel values reflective of interests of dominant classes from values reflective of real human needs and interests. And it can generate alternative ideologies and visions of ways of life and social policies, conducive to the unfolding and actualization of everyone's innate potential, and to the emergence of an institutional order based on social justice and social equality, freedom and comprehensive democracy, and the affirmation of life in harmony with nature.

While critical consciousness, were it stimulated and used widely, could enable humankind to transcend prevailing, destructive and self-destructive practices, the societal tendencies and biological constraints discussed above seem to inhibit its widespread use.[25] These survival-threatening circumstances necessitate ever more intense efforts to overcome obstacles to the unfolding of critical consciousness, by individuals and social movements who have realized that critical thinking, and action based on it, are the key to a meaningful existence, and, perhaps the last hope of the human species.[26]

FORCES AFFECTING HUMAN NEEDS, SOCIAL CHANGE AND SOCIAL POLICIES

To round out the discussion of a theory of social policy, it is necessary to identify the major forces whose interactions affect human needs, processes of social change, and development of social policies. These forces include:

—attributes of the natural environment, and changes in it
—biological and intrinsic psychological and social attributes and tendencies of people, and their socially shaped elaborations
—demographic developments and changes in the ratio of population size to natural and human-created resources
—generation of economic surplus and related social, occupational, and spatial differentiations, and differentiations of rights and perceptions of interests; emergence of social classes and of class consciousness; conflicts resulting from these developments within

and among societies, especially concerning the control of resources, the division and organization of work, the exchange and distribution of products of work, and the disposition of economic surplus
—development of ideas, knowledge, science, technology, and skills
—interactions among different societies, and diffusion of alternative ways of life and consciousness

The process of social life and the development of social values and policies which reflect and sustain it, originated in interactions within human groups and between these groups and particular natural environments. Hence, attributes of natural environments and natural and human-wrought changes in them, as well as intrinsic attributes of humans and their socially shaped elaborations, are the basic forces of societal evolution. The powerful effects of environmental scarcities and abundance on social organization can be gleaned by comparing the institutions, values, and policies of societies living in deserts and in fertile river valleys. Clearly, the intrinsic possibilities of natural environments constitute facilitating as well as limiting conditions for patterns of social life. Equally powerful facilitating and limiting conditions for these patterns are inherent in the biological, psychological, and social attributes of the human species.

The fundamental existential issue, which all societies must resolve, is securing a steady, adequate flow of suitable, life-sustaining, and life-enhancing resources from their environment while, at the same time, protecting and conserving that environment and its regenerative capacities. In other words, humans must achieve and maintain a balanced relationship between their needs and the environment's capacities to meet these needs. This essential balance may be enhanced, as well as upset by changes in the productivity of the environment and/or of people. Such changes can result from natural processes, and also from survival-pursuing activities of people, which may involve improvements in production, but also excessive use and waste of natural resources and, at times, abuse and destruction of the environment's regenerative capacities.

A major force which can upset the essential balance between people and the carrying capacity of the environment is unchecked increase in the size of human populations in the context of real limits on necessary resources, and resulting changes in the relation between people and their needs. When this relation reaches a critical level, human groups may cease to exist, unless they can migrate to alternative environments in which they can live by their accustomed ways and policies, or they discover and develop new existential patterns which reestablish an adequate balance between them and their old environment. History over the past ten thousand years is, in a sense, a record of efforts by human groups to maintain or regain balanced relations with their environment, in spite of population increases which have gradually assumed massive proportions in numbers and density relative to the carrying capacity of Earth.[27] Population pressure on the environment and efforts to deal with its consequences underlie the discovery and development of new modes of production such as the shifts from hunting and gathering to animal husbandry and agriculture, crafts, trade, and industry. They also underlie the emergence of a wide range of societal processes and human practices, some of which involve serious threats to human development and survival.

The evolutionary shift from hunting and gathering to animal husbandry and agriculture, some ten thousand years ago, has had revolutionary consequences for patterns of social life, social values, and social policies. Hunting and gathering did not yield a regular surplus as people produced usually about as much as they consumed. Nearly everyone had to participate in food production, and whatever division of work was practiced, was based mainly on sex, age, and physical conditions, not on social criteria, such as family, clan, tribe, race, religion, caste or class, as during later stages of social evolution. Societies were relatively small and isolated from one another during this early stage. Their social organization tended to be based on egalitarian, communal, and cooperative principles, and did not involve significant differentiations in circumstances of living. The level of internal conflicts of interest was relatively low, and so were the rates of population increase and social change.[28]

These conditions and tendencies changed once unchecked increases in population and resulting scarcities of food and land spurred the development of animal husbandry and agriculture—modes of production yielding gradually a significant economic surplus which became a major source of social development, as well as of conflicts within and among societies. Increases in food supplies from herding and agriculture enabled some people to withdraw from food production and to pursue instead alternative occupations and roles, including crafts and trade; arts, science, and technology; armed forces and ruling elites; and spiritual, cultural, and ideological functions. The emerging division of work and functions led also to spatial differentiation into rural and urban settlements; to systems of social stratification consisting of dominant, exploiting, and privileged, and dominated, exploited, and deprived castes and classes; to corresponding differences of rights, consciousness, culture, and perceptions of interests; and to overt and covert conflicts between dominant and dominated social groups concerning the control of resources, the disposition of the economic surplus, and the terms of exchange for their respective work and products.

Exchanges between individuals and groups controlling different resources and performing different tasks in the division of work of a society can be fair and balanced or unfair and unbalanced in terms of human energy and material resources invested in their respective products and services. Balanced exchanges tend to be voluntary, as both parties share the economic surplus fairly and receive roughly equal benefits. Unbalanced exchanges, on the other hand, require usually physical and/or ideological coercion, as one party exploits the other by appropriating as much as possible of the economic surplus, and by receiving consistently larger benefits than the other. The processes of social, occupational, cultural, and spatial differentiation which followed the agricultural revolution resulted usually in coercively instituted and maintained unbalanced economic exchanges and conflicts of interests within and between societies. Over time, the processes of coercion induced counter violence by dominated and exploited social groups, which was usually followed by intensified coercion and repression—a vicious circle of violence, reflected in such violent, though "legitimate" institutions as colonialism, slavery, serfdom, "wage-labor," unemployment, and poverty, on the one hand, and concentrations of wealth and power, on the other.[29]

The differentiations and tendencies which followed the development and spreading of agriculture, the interplay between them, and reactions to them on the part of competing interest groups within and among societies, have become major forces propelling the evolutionary and, at times, revolutionary developments and changes of human societies and their social policies. Social policies may thus be viewed as expressions of the evolving differentiations and conflicts within and among societies, for they derive from and support the differentiations, and they spur the conflicts.

Once initiated, processes of societal evolution, and the parallel processes of social policy evolution, continued as a result of conflicts of interest among individuals and social groups who gained control over different levels of resources, and who differed consequently in rights and power. Past inequalities in the organization of work, and in the resulting distribution of rights, tended to be perpetuated, since individuals and groups who achieved control over disproportionately large shares of resources, and over more desirable and influential positions in the work system, were in an advantageous power position to assure continuation of these inequalities, and even to increase them in their favor. Also, institutionalized legal and political systems tended to reflect the status quo of power relations among competing interest groups, and were unlikely to upset temporary equilibria prevailing among them.

One consequence of economic surplus and of the social and occupational differentiations and specializations which it made possible, was the emergence of intellectual and spiritual elites, whose major function became development and dissemination of ideas, knowledge, science, and technology, as well as of ideologies and interpretations of unknown and unknowable aspects of life and the universe. The contributions of these elites were usually not intended as a force for social change, but were meant to serve social continuity and enhancement of the quality of life within established societal patterns; their search for "truth" and knowledge has, nevertheless, led to important changes and advances in ways of life of societies and in their social policies. Moreover, many intellectuals, throughout history, have viewed their mission as enriching human life and overcoming obstacles to individual and social development. They have, therefore, assumed major roles in social movements toward social and economic justice.[30] On the other hand, many intellectuals, induced apparently by their privileged social position and circumstances, and their close association with political and economic elites,

Chart # 2.2 FORCES AND VARIABLES UNDERLYING AND AFFECTING THE EVOLUTION OF HUMAN SOCIETIES AND THEIR SOCIAL POLICIES

A. FACILITATING AND LIMITING CONDITIONS

1. attributes of the natural environment and changes in it;

2. biological and intrinsic psychological and social attributes and tendencies of people and their socially shaped elaborations;

3. basic and perceived human needs: biological-material, social-psychological, productive-creative, security, self-actualization, spiritual

4. demographic developments and changes in the ratio of population size to natural and human-created resources;

B. INTRA-AND INTERSOCIETAL DYNAMICS

1. generation of economic surplus and resulting social, occupational, and spatial differentiations and differentiations of rights and perceptions of interest; emergence of social classes and of class consciousness; conflicts within and among societies concerning control over resources, organization of work, exchange and distribution of products and rights, and disposition of the economic surplus;

2. development of ideas, knowledge, science, technology, and skills;

3. interactions among different societies and diffusion of alternative ways of life and consciousness;

C. SYMBOLIC UNIVERSE AND THEMES OF CONSCIOUSNESS

1. images of: established ways of life, institutional systems and social policies, customs and traditions, circumstances and quality of life, power and social relations;

2. systems of ideas, beliefs, and meanings; conventional wisdom;

3. perceptions of individual and collective needs and interests;

4. social values and personal values; value dimensions relevant to social policies: equality vs. inequality; liberty vs. domination, exploitation and oppression; self-orientation and individuality vs. selfishness and individualism; life-affirmation vs. disregard for life; collectivity-orientation and mutualism vs. disregard for community; cooperation vs. competition;

5. ideology;

6. critical consciousness: reflections questions, challenges concerning the established way of life and social policies; alternative visions;

D. SOCIAL POLICIES

1. operating variables:
   a. development, management, and conservation of natural and human-created resources
   b. organization of work and production;
   c. exchange and distribution of goods, services, rights and responsibilities;
   d. governance and legitimation;
   e. reproduction, socialization and social control;

2. outcome variables:
   a. circumstances of living of individuals, groups, and classes;
   b. power of individuals, groups, and classes;
   c. nature and quality of human relations among individuals, groups, and classes;
   d. overall quality of life;

NOTE: The forces and variables presented in this chart interact with one another in multiple and circular ways.

63

have, through their work, supported destructive societal patterns and policies, and provided pseudoscholarly justifications for oppressive and exploitative tendencies.

Finally, of considerable importance among the forces propelling change within and beyond societies, are interactions among members of different societies on personal levels, as well as through economic, cultural, and political relations. Such interactions result, inevitably, in exposure to alternative ways of life, consciousness, ideas, knowledge, and technology. Individuals and groups involved in them may be stimulated by these exposures to examine critically their own ways of life and consciousness, an essential step toward social change.

The significance of these interactions has increased throughout history as their scope widened and their quality intensified due to global population growth, territorial expansion of societies, and technological developments, especially in land, sea, and air transportation, and in worldwide, instantaneous communications.

SUMMARY

Chart 2.2 (p.63) summarizes schematically the forces and variables which underlie, and affect through their multifaceted interactions, the evolution and change of human societies and their social policies. Awareness of the complex interrelations among these forces and variables is essential to the analysis of social policies, the development of alternative policies, and to social and political action aimed at human survival and liberation on local and global levels.

NOTES

1. Berger, Peter L. and Luckman, Thomas, *The Social Construction of Reality: A Treatise in the Sociology of Knowledge* (Garden City, NY: Anchor Books, 1967).

2. John Dewey, *Liberalism and Social Action* (New York: G.P. Putnam's Sons, 1935); Erich Fromm, *The Sane Society* (Greenwich, CT: Fawcett, 1955); Abraham H. Maslow, *Motivation and Personality* (New York: Harper & Row, 1970).

3. Manheim, Karl, *Ideology and Utopia* (New York: International Library of Psychology, Philosophy, and Scientific Method, 1936).

4. Marx, Karl, "Economic and Philosophic Manuscripts of 1844" in *Early Writings.* (New York: Vintage Books, 1975); Gil, David G., "Social Policy and the Right to Work," *Social Thought* (Winter 1977); Gil, David G. & Gil, Eva A., eds., *The Future of Work* (Cambridge, MA: Schenkman, 1987); Gil, David G., "Work, Violence, Injustice and War," Journal of Sociology and Social Welfare, Vol. XVI, No. 1 (March 1989) see also ch. 6, 10, 14 in this book.

5. Theordorson, George A. and Theordorson, Achilles G., *A Modern Dictionary of Sociology* (New York: Thomas Y. Crowell Co., 1969).

6. Sharp, Gene, "Power and Struggle," Part I of *The Politics of Non-Violent Action* (Boston, MA.: Porter Sargent, 1973).

7. Eleanor B. Sheldon and Wilbert E. Moore, ed., *Indicators of Social Change—Concepts and Measurement* (New York: Russell Sage Foundation, 1968); Jan Drewnowski, *Studies in the Measurement of Levels of Living and Welfare* (United Nations Research Institute for Social Development, Report No. 70.3, Geneva 1970); Jan Drewnowski, Claude Richard-Proust & Muthu Subramanian, *Studies in the Methodology of Social Planning* (United Nations Research Institute for Social Development, Report No. 70.5, Geneva 1970); Donald V. McGranahan. "Analysis of Socio-Economic Develoment Through a System of Indicators," *The Annals,* Vol. 393 (January 1971); Jan Drewnowski, "The Practical Significance of Social Information," *The Annals,* Vol 393 (January 1971).

8. Polanyi, Karl, *The Great Transformation* (Boston: Beacon Press, 1957); Weber, Max, *The Protestant Ethic and the Spirit of Capitalism* (New York: Charles Scribner's Sons, 1958); Tawney, R.H., *Religion and the Rise of Capitalism* (New York: Harcourt, Brace, & Co., 1926).

9. Samuelson, Paul A., "From GNP to NEW," Newsweek, April 3, 1973; Nordhaus, William & Tobin, James, *Is Growth Obsolete?* (New York: National Bureau of Economic Research, 1972).

10. Smith, Adam, *The Wealth of Nations* (Indianapolis: The Bobbs-Merrill Co.. 1961).

11. Kropotkin, Petr, *Mutual Aid—A Factor in Evolution* (Boston: Porter Sargent, 1956).

12. Berger, Peter L. and Luckman, Thomas, *The Social Construction of Reality*.

13. see pp. 15 and 16 in this chapter.

14. see pp. 16–20 in this chapter.

15. This argument is similar to Freud's psychoanalytic theory of the Unconscious. See Freud, Sigmund, *Basic Writings*, edited by A.A. Brill (New York: The Modern Library, Random House, 1938).

16. Gramsci, Antonio, *The Prison Notebook* (New York: International Publishers, 1971).

17. While priesthoods and organized religions have usually supported and disseminated values representing the needs and interests of dominant social classes, the sources of religions and their "prophetic traditions" reflect values which represent the real needs and interests of all people. The prophets, in opposition to priesthoods, advocated social justice, equality of people, love, and mutualism, and they called for establishment of just social orders "here and now," rather than in an "afterlife" of a "kingdom of heaven." The Bible, and especially the books of the prophets and the gospels, as well as sacred scriptures of other religions, provide ample evidence for the roots of religions in the yearnings of people for social justice, equality, and liberation from oppression. "Liberation The-

ology" is the contemporary expression of this strong counter current in religious consciousness. See: Gutierrez, Gustavo, *A Theology of Liberation History, Politics, and Salvation* (Maryknoll, NY: Orbis Books, 1973).

18. Sharp, Gene, *Power and Struggle.*

19. Tawney, R.H., *Equality* (London: George Allen and Unwin, 1964)

20. See pp. 16–18 in this chapter.

21. See pp. 42 and 43 in this chapter.

22. Commoner, Barry, *The Closing Circle* (New York: Bantam Books, 1972).

23. See p. 14 in this chapter.

24. Theodorson, George A. and Theodorson, Achilles G., *A Modern Dictionary of Sociology.*

25. See pp. 45 and 46 in this chapter.

26. Freire, Paulo, *Pedagogy of the Oppressed* (New York: Herder and Herder, 1970).
Freire Paulo, *Education for Critical Consciousness* (New York: Seabury Press, 1973)
Gil, David G., *The Challenge of Social Equality* (Cambridge, MA.: Schenkman Publishing Co., 1976). See especially Part III "Inquiry into Political Practice."

27. Weeks, John R., *Population: An Introduction to Concepts and Issues* (Belmont, CA.: Wadsworth Publishing, 1981).
The World Bank, *World Development Report 1984* (Washington D.C.: World Bank, 1984).

28. Eisler, Riane. *The Chalice and the Blade* (San Francisco: Harper and Row, 1987).

29. Gil, David G, "Work Violence, Injustice, and War." See also chapter 14 in this book.

30. Gil, David G., "Social Sciences, Human Survival, Development and Liberation," in *Basic Principles for Social Science in Our Time*, ed. Kenneth Westhues (Waterloo, Ontario: University of St. Jerome's College Press, 1987). See also chapter 11 in this book.

3

A Framework for Analysis and Development of Social Policies

INTRODUCTION

In this chapter a framework for systematic analysis of existing or proposed social policies, and for development of alternative policies, is derived from the conceptual model presented in the preceding chapter. The framework should facilitate attainment of the following separate, but related, objectives.

The first objective is to gain understanding of the issues that constitute the focus of a specific social policy which is being analyzed or developed. This involves exploration of the nature, scope, and distribution of these issues, and of causal theories concerning underlying dynamics.

A second objective is to discern the chain of substantive effects resulting, or expected to result, from the implementation of a given social policy, including intended, unintended, and short and long-range effects. This involves explication of policy objectives with respect to the focal issues, of value premises underlying these objectives, and of hypotheses guiding the strategies and provisions of a policy. It also involves specifications concerning the size, distribution, and relevant characteristics of target populations, and determination of the extent to which actual effects of a policy match, or are expected to match, its objectives. Once the substantive effects of a policy have been clarified, implications for the structure of society and for the entire system of social policies can be discerned in terms of changes in the operating and outcome variables of social policies. This requires also exploration of the forces affecting a policy and its implementation, for understanding interactions between a policy and the social environment seems essential to predicting its likely consequences.

A third objective of policy analysts is to suggest alternative policies aimed at the same or at different objectives concerning the focal issues. Different policies can then be compared and evaluated in terms of social policy relevant value premises, attainment of specified policy objectives, implications for social structure and the policy system as a whole, unintended effects, and overall costs and benefits.

The framework presented here is geared to the attainment of the foregoing objectives. Section A corresponds to the first objective, sections B through D to the second objective, and section E to the third objective. An analysis grows more complex as the number of objectives increases, and analysts may therefore decide that for certain purposes, a policy analysis should be limited to the first two objectives, or merely parts thereof. When it is decided to limit the scope of analysis of a specific policy, appropriate sections of the analytic framework can be used.

The proposed framework consists of a standard set of foci to facilitate systematic coverage of aspects relevant to the understanding of social policies and their consequences. The utilization of these foci should reduce differences in findings among analysts studying the same policy, since such differences seem often due to variations in the scope of issues explored.

Social policies vary in content, scope, and objectives. Hence the extent to which the foci of the framework are relevant in the analysis of any given policy will vary. Some foci may be of little or no relevance to certain policies and may consequently be omitted in the analysis. A certain measure of overlap is unavoidable among the sections and foci of the framework, since these sections and foci examine the policies from different perspectives.

The quality and reliability of available data, and the validity of specialized indicators, are likely to vary with respect to the foci of the framework. Moreover, it is possible that reliable data cannot be obtained, and that valid indicators are not available or cannot be developed, with respect to certain foci. Such negative findings concerning the data base of certain foci are, however, in themselves, important information, since in developing predictions with the help of the framework one needs to be aware of what cannot be known.

Before a given social policy can be analyzed, its provisions should be specified. If the policy has been enacted into law, administrative regulations and judicial decisions concerning it should be taken into consideration along with the language of the law. If a policy proposal rather than an enacted policy is being analyzed, specificity concerning operational aspects of the proposed policy should be provided. The framework is presented below, and its sections and foci are then discussed.

CHART #3.1

FRAMEWORK FOR ANALYSIS AND DEVELOPMENT OF SOCIAL POLICIES

SECTION A: ISSUES DEALT WITH BY THE POLICY

1. Nature, scope, and distribution of the issues
2. Causal theory(ies) or hypothesis(es) concerning the issues

SECTION B: OBJECTIVES, VALUE PREMISES, THEORETICAL POSITIONS, TARGET SEGMENTS, AND SUBSTANTIVE EFFECTS OF THE POLICY

1. Policy objectives: overt objectives and covert objectives
2. Value premises and ideological orientations underlying the policy objectives: explicit and implicit value premises
3. Theory(ies) or hypothesis(es) underlying the strategy and the substantive provisions of the policy
4. Target segment(s) of society—those at whom the policy is aimed:
   a. Ecological, demographic, biological, psychological, social, economic, political, and cultural characteristics
   b. Size of relevant subgroups and of entire target segment(s) projected over time
5. Short- and long-range effects of the policy on target and nontarget segment(s) in ecological, demographic, biological, psychological social, economic, political, and cultural spheres
   a. Intended effects and extent of attainment of policy objectives
   b. Unintended effects
   c. Overall costs and benefits

SECTION C: IMPLICATIONS OF THE POLICY FOR THE OPERATING AND OUTCOME VARIABLES OF SOCIAL POLICIES

1. Changes in the development, management, and conservation of natural and human-created resources
   a. Changes in ownership, control, and locus and criteria for decision-making
   b. Changes in types, quality, and quantity of goods and services produced
   c. Changes in priorities concerning resource allocation and conservation
   d. Other changes

2. Changes in the organization of work and production
   a. Development of new models, roles, and practices
   b. Strengthening of existing models, roles, and practices
   c. Elimination of existing models, roles, and practices
   d. Changes in criteria and procedures for access to positions in the work and production system
   e. Changes in the definition of work
   f. Changes in the design of work processes and in the quality of work life
   g. Other changes

3. Changes concerning exchange and distribution of goods, services, rights, and responsibilities
   a. Changes in the quality and quantity of general and specific entitlements, task- or role-specific rewards, and general and specific constraints
   b. Changes in the proportion of rights distributed as entitlements and as rewards, or in the extent to which the distribution of rights is linked to specific roles in work and production
   c. Changes in the proportion of rights distributed directly, in kind (e.g., public provisions and services), and rights distributed indirectly, as "right equivalents," purchasing power, or money
   d. Changes in the specifications of minimum levels of rights, e.g., "official poverty line," and in the extent to which the distribution of rights actually assures coverage of such a minimum level
   e. Changes in the relative distribution of rights, the terms of exchange of work products, and the degree of inequality of rights among individuals, groups, and classes
   f. Other changes

4. Changes in processes of governance and legitimation

5. Changes concerning reproduction, socialization, and social control

6. Consequences of changes concerning resources, work and production, rights, governance and legitimation, and reproduction, socialization, and social control, for:
   a. Circumstances of living of individuals, groups, and classes
   b. Power of individuals, groups, and classes
   c. Nature and quality of human relations among individuals, groups, and classes
   d. Overall quality of life

SECTION D: INTERACTIONS OF THE POLICY WITH FORCES AFFECTING SOCIAL EVOLUTION

1. History of the policy's development and implementation, including legislative, administrative, and judicial aspects

2. Political groups in society promoting or resisting the policy prior to, and following, its enactment: their type, size, organizational structure, resources, strength, extent of interest, value positions, and ideological orientation

3. Attributes of the natural environment and changes in it

4. Intrinsic attributes and tendencies of people and their socially shaped elaborations

5. Basic and perceived needs of people

6. Demographic developments and changes in the ratio of population size to available natural and human-created resources

7. Economic surplus and its disposition

8. Social, occupational and spatial differentiations, and differentiations of rights and perceptions of interests; class structure and class consciousness; conflicts concerning resources, work, rights, and the disposition of the economic surplus

9. Development of ideas, knowledge, science, technology, skills

10. Prevailing symbolic universe and consciousness including images of established ways of life; customs and traditions; systems of ideas, beliefs, and meanings; conventional wisdom; perceptions of needs and interests; value positions; ideology
11. Critical consciousness and alternative visions
12. Interactions with other societies and exposure to alternative ways of life and consciousness
13. Social and foreign policies relevant to the focal issues of the policy
14. Summary and conclusions concerning the policy's interaction with the forces affecting its development and implementation

SECTION E: DEVELOPMENT OF ALTERNATIVE SOCIAL POLICIES; COMPARISON AND EVALUATION

1. Specifications of alternative social policies
   a. Aimed at the same policy objectives, but involving alternative policy   measures
   b. Aimed at different policy objectives concerning the same policy issues
2. Comparison and evaluation: each alternative policy should be analyzed in accordance with the framework and compared with the original policy and other alternative policies.

DISCUSSION OF THE FRAMEWORK

The main sections of the framework are designed to elicit answers to five basic questions concerning a policy:

A—Which of the many domains of concern to a society constitute the focus for this policy?
B—How would the policy affect this domain in substantive terms?
C—How would society as a whole be affected by the substantive consequences of the policy?
D—What effects may be expected from the interaction of the policy with various forces within and outside the society?

E—What alternative policies could be designed to achieve the same or different policy objectives concerning the specified domain?

A—Both policy analysis and policy development should begin with the identification and exploration of the issues to be dealt with by given policies. The use of the term "issues" rather than "problems" in this context may require clarification, since social policies are usually considered to be measures for the solution or amelioration of specific social problems. According to the conception presented here, however, social policies are not merely societal responses to perceived problems, but constitute a system of human-designed principles for shaping the quality of life, the circumstances of living, power, and social relations within society. Consequently, while many social policies are indeed designed to solve or reduce specified, perceived social problems, such as poverty, many others deal with issues which are not necessarily perceived as social problems, such as the provision of education, the maintenance of health, etc. It seems therefore preferable to denote the general focus of social policies not as "problems", but as "issues." Obviously, this latter term includes also the notion of "problems."

Two related propositions are implied in the title of the first section of the analytic framework. One is that each social policy does have specific, identifiable foci—the issue or issues with which it deals. The other is that the various issues with which specific social policies deal are all components of the general domains of social policies. The purpose of the first section of the analytic framework is to identify and examine the specific issues dealt with by a policy as basis for the analysis of this policy and for the development of alternative policies. Such identification and examination involves two sets of questions, one set on a descriptive level and the other on an analytic-dynamic level.

A-1— The manner in which given issues are to be identified and described will depend to a considerable extent on their intrinsic nature and on the state of established knowledge concerning them. In general, issues should be identified and described within the context of the operating and outcome variables of social policies, rather than in terms of specific provisions of given policies. Thus, a given policy may make provisions for retirement income for a specific occupational group, e.g., railroad employees. The issue with which this policy deals should be defined as "retirement income maintenance," or perhaps even more comprehensively as "rights distribution through income maintenance," rather than as "railroad retirement income". Broad definitions of issues make it possible to examine and evaluate the effectiveness of policies in relation to generic societal functions instead of merely in their own limited and fragmented terms. Broad definitions of issues also facilitate the development of alternative policies. It can be seen from these comments that the way policy issues are defined is crucial for the entire analytic process. Care should therefore be taken to avoid definitions which are likely to limit policy analysis, and development of alternative policies, to the same assumptions and patterns of reasoning which led to the formulation of earlier policies.

One further caveat with respect to the proper identification of issues concerns the fact that policies may at times deal with covert issues rather than merely with overt ones. Thus, public assistance policies may deal overtly with income maintenance for economically deprived segments of a population but may, at the same time, deal covertly with the supply of cheap, unskilled workers.[1]

Descriptions of policy issues should identify and clarify major variables concerning the issues. If indicated, a classification or typology of the issues should be developed, problem areas should be specified, and the background and history of the issues should be reviewed. The scope and social significance of issues should be assessed in general terms, and, if appropriate, also in terms of prevalence and incidence rates throughout society, as well as relative prevalence and incidence rates among relevant subgroups of society.

A-2— Policy analysis and policy development require not only descriptive knowledge of issues but also insights into their underlying dynamics. Such insights can usually be derived from theories or hypotheses concerning the configuration of forces involved in the issues. This focus of social policy analysis and development involves, accordingly, a critical review of relevant scientific writings aimed at ascertaining the existing state, and the validity, of applicable theory.

B— The second section of the framework focuses on the objectives of a given policy with respect to the issues it deals with, values relevant to social policy underlying these objectives, theoretical positions underlying the strategy and provisions of the policy, and the substantive effects of the policy on target and other segments of the population.

B-1—The objectives of social policies constitute key criteria for the evaluation of their social significance and the analysis of their effectiveness. Objectives of policies need, therefore, to be explicated as clearly as possible. The importance of specification of objectives for policy analysis and development is widely recognized but, nevertheless, such specifications are often neglected. One reason for this seems to be the tendency of some analysts to be more concerned with the technical aspects, or means, of a policy than with its objectives. Technical aspects of policy implementation are, of course, important, and alternative means need to be evaluated and compared in terms of their respective effectiveness and efficiency. However, unless objectives have been explicated, and are kept in mind constantly as yardsticks for policy evaluation, the examination of means and of technical aspects is likely to be of questionable utility.

One consequence of the dominant interest in policy means is the tendency to substitute technical means for social goals. Thus, for instance, "constructing houses" may come to be viewed as a policy objective, replacing the socially more appropriate objective of "housing people." Constructing houses is, no doubt, an important means toward the objective of housing people. However, when this means is elevated to the level of an objective, its pursuit may, under certain conditions, produce adverse consequences for the policy objective of "housing people." This has actually happened in the United States when several decades of public housing, slum clearance, and highway construction policies resulted in a net decrease of adequate housing for the population. This is not the place to explore the fascinating process of social policy goal displacement and the social forces underlying it. The process is mentioned here merely in order to alert analysts to its existence, and to the importance of distinguishing clearly between social policy objectives and social policy means when attempting to explicate the former. One further difficulty concerning the identification of social policy objectives is the distinction between overt and covert objectives. This distinction corresponds to the one made above between overt and covert issues dealt with by policies. Overt objectives tend to be expressed in the preambles of policy documents, while covert objectives can only be inferred from provisions in the operational sections of such documents, or from administrative regulations and practices, and subsequent court decisions during the implementation of a given policy. Frequently overt and covert objectives conflict with each other, and awareness of such built-in conflicts is, therefore, important in analyzing the consequences of a policy. Policy means designed originally for the achievement of overt policy objectives are occasionally transformed into covert policy objectives by way of the earlier mentioned substitution process. Thus, policies aimed at the elimination of hunger in the United States were gradually shifted in emphasis toward subsidizing agricultural production and disposing of agricultural surpluses.

B-2—Next to be examined in social policy analysis and development are values relevant to social policy implicit in the overt and covert objectives of a given policy. Clarification of these values is likely to encounter difficulties similar to those discussed in connection with the specification of policy objectives. Values underlying overtly expressed objectives are likely to be openly stated or clearly implied in these objectives. On the other hand, values which underlie covert objectives will have to be inferred in the same way that these objectives are inferred, namely, on the basis of detailed aspects of the policy and the manner of its implementation. Once the two sets of values have been discerned, the extent of conflict between them, as well as of possible conflict between them and the dominant value orientation of society, needs to be assessed.

Clarification of value premises underlying the objectives of given social policies, and of the extent to which these value premises may be in conflict with a society's dominant value premises, is of crucial importance for social policy analysis and development since dominant value premises act as constraining forces with respect to the malleability of social policy systems. Knowing the value premises inherent in a policy seems, therefore, to be a prerequisite for predicting the manner of its implementation and its actual consequences for society. At any point in time a society upholds many different values. The extent to which these different values influence social policies varies widely. Some values exert considerable influence on the policy system while the influence of others may be negligible. For purposes of social policy analysis, consideration should be given mainly to value dimensions which are most likely to affect attitudes, decisions, and actions concerning resource control, work organization, and rights distribution. These value dimensions, denoted here as social policy relevant value dimensions, were identified in Chapter Two. The value premises of given policies should be examined in relation to these specific value dimensions.[2]

B-3— Once the objectives and value premises of a policy are clarified, theories or hypotheses underlying its strategy and its concrete provisions should be made explicit, and their scientific validity should be examined. The extent to which the strategy and the concrete provisions of social policies are derived from theory is likely to vary from policy to policy. Some policies may not involve any theories or hypotheses. Others may have been intentionally designed in accordance with specific theories, while still others may not have been designed in accordance with theory, but may nevertheless reflect certain theoretical positions in their strategy and concrete provisions. Whatever the extent and nature of the theoretical underpinning of a given policy may be, the analysis should bring it to light. Furthermore, the analysis should also clarify whether the theories that underlie the strategy and the provisions of a given policy are compatible with the theories that explain the dynamics of the issue with which this policy is expected to deal. These latter theories, it will be recalled, are to be explored under the first section of the framework.

A few illustrations may aid in clarifying the connection between social theory and social policy. Social science offers several theories to explain the phenomenon of poverty. One theory views poverty as resulting from a deviant subculture—the "culture of poverty"— which supposedly is handed down from generation to generation. Another theory interprets poverty as the result of economic reality factors, such as economic depressions and extended unemployment, and adaptation to these factors on the part of population segments exposed to them for some time. A third theory explains poverty as the result of socially structured and legitimated inequalities with respect to the control of resources, the organization of work and the distribution of rights in society. Social policy measures aimed at combating poverty can be devised in accordance with each of these theories. Educational approaches such as "Headstart," "Upward-bound," and various work training and work experience programs are anti-poverty policies derived primarily from the "culture of poverty" theory. Income maintenance programs, work guarantee programs, and minimum wage laws reflect a theory interpreting poverty as the outcome of particular economic realities and antidiscrimination policies, and other policies eliminating obstructions to equal access to resources, work and rights, reflect the poverty theory of "socially structured and legitimated inequality."

While compatibility between a theory explaining the dynamics of a policy issue and a theory underlying the strategy and concrete provisions of that policy seems to be a necessary condition of policy effectiveness, it is not sufficient to assure such effectiveness, since both theories may be invalid, or since policy objectives may be set at an inadequate level. Such inadequacies in the level of policy objectives may in turn reflect the values underlying the objectives. It can be seen, thus, that policy objectives, value premises underlying them, and theoretical positions concerning the strategy and provisions of a policy, have to be examined as interacting variables which affect policy outcomes jointly, rather than singly as independent forces.

B-4— In theory, every social policy affects every member of a given society to some extent. For purposes of social policy analysis and development, not all effects are of equal significance, however. Every social policy tends to be aimed primarily at specific groups of a society who constitute the "target segment(s)" for the intended effects of the policy. The remainder of the population, "the nontarget segment," is likely to be subject to indirect effects, most of which may be unintended, and some of which may be of limited significance only. No doubt, this division of a population into target and nontarget segments, and of policy effects into intended and unintended ones, is a somewhat arbitrary dichotomization. It seems, however, to be a useful device for social policy analysis, provided analysts do not interpret these divisions as valid representations of reality but merely as schematic approximations. Before the effects of a given social policy can be explored, the characteristics of target segments within a society must be investigated with respect to the following spheres which are relevant to social policy: ecological, demographic, biological, psychological, social, economical, political, and cultural. The more complete and reliable the information obtained in each of these spheres, the more reliable can be the analysis of the policy and the prediction of its effects. In gathering information on the target segments in these spheres, analysts should proceed from general toward specific levels, but should avoid specificity beyond a level expected to be utilized in the analysis. The optimum scope of information concerning the several spheres, and the optimum level of specificity, will also depend on the nature of the issue dealt with by the policy, the policy objectives, the policy strategy and provisions, and the theoretical position underlying the strategy and provisions.

Besides describing relevant characteristics of target segments of the population, their numerical size (as well as the size of appropriate subgroups among them) should be clarified, both in absolute terms and relative to the size of the entire population. Furthermore, projections into the future of these absolute and relative numerical sizes should be calculated as a basis for predicting long-range consequences of a given social policy. Published census data and, when indicated, special compilations of raw census data, available from the Bureau of the Census, are the best sources for this type of information in most instances.

B-5—The final focus of the second section of the framework calls for an examination of the chain of effects set in motion by a given social policy throughout the target and nontarget segments of society. In this examination, analysts should review first the intended effects of a policy, the "policy objectives," and the extent to which these intended effects actually occur. However, not less important than the review of intended effects and the degree of their realization is a search for possible occurrence and scope of unintended and unanticipated effects of a policy. Both types of effects may occur in the spheres of population characteristics mentioned above. Obviously, not every single policy will have noticeable effects in all these spheres. However, checking each sphere for possible effects will reduce the probability of errors due to oversight.

Once the intended and unintended effects of a policy have been established, they should be examined in terms of their overall costs and benefits. This examination should discern not only economic costs and benefits, but also social costs and benefits, although it may be much more difficult to estimate the latter. The translation of policy effects into cost-benefit terms may be useful for comparing alternative policies dealing with the same policy issue with respect to their relative effectiveness and efficiency.

C—The third section of the framework is based on the conceptual model of social policies and is designed to explore the effects of specific social policies on the structure and dynamics of society as a whole by discerning the extent to which the provisions and consequences of these policies result in significant modifications of the operating and outcome variables of social policies.

C-1— Important issues to be examined under this focus are whether the concrete provisions of a policy cause changes in ownership and control of resources; in participation in decisions concerning use, allocation, and conservation of resources; and in the criteria by which these decisions are made. Ownership, control, and decision making can be concentrated or dispersed, public or private, centralized or decentralized, regulated or unregulated. Changes in social policies can cause shifts and different combinations concerning these dimensions. Policy controversies concerning ownership, control, and decision making regarding resources are illustrated by eminent domain and zoning laws, rent control, worker ownership, and capital gains and inheritance taxes.

Criteria for decision making concerning resources may be modified by social policies along such dimensions as individual vs. public interest, short-term vs. long-term goals and interests, maximization of profits vs.

satisfaction of people's needs and promoting consumer interests, and maximum exploitation of resources vs. use of resources in harmony with requirements of conservation.

Priorities concerning resource allocation tend to reflect the preferences of individuals, groups, and classes who own and control the resources and who are, therefore, in a privileged position to make decisions concerning them. Priorities tend to change when policies effect changes in the relative power of interest groups and corresponding shifts in patterns of ownership and control. Shifts in value premises may have to precede such changes in policies. Movements for peace and economic conversion, which aim to shift resources from military uses toward meeting human needs and protecting the environment, illustrate intrasocietal conflicts concerning priorities in resource allocation.

Social policies effecting changes in the types and quality of goods and services are illustrated by policies promoting shifts from large, energy-wasting to small, energy efficient cars; from transportation by private cars to public transportation by trains and buses; from privately purchased medical care to publicly maintained health services; from products made of nonrenewable and nonbiodegradable materials (e.g., plastics), to products made of renewable and biodegradable materials (e.g., wood, wool, and cotton); and from low-quality products with built-in obsolescence, to be discarded and replaced after relatively short use, to high-quality products designed for long-term use. Qualitative changes may result also from policies conducive to the development of new products and services, and to the discontinuance of existing ones, such as the introduction of personal computers and their penetration into many spheres of life, and the closing of public libraries on weekends, respectively.

Policies supportive of qualitative changes in resource use will usually result also in quantitative changes, since the introduction of new or modified goods and services tends to be followed by changes in utilization patterns and in demand for earlier products. In turn, policies promoting significant changes in quantity of production will often lead to qualitative changes, as illustrated by declines in quality and increase in waste associated usually with shifts to mass production.

An important social policy issue concerning resource use is whether the quantities produced of such goods and services as food, clothing, housing, health care, education, recreation, and transportation correspond to the actual levels of need in a population or merely to "effective demand" or "purchasing power" as manifested in "free markets." Whenever the scope of production of such goods and services is geared to effective demand, the needs of many people with insufficient purchasing power will simply not be satisfied. Hunger, homelessness, and disease are some of the unintended, though usual, consequences of resource allocation policies which set production levels without regard for levels of need.

C-2— The organization of work can be affected and changed by social policies in many ways. Old patterns, such as serfdom and slavery, were abolished, and new patterns, such as democratically managed worker-cooperatives, may be established. Policies may also strengthen established models of work organization—private or public enterprises involving wage labor—and inhibit the development of alternative models through mechanisms such as licensing, incorporation, and taxation.

Social policies can facilitate or inhibit the representation of workers by unions, and they can promote or retard health and safety and other qualitative aspects of work life, such as the length of work days, weeks, and years; rest and vacation periods (including paid parental leave, educational leave, and sabbaticals); and provisions for the care of children of working parents.

Policies can also change the very definition of the concept of work by expanding or narrowing the range of activities which are regarded and rewarded as work. Are people "working" when they care for their own children or when they nurse disabled parents or relatives, or are such activities considered work only when carried out by an unrelated person? Are people working when they engage in activities which damage or endanger other people or the environment and its resources? Policy solutions of such definitional issues and dilemmas have implications for inclusion of activities within the GNP or their exclusion from it, and for social recognition and economic rewards for persons engaging in the activities, by choice or necessity.

A major policy issue concerning the organization of work is whether all people are expected and entitled to participate in accordance with their capacities, or whether some people may be excluded from participation through delayed entry, forced unemployment, or forced retirement. A related issue concerns the criteria societies use for selection, preparation, and assignment of individuals and groups to different positions within their system of tasks and functions. Access to all positions may be open to everyone on an equal basis, as would be the case in an egalitarian, democratic society, or access may be determined almost completely by birth and origin, as in caste systems. Between these extremes, many intermediate types of access to tasks and positions are possible, and can be designed by social policies. Policies dealing with socialization, education, training, apprenticeship, and inheritance, and with discrimination by age, sex, race, ethnicity, religion, political views, etc., are relevant to this important issue. Modifications of these policies would, therefore, be reflected in gradual changes concerning people's access to tasks and positions in a society's work system.

One other issue concerning work which social policies influence is the design of processes of work and production. Designs vary in consequences for human development and self-actualization. Designs will inhibit development when people are not expected to use their intellectual faculties and creativity in their work, as is the case when workers are viewed as "factors of production" and "attachments to machines." Automated assembly lines and minute subdivision of processes of production illustrate such dehumanizing designs.[3] On the opposite end of this dimension are work designs and contexts of creative artists who use their intellectual, emotional, and physical faculties in an integrated manner while working, and who exercise a relatively high degree of control over their work. Many variations are possible between these extremes, and social policies can reduce dehumanizing tendencies and facilitate the emergence of development-conducive ones.

C-3— Analysis of the effects of social policies on the exchange and distribution of goods, services and rights involves several aspects. One of these is the discernment of changes in general and specific entitlements, in task-specific rewards, and in general and specific constraints.

Illustrations of such changes in policies are: the establishment of a universal national health service, or health services for retired, aged individuals—a general or specific entitlement, respectively; increases in the legal minimum wage and in the compensation of members of Congress—task specific rewards; and changes in the rates of income tax and capital gains tax—general and specific constraints, respectively.

Related to policy changes concerning entitlements, rewards, and constraints are consequences of these changes for the ratio of rights distributed as entitlements to rights distributed as task-related rewards. Were a society to establish a system of free food distribution or a minimum annual income as general entitlements, the ratio of rights distributed as entitlements to rights distributed as task-specific rewards would change significantly, and the extent to which the distribution of rights is linked to people's specific positions in the work system would be greatly reduced.

Another ratio relevant to social policy is that of rights distributed directly, in kind (e.g., publicly supplied provisions and services), to rights distributed indirectly in the form of right-equivalents (such as money, which recipients can transform into a variety of rights at their discretion). Using the foregoing illustrations, a system of free food distribution would increase the proportion of rights distributed in kind, while a guaranteed cash income would increase the proportion of rights distributed in the form of right-equivalents or purchasing power.

A society's changing concepts of the levels of minimum rights which it guarantees to all its members is an important aspect of its system of rights distribution. The specifications of such levels, and changes in these specifications over time are, therefore, important social policies. These specifications have taken different forms throughout history. Major policy instruments such as the Magna Carta, the U.S. Constitution, and the Bill of Rights defined basic levels of civil and political rights. A more recent administrative method of such specifications are "official poverty lines."[4]

Social policies do not merely specify the levels, nature, and scope of minimal rights, but determine also the extent to which coverage of these levels is to be provided in practice. This latter function of social policies is perhaps even more significant for the actual distribution of rights in a society than the formal designation of the minimum levels. Obviously, social policy analysis and development need to be concerned with both aspects, the specifications and the extent of coverage.

A further aspect for analysis concerning the distribution and exchange of goods, services, and rights is whether a policy causes changes in prevailing relative distributions or in degrees of inequalities among individuals, groups, and classes. The ultimate sources of inequalities are coercively initiated and maintained differences in social and economic valuations of the work and products of different people and classes. These are reflected in consistent imbalances in exchanges of work and work products within and among societies. For policies to effect changes in relative distributions of goods, services, and rights, and in degrees of social inequalities, they would have to involve changes in the social and economic valuations of all types of work and workers, and they would have to reverse the coercive perpetuation of imbalances in exchanges of work and work products. For real social equality can be achieved only by policies which equalize the social and economic worth of all necessary work, and which eliminate structurally enforced imbalances concerning control over resources and exchanges of work and goods, services, and rights.

C-4— Social policies may effect changes in structures, processes, and responsibilities of governments at various levels, as well as in criteria for election and access to, or participation in, government bodies and institutions. Policies should, therefore, be examined for possible changes concerning these aspects of governance.

Legitimation can be accomplished through simple, formal processes, as well as through complex, subtle, symbolic, and informal ones. Analysis of social policies should discern possible changes in all these types of legitimation.

C-5— Social policies can affect and change processes of reproduction, socialization, and social control in many different ways. In fact, this diversity is so broad, that anticipating and mapping it does not seem possible. Analysis of discrete policies requires thorough exploration of their possible effects on these important variables of social life and societal evolution.

C-6— Once the effects of a policy on resource management, work organization, rights distribution, governance, legitimation, reproduction, socialization, and social control have been identified, the combined effects of these variables on circumstances of living, power, social relations, and the quality of life should be examined. These effects would be reflected in the spheres discussed above concerning the "target segments" of populations (Section B, 4 & 5). Information developed at that stage of an analysis should be used here from a social structural perspective to trace possible shifts in the circumstances and power of various groups and classes, and their consequences for social relations and the quality of life. Clearly, not every policy will affect every sphere. Nevertheless, each sphere should be examined for possible effects.

In discerning policy effects on the circumstances of living and power of people, and on the overall quality of life, a distinction between objective indicators and subjective perceptions is required. Illustrations of objective indicators of various spheres are: pollution levels, highways, housing, and parks—ecological; population density, rates of births, deaths, marriages, divorces, and migration—demographic; infant mortality, morbidity rates, and genetic disorders—biological; incidence of mental illness and suicide—psychological; social participation, social alienation, and social deviance—social; levels of production, distribution of goods and services, distribution of income and wealth, employment rates, and cost of living—economic; citizen participation, civil and political rights—political; science, education, recreation, art—cultural. [5]

Measures of subjective perceptions of the quality of life, circumstances of living, and power are usually not readily available unless special surveys are conducted. When surveys are conducted, they should elicit feelings, attitudes, and opinions before and after the implementation of specific social policies. Responses of individuals obtained by such surveys can be aggregated into quantitative measures of subjective perceptions. Eventually such surveys could be carried out routinely.

A comment seems indicated concerning the difference between the concepts "quality of life" and "circumstances of living." The former refers to phenomena on an aggregate level as encountered by society as a whole. The latter, on the other hand, refers to specific living conditions of individuals and social classes. The concepts are related, yet they refer to different aspects of the same reality.

While objective changes in quality of life, circumstances of living, and power can be observed and often measured directly, changes in intrasocietal relations may be less noticeable, especially when the changes are merely minor. Some of these changes will be on the level of formal, institutionalized relations, such as changes in doctor-patient relations upon the establishment of a national health service, or changes in relations between employers and employees once social policies sanction labor unions as bargaining agents. Other changes may be more subtle, such as changes in informal and formal intrafamilial relations upon the introduction of income maintenance schemes, such as children's allowances, parents' wages, retirement benefits, negative income taxes, or universal demogrants.

A useful approach toward detecting changes in human relations involves identification of sets of intrasocietal relations which are likely to be affected by specific social policies. Once these sets are identified, possible changes in their relations may be discerned.

D— The fourth section of the framework examines social policies in relation to forces represented in Chart #2.2 of the preceding chapter. The purpose of this analysis is to study the effects of interactions between specific policies and forces within and outside a society which surround the development and implementation of social policies.

D-1— In preparation for studying these interactions, the history of specific policies should be reviewed. Attention should be given to political, legislative, administrative, and judicial aspects. Information gathered for Section A, when analyzing issues dealt with by specific social policies, is likely to be relevant to the historical review.

D-2— The second item of this section is actually part of the historical review. Yet, because of the importance of political forces for the development of social policies, they should be examined separately. Not all political forces in a society are, however, relevant to the analysis of every social policy. Only those political forces should be examined which were involved in the evolution of specific policies, or are likely to become involved in the future.

D-3 and *D-4*— Next, interactions of a policy with facilitating and limiting aspects of the natural environment, and of biological, psychological, and social attributes of people should be examined. The importance of the former can be grasped by studying differences in the evolution of social policies among nomadic societies living on the fringes of deserts, and sedentary societies inhabiting the fertile valleys of major rivers. As for the latter, biological, psychological, and social characteristics of people are relevant to social policy analysis since they underlie specific behavioral and motivational patterns. Assumptions concerning these patterns tend to influence the design of social policies. Thus, for instance, work incentive features in income maintenance policies, and tax reduction features as incentives to philanthropic gifts or capital investments, reflect certain assumptions concerning human behavior and motivation implicit in the notion of "rational, economic individuals" who act to maximize perceived self-interests.

While human attributes reveal usually a high degree of continuity, they are nevertheless subject to change under the influence of different societal patterns and social policies. This plasticity of human characteristics is revealed in the development of individuals who are transplanted from one societal context to a vastly different one. Behavior and motivation should therefore not be regarded as unchangeable factors in the analysis and development of social policies. Biological properties of people and of the natural environment, on the other hand, seem to be less plastic than psychological and social characteristics, and physical properties of the natural environment tend to be most resistant to change through human intervention. These differences in plasticity should be kept in mind when examining interactions of social policies with the facilitating and limiting characteristics of people and of natural environments.

D-5— Basic and perceived human needs are assumed to be the sources of social evolution, social change, and social policies. In accordance with this assumption, it was suggested in Chapter Two that the extent to which people are able to realize their needs was an appropriate criterion for evaluating ways of life and social policies.[6] Analysis of interactions between specific social policies and basic and perceived human needs should, therefore, discern possible changes, associated with the implementation of the policies, in the extent to which people of different groups and classes can satisfy their needs. Analysis should also trace changes in people's perceptions of their needs associated with given social policies, and how policies, in turn, are shaped by people's basic and perceived needs.

D-6— Demographic developments may cause changes in the aggregate level of needs of a population and thus affect the interactions of social policies with basic and perceived human needs. Changes in population size and in age distribution can cause conflicts related to emerging imbalances concerning resources, production, and distribution of goods and services. These conflicts and imbalances are often dealt with through policies aimed at restoring a balance and managing the conflicts. Analysis should trace demographic trends and examine whether, and how, they are reflected in specific social policies and changing societal practices. It should also examine how policies, in turn, affect demographic trends.

D-7— The capacity of human groups to produce more than necessary for survival and reproduction has posed challenges to them ever since they succeeded in generating a regular economic surplus. Major policy questions in this regard include: how, and by whom, is the surplus produced; what should be its form; who should share in its use and consumption; and how are rules concerning the production and distribution of the surplus to be enforced. Many social policies deal directly or indirectly with these issues. Analysis should, therefore, discern how the dynamics of surplus production and disposition are reflected in given policies, and how these policies influence and change these dynamics.

D-8— Differentiations within societies by occupation, location, rights, life style, social class, consciousness, and perceptions of interests are results of historic processes set in motion and perpetuated by the production of economic surplus, and conflicts and struggles over its allocation and distribution. Social policies serve as ex-post-facto ratifications and legitimations of these intrasocietal differentiations. Some differentiations may benefit everyone in a society (e.g., improvements in productivity and in the overall quality of life due to competence gained by specialization), while other differentiations may benefit only special groups and classes who monopolize control over resources and access to privileged roles, functions, power, and life styles. While differentiations which benefit all people in a society evenly tend to evolve without coercion, differentiations which serve mainly the interests of special groups and classes are usually established and perpetuated through the use of overt and covert coercion.[7]

Policy analysis should examine the influence of established intrasocietal differentiations, and of tendencies and conflicts inherent in them, on new policies. It should also examine likely consequences of new policies for prevailing differentiations, their reinforcement, and possible changes in them.

D-9— Ideas, knowledge, science, technology, and skills are products of intrasocietal differentiations, which have important implications for social evolution, social change, and social policies. Social policies, in turn, affect the development of ideas, knowledge, science, technology, and skills. Societies at different stages of development concerning these cultural dimensions generate different systems of social policies, which, in turn, are reflected in differences concerning the development of ideas, knowledge, science, technology, and skills. These interactions are not always taken into account in social policy analysis and development. Disregarding them has often resulted in unintended and unexpected consequences of specific social policies. A well-known illustration of this is the invention, and subsequent evolution, of the automobile, and the sequence of social policies which this invention stimulated. Interactions between this invention and these policies on the one hand, and many aspects of life in the United States and in foreign countries on the other, have gradually revolutionized the overall quality of life, the circumstances of living, and the nature of human relations on an unprecedented and unexpected scale. Had the attention of policy makers been focused on these multifaceted interactions when they formulated social policies which subsequently became important factors in the evolution of the automobile, many undesirable side effects of the unrestrained development of the automobile could, perhaps, have been prevented.

To prevent unintended consequences such as these, analysis of new social policies should examine whether, and how, they are influenced by established ideas, knowledge, science, technology, and skill; whether they reinforce them, and if so, with what consequences; or whether they transform them, and if so, in what ways.

D-10— The "symbolic universe" or "socially constructed reality" of people, including the major themes of consciousness reviewed in Chapter Two, exert a constraining influence on the formulation of new social policies and on modification of established ones.[8] Analysis should, therefore, examine the effects of themes of consciousness on new policies, and consequences of new policies for the reinforcement or modification of prevailing consciousness. It is especially important to clarify whether the value premises and perceptions of interests implicit in a policy are internally consistent and compatible with the dominant beliefs, values, perception of interests, and ideology of society. Internal inconsistencies and lack of compatibility concerning these aspects should alert analysts to likely difficulties and conflicts during the implementation of a policy.

D-11— Critical consciousness and alternative visions of social life are among the major themes of consciousness.[9] Their influence on social policy development should nevertheless be examined separately because of their crucial role in social evolution and change. The spread of critical consciousness among members of a society is a necessary element of all significant social change. The influence of critical consciousness on new policies, as well as consequences of new policies for the expansion of critical consciousness, should therefore be examined in any policy analysis.

D-12— The ways of life of nearby and distant societies have always exerted an influence on the consciousness of people, and, therefore, on the development of social policies. This influence has intensified greatly in the twentieth century, due to technological improvements in transportation and communication, and resulting increases in intersocietal contacts and flow of information. Policy analysis should discern the extent of this influence in relation to specific social policies, as well as the influence of new policies on the scope of ongoing intersocietal relations. Illustrations of policies reflecting mutual influences among societies are worldwide similarities of programs for social security. Illustrations of policies designed to inhibit intersocietal contacts and the flow of information on different ways of life are restrictions on the entry into a country by individuals espousing "undesirable" views, and censorship on foreign newspapers and books.

D-13—From a theoretical perspective, every social policy interacts to a certain, extent with every other social and foreign policy. From a practical perspective, however, analysis should be limited to interactions with policies which are likely to result in significant rather than in minor effects. Policies which deal with the same and with related societal issues should certainly always be considered.

Interactions between social and foreign policies are not always considered in the analysis of social policies although, especially during periods of foreign wars, foreign policies exert considerable, manifold influences over decisions concerning intrasocietal resource management, organization of work, and rights distribution. And, in turn, social policies exert similarly important influences over foreign trade and other aspects of foreign policy, such as economic aid, capital investments, cultural relations, territorial expansion, migration, and war and peace. Examining effects of actual and potential interactions between specific social policies and relevant foreign policies is, therefore, as important an aspect of social policy analysis and development as the study of interactions among the various social policies of a society.

D-14—The substantive items of section D of the framework are closely interrelated since they all focus on interactions between specific social policies and various sets of forces within and beyond the same society. They are thus dealing with the same question from different perspectives. It seems, therefore, important to go through the analysis of all the substantive items of this section before predicting the probable fate of specific social policies, rather than attempting such predictions on the basis of information gathered in relation to merely one or some of the items.

E—Section E moves beyond the analysis of specific social policies to the development and study of alternative policies, and to the systematic comparison of these social policies in terms of specified evaluative criteria. The development and study of alternative social policies is perhaps the most important aspect of policy analysis, and thus the most constructive use to which the framework may be put. For ancient social problems which have defied solution when attacked through conventional, incremental policy strategies may yield to innovative approaches involving significant restructuring of the major processes of social policies, the existing configurations of which maintain the alienating status quo and sustain its social problems.

E-1—In general, the development of alternative social policies involves determination of the nature and scope of changes which need to be made in the policy processes of resource management, work organization, rights distribution, governance, and socialization in order to attain selected objectives on the outcome variables of social policies. These changes are then transformed into substantive program elements which are incorporated into newly generated policies. It should be reemphasized that specified policy objectives depend for their realization on specific configurations of the policy processes, and that unless these specific configurations are attained by means of appropriate modifications, the objectives can simply not be realized.

More specifically, development of alternative social policies involves one or the other of two approaches, or combinations of these approaches. The first approach is concerned mainly with assuring effectiveness and increasing efficiency in relation to constant policy objectives. Alternative policies developed along this path are unlikely to result in significant social-structural breakthroughs or major modifications of social policies. They will merely increase the probability that specified policy objectives are indeed achieved, that resources are not wasted in the process, and that undesirable side effects are minimized.

An illustration of policy alternatives of this type would be different policies aimed at the identical objective of closing the official " poverty gap." Closing the poverty gap involves transferring income from groups in the population with incomes above the official "poverty line" to groups with incomes below that line in amounts sufficient to close the income gap for all persons whose income is below the poverty line. A number of approaches are available to achieve this objective. Income could be transferred through "negative income taxes" involving work incentive features at varying levels, and administered through different procedures; through "universal demogrants" at, or above, the level of the poverty line, distributed to all members of society, with surplus income recouped through various provisions in the tax laws; through a combination of measures including increases in minimum wages, creation of public service and other jobs, extending social security to currently not covered groups of the population, and increasing minimum social security payments to the poverty level. Obviously, several other policies could be devised to close the poverty gap. Analysis by means of relevant sections of the framework would indicate the extent to which each approach achieved the specified objective of eliminating the poverty gap, what other consequences would occur, and what overall societal costs and benefits would be involved. All these alternative policies would, however, accept, by implication, the closing of the poverty gap as an appropriate policy objective in relation to the underlying policy issue of income distribution.

The second approach to the development of alternative social policies begins with questions concerning the appropriateness of given policy objectives with respect to the issues to be dealt with by these policies. If existing objectives do not seem suitable, alternative, more suitable ones are specified, and policies corresponding to these alternative objectives are then generated. Thus, in relation to the issue of income distribution discussed above, questions could be raised concerning the appropriateness of the objective of eliminating the poverty gap. Such an objective might be considered inappropriate by some analysts as it could, in their view, undermine motivation to work and to support oneself and one's family, and lead to a general decline of individual responsibility. Proponents of such views might suggest, as alternative policy objectives, (1) closing merely a portion (e.g., one half) of the poverty gap in order to protect poor individuals and families against extreme hardships while maintaining pressures on them to seek employment; or (2) closing the poverty gap only for groups in the population who are not expected to support themselves by working, such as children, aged individuals, and people with disabilities. Other analysts might view the objective of closing the poverty gap as inadequate since its redistributive effects may seem to them insignificant in terms of equalizing rights and opportunities throughout society, and since, even as a minimum standard of living, the poverty level would be judged by them to be totally inadequate and inhumane. Proponents of these latter views might suggest, as an alternative policy objective concerning the issue of income distribution, to close the income gap up to an objectively measured standard of decent living, such as the Bureau of Labor Statistics' "low" standard of living which is nearly twice the amount of the official "poverty line." It is clear from these illustrations that the selection of policy objectives tends to be influenced by value premises, ideological positions, and theoretical assumptions of different policy analysts, and that such selections are therefore based only partly on objectively established facts.

Value premises, ideological positions, and theoretical assumptions concerning human behavior and motivation influence not only the selection of policy objectives but also the selection of policy means. Illustrations of this would be differences in the scope of work incentive features and in procedures for verifying resources of recipients and establishing eligibility, among alternative income maintenance policies geared to the identical policy objective of eliminating the poverty gap. Another illustration would be the choice between "selective" approaches (such as the negative income tax) and "universal" approaches (such as parents' wages and children's allowances) as means of closing the poverty gap. Selective approaches would maximize the economic value of efficiency, while universal approaches would sacrifice economic efficiency to the value of social integration.[10]

E-2—Alternative policies developed at this stage of an analysis, be they aimed at attaining originally selected policy objectives or newly suggested alternative objectives, should be analyzed in accordance with relevant foci in sections B through D of the framework, and compared throughout this analysis with the original policy and other alternative policies. These comparisons and evaluations constitute the summation of a policy analysis, and should answer the following questions:

—What values would be maximized by the original and the alternative social policies in terms of social policy relevant value dimensions?

—What are the objectives of the different social policies with reference to the issues dealt with by them, and how effective would each policy be in realizing its respective objectives?

—What would be the impact of these different policies on the structure of society, the processes of social policies, and the entire system of social policies?

—What unintended side effects could be expected from the several policies?

—And, finally, what would be the overall benefits and overall real costs to society as a whole of every one of these policies?

SUMMARY

To conclude the discussion of the framework for the analysis and development of social policies, several general observations seem indicated. First of all, it needs to be reemphasized that the framework is not meant to yield automatic solutions to policy questions. It is definitely not designed as a substitute for informed and critical human intellect, but merely as an important aid to it. The more thoroughly policy analysts understand the complex dynamics of their society and the substantive issues dealt with by specific policies, the more useful the framework could be in their work.

Few policy analysts can be expected to have sufficiently mastered all the relevant scholarly disciplines dealing with societal dynamics and substantive policy issues such as biology, ecology, demography, psychology, sociology, anthropology, economics, political science, history, etc. It would appear, therefore, that in order to achieve optimal results with the aid of the framework, policy analyses should, preferably, be carried out by multidisciplinary teams rather than by individual analysts working independently. Such teams, because of the collective competence of their members, will be skilled in identifying and utilizing the types of data needed to carry out complete policy analyses, and they will know where and how these data can be secured efficiently. Moreover, teams of policy analysts working under the auspices of government bureaus, policy institutes, or of citizens' organizations, could develop and maintain permanent files of relevant series of data, instant availability of which would greatly facilitate and accelerate the systematic analysis and development of social policies.

While, then, the implementation of comprehensive, valid, and reliable policy analyses requires considerable resources because of the complex nature and scope of the task, it is nevertheless possible to utilize the framework in a flexible manner on a lesser scale of effort and investment. This can be done by individual analysts or by small ad hoc teams working outside well-equipped organizations. Such less complete analyses may often be sufficient for purposes of orientation concerning specific policies. Abbreviated analyses should utilize the five general questions listed on page 74, each of which corresponds to one section of the framework. From these general questions, analysts could proceed to deal with the first-order (numbered) items of relevant sections of the framework, bypassing the second-order (lettered) sub-items. The reliability of shortened analyses will be lower than that of the complete analyses, and interpretations, conclusions, and predictions based on them will have a wider margin of error. Yet, nevertheless, there are likely to be many instances when such shortened analyses will be all that is required, and when it would even be wasteful to carry out more comprehensive analyses.

One further comment concerns differences in the use of the framework in the analysis of existing or proposed policies, and in the development of new ones. In either case, it is important to start with a study of the issues to be dealt with by a policy—section A of the framework. However, when analyzing an existing or proposed policy, the remaining sections of the framework are followed in proper sequence from B through E, while in developing new policies work on section A is followed by sections, E, B, C, and D, in that order. Also, when generating new policies it is important to develop specific statements of the provisions of the proposed policies before proceeding with sections B through D of the framework. Without such specific policy statements the analysis could not be carried out properly.

The foregoing discussion of the framework and its utilization in the analysis and development of social policies has probably left several unanswered questions in the minds of readers. These questions, it is hoped, will be clarified in Appendix I through an illustration of the application of the framework in the analysis and development of one specific social policy. This illustrative analysis was carried out by one analyst working by himself, and it is, therefore, not as thorough and reliable as it could be, were it undertaken by a multidisciplinary team competent in all relevant social and life sciences. Shortcomings of the following policy analysis reflect thus limitations of the analyst, but not of the method, and are, therefore, not expected to thwart the purpose of the illustration, which is to further clarify the analytic approach, rather than to fully analyze one specific social policy.

NOTES

1. Piven, Frances Fox and Cloward, Richard, *Regulating the Poor: The Function of Public Welfare* (New York: Pantheon Books, Random House, 1971).

2. See Chapter Two, pp. 51–55

3. Braverman, Harry, *Labor and Monopoly Capital: The Degradation of Work in the Twentieth Century* (New York: Monthly Review Press, 1974); Pope John Paul, II,. *Encyclical on Human Work* (Boston, MA: Daughters of St. Paul, 1982).

4. Orshansky, Mollie, "Counting the Poor: Another Look at the Poverty Profile," *Social Security Bulletin*, January 1965.

5. Eleanor B. Sheldon and Wilbert E. Moore, ed., *Indicators of Social Change—Concepts and Measurement* (New York: Russell Sage Foundation, 1968); Otis Dudley Duncan, *Toward Social Reporting: Next Steps* (New York: Russell Sage Foundation, 1969); U.S. Department of Health, Education, and Welfare, *Toward a Social Report* (Washington, D.C: U.S. Government Printing Office, 1969); Raymond A. Bauer, ed., *Social Indicators* (Cambridge, MA, and London, England: The M.I.T. Press, 1966); Jan Drewnowski, *Studies in the Measurement of Levels of Living and*

Welfare, United Nations Research Institute for Social Development, Report No. 70.3 (Geneva 1970); Jan Drewnowski, Claude Richard-Proust & Muthu Subramanian, *Studies in the Methodology of Social Planning,* United Nations Research Institute for Social Development, Report No. 70.5 (Geneva 1970); Donald V. McGranahan, "Analysis of Socio-Economic Development Through a System of Indicators," *The Annals,* Vol. 393 (January 1971); Jan Drewnowski, "The Practical Significance of Social Information," The Annals, Vol. 393 (January 1971).

6. See Chapter Two, p. 19

7. See Chapter Two, p. 61

8. See Chapter Two, pp. 43–58

9. See Chapter Two, p. 57

10. Reddin, Mike, "Universality Versus Selectivity," in William A. Robson and Bernard Crick, ed., *The Future of the Social Services* (Harmondsworth, Middlesex, England: Penguin Books Ltd., 1970).

Political Action Toward Social Equality

4

Implications for Social and Political Action

INTRODUCTION

What implications for social change toward egalitarian and humanistic ways of life can be derived from the conceptual model of social policies developed in this study?[1] This question concerns the application of insights unravelled with the aid of the model to the everyday world of real human problems. Developing alternative social policies and understanding their dynamics and consequences are only first steps toward humanly satisfying systems of social policies. These steps must be followed by constructive political action so that significant changes suggested by policy analysis can become social realities. Conventional political approaches are, however, unlikely to suffice for this purpose, as chances for promoting and implementing policies which involve significant departures from the established social order and its dominant value premises are slim, indeed, within the political system of that order. The central question to be addressed, therefore, is, "what alternative guiding principles for social and political action toward egalitarian and humanistic social orders can be deduced from insights developed in this study?"

CONVENTIONAL POLITICS IN THE UNITED STATES

Before answering this question it is important to clarify intrinsic dynamics of the political system in the United States and of the conventional approach to the development and promotion of social policies. For these dynamics derive from, and perpetuate, the prevailing non-egalitarian, individualistic, competitive, alienating, and oppressive social and economic order. It is necessary to comprehend these dynamics in order to avoid being caught in them when designing alternative political

approaches which should facilitate the evolution of a different order.
Development of social policies in the United States (and in many similarly organized societies) tends to proceed in a fragmented manner in relation to different elements of the common domains of social policies such as wages, pensions, profits, and wealth; labor, commerce, industry, and agriculture; housing, education, health, and recreation; the needs and rights of children, women, families, and the aging; intergroup relations; social deviance, etc. The fragmented and inconsistent quality of the "normal" processes of social policy formulation reflect their political nature, that is, their roots in conflicts of real or perceived interests of diverse groupings within society at large.

The various groups which compete in the "pluralistic" political marketplace constitute, frequently, ad hoc rather than stable organizations. They tend to organize not around explicit values and ideologies such as liberty and equality (which inspired political movements spearheading the American, the French, and several other social revolutions) but around pragmatic and concrete interests, related either to personal and group characteristics such as age, sex, race, religion, social class and status, locality, etc., or to substantive issues, such as health, education, housing, income, taxes, etc.

Several observations concerning the foregoing organizing principles of political forces in the United States seem indicated. Firstly, the personal and group characteristics, and the substantive issues around which political forces tend to crystallize, do not constitute mutually exclusive entities, but overlap in multiple ways. Consequently, individuals and groups tend to join different political organizations at the same, or at different, times, depending on the extent to which their perceived interests correspond to the objectives pursued by given "special characteristics" or "special issue" organizations. Secondly, the relative stability of the major political parties in the United States does not negate the organizing principle of identity or similarity of perceived interests. For the durability of these parties seems to derive from their function of building "grand electoral coalitions" among groups pursuing diverse interests, usually on the basis of vague and ambiguous promises, trade-offs, and compromises. Thirdly, while political forces tend to organize in the United States primarily around special, concrete interests, rather than around explicit sets of social policy relevant values and ideologies, the dynamics of political processes and organizations reflect, nevertheless, an intrinsic, though covert, commitment to an underlying ideological position. Not unexpectedly, the ideology and values implicit in these political processes correspond to the dominant value premises of the United States, namely pursuit of self-interest, competitiveness, and defense of established and newly evolving social and economic inequalities.

Social policies are thus shaped in the United States by an unceasing process of intergroup conflicts of interest and competition in the political arena, where, supposedly, every citizen and every group of citizens have equal opportunities and equal civil and political rights to promote their self-defined interests. Even if this image of the political arena were a true reflection of reality, this approach to the development of social policies would still be seriously deficient with respect to the promotion of policies concerning collective interests. For such policies, by definition, are no one's private interest, and they may, consequently, be left without adequate sponsorship in the competitive political marketplace.[2] The "ecology crisis," which has become such a prominent issue since the sixties, illustrates the serious neglect of overall societal interests within the established political system. Such interests tend to be overlooked or shortchanged until they reach critical dimensions.

Yet, as has been shown in many studies, the reality of the political marketplace bears little resemblance to the idealized image of "fair competition" under conditions of equal opportunities and equal civil rights and political power. For social and economic resources and opportunities have always been distributed unequally among individuals and groups in the United States, and "real" civil rights and political power are usually correlated with the distribution of social and economic resources and opportunities. It is, therefore, not surprising that "free competition" in the political marketplace in pursuit of self-interest under existing conditions of inequality tends to perpetuate or enhance advantages of individuals and groups who enter the competition from an advantageous position with respect to command over social and economic resources and opportunities, and tends to perpetuate disadvantages of individuals and groups who enter this free political competition handicapped by inferior social and economic opportunities.[3]

Several prominent characteristics of the political system of the United States seem to derive from its principal source of energy, the continuous competition among different social groups in pursuit of their perceived self-interests. Perhaps most important among these characteristics is the fact that the social policy system is undergoing perpetual change as a result of ceaseless pressures and counterpressures among various interest groups whose relative power shifts continuously as their political support increases or decreases, and as they enter into temporary coalitions or long-range alliances in pursuit of specific substantive objectives. Yet, paradoxically, in spite of perpetual changes of specific substantive policies, significant changes in major processes of social policies—that is, in resource control, organization of work, and especially, in rights distribution—tend to be extremely rare. That does not mean that no changes occur in these processes for, by definition, any substantive change in a specific social policy reflects some underlying change in one or more of these processes. However, the existing political dynamics of interest-group competition tend to facilitate merely minor, incremental changes of these processes which are often also accompanied by compensatory changes such as special "loop-holes" in tax provisions for powerful, privileged interest groups. Thus, the eventual results of extended, and often frantic, political struggles tend to be merely new variations on long established patterns with respect to the organization of work, the distribution of rights, and the control and development of societal resources. The entire process may well be summarized in the cynical adage: "the more things change, the more they remain the same."

Recent illustrations of this phenomenon are the War on Poverty and the Model Cities Program of Democratic administrations, and the Family Assistance Program and the New Economic Plan of Republican administrations. None of these programs resulted in thorough changes in the relative power and circumstances of living of major socioeconomic subsegments of the population, in the overall quality of life in society, or in intrasocietal human relations.[4] Yet, all these policies have been promoted by their sponsors as measures designed to lead to major improvements in critical, social, and economic conditions.

Explanations for the intrinsic futility of the perpetual changes of social policies may be found in certain assumptions or, perhaps, illusions which seem to be shared by a majority of individuals and interest groups who compete in the political arena. These assumptions include the belief that the existing social, political, and economic systems of the United States are structurally sound, and that, therefore, policy reform should not be concerned with structural elements, but should deal merely, one by one, with specific deficiencies which may exist in certain areas (such as housing, health, education, etc.) and which may be corrected through specific technological and professional interventions in each of these separate areas. This approach leads to a preoccupation with isolated symptoms, but leaves underlying structural causes and sources of social and economic problems untouched.

Related to the foregoing assumptions concerning the essential soundness of the institutional structure of society is the corollary that social problems tend to result from personal failings of individuals affected by these problems, rather than from the societal context in which these individuals find themselves. The widespread notions that "poor people are lazy," and that "their poverty results from their laziness," illustrate this way of thinking about social problems. Such an approach leads unavoidably into dead-end streets in terms of social policy development and intervention, for it generates policies and programs aimed at changing individuals rather than the social reality with which they are confronted.[5]

Further reasons for the futile nature of most changes in social policies in the United States can be discerned in the strategies and tactics used by the various competing interest groups, or in what is often referred to as the "rules of the political game." Central to these strategies and tactics are such notions as "feasibility," "flexibility," "compromise," "a little is better than nothing," etc.[6] Implicit in these notions is a tacit acceptance of the power relations existing in the established order, and a questionable readiness to forego responsibilities of political leadership and political education, based on unambiguous commitment to humanistic values and principles. These notions may, at times, also reflect a certain ambivalence concerning the "costs" of real changes in social policies, which may be higher than the sponsors of the changes are willing to pay. Thus, while many reform-minded, "liberal" individuals and groups would like to eliminate poverty, exploitation, and discrimination, they seem reluctant to forego the material advantages made possible for them by the continued existence of these conditions. Because of this, they may be inclined to accept "feasible compromises" which involve merely minor improvements in the circumstances of poor, exploited, and discriminated-against segments of the population, but do not affect adversely the advantageous position of privileged groups. While political compromises under the current system may, at times, yield limited benefits for disadvantaged groups, and may have to be accepted temporarily on this basis, it seems important not to get caught in illusions and to mistake such incremental improvements as real and meaningful changes.

One further characteristic of the existing approach to social policy development needs to be mentioned here since it, too, derives from the dynamics of interest group competition, and since it, too, is an important factor in keeping the social policy system essentially unchanged as far as the major processes and common domains of social policies are concerned. This element is the manipulative approach employed by political leaders and organizations in order to generate support (for themselves and their objectives) from individuals and groups in society. Essentially this approach involves telling people what they like to hear, whether one believes in it or not; creating the impression that one agrees with, and would promote, the perceived interests and biases of potential supporters, even if one has no intention of doing so; and, in general, using any handy means to obtain support and votes for one's political endeavors, whether these means are honest and ethical or not. This manipulative approach is often rationalized by futile expectations, according to which, once one achieves political power, one would use it to promote the "common good." However, in reality, political leaders and organizations who make ambiguous and vague commitments to groups pursuing different and even conflicting interests in order to gain political support from these groups will find their options greatly constrained after gaining power and office, as these diverse supporters will rightfully demand fulfillment of campaign promises. And, as many political leaders and organizations may often be more concerned with the effects of their actions on their future political fortune than on the quality and circumstances of life in society, they are likely to be reluctant to disappoint their various political supporters. Hence, they will be caught in their own past manipulative schemes and promises, and will hesitate to promote real changes in the social policy system. Instead, they will "play it safe" by promoting policies involving merely incremental, non-significant changes, yet they will tend to present these policy proposals as major advances.[7] Campaign promises are rarely specific under this manipulative approach, and it is thus not too difficult to present such incremental steps as fulfillment of vague promises made in the past to groups of varying political persuasions.

TOWARD ALTERNATIVE POLITICS

There would be little reason to explore alternative approaches to the development and promotion of social policies if the existing system would result in a social and economic order in which all members of society would lead meaningful, satisfying, and self-fulfilling lives. Since, however, the circumstances of living of large segments of society, as well as the overall quality of life and of human relations, continue to be unsatisfactory in many respects and to varying degrees, it seems imperative to search for alternative political strategies, and for approaches to the development and promotion of social policies which would assure equal rights and opportunities for self-realization to all members of society. The tentative ideas sketched below for such an alternative political approach presuppose an interdependence between the dynamics of political systems and the nature of social policies they generate, an assumption which is supported by observations of the workings of the political system in the United States and its social policy output. To the extent that this assumption is valid, it seems necessary to modify the established approach to political action, if one desires to replace the now prevailing societal order with one based on social, economic, civil, and political equality, and on humanistic values.

Perhaps the most important change in this context concerns the organizing principles of political movements. The existing principle of organizations, which reflects a model of competition in a pluralistic marketplace among groups in pursuit of their perceived self-interests, needs to be replaced by an alternative principle, namely, commitment to an explicit set of social policy relevant value premises. For equal rights and opportunities for all individuals and groups, and the collective interests of society as a whole, can simply not be realized as long as social policies are left to emerge from a process of intrinsically unfair competition among social classes commanding unequal resources and power, and striving to perpetuate and enhance advantageous positions. Thus, the existing competitive model of political action sustains, implicitly, an ideology of inequality, as competing individuals and groups merely seek to improve their own circumstances of living relative to other individuals and groups; no one promotes equality of rights for all members and groups of society.

One destructive consequence of the competitive approach tends to be that deprived groups perceive each other as threats to their respective, narrowly defined interests, and do not realize that the real threat to their joint interests is the principle of inequality which pervades the entire structure and fabric of society. These perceptions or, rather, misperceptions of deprived groups in society result often in fierce conflicts among them, with respect to the limited resources which powerful and privileged classes permit to "trickle down" through conventional, incremental social policies. The animosity between "poor Whites" and "poor Blacks," and local conflicts surrounding Model Cities and Office of Economic Opportunity funds and programs, reflect the sad consequences of the competitive approach, as well as the underlying, ancient, and cynical device of powerful ruling classes: "divide et impera."

Explicit value premises (such as equality of social, economic, civil, and political rights and liberties) would provide political movements organized around them with definitive criteria for evaluating existing or newly proposed social policies, and for developing alternative policies, irrespective of the substantive content of given policy issues. It would thus no longer be necessary to mobilize separate political action groups and lobbies whenever different issues or interests demand attention. The inefficient use of political energy, and the self-defeating fragmentation and inconsistencies which now characterize political action, could thus be avoided. Political movements committed to such value premises would also eschew existing tendencies of social policies to deal merely with the symptoms rather than the causes of social problems, and the futility of incremental, illusory changes in policies. Such movements would focus policy development on the key issues of controlling resource development, reorganizing work, and redistributing rights, and would work for an adjustment of these variables in accordance with the notion of social equality. While such movements might have to accept "feasible compromises" on a temporary basis so as to ease the circumstance of living of deprived population segments, they would neither mistake nor misrepresent such compromises as real solutions, and would continue to work for policies which conformed in every respect to an egalitarian ideology.

Political movements of the kind envisaged here would be guided in policy development by assumptions concerning the causation of social problems, which differed from the assumptions implicit in the political actions and social policy proposals of the majority of existing political forces. Their assumptions would derive from the application of egalitarian yardsticks to the analysis of social issues and problems in the United States and throughout the world. Such analyses would systematically bare the causes of existing individual, social, and economic problems in the structure and fabric of society, rather than disguise these causes, as is done now, by blaming individuals and groups for their problems and deprived circumstances. Social policy proposals derived from this kind of analysis would, therefore, avoid futile programs for rehabilitating the victims of destructive social and economic conditions without simultaneously eliminating these conditions. They would focus instead primarily on restructuring society as a whole, so that all members and groups would live in circumstances conducive to the fullest possible development of their innate human potential.

Intrinsic to the egalitarian and humanistic philosophy of such alternative political movements would be the unequivocal rejection of intergroup political competition in pursuit of special interests. For true equality of rights is only possible when no single individual or group maintains a privileged position in relation to all other individuals and groups. Consequently, political movements committed to equality would have to work for the rights of all people rather than merely for the special interests of some groups such as currently deprived segments of society. Such movements could not be directed against any segment of society. They would struggle actively against the principles and institutions of privilege, inequality, exploitation, injustice, oppression, and inhumanity, but not against individuals and groups who benefit from the workings of these principles. Perhaps a major source of failure of political movements committed to egalitarian principles has been their tacit or explicit acceptance of competitive and manipulative political models. They became involved in destructive and violent conflicts with powerful and privileged classes and the latter's political allies from deprived classes, rather than engaging in constructive efforts to overcome the dynamics of inequality and privilege, so as to benefit all members and groups of society, and to establish a social order conducive to development and self-actualization for all. It should be emphasized that interpersonal and intergroup coercion and violence would be contrary to the egalitarian values implicit in the political approach suggested here, as coercion and violence always involve inequalities between their agents and victims.

The ideas discussed here raise questions concerning appropriate strategies and means to be utilized by such alternative political movements. Important departures from the existing political system are indicated in this respect. The overriding guiding principle seems to be that the strategies and means must never be in conflict with the egalitarian and humanistic philosophy of the movements. Manipulation in any form, exploitation, deception, dishonesty, and physical force (be they directed against opponents or potential supporters) are therefore ruled out as acceptable means. Clearly, then, alternative political movements would have to evolve a radically different political style from the one fitting the existing political system and its competitive philosophy. If all human beings are valued for their intrinsically equal worth and dignity, and if they are respected by political leaders and movements, it is inconceivable that such movements and leaders should deceive and manipulate them, and withhold important information from them.

What options for constructive, nonviolent political action are then available to movements committed to egalitarian and humanistic value premises? One most appropriate focus of intervention for political action seems to be the system of dominant beliefs and values of society. When discussing in Chapter Two the conceptual model of social policies, it was suggested that a society's dominant values and ideology exert a constraining influence on the malleability of its social policy system. Therefore, if policy changes are sought beyond the range set by existing dominant value premises, these premises need first to be changed, so as to widen the scope of options for the development of alternative policies. Movements committed to the establishment of an egalitarian social order need, therefore, attempt to gain acceptance of their ideology among large segments of society.

Changing a society's dominant value premises is, of course, a complicated undertaking since these values pervade all aspects of its culture, its institutional structure, and its system of socialization and education. Social and behavioral sciences offer only uncertain guiding principles for large scale value change. It seems, however, valid to assume that self-interest as perceived by the majority of a population constitutes a major source of energy for maintaining, as well as for changing, a society's system of values. Changes in dominant values may therefore depend on changes in the perceptions of self-interest of large segments of society. Accordingly, a crucial issue to be raised by political movements pursuing radical change of the social policy system, by way of thorough modifications of its dominant value premises, is whether the existing value premises of competitiveness, pursuit of narrowly perceived self-interest, and inequality of rights and opportunities are indeed conducive to the realization of the self-interest of people. Characteristic features of the existing social policy system which reflect these dominant value commitments are attitudes and practices of exploitation toward the natural environment and toward human beings, inequalities in circumstances of living and power of members and groups of society, and a high incidence of alienation in human experience and relations. The question to be examined then is whether these values and these aspects of the social policy system serve indeed the true interests of the people.

There is, of course, no "correct" way for selecting criteria to establish the "true" interests of an individual and of an entire society or its subsegments. Any criteria one selects would involve certain value positions. The criteria suggested here are derived from an intrinsic aspect of the human condition, namely, an innate bio-psychological drive to survive, to develop, and to satisfy basic needs, and from the value premise that all people should be entitled equally to realize this basic, common, human drive. Based on these criteria, it seems that only social policies which sustain life, and which enhance the quality of life and the circumstances of living of all members of a society, meet the test of true or real interest; and that social policies which undermine life, and which adversely affect the quality of life and the circumstances of living, even of some members of a society, do not meet that test.

Were one to apply this test of true interests to conditions prevailing at present in the United States, it would become obvious that the existing dominant values, and the social policies based on them, certainly fail to promote the true interests of deprived segments of the population. Their very state of deprivation, exploitation, and alienation provides ample evidence for this judgment, whatever their own perceptions concerning the realization of their interests may be.

It may help to get at this point a sense of the scope of material deprivation in the affluent society of the United States. Using as a rough measure the "low" standard of living of the Bureau of Labor Statistics, one finds that approximately one-third of the population is deprived in a material sense, for their income is below that low standard of living. Furthermore, over half the population live in households with incomes below the B.L.S. "intermediate" standard. No doubt, then, the true interests of the majority of the population, the deprived and near-deprived segments, would benefit from policy changes aimed at eliminating their deprived circumstances by equalizing rights and opportunities for all.

Turning next to the less than 50 percent of the population who constitute the nondeprived, privileged segments, one finds that material affluence in itself does not assure a satisfactory quality of life, fulfillment of social, psychological, and spiritual needs, and realization of true interests. The middle and upper classes in the United States seem to be in a state of social and cultural crisis. This statement could be supported with recitations of ample evidence. It should suffice, however, to mention here drug problems, alienation, and disaffection among middle and upper class youth, and the "rat race syndrome" of white-collar, professional, and managerial strata. These are, no doubt, symptoms of social crisis. The conclusion suggested by these brief observations is that privileged classes fail under current conditions to realize their true human interests just as the deprived classes fail to realized theirs. The existing system of social policies and the value premises underlying it seem thus to have destructive consequences for all segments of this society. Accordingly, major changes in values, and in the social policies derived from these values, would seem to be in the true interest of all segments of society. The commitment to rugged individualism, competitiveness, and inequality seems detrimental to the well-being of all, the deprived and the privileged, and those in between. This analysis suggests that political movements interested in promoting radical changes of values and policies through nonviolent means would have to engage in active interpretation and education among all population groups in order to facilitate a more realistic understanding of the social context and its destructive and alienating dynamics, and of the extent to which the true human interests of all people are now not being realized. Such political education or interpretation aimed at spreading critical consciousness would have to be thorough, factual, and honest, rather than superficial, misleading, and manipulative, and it would have to be on an intellectual, rather than on a charismatic, emotional, nonrational basis.

The major difficulty to be coped with in this educational and interpretational effort are the misconceptions and the "false-consciousness"[8] which most people in the United States tend to develop through exposure to often stultifying and mind-crippling educational systems, mass media of communication geared to a below-average mentality, and exhortations by public officials and political leaders, all involving over-simplified presentations of complex issues, and avoiding responsible, intellectual inquiry. These combined, lifelong influences along with the normal experiences of everyday life tend to indoctrinate people into the dominant value system by reinforcing the notion of the structural soundness and superiority of "the American way of life," and a broad range of social and economic inequalities intrinsic to it. Eventually these influences add up to an utterly distorted view of the United States, the world, and reality.

Alternative political movements would endeavor to overcome the false consciousness of the population (and to counter the foregoing destructive influences) through recruitment of members and organization of support groups and networks on local, regional, national, and international levels, and through personal influence by their members on everyone they come in contact with, be it in an informal, social, or a formal, occupational context. Teachers on all levels of educational systems, human services workers, and other professionals working with individuals and groups are likely to have many opportunities for educational and interpretive work, since students and intellectuals appear to be most ready to respond to such efforts. However, the messages of such movements must reach every member of society. Elitism must be avoided, and efforts would have to be made to involve all strata of society, and to organize political support on the broadest possible level.

Members of such movements would have to view themselves as "educational agents," since the movements' principal strategy would consist of political education. Lest this notion be viewed as unethical by teachers and other professionals who might consider education a politically neutral process, it needs to be emphasized that education involves always overt and covert political components. Education involves preparation for life through expansion of understanding and awareness of societal processes. In this sense it is a political process both by what it communicates, and by what it fails to communicate. It seems entirely ethical to recognize and affirm the political dimension of education, and to consciously assume responsibility for it, rather than to deny its existence and to let it happen subconsciously. Furthermore, political education, as suggested here, is not to be confused with propaganda or indoctrination. Rather, it is to be a serious, exploratory process leading to thorough understanding of the dynamics of the United States and world society.[9]

Adherents of such political movements, who would be their educational agents, would have to assume this role in addition to their social, occupational, and professional roles. Adding to one's occupational role the role of educational agent for political movements may lead to conflicts in occupational settings, since such settings are usually linked in various ways to the existing social order and its policies and value premises, and since they also obtain their resources from that order. There are no simple solutions to this dilemma, yet responsibility for ethical action in accordance with one's conscience may have to take precedence over blind loyalty to the organization in which one is employed. By engaging in political education in their social and occupational settings, movement members could gradually become links in a network of an emerging counterculture.

The approach to political action sketched here seems to follow logically from the preceding line of argument, according to which social problems are products of established social policies which must be changed radically if the problems are to be eradicated. Such radical changes of social policies require prior changes in value premises, and such changes in value premises depend in turn on revisions in the perceptions and consciousness of large segments of the population with respect to their true interests and the reality in which they live.

Critics of the political philosophy and approach presented here tend to argue that people cannot overcome their narrow self-centeredness, that they are greedy and competitive by nature, and that the proposed political movements would be working against human nature. Science offers no definitive answers to the hypotheses implied in such claims and counterclaims. People certainly seem to have an innate potential for self-centeredness, greed, and competitiveness. Yet they also seem to have an innate potential to act cooperatively and to pursue fairness and justice. Besides, they have intellect and a capacity for learning from past experiences and future possibilities, and they can distinguish between different levels of interest, immediate and long-range. Which of people's many innate potentialities become dominant, manifest traits seems to depend on socializing influences in their environment. There certainly have always been societies which practiced cooperation, and in which people do not act as greedily, and do not compete as savagely, as they tend to do in the United States.[10] It consequently seems that the movements may not be going against human nature after all. Certainly, until more definitive evidence becomes available, it would be as valid to assume that social conditions can be designed to bring out people's potential for living cooperatively in a just and egalitarian social and economic order, as it would be to assume that people are incapable by their very nature to live in such a way.

What chances to achieve their goals do such alternative political movements have within the existing context of the United States? Is it not naive to assume that small, politically conscious, intellectually oriented, and ideologically committed minority movements could stem and reverse an overwhelming tide, and bring about a radical restructuring and reorientation of society, especially when these movements are also committed to avail themselves only of nonviolent and ethical means? Perhaps so; therefore, no assumptions are made here concerning the probabilities of success of such political movements. The dynamics and motivations of these gradually evolving and growing movements, in the United States and abroad, are not based on calculations of probabilities of success. Such movements are emerging because they stand for social justice which requires no justification and no assurances of success, and because growing numbers of people realize that destruction looms ahead if we continue to live by the dominant value premises of this culture, its dehumanizing social policies, and the competitive and manipulative political processes through which it perpetuates itself.

Once people fully comprehend the true situation today, they seem to have no choice but to join movements for radical change, and to ask others to do the same, even though they are aware of the odds against such movements, and even though they know nothing of probabilities of success. The road ahead for such movements is uncertain, of course, and would have to be evolved mainly by avoiding routes which lead toward destruction, and by being guided by principles of social justice, equality, real democracy, and humanism. Groping their way in that direction people would know that they have turned away from destruction and death toward the probability of life.

TOWARD A GLOBAL PERSPECTIVE

To broaden the scope of these thoughts beyond the United States, it should be noted that social problems and social policies within any society tend to interact in many ways with that society's worldwide, international relations. Because of this linkage between social and foreign policies, solutions of social problems within the United States, in accordance with the philosophy suggested here, seem to depend also on the pursuit of foreign policies shaped by the same egalitarian, cooperative, democratic, humanistic, and nonviolent principles. To clarify further the linkages between social and foreign policies, several observations are necessary concerning "boundaries" of national societies and the general domain and functions of foreign policies.

International boundaries constitute human-drawn lines which reflect the workings, over time, of ecological, biological, psychological, social, cultural, economic, and political forces within, and between, separate human societies. Such boundaries seem to fulfill on a worldwide scale the same functions as variously defined dividing lines between segments of national societies. In either context, boundaries identify, and set apart, one aggregate of human beings from other aggregates in order to establish, promote, and defend exclusive claims with respect to certain rights for members of specified groups. Hence, from the perspective of humankind, the relations of national societies to worldwide society are analogous to the relations of segments of national societies to their respective national societies. The dynamics of international relations and of foreign policies on a worldwide scale are consequently similar, in principle, to the dynamics of intergroup relations and of social policies within national societies.

The foregoing argument suggests that the conceptual model of social policies, the framework for policy analysis and development, as well as the implications of the conceptual model for social and political action, can be extrapolated to a worldwide scale by expanding the notion of "society" to encompass all of humankind. The variables of the conceptual model and the foci of the framework can, therefore, be used in the analysis and development of foreign policies, the common domains of which include (a) the overall quality of life on earth, (b) the circumstances of living and power of various segments of world society, and (c) the relation among nations. Such analyses would reveal that just as social problems within the United States are rooted in the fabric of its non-egalitarian social and economic order, and in its dominant value premises of individualism, competitiveness and inequality, many worldwide social problems and international conflicts are rooted in the ethnocentric and competitive dominant value premises of nations. This creates a world order involving multifaceted inequalities with respect to the control, development, distribution, and allocation of life-sustaining and life-enhancing resources, rights, and work. The United States, it may be noted, occupies a highly privileged position in the existing world order as it controls roughly 30 to 40 percent of the world's resources and annual output, while constituting less than 6 percent of the world's population. It thus shares major responsibility for maintaining worldwide social and economic inequalities.

Problems in international relations seem, at times, even less amenable to reasoned solutions than social problems within national societies, since forces involved in international affairs tend to be more complex, uninhibited, and violent, and less susceptible to rational influences than intrasocietal forces. However, since intrasocietal and international problems seem to involve similar dynamics, though on different scales, and since both types of problems can be understood in terms of the same conceptual model, the guiding principles derived from that model for dealing with social problems within the United States seem equally valid for developing constructive, just, humane, and peaceful foreign policies. For, in spite of uncertainties concerning probabilities of eventual success, the political action philosophy based on principles of equality, cooperation, humanism, democracy, and nonviolence seems to constitute the most promising approach to resolving social problems and conflicts not only on the level of local communities and national societies, but also on the international, worldwide level.

BEYOND FEAR AND SCARCITY

In concluding these observations, one important source of resistance to social and foreign policies, based on the political philosophy advocated here, should be noted: a widespread fear on the part of more affluent societies (and privileged segments within many societies) of significant reductions in their accustomed standards of living. Such reductions in living standards are feared to ensue, should an egalitarian social and world order replace the prevailing non-egalitarian one. This fear seems rooted in long-established cultural patterns and attitudes which reflect people's traditional response to conditions of real scarcity: fierce competition for limited resources to satisfy immediate needs, and to provide security from future want for oneself, one's family, and one's social group by accumulating wealth. Over time, such competitive and acquisitive patterns became thoroughly institutionalized in many societies. By now these traits pervade many aspects of intrasocietal and international human relations, and they are widely perceived as intrinsic to human nature and as essential to survival. Yet there is ample evidence that modern science and technology, and the existing worldwide economic potential could enable humankind, through cooperation rather than through competition, to organize the development and distribution of life-sustaining and life-enhancing resources in a manner which could avoid waste and destruction and assure to all adequate living standards and meaningful, satisfying life experiences. The fears noted above would thus seem to be largely unfounded.

It thus appears that competition and acquisitiveness in human relations within and among national societies may no longer be necessary or appropriate, but may, by now, be definitely dysfunctional, and may pose serious threats to human well-being and survival. Yet irrational fears, based on "false consciousness" with respect to existing human realities on the part of large segments of the world population, sustain the continued dominance of these dysfunctional and potentially destructive patterns. Constructive changes in consciousness, attitudes, policies, and actions become thus very difficult to achieve. Social and political action and education aimed at establishing a just world order, need, therefore, to counteract the widespread ignorance, misconceptions, and fears which now underlie resistance to necessary changes in social and foreign policies, by demonstrating the feasibility and long-range advantages for all individuals and all nations, of an alternative order involving worldwide cooperation toward social and economic equality and justice. For it seems that political movements promoting the implementation of egalitarian, noncompetitive, non-acquisitive, and humanistic social and foreign policies will gather momentum only if, and when, ever-increasing numbers of people all over the world will come to realize that a social and world order based on such policies would serve their real interests, since it could indeed assure to all people peace, adequate and enriching circumstances of living, improvements in the overall quality of life on earth, and enhanced opportunities for meaningful human relations and self-fulfillment.

NOTES

1. See Chapter Two, especially Chart #2.2.

2. Roger Strait, "We CAN Become Responsible," *Journal* (United Church of Christ), Vol. 9, No. 4, (Jan.-Feb. 1971), p.4-11.

3. Gabriel Kolko, *Wealth and Power in America—An Analysis of Social Class and Income Distribution* (New York, Washington, London: Praeger Publishers, 1962).

4. Peter Marris and Martin Rein, *Dilemmas of Social Reform* (New York: Atherton Press, 1967).
   Stephen M. Rose, *The Betrayal of the Poor* (Cambridge, MA: Schenkman Publishing, Co., 1972).
   Roland L. Warren, "The Sociology of Knowledge and the Problem of the Inner Cities," *Social Science Quarterly*, December 1971.
   Eveline M. Burns, "Welfare Reform and Income Security Policies,"in *The Social Welfare Forum*, 1970 (New York and London: National Conference on Social Welfare, Columbia University Press, 1970), pp. 46-60.
   Alvin L. Schorr in "Two Views on the Welfare Plan," *The New York Times*, December 1, 1970.

5. William Ryan, *Blaming the Victim*, (New York: Pantheon Books, 1971).

6. Robert Morris and Robert H. Binstock, with the collaboration of Martin Rein, *Feasible Planning for Social Change* (New York and London: Columbia University Press, 1966).

7. An apt illustration of this tendency is Dr. Daniel P. Moynihan's article "One Step We Must Take" (*Saturday Review*, May 23, 1970, pp.20-23), in which he describes President Nixon's Family Assistance Program in the following manner:

   ... Then came the Family Assistance Plan, the single most important piece of social legislation to be sent to the Congress in a generation (or really two generations as we count them today) and the social initiative that will almost surely define the beginning of a new era in American social policy. The legislation establishes a floor under the income of every American family with children. It provides incentives for work and opportunities for work training, job placement, and child care.

The Family Assistance Plan is not an incremental change—a marginal improvement in an old program. It is a new departure in social policy, emerging from a new mode of analysis of social processes. Indeed, it is something more than just that. The Social Security Act, the only comparable legislation in American history, was after all mostly a compendium of ideas we had got from Lloyd George, who had got them from Bismarck. With Family Assistance, the United States takes its place as the leading innovator in the world in the field of social policy. Soon, I expect, we shall be seen as an exporter of social programs to Europe, reversing a century in which the flow has been from Europe to us.

... Yet at this very moment it is within the power of that great majority of the American people who love their nation—who wish to see it healed and whole— to enact a social program that will cause future generations to regard us as an anguished and often agonizing people who were somehow touched with glory. Others would say, and I would not deny, that recognizing it or not, what posterity will in fact be contemplating is a generation of Americans who for all their failings were capable of great things and did great things."

When writing this article, Dr. Moynihan was Counselor to President Nixon and was actively promoting the administration's welfare reform plan which he had helped to design. The income floor referred to in this excerpt was to be $1,600 in cash and $894 in food stamps per year for a family of four. This amount was merely two-thirds of the government's own, unrealistically low, poverty threshold ($3,720 in 1970). It was also lower than public assistance rates prevailing at the time in 42 states. Thus, in spite of the rhetoric in this article, implementation of the Family Assistance Plan as proposed by president Nixon and passed by the House of Representatives in 1970, and again in 1972 in a somewhat different version, would have hardly changed the relative distribution of rights, work, and resources among socioeconomic strata of the U.S. population.

8. For a discussion of the concept "false consciousness" see: Karl Mannheim, *Ideology and Utopia* (New York: A Harvest Book—Harcourt, Brace, and Company, 1936). First published in Germany in 1929. See especially Chapter II, section 9: The Problem of False Consciousness, pp. 94-97.

9. Freire, Paulo, *Pedagogy of the Oppressed* (New York: Herder & Herder, 1970).

10. Petr Kropotkin, *Mutual Aid—A Factor of Evolution* (Boston, Mass.: Extending Horizons Books, Porter Sargent 1956, originally published in 1902). Ruth Benedict, "Synergy—Patterns of the Good Culture," Psychology Today, June 1970.

PART III

Critical Essays on Policy Issues

5

Clinical Practice and Politics
of Human Liberation *

This essay explores the proposition that clinical practice in human services should become an integral part of political struggles toward human liberation. This proposition conflicts with the prevailing view that mixing politics and clinical practice is unethical and unprofessional since practitioners ought to be tolerant of all political positions, and that clinical practice should, therefore, be politically neutral. In accordance with this view, practitioners in human service fields such as health, education, welfare, etc. tend to view politics as a domain apart from their practice. Hence, when they participate consciously in politics they consider this a private affair separate from their practice, to be engaged in, in their spare time, away from practice settings.

THE ILLUSION OF POLITICAL NEUTRALITY

Upon examination, the norm of political neutrality of practice reveals, however, unintended political consequences. Since political neutrality requires practitioners to refrain from taking sides on political issues in the course of practice, they may neither advocate nor challenge the societal status quo, its values, institutions and dynamics. Not challenging what already exists is, however, not the same as being neutral towards it, for not challenging an established order implies tacit acceptance of it. Thus the norm of political neutrality transforms practice into a tool for systems maintenance, but prevents its transformation into a force that

*Journal of Clinical Child Psychology, Vol. 5, No. 3 (Winter 1976). Catalyst Vol. 1, No. 2, 1978, David G. Gil, Beyond the Jungle (Cambridge, MA: Schenkman Books and Boston: G. K Hall, 1979).

challenges the status quo. Enforcement of that norm is thus in itself a powerful political act in defense of the established order.

One other aspect of practice renders the claim of political neutrality meaningless. This is the tendency to interpret problems dealt with by human services as rooted in characteristics of individuals rather than in interactions of individuals with prevailing societal dynamics. This interpretation is reflected in interventions and therapies which put the onus for change upon individuals and expect them to adapt to existing societal realities which are viewed as essentially sound and relatively constant. Clearly, such a conception of the etiology of human problems, and treatment approaches derived from it, support the prevailing societal order.

Since political consequences appear to be inescapable aspects of practice in human services, though practitioners are usually unaware of them, the prevailing view that mixing politics and practice is unethical and unprofessional does not seem valid. To replace prevailing, unintentional, covert political aspects of practice with conscious, overt ones and to hold practitioners responsible for the political perspective of their practice would seem a more honest, and hence more appropriate, course in ethical and professional terms.

OBJECTIVES OF PRACTICE

A conscious political perspective for practice in human services should be compatible with practice objectives and value premises underlying these objectives. The practice objectives suggested below are derived from egalitarian-humanistic principles, according to which all humans ought to be considered of equal intrinsic worth in spite of manifold differences among them. Hence, they ought to be entitled to equal rights in every sphere of life, especially the right to actualize their individuality freely and fully, subject only to constraints intrinsic in the same rights for all others. In accordance with these value premises, the common objective of clinical practice is to help humans achieve self-actualization, and the corresponding objective of political practice is to transform the prevailing social order into one conducive to the self-actualization of every human being. The objectives of clinical and political practice are thus complementary. Clinical practice involves helping humans maintain or regain optimum physical, psychological, and social health, and overcome obstacles to free and full development of their potentialities. Political practice involves working for change of social values and consciousness, and of social, economic, and political institutions so that circumstances of living, human relations, and the quality of life should become conducive to optimum human development. Political practice as conceived here aims to advance social development, defined as evenly shared enhancement of the quality of life.[1] It differs from the familiar model of political practice which consists mainly of competitive struggles for power, personal gain, advantages of interest groups, and control and exploitation of others.

HUMAN NEEDS, HEALTH, AND SELF-ACTUALIZATION

Given the common value of social equality and the common objective of human self-actualization, effective clinical and political practice require a theory of human needs, of human development and of social organization; they require also a theory of physical, social, and psychological health and of the dynamics of ill health; finally, they require a practice-theory for overcoming forces which obstruct development and cause ill health, and for restoring the momentum of interrupted development and impaired health.

Health and development of humans are thought to be functions of intrinsic life forces. They depend, however, for their actualization on regular satisfaction of basic and complex existential needs on physical, social, emotional and intellectual levels. In accordance with these assumptions, all types of ill health and disturbances of development are essentially results of the thwarting of some human needs through deficits, delays, or surfeit.

Human needs are rooted in the fact that humans are not self-sufficient, but depend on relations and interactions with others, and on exchanges of materials and energy with their environment. All social orders of human groups, in spite of many differences among them in values and institutional patterns, constitute different solutions to the existential requirements for steady patterns of human relations, and for a steady flow of life-sustaining and enhancing materials and energy among humans and their environment.

Several kinds and levels of closely related and interacting human needs which differ in focus, intensity, and flexibility have been identified.[2] First, there are basic needs for food, shelter, clothing, health care, and other concrete, life-sustaining and enhancing goods and services, along with the psychological need for a sense of security that these concrete needs will be regularly satisfied. Next, there are needs for reciprocal, meaningful, and satisfying human relations: not to be alone and isolated but to belong, as a whole being with an identity of one's own, to a community; to be cared about and acknowledged as an authentic and autonomous subject and to care about and acknowledge others in a like manner. Finally, there are needs to discover, express, and actualize one's whole being by engaging in meaningful, self-directed, productive, and creative work.

Human needs, irrespective of kind and level, derive from biological sources. Their manner of manifestation and scope of satisfaction or frustration are shaped, however, largely by specific societal contexts. Societies which differ in values and institutions differ also in definitions of human needs, and tend to sanction different levels of satisfaction for different needs and for different segments of their population. Hence, societies vary in the extent to which different kinds and levels of needs are acknowledged, resources are provided for their satisfaction, and individuals are able to satisfy needs, maintain health, and develop their potentialities.

VALUE CLUSTERS AND INSTITUTIONAL PATTERNS CONDUCIVE TO HEALTH AND SELF-ACTUALIZATION

Since levels of needs satisfaction, health, and self-actualization are influenced by the values and institutional patterns of societies, it is possible to identify value clusters and institutional arrangements conducive to optimum health and development. In our modern, crowded, and interdependent world, genuine self-actualization and comprehensive satisfaction of material, social, and psychological human needs seem unattainable for individuals unless they are assured for everyone. Frustration of the developmental needs of any one individual tends to threaten, directly or indirectly, the satisfaction of the needs of others. Hence, value clusters and institutional patterns conducive to health and self-actualization will have to reflect the needs and interests of the "self" as well as those of all others. The interests of the "generalized other" thus become part of "sophisticated self-interest."

Values: Everyone would have to be regarded and treated as an autonomous subject of equal intrinsic worth and of equal entitlement, rather than as an object to be used, exploited, and dominated in the selfish designs of others. Mutual aid rather than competition would have to shape human relations at work and in other domains, since a competitive mentality tends to negate the individuality, needs, and rights of others who are perceived as potential means to one's ends, whereas a cooperative mentality affirms the individuality, needs, and rights of self and others. Freedom, self-reliance, and self-determination would also be part of the value cluster, since individuality and self-actualization for everyone are unattainable under conditions of domination, dependence, and subordination to the will of others.

Institutions: The basic institutional principle for a social order shaped by the foregoing values is an inalienable right of everyone to use, but not to own or waste, natural and human-created productive resources such as land, raw materials, energy, knowledge, technology, tools, etc. Accumulation and concentration of control over these productive resources—the sources of livelihood of people—by private or corporate owners or by state bureaucracies would thus be precluded. For the right to use productive resources is a sine qua non for genuine freedom and self-reliance of people through self-directed, productive work in contexts free of exploitation and dehumanizing and alienating structures and processes.

Transferring, or rather, returning, the right to use productive resources to producers themselves, and organizing the division of labor and processes of production rationally around the central criterion of satisfying material, social, and psychological human needs rather than profits for owners, would assure to everyone security in the provision of needed goods and services. It would also secure to everyone the right to participate in meaningful, productive activities, conducive to the integrated use of one's physical, intellectual, and emotional faculties and talents, and in this way work would provide opportunities for self-expression, self-discovery, and self-actualization, and for caring, reciprocal human relations. The insane phenomena of unemployment and of waste and destruction of human and other natural resources could thus be eliminated.

In such a social order all humans would be respected regardless of their roles, since all tasks performed would be rational contributions to everyone's well-being. Everyone would also enjoy equal economic, civil, and political rights. Public affairs would be conducted through participatory democracy on local community levels and through networks of assemblies representing communities, not individuals, on regional and wider levels up to the global level. Local and trans-local assemblies would be guided in their decisions and actions by shared commitments to egalitarian, libertarian, and cooperative values and institutions which alone can assure rational development, use, distribution, and preservation of the aggregate global productive potential for the collective survival and well-being of humankind.[3]

NEEDS-SATISFACTION, HEALTH, AND DEVELOPMENT IN THE PREVAILING SOCIAL ORDER

The value clusters and institutional arrangements of the established social order in the United States differ in many ways from the ones identified above as conducive to human development, health, and self-actualization. Hence, it is not surprising that material, social and psychological needs remain now unsatisfied for large segments of our population, that physical, social and emotional ill health is widespread, that human development of many individuals is stunted, and that self-actualization is hardly ever achieved.

Human existence in this society is shaped by a selfish, competitive, and acquisitive mentality. Life is perceived as a zero-sum, win-lose context. Humans consider one another as objects or means for ends pursued by the self. They are usually ready to use, manipulate, and exploit one another, and they do not relate to others as whole beings but tend to interact as "roles" or "functions." They do not care about others and do not feel cared about by them. People are considered to be unequal in worth, and they tend to think of themselves and others in comparative terms. Many are considered, and treated, as worthless. Being considered unequal in worth serves as justification for vast inequalities of rights in every sphere of life—social, psychological, economic, civil, and political. The established institutional order reflects the foregoing value cluster and recreates and reinforces it. The central institutional feature is private appropriation and control of productive resources. This has led to dynamics of acquisition through competitive drives and to massive accumulation and concentration of wealth. By now less than 5 percent of the population own and control over 80 percent of all productive wealth. The majority are therefore dependent for their livelihood on a small minority who provide "employment" with the resources they own and control, on terms advantageous to them.

The work and production context under these values and institutional arrangements is dehumanizing and alienating. The profit motive which underlies the design of work, and the criterion of efficiency which usually does not include consideration of social and psychological human needs, have brought about a mode of production to which most workers contribute only physical capacities, while their intellectual and emotional faculties remain unused and wasted. Workers have little to say in designing the products of their work and the processes of production, and thus have no opportunity to express and discover their true human potential at work. They rarely take pride in their products, and they can not actualize themselves in their work life. Work becomes an inevitable burden and "real life" is imagined to be away from work, somewhere at "leisure." And yet, in spite of its alienating qualities, "employment" is sought after eagerly, and struggled for competitively, since it is the only means for most people to attain a livable existence. To be "unemployed" has worse consequences for existence than to be working. The fate of millions of unemployed "surplus" persons serves to illustrate this point, and to drive those who are "lucky" to have jobs back to their jobs day after day, however distasteful the jobs may be.

Work is usually carried on in large, hierarchically structured organizations in which people at every level feel dominated by people on "higher" levels, and where they must dominate and control people on levels below theirs. Human relations in such organizations are structured to be impersonal and competitive. They are shaped by "mobility" dynamics, which means constant efforts to get ahead of others.

The distribution of economic goods and social services and of social prestige and psychological rewards in this social order is linked closely to one's relative success in competing for "higher" strata of the work organization. The highest rewards are usually reserved for owners of productive resources, irrespective of their role in production. Managerial and professional strata tend to be more handsomely rewarded, while production and service workers receive the smallest shares of goods, services, and recognition, and the "unemployed" must usually make do with less than the lower wage earners.

One other consequence of the dynamics intrinsic to the values and institutional arrangements of the prevailing social order is an exploitative, thoughtless, and wasteful attitude toward the natural environment and its nonrenewable resources. This attitude, and actions based on it, cause serious consequences for the quality of life, not only of the present, but of future generations as well.

Within the value and institutional context of this society, many, and perhaps most people lack a sense of security concerning the satisfaction of their most basic material needs throughout their lives. Unemployment and related material, social, and psychological deprivations are a potential experience for many individuals. Many others who succeed in holding on to jobs find themselves in dead-end, marginal positions which offer limited economic rewards, too little for an adequate material existence. Still others, whose jobs are not in a "dead-end" category, may nevertheless not be promoted for various arbitrary, bureaucratic reasons. And nearly everyone, upon reaching "retirement," which more often than not is involuntary, faces living on a reduced income. Finally, cessation of income because of illness, high costs of health care, or death of a wage earner causes many families to lose their economic base and to drift into poverty. There are, of course, certain economic safety mechanisms in operation in this society (e.g. public welfare, social security, unemployment compensation, etc.) which are intended to assure the physical survival of victims of blind market forces. However, these mechanisms provide, at best, a marginal existence at high social and psychological costs, and their potential availability does not provide people with a sense of security. Hence, one must conclude that this society does not satisfy the most basic human needs for material goods and psychological security.

The next level of needs, meaningful human relations, can also not be satisfied given the prevailing values and institutional arrangements. Meaningful human relations do not usually thrive in the context of competition, manipulation and exploitative attitudes, and hierarchical structures. Furthermore, insecure and psychologically deprived individuals who grew up in tense and inharmonious homes and in regimented schools which socialize them for the competitive and alienating reality of adult life are internally handicapped in entering human relations.

The need for genuine self-actualization is also unlikely to be satisfied within the prevailing social order. The work context sketched earlier dooms nearly everyone to engage in activities and situations which are antithetical to the requirements of self-actualization.

IMPLICATIONS FOR PRACTICE

Based on this analysis, health in a comprehensive sense and free and full development of human potential seem unattainable in the existing societal context. Erich Fromm, reaching similar conclusions in an incisive analysis more than two decades ago, referred to this societal context as insane.[4] He observed that when people are forced to adjust to an insane reality which frustrates their material, social, and psychological needs, they tend to develop various forms of ill health and to defend themselves by escaping or by acting aggressively.

Practice toward health and human development in the existing insane context begins with acknowledging its injurious dynamics, rejecting the established order, and working for its radical transformation into a humanistic-egalitarian society along the lines sketched earlier, a society capable of releasing intrinsic life forces by consistently satisfying material, social, and psychological needs. If clinical practitioners accept human self-actualization as the goal of practice, then they must reject the dominant therapeutic model which affirms the established order by implication, and assists humans to adjust to the insane logic of that order and the constant frustration of their inner needs—the sources of their suffering and ill health. They must adopt instead an alternative therapeutic model which helps humans unravel the causes of suffering and ill health in the existing social order, their reactions to it, and their defenses against it, and which helps them transcend their system-shaped consciousness and to release their intrinsic life-forces by discovering steps toward self-liberation in the context of collective human liberation. Implicit in this alternative therapeutic model is a conscious political perspective and unequivocal commitment to humanistic-egalitarian values and institutions, the societal prerequisite for human health and self-actualization through satisfaction of intrinsic human needs.

Freud stressed two principles which seem relevant also to an alternative therapeutic approach: to overcome ill health, one has to discover its sources by reexperiencing them in a corrective "transference" relationship; for therapists to help patients in the discovery and experience of sources of ill health, they must first explore and experience such sources in themselves. Clinical practice identified with politics of human liberation expands these Freudian principles from psychological to societal dynamics. It helps humans become conscious of hidden societal sources and dynamics which undermine health and prevent full development, and it does this in the context of a genuine human relationship between practitioners and individuals seeking to regain health.

One cannot practice in this manner unless one first discovers the alienating consequences of the existing social order for one's own life. Practitioners must recognize how their human needs are frustrated in their places of employment and in their personal lives, and how they themselves fail to actualize fully their human potential. They must overcome the conventional denial of their own systemic oppression, and they must broaden their consciousness of the dynamics of the existing social order. They must realize that their own human experience is essentially similar to that of the "patients," that they and the patients are brothers and sisters in oppression, and that they must unite in solidarity in the common struggle for human liberation. Radical clinical practice rejects the conventional, hierarchical, controlling conception of therapy and replaces it with an egalitarian one according to which patient and therapist are in the same boat, on a joint journey toward a sane society, individual health, and human fulfillment.

Politically conscious practice as suggested here derives from a political strategy which aims to spread consciousness of the true nature of the existing social order and its destructive consequences, as well as of feasible alternatives that are conducive to a rewarding life for all. Enhanced consciousness by large numbers of people seems necessary for transforming the established social order into an alternative one. Practitioners in all human services who communicate with people around human needs and problems have many opportunities as part of their work to enhance people's consciousness concerning current reality and possible alternatives. When practitioners adopt such a conception of their work, their conventional systems-maintenance function is transformed into an attack on the roots of human problems, and practice shifts from amelioration to "primary prevention."

EPILOGUE

It follows from the arguments presented here that individual practitioners in the human services must make a conscious choice between antithetical modes of practice. They can choose to conform to now dominant, status quo preserving, symptom-ameliorating practice models—the models of service organizations which operate within the sanctions and resources of the prevailing social order. Alternatively, practitioners may reject these models, challenge the ideology of existing service organizations, and choose to participate in the development of radical, innovative, system-transforming practice. Such radical practice and its practitioners should become integrated into political movements for human liberation and social equality, and against the systemic roots of inequalities which obstruct human development, causing social and psychological problems and ill health.

This essay has dealt mainly with a rationale for radical practice. It presented no blueprints and it bypassed many theoretical and practical aspects. I would suggest, however, that we refrain from developing blueprints for radical practice. Their absence can actually be a source of strength, for practice blueprints tend to become control mechanisms of hierarchically structured organizations and obstacles to self-direction of practitioners .

Radical practice ought to be developed through the individual and collective creativity of practitioners who are consciously committed to its political perspective and social ends. Once we develop a critical political analysis, philosophical clarity, and personal commitment, and once we come to view the people whom we serve as equals rather than as inferior and dependent beings, we should be able to create radical practice approaches for the diverse settings of the human services and for the diverse circumstances which people encounter.

One essential element in the development of radical practice is cooperation and solidarity among its practitioners. Such cooperation and solidarity which are negations of the dominant, competitive mode of human relations in most work places could gradually lead to the emergence of support groups and work place collectives among practitioners, and later on, of networks of such groups and collectives. Transformations toward cooperative and egalitarian patterns of individual and collective life styles among practitioners are likely to set in motion powerful dynamics toward radical practice. For we should realize that radical practice is not a technology. It is a philosophy and a way of life which will be created through dialogue and praxis among practitioners and the people they serve.

I do not intend to underestimate theoretical and practical difficulties inherent in the development of radical practice, nor to belittle the resistance such development will encounter from powerful, established institutions and human services agencies. Yet we must not forget that the power of the established order and its agencies is sustained by the multidimensional divisions it generates among people, and by its ideology which people internalize in the course of their socialization. As we learn to pierce that ideology and to overcome these divisions, we may find ways to counter the oppressive potential of existing institutions and to overcome resistance to the development of radical practice and radical movements.

NOTES

1. See the essay, "Social Policy and Social Development," in my book *The Challenge of Social Equality* (Cambridge, MA: Schenkman Publishing Company, 1976).

2. Abraham Maslow, *Motivation and Personality* (New York: Harper and Row, 1970).

3. For a detailed discussion of the institutional order sketched here, see the essay "Resolving Issues of Social Provision," in my book *The Challenge of Social Equality* (Cambridge, MA: Schenkman Publishing Company, 1976).

4. Erich Fromm, *The Sane Society* (Greenwich, CT: Fawcett, 1955).

6

Social Policy and The Right To Work *

This essay explores several related questions concerning a central human function—work. The questions are:

1. *Does our society acknowledge a right to work, and, if so, is everyone free to exercise this right?*
2. *If such a right is not acknowledged now, are an acknowledgement and guarantees to exercise a right to work desirable political goals?*
3. *What does right to work mean, and what are the implications of different meanings of this notion?*
4. *Upon what societal conditions does the exercise of a right to work depend, given different meanings of that notion?*
5. *What recommendations for social policy follow from these explorations?*

For a philosophical and political discourse to be productive, concepts and values should be made explicit. I begin, therefore, with a clarification of key concepts and will state my values before discussing recommendations for social policy.

SOCIAL POLICIES[1]

Social policies are human-created rules which shape and maintain social orders. These rules have evolved throughout history out of choices humans made while struggling to satisfy biological, social, and psychological needs in pursuit of survival in environments characterized by relative scarcities.

*Social Thought, Vol. 3, No. 1 (Winter 1977).

©1977, *National Conference of Catholic Charities*, Washington, D C.

David G. Gil, *Beyond the Jungle* (Cambridge, MA: Schenkman Books and Boston: G.K. Hall, 1979).

Social policies maintain social orders by regulating several related, existential processes for which every human group must evolve solutions to assure its viability:

1. Development and control of natural resources and of human-created material and nonmaterial wealth
2. Organization of work necessary for production and distribution of provisions suitable for sustaining life and enhancing its quality
3. Definition, recognition, and distribution of civil, social, psychological, political, and economic rights
4. Procedures for making decisions and for conducting societal affairs

By regulating these processes, social policies shape, indirectly, the conditions of living of members of a society, the quality of human relations, and the overall quality of life. Significant changes in living conditions of individuals and groups, in their relations with one another, and in the total existential milieu of a society are, therefore, predicated upon prior significant changes in the stewardship of natural and human-created wealth, the organization of work, the distribution of all rights, and the processes of governance.

SOCIETAL VALUES RELEVANT TO SOCIAL POLICIES

The dominant values of societies are crucial factors in the evolution and stabilization of social policies and, hence, of entire social orders and their dynamics. Like social policies, values, too, are products of human choices. They are rooted in human needs and reflect perceptions of human interests. The following value dimensions seem to be of special relevance to the evolution of social policies: equality/inequality; liberty/domination; cooperation/competition; collectivity-orientation/selfishness. Because of their importance to the evolution and maintenance of social orders, significant shifts must be attained along these value dimensions if major changes are to be brought about in an established institutional order. Achieving such shifts in the consciousness of large segments of a population is undoubtedly a complex, though not impossible, undertaking, while bringing about significant changes of social policies and of institutional orders without such shifts in values and consciousness may not be possible at all.

RIGHTS

The definition, recognition, and distribution of civil, social, psychological, political, and economic rights were identified above as one basic existential process which human groups regulate through social policies. This means that rights of humans living in societies are established and sanctioned through societal processes, and that "natural" or "inalienable" rights do not exist unless they are socially acknowledged. The source of all socially defined and acknowledged rights is natural or socially evolved human needs. Needs do not become rights automatically, however, but only when a society, through its social policies, acknowledges them, defines them as rights, explicitly or implicitly, and allocates appropriate resources out of its aggregate wealth for their satisfaction. A society may transform given needs into rights for everyone experiencing them, or merely for individuals belonging to certain groups, e.g. children, men, hunters, owners of wealth, black-skinned people, etc.

An illustration of the societal nature of rights, and of the difference between needs and rights, is the fact that everyone needs food, shelter, education, health care, etc., but many millions in our own society suffer from hunger, live without adequate shelter, and lack access to adequate education and health care. Their needs, in contradistinction to identical needs of so many others, have not been acknowledged as rights in a real sense. Their inability to satisfy these basic needs is not in conflict with prevailing "law and order," but is the result of past and present social policies and is in full accord with them. Hence, the frustration of their needs is as legitimate as the satisfaction or wasteful over-satiation of identical needs of others, which have obviously been acknowledged as rights.

The foregoing illustration concerns needs for goods and services which are transformed into effective rights (i.e. legitimate claims against society's aggregate stock of goods and services) when they are acknowledged through social policies. The same logic applies to civil, social, psychological, and political rights. These rights, too, derive from human needs, such as the need to participate in the productive processes and the governance of one's society, the need to be free and self-directing, the need for social recognition or prestige, etc.[2] Like the needs for material goods and services, these needs, too, become effective rights when they are defined as such, either for everyone, or merely for certain individuals and groups. Thus participation in decisions affecting one's life may be assumed to be a common human need, independent of sex, age, ethnicity, etc. Yet that need was transformed into the right to vote and to be elected to public office at different times for different groups in our society.

A formal explicit definition of a need as a right through social policies is, however, neither sufficient nor essential for the exercise of a given right. It is insufficient whenever the exercise of a right depends on access to and use of various resources, as is the case with respect to work. In such situations, a need becomes a right in a real sense only when necessary resources are allocated through appropriate societal processes.

On the other hand, rights need not always be defined explicitly, but can be established indirectly or by implication through the allocation of needs-satisfying resources to everyone or to certain individuals and groups. When rights are established in such an indirect manner, individuals to whom social policies allocate resources are free, within socially defined limits, to transform needs into rights at their own discretion. Societies make widespread use of indirect distribution of rights by regulating, through social policies, the distribution of wealth and income. Money (i.e. purchasing power) is a convenient mechanism for such indirect rights-distribution. It is a neutral right-equivalent which is easily transferable to, and easily transformed into, different needs-satisfying, concrete, and symbolic goods and services. In many societies, money is also necessary, or useful, to transform civil, social, psychological, and political rights into effective rights, and the distribution of these rights, too, can therefore be influenced indirectly through social policies which regulate money income and wealth holdings.

Rights and resources can be distributed as universal or specific entitlements by virtue of belonging to a society, or to special groups within society, or as differential, role, or status-related rewards. They can be distributed directly "in kind," or indirectly as "purchasing power." Illustrations of entitlements are demogrants, children's allowances, universal health services, public education, etc. Illustrations of role or status-related rewards are salaries, fringe benefits, stock options, rents, dividends, interest, royalties, etc.

WORK

The organization of all work deemed necessary by societies to secure life-sustaining and life-enhancing provisions has also been identified as one of the basic, existential processes which human groups regulate through social policies. Work seems rooted in universal aspects of the life process and of the human condition. It evolved as a response to needs inherent in the drive to survive. Live organisms are not self-contained beings. Hence, survival of humans, satisfaction of their needs, and the quality of their existence are predicated upon complex interactions and exchanges with their natural environment. The multifaceted mental and physical activities involved in these interactions and exchanges, all of which are intended to procure life-sustaining and enhancing resources, constitute the aggregate of human work.

Several aspects of work can be derived from this conception:

a. Work, in its original and undistorted manifestations, is a rational response to human needs and is motivated by the urge to satisfy these needs. It is a requirement for human survival, self-reliance, independence, and freedom. The "work ethic," which is a positive societal valuation of work, is a logical derivative from these original aspects of work.

b. Work involves the use of intellectual and physical human capacities to conceive, design, and evaluate solutions to existential problems in the mind, and to try out and implement these solutions in the material world. Work makes use of accumulated, transferable human experiences, knowledge, and skills.

c. Being motivated by human needs which it aims to satisfy, work is affected by, and in turn, affects human emotions. Hence, work has a psychological component in addition to intellectual and physical components.

d. Being a central aspect of human activities, work has evolved into a major constituent of human consciousness. Accordingly, work has significant implications for human self-definition, self-image, and identity, and is a medium for human relations, self-discovery, self-expression, and self-actualization. The crucial functions of work for human existence, perceptions, and interests were always reflected in societal values concerning work, such as the earlier mentioned "work-ethic."

e. All work involves combining resources from the natural environment with past and present human capacities. Past human capacities are stored in products of past work, namely discoveries, inventions, science, technology, tools and other material products, all of which are required to work in the present. Work in the present, therefore, depends on rights to use natural resources and products of past human work. To think of work apart from such rights results inevitably in conceptual confusion since issues related to work can be fully grasped and resolved only in the context of the development and control of a society's natural and human-created resources.

f. Throughout human history, social, psychological, economic, political, and ideological developments, as well as developments of science and technology, have resulted in increased complexity of work processes and work organization, in specializations in the division of labor, and in refinements of criteria of access to, and preparation for, different work roles. These developments regarding work became important factors in the emergence of systems of social stratification, the distribution of all kinds of rights, the circumstances of living, the quality of human relations, and the overall existential milieu of human societies. The extent to which access to work in general, and to specific work roles, is open rather than restricted, and the extent to which all kinds of rights are distributed as rewards linked to the division of labor, rather than as entitlements by virtue of belonging, have consequently become central issues of social philosophy and of political struggle.

Based on the discussion of the concepts of social policy, societal values, rights, and work, we can now tackle the questions raised above.

1. Does our society acknowledge a right to work, and is everyone free to exercise it?

No; we do not now acknowledge an explicitly defined, unconditional right to work. At the same time, we do not explicitly deny such a right, except in certain specified circumstances (e.g. "aliens," women, children, etc.). In a formal sense, people in our society are mostly free to work, on their own when they control resources with which to work, or as "employees" when others who control productive resources find it in their interest to hire them on terms advantageous to the employers. It follows that the right to work in general, and access to specific positions within the work system, is regulated indirectly through social policies which determine ownership and control of natural and human-created, productive resources, the use of which is a sine qua non for work.

As a result of social policy evolution, ownership and control of productive resources became concentrated within a small segment of our society through processes involving "legitimate" expropriation of the majority.[3] The expropriated majority now has access to work only when it serves the interests of those in control of our societal wealth, and they do not enjoy a right to work in a real sense.

Decisions of owners of productive resources in our society tend to be shaped by considerations of profit and further accumulation of capital. Accordingly, they perceive an unconditional right to work as contrary to their interests, since a surplus of idle individuals tends to depress wages, to increase profits, and to check inflation, given the dynamics of the existing institutional order. Restricting access to work selectively is, therefore, a social policy favored by many owners of productive resources.

The expropriation of the majority of our population has resulted not only in restrictions on their use of productive resources, and thus on their right to work, it has also resulted in limitations on their "income" and on economic, social, civil, political, and psychological rights which tend to be closely related to income. Furthermore, it has resulted in the transformation of work itself into a context for economic exploitation since the product of work does not belong to the workers, and since workers are routinely deprived of the full value of their labor through a wage system which reflects the relative social, economic, and political power of employers and employees rather than the full value of work in production. The nature of products, work processes, and the quality of work and human relations at work have also been shaped largely by considerations of profitability rather than by considerations of needs and priorities of the population, and the physical and psychological needs of workers engaged in production. Workers have no say in what they produce, how they produce it, and what is done with their finished products. They are not masters of production, but means or "factors" of production. They are controlled by others while at work, and because of their dependence on their jobs, that control tends also to permeate their lives outside the work place. The labor of workers is treated as a commodity which is exchanged for units of money, a neutral means of exchange in markets.

In these transformations, the products of work tend to lose meaning for workers. This loss of meaning is facilitated also by an "efficiency-oriented" production technology which reflects little concern for human needs of individual workers, splits production into minute tasks that lack intrinsic meaning, and separates intellectual and design functions from actual production work. Workers cannot develop a sense of pride and accomplishment in products which they hardly know and comprehend in their wholeness, and in whose design they have no part. Workers make little use of their intellectual faculties on most jobs and they become extensions of the machines they serve. Obviously, this production context is usually not conducive to self-expression, self-discovery, and self-actualization but to a pervasive sense of frustration, inadequacy, oppression, and alienation. This experience at work tends to be suppressed from consciousness but results frequently in emotional and psychosomatic ill health, escape into substitute gratifications, and over-compensation through meaningless "entertainment."

Another consequence of the existing work context and of the dependence of propertyless workers on owners of productive resources is intensive competition among individuals and groups for access to scarce jobs and for entry into preparatory channels, for holding on to jobs once hired, and for promotions to more desirable positions in hierarchical systems. As a result of this socially structured, competitive context, human relations tend to be remote and alienated on and off the job. The competitive dynamics affect especially the middle and higher strata of the work force whose members have opportunities, and hence aspirations, for climbing up the ladder of "success." Members of lower and marginal strata tend to be less ambitious and less competitive, since opportunities for "upward mobility" are usually blocked for them.

It is unrealistic to expect a positive valuation of work by workers themselves and by others given the existing work context. A positive work ethic can not coexist with economic exploitation and emotional deprivation at work. Rather, such conditions will breed negative attitudes toward work, a "work-avoidance" ethic and a celebration of leisure. In accordance with these attitudes, which are perfectly rational under the circumstances, workers tend to reduce the quantity and quality of their work and effort as far as is possible while holding on to a job. Whatever motivation to work is left in this context seems to be due not to an honest, positive work ethic but to fear of losing the job and of sinking into poverty.

2. Are acknowledgment of an unconditional right to work and guarantees to exercise that right desirable political goals?

While the preceding question could be answered on the basis of a factual analysis of the prevailing work context, answers to this question depend on one's values. A sketch of my value premises is therefore necessary at this point. We know from science that humans, anywhere and anytime on earth, are part of the same life process. We all belong in a real sense to the same human family, and hence everyone ought to be considered intrinsically equal in worth in spite of individual uniqueness and differences. Being considered of equal worth implies entitlement to equal social, economic, civil, political, and psychological rights. This, in turn, requires societal structures and dynamics conducive to the exercise of equal rights by all in every domain of human existence and on every level of social organization—local, trans-local, and global.

Equality of rights implies equal liberties and equal responsibilities for all. It implies equal shares in decision making or genuine democracy;

equal claims to the natural resources of the globe, and to human-created material and nonmaterial wealth; and equal freedom from all forms of exploitation, domination, and oppression.

Social equality, however, does not mean sameness or uniformity. It means equal rights to be and become oneself, or equal rights to individuality, to self-actualization, and to satisfaction of individual needs within constraints implicit in limitations on natural and human-created wealth, and in the same rights to needs-satisfaction of all others.[4]

From this value perspective, the answer to the present question is unequivocally yes. An unconditional right to work is not only a desirable political goal; it is an essential requirement if social orders are to be conducive to survival, liberty, and self-actualization for all humans. When discussing the sources and functions of work, we identified rational-objective ones (namely, procurement of needs-satisfying, life-sustaining, and life-enhancing goods and services); subjective-psychological ones (namely, self-discovery, identity, self-expression, and self-actualization of individuals); and social ones, (namely, shaping meaningful human relations through interactions in complementary roles). All this implies that to be fully human, one must participate freely, as an equal, in the work system of the human group of which one is a part; being excluded from such participation tends to dehumanize an individual. To overcome and prevent such dehumanization at its structural roots requires the development of work systems, the primary principle of which is assured participation for all as self-directing workers or masters of production. This requires socially acknowledged equal rights of access to, and use of, natural resources and human-created productive wealth, and a socially acknowledged and guaranteed equal right to work.

3. What does right to work mean, and what are implications of different meanings?

Slavery represents one possible meaning of a right to work. This paradoxical statement and the earlier discussion of "wage-labor" in our society illustrate the variability of work organization, and hence of the meanings of a right to work. It is obviously important to be clear as to the work context one has in mind when one advocates a socially acknowledged and guaranteed right to work.

One approach to conceptualizing different possible meanings of work is to think of different work contexts as defined by their position on several work-relevant dimensions. One such dimension is the rational-objective function of production, the procurement of needs-satisfying, life-sustaining and enhancing goods and services. Production of food, homes, clothing, and promotion of public health, education, etc., would rank high on this dimension, while production of cigarettes, nuclear bombs, defoliants, etc., would rank low. Some of these examples may be controversial since they do derive from my values. The general idea should nevertheless be clear.

Another relevant dimension is the subjective-psychological function of work. Creative, self-directed work, integrating intellectual, physical, and emotional faculties of humans, and conducive to self-discovery, self-expression, identity, and self-actualization (such as the work of artists or skilled craftsmen) would rank high on this dimension, while work in an hierarchically controlled, economically exploitative, and psychologically alienating context which precluded the integrated use of human faculties would rank low. Assembly line work in many contemporary industrial enterprises illustrates the latter work context.

One further dimension is the social function of work, the consequences of a work context for human relations, social integration, and for a sense of belonging. Cooperative work in a worker-controlled and directed setting would rank high on this dimension, while competitive work in hierarchically structured and controlled settings, such as university or government departments, would rank low.

Any specific work process and work context can be located on each of these dimensions. The total meaning of a given work context would depend on its position on each of the dimensions.

When one talks of guaranteeing a right to work, one needs to be explicit as to the nature, circumstances, and quality of work to which humans should be entitled, and whether one considers everyone entitled to work ranking high on the dimensions sketched here, or whether one considers certain individuals and groups in society entitled to work ranking high, while for others any kind of work should do.

Implications of alternative meanings of a right to work seem clear. If a right to work meant entitlement for everyone not merely to any kind of "job" within the existing, privately controlled system of production, but to work which is rational and meaningful in terms of objective human needs, and which is self-directed, nonexploitative, and conducive to self-actualization and to cooperative and caring human relations, then we would have to redesign our systems of resource control and production so that all roles within these systems were fit for authentic human beings. If, on the other hand, a right to work meant assuring everyone of a position within the exploitative, dehumanizing, and alienating work system as it now exists in our society, it would be a caricature of a right to work understood in humanistic terms, and only marginal adjustments would be required in the prevailing systems of resource control and production. Such a right to a "job" may nevertheless be a desirable interim reform, as it would ameliorate suffering due to unemployment, one destructive symptom of our unjust social order. One would have to be clear in advocating such a reform that guaranteeing jobs in the existing productive system would not eradicate (it might possibly even perpetuate) the roots and dynamics of injustice and inequality, namely, the long-standing expropriation of the majority of the population and their separation from productive resources without which they can not work freely and regain self-reliance.

4. Upon what societal conditions is the exercise of a right to work predicated, given different meanings of that notion?
In searching for answers to this question, one needs to overcome the widely believed myth that some level of unemployment is inevitable in a modern industrial productive system and that inflation is an inevitable consequence of reduction or elimination of unemployment. This proposition which many economists, journalists, and governmental leaders in our society believe to be universally valid, is, as a matter of fact, valid only in societies shaped by dynamics of competition, acquisitiveness, mutual exploitation, and waste. Societies which would use natural and human-created resources rationally to produce and distribute goods and services to meet the needs of all their members, rather than to serve narrowly perceived interests of privileged minorities, could divide the aggregate of required work into as many tasks as there are people available to do the work, and could organize the division of labor in a

manner conducive to a harmonious match of people and tasks. Such rational-humanistic institutions could emerge also in our society if we shifted our dominant values significantly toward equality, liberty, cooperation, and collectivity-orientation.

In discerning conditions essential for implementing any version of a right to work, one needs to recall that all work depends on use of natural and human-created resources. Hence, even a limited, non-humanistic version of a right to work, one which involved assuring a "job" to everyone without changing significantly the nature and quality of existing products, work processes, work experiences, and human relations, could not be implemented without some modifications of, or constraints on, now existing property rights over productive resources. Shifting from a work system which normally excludes large numbers of workers to one in which everyone is entitled to a job requires reallocations of productive resources, so that currently idle workers can be included in the aggregate of productive activities. Such essential reallocations tend to be judged "inefficient" in accordance with conventional profit and accumulation criteria, but would have to be judged "efficient" by criteria of need of idle workers whose right to a job can only be implemented through access to productive resources. This conflict of interests between current owners of productive resources and idle workers has no satisfactory solution within the logic and dynamics of now prevailing property rights, and can be resolved only by transcending the institutional order and dynamics defined by these rights.

These observations on conditions for a limited version of a right to work reveal that, in general terms, any expansion of rights to work requires corresponding modifications of, or constraints on, the rights of ownership and control over productive resources. An unconditional right to work for everyone can simply not coexist with an unconditional right of a minority of property owners to control, and withhold from use, productive resources essential to the exercise of rights to work.

It is relevant to point out in this context that concentration of control over a society's productive resources by small minorities is, by no means, a natural, inevitable human condition. It has emerged, as a legitimate institution among many human groups, only as a result of complex societal developments which brought about a gradual expropriation of majorities by means of physical force, ex-post-facto legitimation of the status quo of expropriation, and subsequent continuous socialization and indoctrination into a consciousness shaped by the established "law and order." Many human societies have never sanctioned private appropriation and concentration of control over their productive resources. Instead, they evolved their institutions on principles of communal ownership and control of these resources, and equal rights and responsibilities for all to work with these resources in a spirit of mutual aid. [5]

Many societies which instituted private control over productive resources early during their evolution have experienced repeated attempts throughout their history to challenge, reduce, or eliminate these institutions. Many of these attempts employed physical force while others involved nonviolent strategies. At the present time, private control over productive resources is being challenged in many parts of the world as growing numbers of people come to realize that achieving a worldwide human order, guided by reason and conducive to free and full development of all humans, requires liberation of the globe's productive resources from control by vested interests of small minorities. Self-reliance of people on every level of social organization is predicated upon rationally designed, democratically controlled, unobstructed use of productive resources, or, in terms of this essay, upon comprehensive, humanistic versions of a right to work for all.

5. What recommendations for social policy follow from these explorations?

The social policies suggested below are derived consistently from egalitarian, libertarian, cooperative, and collectivity-oriented value premises. They are designed to be conducive to the exercise of a comprehensive, humanistic version of the right to work. The policies reflect long-range goals for radical transformations of the four basic existential processes of human societies: the stewardship of natural and human-created resources, the organization of work, the distribution of goods, services, and other rights, and the governance of public affairs. Short-range policies can be formulated and evaluated in terms of their correspondence with the suggested long-range objectives.

Resources:

The most important policy for a humanistic version of the right to work, one without which such a version does not seem feasible, is the establishment of a "public trust" for the stewardship of all productive resources on local and trans-local levels.[6] Everyone would be equally entitled to use appropriate shares out of the public trust to work with, but not to own and accumulate. These freely available and circulating material and nonmaterial resources would be a permanent basis for everyone's participation in productive processes, and hence, for optimum satisfaction of human needs throughout the life cycle. The public trust would constitute a guarantee for all against domination and exploitation by others, as no one would depend on others to gain access to, and use of, resources necessary for a free and self-reliant existence .

The liberation of productive resources from private control and from exploitation for selfish ends will be reflected in radical modifications. Under the stewardship of a public trust, resources can be used rationally, efficiently, in accordance with scientific knowledge, and geared to the interests of the collectivity. Use and conservation can be balanced to assure adequate supplies for present and future generations, and waste and destruction can be reduced to a minimum. Emphasis can be placed on quality and durability of products, and on the use of renewable materials and of energy from abundant sources: the sun, the oceans, and the winds. Resource allocation can be guided flexibly by priority considerations derived from a hierarchy of human needs.[7] It needs to be stressed, however, that the notion of public trust does not imply a monolithic, centralistic, bureaucratic hierarchy which makes all allocative decisions. Public trust is used here in an abstract sense. It indicates that all productive resources belong jointly to all the people and that allocative decisions are evolved collectively, on decentralized levels through genuinely democratic processes.

Those who argue that the ultimate scarcity of global resources renders the competitive drive for shares inevitable disregard the fact that struggles to secure resources and privileges for oneself, one's family, group, or nation, result, invariably, in waste and destruction of resources, in irrational uses, and in distorted production priorities, all of which merely intensify existing scarcities and the vicious cycle of competition. The scarcity and zero-sum mentality of competition accelerates the shrinkage of local and global wealth and is thus patently self-defeating. It needs to be replaced by a plus-sum mentality of pacific cooperation, sharing, and joint planning, which alone can stretch and preserve scarce resources, and allocate them rationally and efficiently for the common good. Obviously, humankind must also adjust its numbers to the total global resource base. The only feasible way for doing this, however, is through cooperation, sharing, collectivity-orientation, and reason, not through competition, accumulation, selfishness, and irrationality.

Establishment of a public trust for productive resources implies abolition of private ownership and control over these resources. This change, it must be stressed, is to serve the genuine human interests for security and self-actualization of all humans, including the minority of individuals and groups who now own and control most productive resources. The radical transformations proposed here are not directed against propertied individuals and classes but against a social system that oppresses people, reduces the quality of life for all, and threatens the survival of the human species. Transition to a classless social system organized around a public trust of productive resources is meant to enhance the quality of life for all by securing the satisfaction of everyone's material, social, and psychological needs, and by relieving everyone from competitive and alienating struggles for false security and prestige derived from material possessions accumulated in an endless rat race.

Work:

Once productive resources are administered as a public trust, radical changes in the work context become possible. These changes concern the direction of work, the nature of products, the quality and technology of productive processes, and the quality of human relations and human experience at work. All these changes are related to one another, and they depend upon the fundamental change in the control of productive resources.

All work would be directed by workers themselves, individually when they choose to work by themselves, and collectively when they prefer working in groups. All workers would be well-trained and skilled, and thus competent to participate in designing, directing, and executing their own work. As far as possible, individuals would choose their work in accordance with capacities, talents, interests, and preferences. Products would be geared to genuine needs of people in type, quality, and quantity. Production technology and work processes would be adjusted to the needs of workers for a creative and meaningful experience and for an integrated use of their capacities and talents. Machines would be designed to fit these qualitative requirements, so that industrial processes would serve the needs of people rather than the other way around. Finally, the quality of human relations would change as exploitation and competition are replaced by cooperation, mutual recognition, and caring. To sum up, work would be thoroughly humanized: it would be shaped by human needs on every dimension and would be conducive to human self-actualization.

In spite of these radical changes of the work context, not all work tasks can be made equally satisfying. To compensate for inequalities of satisfaction intrinsic to different tasks, undesirable and less desirable tasks could be shared by all through rotation when their performance by machines is not feasible or is contraindicated for reasons of resources and energy conservation. Work rotation may be a desirable policy not only to deal with less satisfying work, but also in order to enhance the quality of work experience throughout the life cycle.

The work context sketched here does not imply elimination of specializations and of a rational division of labor. Individuals and communities should not aim to become autarkic through their productive work. Self-reliance does not mean self-sufficiency. Different individuals and communities would produce different goods and services in relation to available natural resources and human skills, and would exchange their products with other individuals and communities on egalitarian, nonexploitative terms of trade. In such exchanges, equal time units of work are considered equal in value, irrespective of differences in products, provided the products satisfy acknowledged human needs.

Rights:

The long-range social policy goal concerning the distribution of rights is to distribute goods, services, and nonmaterial rights as universal entitlements in accordance with individual needs, rather than as differential, task-specific rewards. Everyone would work at different tasks and would thus contribute to the aggregate product of his or her community and society. Irrespective of the type of work, individuals would be entitled, by virtue of belonging to a community, to have their socially acknowledged needs met out of the aggregate collective product.

Governance:

Self-direction and self-actualization at work for everyone is predicated upon genuinely democratic processes of governance in work places and communities, as well as on trans-local, coordinating levels. In places of work and in local communities or neighborhoods, governance can utilize participatory democracy in open assemblies of entire constituencies. Beyond the local level, governance can function through representative assemblies to which localities send delegates. This system can be expanded to more inclusive levels and to the global level, with assemblies on every level selecting representatives for the next broader level. In this manner, decentralized self-governance of parallel units on every level can be integrated into more inclusive levels, with each level being responsible for dealing with issues which transcend the perspectives and interests of the separate units represented in it. Assemblies on local and trans-local levels would select public administrators to carry out their decisions and policies.

The work of representatives and of public administrators on all levels would be deemed equal in value to other needed work and would entitle incumbents of these roles to the same rights everyone else enjoys. It would not entitle them to additional privileges. Besides, representative and administrative roles would be rotated routinely, with everyone having to share in responsibilities for public affairs.

All processes of governance would be conducted openly, precluding all secrecy, as secrecy is not needed to conduct the public affairs of egalitarian social orders. Secrecy's real function is to cover up existing injustices or attempts to establish new privileges.

Egalitarian social orders, shaped by the long-range social policies sketched here, could come into being through extended transformation processes, rather than through brief, revolutionary events, since they require thorough revolutions of consciousness along with institutional transformations. Steps toward egalitarian orders may be small or large. Whatever their scope, they are part of the total process. Whether a policy is a real contribution to this process depends on whether it is in tune, rather than in conflict, with the long-range goals.

Short-Range Policies:

Limited versions of the right to work can fit into this process, as valid, incremental steps, provided long-range, humanistic goals are not denied or obstructed by implementing an immediate, unconditional right to a job for everyone. Political struggles for such a limited right to work can actually be used to advance the understanding of the larger issues and of the long-range goals.[8]

Limited versions of a right to work can be implemented through "regressive" social policies which reinforce the principle of private control over productive resources, or through "progressive" social policies which place constraints on private control of these resources. Illustrations of regressive policies are government subsidies or investment tax credits to private firms as incentives for the creation of jobs or the implementation of manpower-training programs. Illustrations of "progressive" policies are taxes on productive assets held by individuals or firms and transformation of the tax yield into resources which are made available to idle workers so that they may work. While regressive policies subsidize owners of productive wealth from tax revenues collected largely from propertyless workers, progressive policies subsidize expropriated, unemployed workers from taxes levied on concentrations of productive resources.

A further possibility of incremental, progressive social policies is public expropriation of owners of major productive resources, and management of these resources in the public interest. This can be done through redistribution of such resources for use by expropriated segments of a population (e.g. land reform benefiting landless tenant farmers), or through direct public administration of the resources (e.g. public management of mines, steel mills, and railroads, as in Great Britain). Another potentially progressive policy affects rights to work by sharing rights of ownership and control of productive resources with workers, transferring corporate shares to them, and including their representatives on boards of corporations. Sweden, West Germany, and Peru, among others, have experimented with different versions of "codetermination" in recent years. European welfare states have made wide use of some or all of these "progressive" short-range policies in their efforts to eliminate unemployment, reduce inequalities, and enhance the overall quality of life. The results of these efforts have been mixed, mainly because of contradictions between the objectives of the policies and the dynamics of capitalist states. The United States tends to prefer "regressive," short-range policies in dealing with unemployment. Not surprisingly, our efforts have usually produced unsatisfactory results from the perspective of idled workers.

I want to end with an illustration of a "progressive" policy from our "underdeveloped" society. Anyone using a public library anywhere in the United States can get a glimpse of the long-range solutions advocated in this essay. Books are part of the productive resources of our society. Through a decentralized system of local public libraries, we have established a public trust to make these resources freely available on equal terms. Everyone benefits directly and indirectly through the free circulation of books. No one loses and everyone is enriched the more he uses the library and the more others use it. The stock of books is constantly replenished and renewed.

There were stages in our development when books were owned and read only by a wealthy elite. The establishment of public libraries did not deprive these individuals of opportunities to read by extending the same right to everyone else. Clearly, establishing a public trust of libraries was not a zero-sum game. It did not result in scarcities of reading materials, but brought about an increase, a typical plus-sum outcome.

The success of our public libraries should help us overcome our reluctance to extend the public trust model to other components of our productive resources. Positive experiences along these lines should gradually open our consciousness to the realization that only when we liberate all our productive resources from control by private interests, and make them available for free use and circulation, can we be truly free, and will we enjoy a genuine right to work.

Native American tribes who preceded Europeans on this continent have known these truths for many centuries. They never divided their lands into private parcels. Similarly, Judeo-Christian philosophy teaches that productive resources should belong to all the people: "'The land is mine,' says the Lord" is the symbolic Biblical message.[9] It is time we learned the secret of life and peace from our native brothers and from our early sources, ere it is too late.

NOTES

1. See chapter 2 in this book.

2. See Abraham H. Maslow, *Motivation and Personality* (New York: Harper & Row, 1954, 1970).

3. See James D. Smith & Stephen D. Franklin, *The Distribution of Wealth Among Individuals and Families.* Conference on Personal Distribution of Income and Wealth, Pennsylvania State University, 1972. (New York: National Bureau of Economic Research: Distributed by Columbia University Press, 1975); Gabriel Kolko, *Wealth & Power in America* (New York: Praeger, 1962).

4. See R. H. Tawney, *Equality* (London: Allen and Unwin, 1931). See also my book, *The Challenge of Social Equality*, (Cambridge, MA: Schenkman Publishing Co., 1976).

5. Petr Kropotkin, *Mutual Aid* (Boston, MA: Porter Sargent, 1956. Originally published 1902).

6. See my essay "Social Policy and Social Development," *Journal of Sociology & Social Welfare,* Vol. 3, No. 3 (January 1976).

7. See Abraham H. Maslow *Motivation and Personality* (New York: Harper and Row, 1970).

8. See Andre Gorz, *Strategy for Labor* (Boston, MA: Beacon Press, 1967).

9. *Leviticus* 25, 23.

The Hidden Success of Schooling
in the United States *

Widespread agreement among parents, students, educators, the media, and the public at large finds the quality and results of education in our schools disappointing. Many children, it is said, graduate without minimal competence in reading, writing, and mathematics, not to mention more esoteric subjects. The search is on for scapegoats and for magical solutions. Parents and educators blame one another. Together they blame administrators, school boards, inadequate budgets and facilities, inappropriate student-teacher ratios, inadequate didactic methods, poor discipline, etc. There is renewed emphasis on "basics," on specifications of concrete learning objectives; on accountability and measurement; on realistic occupational goals; on behavior modification; on increased control over students and teachers; and on grading, scaling, testing, sorting, reviewing. Implicit in these fashionable remedies for the unsatisfactory performance of schools, students, and teachers is the assumption that "technical fixes" can solve these problems. If only some ingenious pedagogue discovered the "correct educational technology," then all students would succeed and perform at an optimum level.

Alas, the alleged failure of our schools and the frustration of parents, students, and teachers will not be overcome in any real sense through the changes proposed in teaching methods, school budgets, control mechanisms, and the like. While marginal improvements are certainly attainable from such measures, effective prevention of school failures and significant improvements in education seem to depend largely on funda-

---

*This article first appeared in *The Humanist*, vol. 39, no. 6. (November/December 1979) and is reprinted by permission.

mental changes in prevailing social values and in the social, economic, and political institutions in which our schools are embedded. These unconventional conclusions follow from a usually overlooked, tragic, and paradoxical aspect of our system of schooling: this system is actually successful in terms of its covert objective while obviously failing individual students on a massive scale. The covert objective of schooling is, of course, to prepare successive generations of students for the total array of tasks and positions which they have to take on as adults in the real world, and not in a world that could or should exist. Such has been the goal of socialization and schooling throughout human history. What has changed over time, along with changes in the patterns of life of human societies, is the form, content, and overt goals of education and schooling—not the underlying, universal mission. Viewed thus, the failures of our schools, which are certainly real and painful from an individual perspective, turn out to be successes in terms of the "aggregate output" required of them by our prevailing way of life, especially our modes of work and production.

If then, we wish to understand the workings of our schools and to evaluate their overt failures and "hidden successes," we need to examine the context of adult life in our society, in particular the prevailing system of work and production into which students are to be absorbed. Such an examination should reveal the characteristics, competencies, and attitudes which every generation of adults requires in order to match the demands at work and elsewhere for which schools consequently must prepare each generation of students. To evaluate results of schooling in terms of abstract educational theories and standards or in terms of achievements of individual students, as educators, parents, and the public tend to do, misses a central criterion of socialization—the performance of entire age cohorts of students upon reaching adulthood. Such conventional evaluations, which focus exclusively on the facade or the overt function of schooling rather than on its underlying mission, merely perpetuate the confusion and illusions which now surround discussions of education in our society. Such evaluations are also unfair to schools and teachers who are being blamed for failures beyond their control, failures which are simply inevitable in the prevailing societal context.

WORK IN THE UNITED STATES

When one examines the organization and quality of work and human relations at places of work in the present stage of our social development, one finds that most adults engage throughout their working years in relatively meaningless, routine tasks and that they are trapped in hierarchically structured, dehumanizing, competitive, exploitative, and alienating organizations. Work usually does not require and stimulate the integrated use of an individual's innate intellectual, creative, emotional, and physical capacities since, given the prevailing division of labor, workers are expected merely to carry out fragmented tasks under the direction of superiors, often without even understanding the process of production and the nature of the products. The less workers understand and think, the more efficiently are production processes assumed to proceed, in the conventional, though fallacious, view of many managers and supposed experts of work design. Accordingly, individuals now participate in production as "specialized functions," as attachments to, or servants of, complex machines which they do not comprehend. They are means toward the ends of managers and owners of settings of production, or—to use a telling phrase of contemporary economics—"factors of production," rather than self-directing subjects working toward their own ends as knowledgeable masters of production. Strange as it may seem, workers are also expected, and they frequently tend, to view the oppressive, concrete, and psychological conditions under which they now labor as valid. They usually consider their superiors as legitimate authority and competent sources of knowledge, and they submit readily, at least on the surface, to authoritarian, nondemocratic forms of management.

A further aspect of our prevailing system of work, one without which workers probably would not submit as readily as they now do to the conditions just described, is the fact that participation in the work force tends to be unstable and marginal for many millions of capable individuals. Many others are excluded altogether from the work force. In the jargon of economics, these conditions are labeled euphemistically "under-employment and unemployment." Economists refrain usually from

CHART 7.1
CUMULATIVE IMPACT OF 1.4 PERCENT RISE
IN UNEMPLOYMENT DURING 1970
(HUMAN IMPACT)

Social Stress Indicator	Stress Incidence 1975	Change in Stress Indicator for a 1.4 % Rise in Unemployment	Increase in Stress Incidence Due to the Rise in Unemployment
Suicide:	26,960	5.7	1,540
State Mental Hospital Admission:	117,480[1]	4.7	5,520
State Prison Admission:	136,875[2]	5.6	7,660
Homicide:	21,730	8.0	1,740
Cirrhosis of the Liver Mortality:	32,080	2.7	870
Cardiovascular-Renal Disease Mortality:	979,180	2.7	26,440
Total Mortality:	1,910,000	2.7	51,570

1. *1972 data, age 65 and under.*
2. *1974 data.*

Source: M. Harvey Brenner, "Estimating the Social Costs of National Economic Policy" (Washington, D.C.: U.S. Government Printing Office, 1976).

detailing the enormous costs in human suffering and the waste of human potential behind their uncmployment statistics (see charts 7.1 and 7.2).

Routine availability of an unemployed labor reserve, consequent difficulties in securing a place in the work system, and ever present fears of losing one's position tend to promote conformity to work place discipline and readiness to work for relatively low wages. The same circumstances are also major sources of fierce competition among individuals and groups for work and for promotions to more desirable, i.e., more highly rewarded, tasks in the work system. This competition tends to poison human relations at work and to divide working people against themselves, thus precluding the emergence of worker solidarity without which managers and employers can not be confronted and

CHART 7.2
CUMULATIVE IMPACT OF 1.4 PERCENT RISE
IN UNEMPLOYMENT DURING 1970
(FINANCIAL IMPACT)

Social Stress Indicator	Classification of Economic Cost	Economic Loss Due to the 1.4 Percent Rise in Unemployment Sustained from 1970-1975 (millions)
Suicide:	Suicide	$ 63
State Mental Hospital Admission:	Hospitalization for mental illness in State and County mental hospitals	82
State Prison Admission:	Imprisonment in State Institutions	210
Homicide:	Homicide	434
Cirrhosis of the Liver Mortality:	1	1
Cardiovascular-Renal Disease Mortality: `	Diseases of the Circulatory System	1,372
Total Mortality	Total Illness	$6,615

¹ Costs not available.

Source: M. Harvey Brenner, "Estimating the Social Costs of National Economic Policy" (Washington, DC.: U.S. Government Printing Office, 1976).

challenged effectively. Discriminatory practices such as racism, sexism, and ageism are also partly rooted in, and tend to be reinforced by, this competition for work.

Perhaps the most amazing aspect of unemployment and under-employment is that marginal and excluded workers tend to regard the work system which abuses and excludes them as legitimate. They often view themselves as inferior to those who secure employment and tend to blame themselves rather than the structured scarcities in our organization of work for their failure to obtain a position.

Only a few individuals (e.g. certain scholars, professionals, managers, artists) are expected to use some of their innate intellectual and creative capacities in the course of their work. Yet their work situation too is frequently dehumanizing, competitive, and alienating, and they too tend to be ignorant of the societal forces which underlie these conditions. Their intellectual capacities are invested largely in the domains of their narrow specializations. They are usually unprepared or reluctant to analyze critically the forces which shape their work settings and cause their stresses and frustrations. Also, their material rewards and working conditions are usually far better than those of other workers. This seems to be a further reason why, like the more severely oppressed and exploited segments of the work force, they tend to conform rather than critique and challenge the established order at their places of work.

SOCIALIZATION AND SCHOOLING: IDIOTS ARE MASS-PRODUCED, NOT BORN

Given the organization of work sketched above and the social, economic, political, and ideological dynamics which maintain that organization, our society requires settings and processes of socialization to prepare entire generations of children to fit smoothly and willingly into the many layers and positions of its skilled and unskilled, professional and managerial work force and its unemployed and under-employed labor reserve. This preparation must accomplish several objectives. First, the rich, innate intellectual, creative and emotional capacities of most children—excepting mainly children from privileged classes, many of whom are expected eventually to fill elite positions in various sectors of society—must be suppressed selectively since the prevailing work and non-work systems have little use for these capacities and creativity. Next, children need to develop a consciousness, or mentality, incorporating attitudes and beliefs which will facilitate adjustment to competitive, exploitative, dehumanizing, and alienating conditions and experiences, both at work and when unemployed. Children must learn to respect and to submit readily to authority as the source of knowledge, well-being, and "law and order." To assure such respect and submission, they need to develop a sense of their own inadequacy and of their dependence upon established, "legitimate" authority. They must also come to believe in the intrinsic superiority, validity, and legitimacy of our prevailing way of life, and its selfish, competitive, and inegalitarian values. A blind attachment to "God and Country" and noncritical admiration for our leaders and heroes, past and present, are also important elements of the desired mentality. And finally, children must learn to live and behave in accordance with these attitudes and beliefs without questioning them, as if they were sacred and unchangeable.

These goals of socialization are attained mainly through experiential learning and, to a lesser extent, through cognitive learning. Much is learned in homes, churches, and other places of worship, and in neighborhoods whose patterns of everyday life are usually permeated by our social and occupational class structures. Children's sense of reality and of themselves, their expectations, their aspirations, and their motivations are all rooted in experiences at home and around the neighborhood. Schools, which are usually associated with and influenced by neighborhoods, merely continue, complement, and reinforce the consciousness and behavior-shaping experiences of home, religious settings, and streets. They echo these experiential teachings and thus lend their support and authority to the intergenerational transmission of our social and occupational class structure.

Schools, families and neighborhoods thus seem trapped in a process of reproducing occupational and social class structures which implies, inevitably, massive failure in terms of the development of individual students. To accomplish their socialization function, schools, like homes, are authoritarian settings in which the motivation of students is further inhibited and undermined through antagonistic relations with teachers and administrators. The innate capacities and creativity of most students tend consequently to atrophy as they are rarely used and expressed because of widespread lack of opportunity, aspiration, and motivation. The suppressed, originally constructive, developmental energy of students does not disappear, however. Rather, it tends to be transformed into destructive and self-destructive energy which is often released through acts of vandalism and aggression in schools and elsewhere. In authoritarian schools, such release of destructive energy by students leads usually to vicious cycles of violence and destruction.

Schools continue the experiential socialization process initiated in homes, churches, and neighborhoods. They promote a predominantly authoritarian milieu based on conventional assumptions according to which children are inherently "evil" and lazy, rather than "good" and self-motivated, and must therefore be controlled and coerced to study. However, it should be stressed that teachers do not intentionally and consciously undermine the capacities and creativity of students in order to assure their adjustment and submission to the dehumanizing conditions of work. Yet such is, nevertheless, the normal aggregate outcome of schooling along with prior and parallel socialization practices in homes and on the streets. The amazing thing about schooling then is that its destructive, covert objectives are attained so well, although most teachers and administrators pursue constructive, overt goals of individual development and achievement for their students and school.

The history of "compulsory schooling"—which is called, euphemistically, free, public education—supports the proposition that schooling in the United States has mainly been shaped by the requirements of our changing modes of production. The mandate of schools since their beginnings seems to have been the preparation and control of the work force, and not the development, education, and cultural enrichment of students. Compulsory school attendance was initiated in Massachusetts in the nineteenth century soon after factories began to replace the earlier production pattern of cottage industries, and large numbers of women were recruited into the new factories. From their beginnings, schools took care of children of working mothers, prepared children of factory workers for the discipline of factory work, and regulated the age of entry into the work force in relation to changing demands for labor. This latter function resulted in the gradual extension of years of schooling during the nineteenth and twentieth centuries, and in the corresponding forced delay of entry into the work force. This extension of schooling did not result however, as is often assumed erroneously, in marked increases in the scope and depth of education of most graduates of public schools, for this obviously was not its real purpose. Rather, that purpose seems to have been to establish a "holding pattern" for the control of large numbers of young and energetic people whose labor was not in demand as industry gradually became more mechanized. The official count of unemployment was, however, reduced significantly by keeping youth in schools longer.

As the structures and practice of public schools evolved, they took on many features of factories and business enterprises. These common features proved to be conducive to the experiential preparation of students for authoritarian, hierarchically structured places of work. Being on time is of crucial importance in factories; life in schools consequently came to be shaped largely by clocks. Authority is the source of all relevant knowledge in factories; it assumed a similar stance in schools, where all knowledge is supposed to reside in and flow from those in authority positions. In both settings, there is a "work force" at the base of the pyramid of power: workers in factories and students in schools. Workers and students are controlled and disciplined by competition-inducing and divisive rewards and sanctions: differential wages, layoffs, and firings in factories; differential grades, punishments and expulsions in schools. Both settings have managers on the premises of local units: school principals and plant managers. And both settings maintain a close watch over their "workers" through classroom teachers and shop floor supervisors. Finally, both settings are controlled by remote, often anonymous, ultimate authority: corporation boards and presidents; school boards and superintendents. School boards, one should note, usually maintain close ties to business elites whose values, perspectives, and perceptions of reality they tend to share and represent.

Throughout their history, public schools in the United States have never been committed in practice to maximum development of intellect, critical consciousness, creativity, imagination, individuality, and penetrating insight into reality. The achievements of most students in these respects usually have been below innate capacity. Yet, cognitive learning has, nevertheless, always been an important component of schooling without which, paradoxically, its covert objectives could never have been realized. Cognitive studies are the medium by which degrees of overt "success" and "failure" are defined, judged, and certified. These studies are also the arena and substance for competition among students, the base for the illusion of that competition's fairness, and the foundation of the ideology of meritocracy which feeds on that illusion. Furthermore, different levels of attainment in cognitive studies provide a rationale and excuse for the material and symbolic inequalities which permeate all spheres of life in our society. And finally, poor performance in cognitive studies provides supposedly objective criteria for blaming individual students for the "failure" of a system of socialization which mass-produces failures through its intimate linkage to our social and occupational class structures. Cognitive studies, then, are needed to disguise the covert mission of our schools: selective destruction of students' capabilities, preparation and regulation of the work force, and intergenerational transmission of prevailing class and occupational structures. In a nominal democracy such as the United States, this patently undemocratic mission could not succeed unless it was disguised behind images of justice, fairness, and mobility and unless large numbers of individuals who are caught up in the schooling process as its victims—students—or its agents—teachers and administrators—actually regarded that process as essentially just, fair, and open.

Cognitive studies are, however, also important in the selection and preparation of technical, professional, scientific, cultural, managerial, and political elites in complex, industrial societies. With respect to these relatively small, yet important, segments of the work force, the overt educational objectives of schooling are valid to an extent. However, elite students, too, are unlikely to realize their innate capacities and creativity in the public and private schools of privileged neighborhoods. These schools, though, and the milieu of their neighborhoods and homes are usually less authoritarian and alienating, and hence less destructive of children's self images, aspirations, motivation, and capacities than the homes, neighborhoods, and schools of less advantaged children. Yet, though their experiences in growing up are more favorable in many respects, their individual development, especially the capacity to think critically and independently, is nevertheless inhibited by the authoritarian and competitive dynamics of everyday life and by divisive and reality-distorting effects of prevailing class structures.

The failure of "successful" elite students to develop penetrating, critical, and holistic insights into reality as well as into the social, economic, and political forces which shape their personal, educational, and eventual occupational experience is as important for the maintenance of our established way of life as the more comprehensive failure of the "unsuccessful," nonelite students. Moreover, the failure of the elite students seems equally inevitable, given the fragmented nature of cognitive studies and the predominantly nondialogical teaching style of most "good" schools and universities where development and transmission of knowledge are usually constrained by conventional departmental patterns and by grading and competitive exams. As a result of these features, students tend to concentrate their studies around narrow, specialized domains and to remain relatively uninformed about areas beyond their "majors." Also, their studies tend to be largely defined and directed by teachers and faculties, rather than by themselves. Thus, in spite, or rather, because of their "good" education in "better" public and private schools and in elite universities, these students usually do not develop a critical and holistic consciousness. They are, consequently, as unlikely as most other students and workers to confront and challenge the societal status quo and its authoritarian and alienating features, especially since that status quo tends to seduce them through ample material and symbolic rewards. It follows that "success" in cognitive studies as defined and organized in the prevailing system of schooling and "higher" education usually means failure in a deeper, existential sense—the development of critical consciousness and practice through which alone existing obstacles to human survival, self-actualization, and liberation may be overcome.

BEYOND DESTRUCTIVE AND DEHUMANIZING SCHOOLING

The analysis of linkages among social and occupational class structures, schooling, and educational "failure" or "success," respectively, reveals that the widespread discontent with schools and education is now largely misdirected, as it focuses on symptoms rather than sources. The real source of inferior schools and of educational failure is not inadequate pedagogical methods and insufficient resources but a social and occupational system which is organized to generate economic profit for society's privileged minorities and does not, therefore, value people and their individual capacities. Most young people in our society have nowhere to go except into alienating work settings or non-work situations. Their capacities are simply not needed and will, thus, continue to atrophy from lack of use. Children usually become intuitively aware of their realistic prospects in life by observing their parents and neighbors. Such awareness and observations tend to undermine, for valid reasons, most young persons' innate motivation to learn. When innate motivation for learning is destroyed, schools inevitably fall short of their stated goals of individual development and achievement, however sophisticated their methods may be. On the other hand, when the motivation of children remains at a high level because their life chances appear to them exciting and challenging, then they are more likely to learn almost anything irrespective of methods and settings.

Schools and the quality of education will change and improve in significant ways when our social order is transformed thoroughly into a way of life in which, to quote Protagoras, "humans will be the measure of all things," a way of life in which all humans will be considered equal in worth and rights and will thus be equally entitled to develop and use their innate capacities, free from domination and exploitation by others. In such a way of life, humans will not be means to the ends of others and hence will be "masters" rather than "factors" of production. Work and production will be redesigned and reorganized to fit and meet the biological, psychological, social, and economic needs of all members of society, rather than the narrow, selfish ends of powerful, privileged minorities who in capitalist states own and control most sources and means of human survival and existence, and who consequently cause the majority of the people to depend on them and be subject to their authority, exploitation, and control.

In a classless, genuinely democratic and egalitarian society, schools would be transformed into centers of study in which all students have ample opportunity to explore and develop their innate capacities. These rich capacities will be in high demand when a transformed way of life and organization of work will make use of everyone's creative, intellectual, physical, and emotional capacities. Socialization in homes, communities, and schools will encourage, and build largely on, the innate motivation and inquisitiveness of children. The guiding assumption of educators will be that humans, when trusted and supported rather than mistreated and controlled, tend, spontaneously, to assume direction of their lives in accordance with their gradually unfolding innate capacities. Accordingly, experiential and cognitive education will be nonauthoritarian, noncompetitive, supportive, and dialogical in agreement with principles practiced over 2,500 years ago by Socrates and advocated and practiced throughout human history by humanistic philosophers and educators.

The goal of socialization and education of such a transformed, egalitarian society will be free and self-directing individuals with critical insight into the human condition, social and ecological reality, and themselves; knowledgeable about science, technology, the arts and culture; able to govern their communities democratically; and able to participate creatively, cooperatively, and skillfully in production and services needed by their communities. This goal is compatible with the universal mission of socialization as well as with the requirements of individual development. Hence, education would not be paralyzed as it is under prevailing conditions by contradictions between overt and covert goals.

To overcome the prevailing, tragic failure of our existing system of schooling requires philosophical and political efforts aimed at creating a broad movement for radical social transformation and human liberation. Nothing less will do. Once the logic of this proposition is acknowledged, we will no longer have to waste time and efforts on a futile search for technical fixes for our failing schools and failing youth. Instead we will be able to concentrate our minds and energy on advancing the revolutionary process toward genuine individual and social liberation.

REFERENCES

Bernfeld, Siegfried. *Sisyphos* (Wien: Internationaler Psychoanalitischer Verlag, 1925).

Bowles, Samuel, and Gintis, Herbert. *Schooling in Capitalist America* (New York: Basic Books, 1976).

Braverman, Harry. *Labor and Monopoly Capital: The Degradation of Work in the Twentieth Century* (New York: Monthly Review Press, 1974).

Freire, Paulo. *Pedagogy of the Oppressed* (New York: Herder & Herder, 1970).

Gil, David G. *The Challenge of Social Equality* (Cambridge: Schenkman Publishing Co., 1976).

Gil, David G. *Beyond the Jungle* (Boston: G. K.. Hall & Co., 1979; and Cambridge: Schenkman Publishing Co., 1979).

Marcuse, Herbert. *One-Dimensional Man* (Boston: Beacon Press, 1964).

Maslow, Abraham H. *Motivation and Personality* (New York: Harper & Row, 1954, 1970).

Pappenheim, Fritz. *The Alienation of Modern Man* (New York: Monthly Review Press, 1959).

8

Overcoming Conventional and Reverse Discrimination at Their Roots *

Social problems such as discrimination in employment can be solved when one deals with the objective and subjective aspects of the context in which they evolve, rather than merely with their surface manifestations. Consequently, if we mean to overcome such problems, we must identify and transform the social arrangements and ideologies in which they are rooted and reproduced. Solutions, however well-intentioned, which fail to confront and eliminate the sources of a problem, can, at best, result in temporary amelioration of its symptoms; variations on the theme underlying the original problem, such as the replacement of conventional by "reverse" discrimination, usually follow.

The objective conditions leading to discrimination in employment can be sketched as follows:

a) Most people in capitalist systems have access to gainful work only when hired by owners or managers of means of production or service establishments

b) People will be hired when, and as long as, their employment serves the perceived interests of their employers

c) The capitalist drive for accumulation and profit is usually aided by the presence of unemployed workers in labor markets, as wages can be forced to lower levels under such conditions

---

*This chapter first appeared in The Humanist Sociologist, vol. 5, no. 2 (June 1980).

d) Production and service enterprises are segmented into sectors with more stable and desirable work and sectors with unstable and undesirable work; within each sector and enterprise, there is further fragmentation into more and less desirable positions

e) Unemployment and segmentation result inevitably in competition for entry into the work force and for mobility to preferred positions; this competition is a major source of internal divisions and antagonistic relations among workers, and leads usually to discriminatory practices such as sexism, ageism, and racism; competition and discrimination are often encouraged overtly and covertly within capitalist systems, so as to counter the emergence of solidarity and class consciousness among workers, a prerequisite toward socialist transformation.

Along with these objective conditions, subjective attitudes and ideologies developed to justify, reinforce, and perpetuate discriminatory practices. People are usually not conscious of the reciprocal links between the objective conditions of competition and discrimination at work and their subjective dynamics. Consequently, they tend to experience and react to racism, ageism, and sexism as if these were discrete phenomena, rather than intrinsic aspects of an exploitative, competitive, hierarchically-structured class society. Real solutions to these discriminatory practices are, however, not possible until these links are made conscious and accounted for when attacking the problems.

Affirmative action policies are merely cosmetic attempts to compensate for long-standing discrimination in employment against women and minorities by allocating a larger share of scarce positions than in the past to women and minorities—and a larger share of unemployment to men and whites—without reducing the total number and rate of unemployed or "excluded" individuals. Therefore, affirmative action means to develop new rules for inclusion and exclusion, a new variation on a standard capitalist theme.

Affirmative action policies make sense only as "first aid" measures. As long range policies, they are actually counterproductive in attaining an egalitarian and democratic way of life. Affirmative action is ineffective because it does not aim to overcome the objective conditions of discrimination sketched above and because it disregards the links between these objective conditions and the subjective dynamics of sexism, ageism, racism, etc. Instead it deals with these discriminatory practices as isolated problems which can be solved without transforming the established capitalist system.

While affirmative action can somewhat ameliorate the existing symptoms of discrimination, although not without transferring the problems elsewhere, it cannot reduce the antagonism which divides working class people. Thus, it further delays the development of their solidarity. Moreover, affirmative action also reinforces the illusion that social problems can be solved without changing the established order, through competitive interest-group politics shaped by the pluralistic ideology of the liberal-capitalist state.

The logical solution to the problem of discrimination in employment which the foregoing analysis suggests is not affirmative action within the context of capitalism, but affirmative action to transform capitalism into decentralized, democratic socialism. This involves transferring the control of production and services from their current owners and managers to workers and communities, and redesigning all work processes and products so that everyone would have an equal right to rewarding work and to free and full development of one's innate human potential. Discrimination, whatever its content and form, will be ended only when no one is excluded, when everyone is entitled to participate in production without being forced to compete—when it is no longer in the interest of a controlling class to perpetuate antagonisms and divisions among an exploited working class.

9

Dialectics of Individual Development and Global Social Welfare*

This essay examines individual development and social welfare in the context of global human relations and egalitarian, humanistic, and democratic values. I first explore the meaning and requirements of individual development and social welfare. Next, I review structural and ideological sources of underdevelopment and "illfare" in capitalist and imperialist dynamics on national and global levels. I then sketch features of an alternative pattern of life—decentralized, democratic-socialism— which many students of the human condition consider compatible with individual development and social welfare everywhere. The essay concludes with comments on political strategy toward the emergence of a global system of democratic-socialist communities and societies.

Some observations on the present human condition seem indicated as background. Many thoughtful observers of conditions of life in the twentieth century have concluded that the human species may not be able to reverse, in time, several interrelated trends which seem to threaten life all over the globe: depletion of food supplies and other important natural resources, unchecked population growth, progressive degradation of the quality of soil, water and the atmosphere, wasteful and destructive processes of production, and proliferation of conventional and nuclear armaments.[1] Along with these threatening material processes, the quality of life and of human relations seems to deteriorate steadily from the household to the global level.

---

*Humanity and Society, vol. 7, no. 1 (February 1983); Brij Mohan, editor, New Horizons in Social Welfare and Policy, (Cambridge, MA: Schenkman, 1985).

Knowledgeable scholars have pointed out again and again that the destructive practices and attitudes of the human species are not inevitable since they do not derive from naturally given "objective" conditions but from cultural ones. "Our principal impediments, at present," says Dr. Hubbert, a noted geophysicist, "are neither lack of energy or material resources, nor of essential physical and biological knowledge. Our principal constraints are cultural ..."[2] Many natural and social scientists have arrived at similar conclusions.[3]

What does it mean that threats to human survival are "cultural," and what implications are suggested by this? It means, first of all, that these threats are inherent in prevailing, fiercely defended patterns of social, economic, and political relations among individuals, groups, classes, and nations, and in consciousness and ideologies which derive from these relations, and in turn, reproduce them. It means, furthermore, that these patterns, consciousness, and ideologies were evolved throughout history by human groups and social classes through frequently antagonistic interactions with one another and with their natural environments in pursuit of survival and perceived improvements in the conditions of life. Finally, it means that since humans are originators, shapers, transmitters, enforcers, and transformers of their patterns of living, they are conceivably capable, through collective, critical reflection and action, to transform survival-threatening into life-confirming patterns along lines conducive to individual development and global social welfare. This perspective and conclusion guide the following discussion.

MEANING AND REQUIREMENTS OF INDIVIDUAL DEVELOPMENT AND SOCIAL WELFARE

In the simplest terms, as well as in a most profound sense, *social welfare means conditions of living in which humans can fare well,* conditions in which their bodies and minds are free to develop through all stages of maturation unto death. Such conditions are predicated upon social structures and dynamics, and upon human acts and attitudes, which will not inhibit spontaneous unfolding of the innate physical, emotional and intellectual capacities of people, but instead will be compatible with developmental processes.

Implicit in this concept of social welfare is an assumption that life organisms are self-propelled toward becoming what they are intrinsically capable of becoming, and that a tendency toward development is inherent in humans in the same way it appears to be inherent in the seeds of plants. Seeds do not grow, however, into healthy mature plants under all circumstances, but only when implanted in nutritious soil, and when sunshine and rain correspond in timing, quality, and quantity to their developmental requirements. Similarly, humans can fare well only when living in social and natural environments compatible with their intrinsic developmental needs.

To further clarify the dynamics and requirements of human development and welfare, one must, therefore, identify developmental and existential needs of humans. Knowledge concerning these needs may be imperfect. However, many students of human development consider fulfillment of the following related needs a sine qua non of healthy human development, and hence of human welfare.[4]

—Needs for regular access to life-sustaining and enhancing goods and services, the scope and quality of which vary among different societies and over time;

—Needs for meaningful social relations and a sense of belonging to a community, involving mutual respect, acceptance, affirmation, care and love, and opportunities for self-discovery and for the emergence of a positive sense of identity;

—Needs to participate in meaningful and creative ways, in accordance with one's innate capacities and stage of development, in productive processes of one's community and society;

—Needs for a sense of security, derived from continuous fulfillment of needs for life-sustaining and enhancing goods and services, meaningful relations, and meaningful participation in socially valued productive processes;

—Needs to become what one is capable of becoming, or in Maslow's terms, self-actualization through creative, productive work.

The quality of life or the level of welfare is always a function of the extent to which the foregoing fundamental human needs can be realized in given natural and socially shaped settings. In turn, the extent to which these needs can be realized depends on the structures, dynamics and values of a society's institutional order, or more specifically, on the manner in which:

1. Life-sustaining and life-enhancing, natural and human-produced resources are controlled, used, developed, and conserved
2. Work and production are organized
3. Goods and services, social and civil rights, and political power are distributed

Interactions among these processes and the values and ideologies which reflect and sustain their specific patterns shape the circumstances of life and the mutual relations of individuals, classes, and societies.[5] It is necessary, therefore, to study the patterns of these processes and corresponding ideologies when one wants to gain insight into the levels of needs realization, the scope of human development, or the state of welfare. And, it may be necessary to radically transform the established patterns of these processes and corresponding values when one wishes to enhance the levels of needs realization, the scope of human development, or the state of welfare on local and global levels.

STRUCTURAL AND IDEOLOGICAL SOURCES OF UNDER-DEVELOPMENT AND ILLFARE IN CAPITALIST AND IMPERIALIST DYNAMICS

The quality of life in the United States and in similarly organized societies is shaped largely by social, psychological, economic, political, and ideological dynamics of advanced capitalism. Because of the global scope of contemporary economic and political relations, these dynamics affect also, directly or indirectly, the developmental context and human welfare all over the world. What are the essential aspects of capitalist resource management, work organization, and rights distribution, and how do these patterns affect the realization of fundamental human needs, the scope of human development, and the state of welfare on local and global levels?

Resource Management

In capitalist societies, a minority of the people own and control most means of production, distribution and exchange including land, raw materials and factories; banks, commercial and service establishments; media of communication and entertainment; knowledge and technology. The majority of people, the propertyless "working classes," do not own and control sufficient resources to survive by working with what they control. They depend, therefore, on being hired at the discretion and in the interest of the propertied classes and their agents.

The working classes are not a homogeneous group. They differ among themselves in origin, race, history and cultural traditions; in sex and age; in education, skills and attitudes; in occupations and income, etc. These differences tend to divide them as they give rise to conflicts of interests mainly around access to employment. These divisions and conflicts usually overshadow the one objective condition which all workers share, namely, the necessity of selling their labor, skills and knowledge for wages to those who control the bulk of productive resources.

Individuals and corporations tend to use the resources they control in the production of goods and services for sales, to generate profits, which they use mainly toward the acquisition of additional productive resources. The quality and quantity of products, the extent to which production corresponds to actual needs of the population, the quality of the labor process, the effects of production on people, communities, the environment, and on the conservation of productive resources—all these considerations are less important in shaping production decisions than criteria of profitability and accumulation and concentration of capital. The competitive striving toward accumulation of wealth and concentration of control over productive resources tends to shape the logic of everyday life and to affect the consciousness, behavior, and mutual relations of people.[6]

Human societies were not always divided into propertied and propertyless classes. Whenever and wherever this division evolved, it was established, not voluntarily, but through coercive processes. Only then did it become institutionalized as "law and order," rationalized and justified through religion, philosophy, and ideology, and transmitted and stabilized through processes of socialization and social control. The maintenance of this human-created division continues to depend on covert, subtle forms of coercion, and not infrequently, on overt violence.

Work and Production

The organization of work and production in capitalist societies derives in multiple ways from the divisions of the population in terms of ownership and control over productive resources. These divisions result inevitably in an antagonistic interdependence. The propertied classes rely on the labor of the propertyless to produce marketable goods and services in order to extract profits by paying workers less in wages than the market prices of their products. The propertyless workers, in turn, rely on employment by, and wages from, individual and corporate owners as their source of survival. In general, the higher the ratio of employment-seeking workers to jobs, the lower will be the average level of wages, and the higher will be the rate of profit. Owners tend, therefore, to favor an over-supply of workers in relation to jobs, which forces workers to compete for scarce jobs.

The reality and threat of unemployment induce fierce competition among individuals and groups which is frequently experienced and expressed not only as personal rivalry, but as racism, sexism, ageism, etc. While these discriminatory tendencies have acquired, throughout history, quasi-autonomous, subjective dynamics, they cannot be overcome as long as propertied classes can exclude propertyless people from employment. In other words, discriminatory practices are intrinsic to the objective reality shaped by capitalist dynamics.

Competition results not only from job scarcities but also from the pyramidal, bureaucratic organization of work, and of wage and prestige systems which reflect and reinforce that pyramidal structure. Competition for entry into the work force and for promotion to more desirable and better paid jobs tends to reduce opportunities for open, mutually caring and meaningful human relations in work places and throughout society. It also tends to inhibit the development among workers and unemployed individuals of class consciousness and solidarity, a sine qua non for the emergence of political movements aimed at eliminating class divisions and transforming the established order into one conducive to human development for all. In personal terms, competitive human relations surrounding access to work and career advancement frequently give rise to loneliness, frustration and alienation which, in turn, may lead to depression, alcoholism, drug addiction, domestic violence, and other destructive and self-destructive behaviors.

Several related economic, social and personal problems result from total or partial exclusion from employment. Unemployment tends to hold down the general level of wages and income throughout the economy. It depresses the self-image of unemployed individuals and induces insecurity among employed workers who may always lose their jobs at the discretion of employers. The insecurity and the depressed sense of self of unemployed and marginally employed workers will usually also affect their families. Emotional suffering thus accompanies material deprivation due to severely reduced income. Unemployment has consequences also beyond directly involved households, since reduced purchasing power of individual households is reflected in the economic realities of communities and society.

While unemployment is dehumanizing, employment under prevailing conditions usually does not provide opportunities to actualize one's potential. Workers are considered and treated as means to the ends of employers, or in the revealing jargon of economists, as "factors of production." Under such a definition of the work context, workers are perceived not as whole and unique individuals but as specific functions or components of production processes. Once they are treated as replaceable attachments to machines, their self-images come to reflect the externally defined reality, and their development as whole persons with multifaceted capacities is stunted.

In efforts to "rationalize production," which means to increase the efficiency and profit rate of enterprises, designers and managers have over many decades reduced the tasks of most workers to routine operations, each being but a step contributing to complex processes and products, which workers need not, and usually do not, grasp in their entirety. Workers, consequently, are no longer competent and knowledgeable masters of production in their fields. Based on their earlier separation from material means of production, workers were separated during the past century from the nonmaterial means, the knowledge component of production. This separation is the ultimate stage of expropriation which deprives workers of their human essence, their sense of integrity and autonomy, and thus completes their transformation into easily marketable and replaceable commodities.[7]

Socialization

The transformation of most work into routines requiring little or no initiative, creativity, and intellectual effort, and of most workers into noncritical performers of routine tasks within authoritarian work settings, has led inevitably, though subtly, to corresponding transformations of child rearing, socialization and formal education. When patterns of work require mainly conforming and apathetic workers, such workers are produced through prevailing modes of life and human relations in homes, schools, churches, neighborhoods, etc. These destructive consequences of child rearing, socialization and formal education do not result from conscious, intentional practices on the part of parents, teachers, and educational authorities. Rather, they come about, almost automatically, from growing up in homes, schools, and neighborhoods whose milieu, sub-cultures and worldview are affected by multidimensional divisions of the population by class, race, origin, sex, occupation, attitudes, ideology, etc. Consequently, though not intentionally designed toward such an end, child rearing, socialization, and formal education in contemporary industrial societies result nevertheless, in massive, differential underdevelopment of the rich innate potential of most children and youth. The result is societies in which most people function below their real potential in many spheres of life.[8]

Systemic Irrationality

One further characteristic of the capitalist mode of production should be noted. Production tends to be planned, rational, and efficient in terms of profit considerations of individual firms. At the same time, aggregate production in a competitive context is unplanned, irrational, inefficient, and wasteful in terms of the real needs of the population, the survival and development of communities, and the conservation of resources and the ecology. This contradiction derives from the fact that production of firms and of the entire economy is not oriented systematically toward actual needs but toward "effective demand" and toward maximizing profits of individual firms. The needs of people who lack sufficient purchasing power are therefore neither considered, nor met, by capitalist production and distribution.

The absence of planning geared to the actual needs of the entire population and to the long-range needs of communities and society is a constant source of the irrationality of capitalist production. It results not only in severe underproduction in terms of people's real needs, but also in wasteful overproduction of unnecessary goods which people with surplus purchasing power are constantly induced to buy by means of sophisticated, yet mindless, advertising. Further aspects of irrationality and waste in capitalist production are frequent, arbitrary changes of models and fashions, and built-in obsolescence requiring premature repair and replacement of products. Massive waste in production is a major, objective source of inflation, intrinsic to capitalist dynamics. Inflation generated by waste, in turn, stimulates subjective, social and psychological tendencies which reinforce the inflationary process.

Lack of planning geared to the needs of all people and communities, and wasteful, inflationary practices lead, inevitably, to periodic economic crises to which individual firms and the economy as a whole respond by cutting back production and by laying off employees. From the perspective of powerful enterprises and the established economic system, such crises are necessary mechanisms to regulate the economy in the absence of planning. From the perspective of individuals, households, small enterprises, and communities, these crises are usually severe disasters.

Distribution of Goods, Services, and Rights

Goods and services are available in capitalist societies mainly through markets. Consequently, purchasing power in the form of money or credit is necessary to obtain goods and services. The quantity and quality of the goods and services which individuals can obtain is therefore largely a function of the sources and size of their income: the scope of their income generating wealth, the stability and compensation level of their jobs, and/ or the amount of transfer payments they receive from governments.

If one studies the distribution of income over time, one finds major inequalities among individuals, households, and social classes.[9] One is also forced to conclude that poverty (understood as a level of income insufficient to secure an acknowledged, minimally adequate standard of living) is built right into the fabric of capitalist societies, since large segments of the population control little or no income generating wealth, and access to gainful employment is not under their own control. These circumstances are reflected in a widespread sense of insecurity which has become a major source of motivation for labor, however alienating conditions of work may be.

Propertyless people who never secured jobs or lost the ones they had, be they young, old, or in between, are usually doomed to poverty. Whatever purchasing power they command derives mainly from government transfer payments or extralegal practices, i.e., crime. Levels of transfer payments to poor people tend to be very low. In the United States, transfer payments usually do not even match the government's poverty index, a measure derived from a short-term, emergency food budget, which corresponds to about 60 percent of the "low-level budget" for urban households as determined by the U.S. Bureau of Labor Statistics. During recent years, about one in eight persons in the United States, or about 25,000,000, were living in households with incomes at or below the official poverty level, and another 40,000,000 were "near poor" in accordance with a 1980 report of the National Advisory Council on Economic Opportunity.[10] The incidence of poverty and "near-poverty" is significantly higher among children, youth, and aged persons; among women, especially in single parent families; and among racial minorities and native American tribes.

However, not only individuals who never secured jobs, lost their jobs, or retired from them tend to exist on incomes below or near the poverty line. In the United States, many regularly employed workers are also forced to live in or near poverty. The legal minimum wage does not assure incomes above the poverty level, and the prevailing wage structure generates an income distribution which leaves about one-third of the entire population in or near poverty.

History since the Middle Ages reveals that when propertied classes exercise a dominant influence over governments and welfare policies, income transfers will not interfere with a handsome rate of profit. This requires a substantial stratum of workers whose wages correspond roughly to a mere subsistence level. To assure an adequate supply of low paid labor and a flexible labor reserve, transfer payments are usually kept at levels below the bottom of the wage structure, so that economic incentives to accept "voluntarily" poorly paid employment should not disappear. Queen Elizabeth I of England acted on this principle when issuing the Poor Laws of 1601. Her insights into the requirements of early capitalism continue to shape income transfer policies in the twentieth century.

In theory, in democratic-capitalist societies everyone is entitled to equal social, civil, and political rights. In reality, however, these rights too tend to be distributed unequally, as they are subtly associated with material wealth and income, and with social class, race, sex, age, occupation, etc. The economically powerful, especially white males, tend to acquire disproportionately large shares of social prestige and political influence. Also, public authorities often treat the well-to-do more politely and more favorably than poor people, especially when the latter are members of racial minorities. Even in courts and in the correctional system, wealthy and prestigious individuals are often able to secure preferential treatment with the help of expensive lawyers.

Access to media of communication to promote views on public issues also tends to be easier for the economically powerful and socially prominent. Consequently, "freedom of the press" seems available mainly to owners, and to individuals and corporations on whose advertising revenue the media depend and to whose views and interests they tend to be especially sensitive. Since political influence and power depend, to no small extent, on access to established media or on economic resources to create alternative media, those who lack ample economic resources usually lack also opportunities to acquire political influence.

Ideology

Ideologies develop in interaction with emerging patterns of basic social processes. They reflect, rationalize, justify, legitimate, and reinforce, at any stage of history, the then prevailing patterns of these processes. The following interrelated value continua strongly influence the patterns of basic social processes. Major tendencies of an ideology can therefore be deducted by discerning its positions on these continua:

1. equality..inequality
2. affirmation of community....................................selfishness
   and individuality
3. cooperation..competition
4. liberty...domination
                                                                              and exploitation

Capitalist ideology seems oriented toward the right poles of these value continua. We proclaim that "all men are born equal," but we seem to accept the premise that individuals, groups, classes, and peoples are intrinsically unequal in worth and are consequently entitled to unequal shares of resources, goods and services, and to unequal social, civil and political rights. We affirm the sanctity of all life, pay lip service to "community spirit," and condemn selfishness in our religious and philosophical traditions, but we do not seem to value the lives and individuality of others, we easily disregard community concerns, and we seem to accept selfishness as a common sense, guiding principle for everyday life and for human relations. We teach children in nurseries to share and to cooperate, but nearly all domains of adult existence are permeated by acquisitive and competitive dynamics. We are enthusiastic advocates of liberty and "human rights" as abstract principles, but we do not seem to hesitate to dominate and exploit other individuals, classes, races, and peoples, and to use them as means to our ends.

Realization of Human Needs

Based on the foregoing sketch, we can now examine the extent to which intrinsic human needs can be realized in capitalist societies. The analysis revealed that regular access to life-sustaining and life-enhancing goods and services is not assured, as most people do not own and control income-generating means of production, nor do they possess unconditional legal rights to gainful employment and adequate income. Unemployment and poverty and their dehumanizing consequences are, therefore, widespread and are a constant threat to the satisfaction of the material needs of many people.

Next, we found little opportunity for the emergence of meaningful, mutually caring human relations conducive to a sense of positive identity. This is due to pervasive, structurally induced competition for profit, for employment and promotions, and for preferred positions and opportunities in spheres of existence shaped by pyramidal, hierarchical systems. Meaningful human relations are usually not possible among individuals who are unequal in prestige, status and power, and who continuously evaluate, control, and use one another as means in the pursuit of selfish ends. Also, meaningful relations are unlikely to develop when people function as separate, competitive, economic units, each trying to survive as best as possible in a noncooperative way of life.

Meaningful and creative participation in socially valued productive processes is beyond the expectations of most people when even any kind of employment is not assured; when most jobs are designed as fragmented, meaningless routines to be performed in alienating, exploiting, and oppressive conditions; and when child care, socialization, and formal schooling result inevitably in massive underdevelopment of innate human capacities.

A sense of security emerges when people's needs for goods and services, for meaningful human relations and for meaningful participation in production can be realized. Since these needs were shown to be unrealizable for most people in the context of capitalist dynamics, few individuals can be expected to develop a genuine sense of security. Most are driven by a nagging sense of insecurity to chase forever after receding mirages of security.

Self-actualization is usually not pursued by people whose material, relational, and security needs are unrealizable. Hence, based on the foregoing analysis which revealed widespread frustration of material, relational, and security needs, we are forced to conclude that few individuals only are likely to realize their innate need for self-actualization.

When people live in environments in which their fundamental human needs tend to be frustrated constantly, their innate capacities do not usually unfold freely and fully. Their development is stunted; they do not fare well. Based on our analysis, capitalist societies seem to be such development-inhibiting environments.

Global Effects

While the dynamics and values of capitalist societies have resulted, within their own countries, in massive underdevelopment of human potential, and hence in low levels of social welfare in spite of ameliorative welfare services, the effects of capitalism on human development and social welfare in Africa, Asia, and the Americas have been even more devastating. These "external" effects too are inherent in the "laws of motion" of capitalism.[11]

Capitalism, by its very nature, is not a static economic system producing goods for direct use in local communities as was the dominant tendency under feudalism. Rather, it is a dynamic system, oriented toward growth and expansion on ever wider scales, by producing commodities for profitable sales to anonymous consumers in close and distant mass markets. It requires, therefore, access to expanding markets and to sources of cheap labor and raw materials, and it had to reach out beyond its origins in Western Europe to encompass eventually the entire globe. This goal was accomplished early in the twentieth century after more than half a millennium of expansion, penetration, and conquest. The period following the World Wars is probably the beginning of the decline of capitalism as a world system.

Capitalism began in Western Europe during the late Middle Ages, simultaneous with the gradual emergence of monarchic nation-states. It evolved out of long-distance commerce, carried on by families, guilds, and trading companies who operated mainly out of cities not subject to the authority of feudal lords. Historians refer to the early stages of capitalism as "mercantilism." This stage involved relatively strong controls over economic activity by central, usually royal, authorities. Under mercantilist policies, nations sought to sell more than they bought in order to accumulate gold and silver bullion which were then considered pure wealth exchangeable into any desired goods or services. Tightly controlled foreign trade was carried on by monopolistic trading companies chartered by the monarchs. Trading territories in Africa, Asia, and in the newly discovered and conquered parts of the Americas were gradually transformed into colonial empires. They were fought over by European nations and plundered and exploited by whoever happened to be the colonial master. The great wealth which was extracted violently from the colonies and the native peoples became the basis for accelerated development and expansion of the capitalist mode of production throughout Western Europe and North America and for massive accumulations of capital which facilitated the industrial revolution in the eighteenth and nineteenth centuries.[12]

In the process of colonization, the indigenous cultures and economies of native peoples were undermined, distorted, and largely destroyed for the purpose of enriching the imperial powers and especially their privileged, dominant classes: the capitalists, courts, and aristocrats. Wherever and whenever native peoples dared to resist domination, European nations and white settlers in the colonies did not hesitate to practice genocide. They also discovered opportunities for generating wealth from the capture, sale, and forced labor of slaves. Finally, they forced colonized peoples to adapt their own economies to the patterns and requirements of the capitalist system. They levied taxes to be paid in money obtainable mainly from wage labor. Native people were thus lured or forced to work on plantations, in mines, in households and in public services. They were also forced, directly or indirectly, to abandon their own modes of production which had, in the past, assured their survival and welfare. Instead, they had to produce raw materials for distant industries or raise single cash crops for the commerce and consumption of the "mother" country. There was little industrial development in the colonies.

As a result of these changes in colonial economies, native peoples became increasingly dependent on imports of basic necessities which they had produced and supplied for themselves prior to the European conquests. In this way, they were integrated into the world markets as consumers and suppliers, paying exorbitant prices for usually inferior imports, while the products of their largely forced labor and the natural wealth of their countries were systematically taken from them, mostly for low prices fixed by monopolistic companies.

The result of colonial practices after several centuries was an enormous accumulation of economic wealth and military power in Western Europe and North America, shared unequally among the people and social classes of the imperial nations, and a corresponding concentration of abject poverty, depressed standards of living, and general individual and social underdevelopment in large parts of Africa, Asia, and the Americas.[13] In most colonies there also emerged a narrow stratum of privileged upper classes of landowners, aristocrats, officials, professionals, and merchants who lived in luxury and who associated with, and assimilated to, the foreign rulers. Members of these classes often assumed governmental roles over the native populations as formal or informal, highly rewarded agents of the colonial powers. The social and economic organization in the colonies gradually absorbed major features of capitalist societies concerning control over resources, organization of work, and distribution of goods, services and rights. Indigenous cultures, too, were penetrated by the ideology, the legal system, and frequently, by the religions of the colonial powers.

Following World War II, the political status of the colonies began to change. By now, nearly all former colonies have secured formal political independence and membership in the United Nations. However, their economic conditions have not changed much, either in absolute terms or relative to major capitalist countries who continue to dominate and exploit many former colonies economically, politically, culturally, and militarily. The distribution of the aggregate global product continues to be skewed heavily in favor of major capitalist countries. The United States, for instance, with about 5 percent of the world's population, controls about 30 percent of the annual global product. Other leading capitalist nations secure similarly disproportionate shares. The majority of the world's people in the former colonies continue, therefore, to live in conditions of severe material poverty. Efforts in the United Nations, over several decades, to bring about by peaceful means a New International Economic Order involving significant reductions of economic inequalities have so far failed. The most recent illustration of resistance to these efforts is last minute objections by the United States government to endorse a U.N. treaty on the Law of the Sea which had been negotiated over seven years and which should give to underdeveloped countries a share of the wealth beneath the world's oceans.[14]

This historical sketch of centuries of relations between capitalist-imperialist nations and the "third" and "fourth" worlds suggests that the vast majority of people in these countries and territories have only limited opportunities to realize fundamental human needs and to develop innate capacities. The quality of their lives has been undermined by the forces and values of capitalism, colonialism and contemporary imperialism, and the levels of overall social welfare are consequently severely depressed.

A GLOBAL SYSTEM OF DECENTRALIZED DEMOCRATIC SOCIALISM

The analysis of individual development and social welfare in the context of capitalist and imperialist dynamics and values, in the centers and on the periphery of the global capitalist system, revealed severe obstacles to the realization of intrinsic human needs, to the unfolding of innate human potential, and to overall social welfare. To overcome these development-obstructing and survival-threatening dynamics, people would have to transform the prevailing international system of competing, chauvinistic states and class-societies into an alternative, development-oriented global order. In the view of many thoughtful students of the human condition, such an order can be developed from democratic-socialist principles which correspond to the left poles of the value continua noted previously: equality, affirmation of community and individuality, cooperation, and liberty.[15] In a democratic-socialist global order, all humans would be considered equal in intrinsic worth in spite of differences among individuals and groups, and everyone would enjoy the same social, economic, civil, and political rights, liberties, constraints, and responsibilities. Everyone would be considered an autonomous subject rather than an object to someone else's ends. No one would be dominated and exploited by others, and institutional arrangements would be designed to facilitate free and full development of everyone's inherent potential. Social equality in the context of liberty does not, however, mean bureaucratically enforced uniformity and suppression of individuality and initiative, as is often assumed erroneously. Rather it means an equal right for all to develop their individuality subject only to constraints inherent in equal rights for all others, limits on aggregate resources, and democratically evolved priorities.[16] To conform to these values and principles, resource management, organization of work and production, and exchange and distribution of goods, services and rights would have to be redesigned along the following patterns. All communities would have to develop through democratic processes their own versions within these general patterns.

Means of production would have to be controlled democratically through community and workplace councils on the local level, and through horizontally coordinated networks of communities beyond the local level. Productive resources would be allocated and used to assure a regular supply of high quality goods and services for all, in accordance with individual needs and with due concern for global human needs, for ecological considerations, and for requirements of conservation. Concern for global human needs would require termination of the privileged position of many nations, and adjustment of their shares of global resources to levels corresponding to their shares of the global population. Reduction of global resource use and resource waste by major countries should enhance the material and overall well-being of people everywhere, and should gradually reduce and eliminate international tensions and the threat of war and nuclear holocaust. Major reductions in resource allocation for defense of prevailing privileged shares by many countries should, in turn, free resources for worldwide human needs.

Production and work would have to be reorganized and redesigned to fit human needs, and to assure everyone's participation in terms of their capacities and stages of development. These reorganizations and subsequent production should be planned and implemented cooperatively by communities and trans-local coordinating bodies. Much current production is neither necessary nor suited to human needs and would have to be phased out, while necessary production which is not carried out now, as it is not profitable, would have to replace phased out work. What is required is not redistribution of the existing "economic pie," but the design of a new social and economic "pie" with different ingredients.

Workers themselves, using their intellectual, physical, and emotional capacities in an integrated fashion, would design, manage, and carry out production cooperatively. Hence, they would have to be well educated as they will have to understand all aspects of their work. In redesigning production they would have to take into account not only the quality and quantity of products, but also the quality of the work experience, as far as that is feasible. People would be free to choose their occupations and to change them in the course of life. Rotation among all workers would assure that necessary tasks, not chosen voluntarily, would be performed nevertheless, including intrinsically unpleasant tasks which cannot be redesigned to be meaningful and satisfying.

Once production is transformed in accordance with the patterns suggested here, it would no longer be permeated by competitive and exploitative dynamics, and could become a context for creative involvement and cooperative behaviors conducive to meaningful human relations in workplaces and communities. The transformed work context should induce corresponding transformations in personal life, home life, community life, child-rearing, socialization, and formal education.

Goods and services would have to be distributed in accordance with individual needs and democratically determined priorities. This means entitlements to goods and services would be based on membership and participation in communities and society, rather than on individual purchasing power, and would not vary with the type of work one did. All work would be valued equally, and differences in work roles would not be a basis for inequalities of rights and differences in living standards.

Trade among individual and cooperative producers of goods and services within and between close and distant communities would have to be based on the principle of exchanging products of equal value to preclude any possibility of exploitation. Calculations of value equivalence would take into account actual costs of production, i.e. work time, materials and their relative scarcity, equipment, transportation, etc.

Social, civil, and political rights would be distributed equally, as there would be no inequalities of wealth and income which now tend to skew the distribution of nonmaterial rights. Public affairs would have to be controlled and coordinated by participatory democratic processes on local levels and by representative assemblies, representing communities pursuing shared rather than antagonistic interests, on regional and global levels. All processes of governance would have to be open and all secrecy concerning public affairs would have to be eliminated, as it is not needed among equals. Representatives and officials would serve on a time-limited basis, would be subject to recall, and would not be entitled to privileged conditions of living. Their work would be valued in the same way as all necessary work. Administrative and representative offices would be filled by elections among volunteers or by rotation when no one volunteered.

Applying the same test of needs realization which we applied earlier to capitalist patterns to the patterns sketched here, we find that realization of needs for goods and services and for participation in meaningful, productive activities would be assured for all, as these patterns are specifically designed to meet these needs. People could also develop meaningful, caring and cooperative human relations and a sense of positive identity, as they would not have to compete with, and to control, judge, and use one another for selfish ends in struggles for survival. Opportunities for all to realize material needs, needs for meaningful relations, for a positive sense of identity, and for meaningful participation in production would be conducive, in turn, to the realization of needs for security and self-actualization. It follows that the societal patterns sketched here would be compatible with requirements of human development and that people would indeed fare well, were the prevailing world system transformed into a decentralized, democratic-socialist, global commonwealth.

POLITICAL STRATEGY TOWARD A GLOBAL SYSTEM OF DECENTRALIZED DEMOCRATIC SOCIALISM

Social changes along lines indicated here depend on sustained political action over many years by movements committed to challenge the dynamics and roots of underdevelopment and "illfare," at home and abroad, rather than to fight merely for amelioration of symptoms. Some notes on political strategies toward a global system of decentralized democratic socialism seem therefore necessary.

General Observations

It is more difficult to develop effective political strategies toward fundamental social changes than to criticize prevailing social realities and past political strategies. Moreover, the validity of proposed strategies can never be known in advance, but only in the future, on the basis of actual experience. Proposals for political strategy should therefore not be considered "correct" solutions, but hypotheses, based on analysis of historical and contemporary conditions and tendencies. Also, strategies should remain open to adjustments based on critical examination of emerging experience.

Political strategies must be designed in relation to the objective realities and the subjective consciousness of people. For, a given strategy could be valid in one historical context and yet be useless in another. Furthermore, strategies should be developed in relation to the goals they are expected to attain, for different goals seem to require different means for their attainment. Thus, for instance, democratic socialism may not be attainable by strategies which might be appropriate toward authoritarian socialism. There may also be contradictions between short-range and long-range political goals. Some short-range goals may be steps toward long-range goals, while others may inhibit progress toward long-range goals.

Political strategies become effective only in practice when people adopt and act on them. They should therefore be designed through collective efforts involving large numbers of people in exploring issues and options, in developing insights and motivation, and in making decisions on actions. Another condition of effectiveness is that strategies should be oriented simultaneously toward local, regional, and global levels. Political action is usually set in motion by people's experience where they live and work. Yet, unless locally generated strategies are relevant also to the needs of people elsewhere, they are unlikely to overcome forces whose reach is often global.

Overcoming Ideological Hegemony

Social orders are maintained and reproduced largely through the everyday behaviors and consciousness of people, who were socialized and who pursue survival in the context of specific institutions, ideologies, and social relations.[17] Fundamental social change requires, therefore, fundamental changes in people's consciousness and behavior. Accordingly, in view of the hegemony of capitalist practices and ideology in the contemporary United States, political movements for radical change in this country must consistently challenge the dominant mentality and practice in order to stimulate the emergence and stabilization of fundamental changes in the consciousness and subsequent actions of growing numbers of individuals.

People have to be helped, through intensive political education, to discover the ugly reality behind the seductive appearances of capitalism—its dehumanizing consequences for individual development and social welfare; the covert links between private troubles and institutional dynamics; the inevitability of unemployment, of waste and inflation, of poverty and crime, of ecological degradation and resource depletion, of discrimination by sex, age, race and class, of mental and physical ills, of loneliness and alienation, of conflicts at home and abroad and wars, etc. People also need to discover that democracy, liberty, equality, and pursuit of happiness, the declared goals of the American Revolution, cannot be attained under a constitution which does not guarantee the equal worth and rights of people, but protects property rights resulting from past, coercive expropriations and from past and present exploitation of the majority by a minority. Next, political education should clarify that authoritarian socialism is not the only possible alternative to the prevailing way of life in the United States. And finally, people need to learn that by upholding the egalitarian and democratic tendencies in this country's culture, they could reclaim their impaired sovereignty and they could develop innovative patterns for cooperative management of resources, humanized modes of production, egalitarian distribution of goods, services and rights, participatory democracy, and mutually caring human relations—all conducive to individual development and social welfare.

Revolutionary changes should, however, not be presented as directed against individual members of propertied classes, but only against the principles and ideology which shape the antagonistic class divisions of the established way of life. Political education should stress that the future social order is meant to enrich the quality of life for all and to enhance everyone's individual development, irrespective of present class position. For, in the prevailing way of life, no one is genuinely free, and everyone is trapped in destructive interactions and falls far short of self-actualization, whatever one's class and conditions. Also, everyone's security and survival are threatened by frequent crises, conflicts and the likelihood of wars. While under prevailing conditions some individuals and groups are relatively comfortable, objectively and subjectively, and many expect that they will improve their condition, all seem inhibited in individual development and human relations. Hence, everyone ought to be urged, and many could conceivably be motivated through reasoned analysis, to join movements toward universal human liberation.

The foregoing critique, goals and values should be widely disseminated in workplaces and neighborhoods by social movements committed to integrating a political mission into the personal, social, and occupational spheres of everyday life. Such dissemination of a democratic-socialist ideology, opposed openly and unequivocally to the hegemonic capitalist ideology and reality, is an essential dimension of revolutionary praxis under prevailing conditions in the United States.[18]

The Range and Goals of Political Action

Actions compatible with the strategy sketched here range from conventional electoral and coalition politics, through struggles by trade unions, special interest groups, and single issue and community organizations, to unconventional "direct actions." The latter involve resistance to and noncooperation with oppressive and exploitative practices, and innovative approaches toward liberation through collective self-empowerment. The long-range goals of all political action, from the perspective presented here, against which every step ought to be evaluated, are to build transformation movements, to promote revolutionary consciousness and conditions, and most importantly, to transfer control over the means of production, exchange, and distribution, and over local and trans-local political institutions, from agents of capitalist-imperialist interests to people in communities and workplaces. Such transfer of control is an essential, though not sufficient, condition of the transformation toward democratic socialism. It is a sine qua non toward the creation of a new social order involving a new culture, new forms of social relations, new qualitatively enriched products and production processes, new attitudes toward the environment, and new patterns of cooperative, sharing and egalitarian relations with communities and people all over the globe.

Electoral and Coalition Politics

As already noted, political action toward an egalitarian and democratic way of life should be shaped by, and should reflect these elements. In other words, the means should contain the ends. Accordingly, in electoral campaigns, democratic socialists should be less concerned with winning offices, though such victories may be important, than with presenting and clarifying fundamental alternatives to programs of capitalist and reformist parties. Joining coalitions seems valid in terms of the strategy suggested here in order to generate political power to improve living conditions of oppressed classes and peoples, and to counter imperialist and other destructive tendencies. Coalitions also provide opportunities to confront the pervasive tendency of dominant classes in the established order to divide exploited groups against one another through exclusion and discrimination. However, participation in coalitions must never lead to concealment of democratic-socialist goals out of concern that potential coalition partners may not be ready to work with advocates of radical change. Such a tactic of self-censorship or deception seems definitely self-defeating in terms of long-range goals, even though it may seem to enhance the unity and strength of coalitions in the short run. Participation in coalitions should also not involve surrender of the right and responsibility to criticize inadequate, reformist solutions to problems inherent in capitalist dynamics and relations.

The comments concerning electoral and coalition politics are also applicable to political work in trade unions, special interest groups, and in various single issue and community organizations. Struggles by such groups to ameliorate effects of capitalist and imperialist dynamics are usually important in their specific terms, as well as in clarifying the links between people's specific troubles and systemic forces. Democratic socialists, therefore, support such struggles and should try to broaden and refocus them from fighting symptoms toward challenging causes, or in Andre Gorz's apt terms, by raising demands for "revolutionary reforms."[19]

Nonconventional Direct Action and Self-Empowerment

Nonconventional political practice involves open rejection of the assumptions, consciousness, and legitimacy of the established social order, and corresponding redefinitions of social reality and social power. People in the United States tend to perceive themselves as powerless when they share prevailing views of reality, according to which citizens confront the state and one another as anonymous, atomized economic actors in pursuit of selfish ends, and power is held mainly by individuals occupying key positions in economic and political institutions. People can extricate themselves from this "common sense" view of social reality by negating it, first through reflection, and then by creating for themselves cooperative and egalitarian relations, structures, and dynamics in everyday life. Through such changes in consciousness and collective behavior, people can begin to reclaim and reassert the power they have heretofore yielded passively to others, or of which they have been actively deprived, and use that power to sustain new realities and relations in every available social space within the prevailing order. Demonstrations, political and economic strikes and boycotts, civil disobedience, tax resistance and refusal of military service illustrate "negative versions" of this approach, while consumer and producer controlled cooperatives and collectives in which people experiment with democratic-socialist principles in everyday life illustrate "positive versions." When carried out in relative isolation, surrounded by capitalist dynamics, such experiments are now inevitably plagued by ambiguities and contradictions in struggles to survive.

It may be possible in the future, however, to expand direct action approaches in ways leading eventually to the necessary transfer of control over economic and political institutions, and based on this transfer, to the transformation of capitalist states into democratic-socialist societies.[20] Workers in and around existing enterprises and institutions could organize themselves voluntarily into social-economic collectives. In a later stage, these collectives could form networks throughout and beyond the country for mutual support, cooperation, and coordinated, self-determined political action. Once such federated workplace collectives succeeded in permeating and establishing themselves in major industries, public services, security forces, and government bureaucracies, they could, at a jointly determined time, assume control over their respective enterprises, and thus over the entire economic and political system. Based on such a simultaneous assumption of control over major economic and political institutions, worker and community councils could proceed to develop a decentralized, horizontally coordinated, democratic-socialist order. By no means do I expect this to be a simple, smooth, conflict-free and sure approach toward revolutionary change. Rather, this strategy, once initiated, is likely to encounter obstacles, resistance, and repression as all other approaches toward revolution. And yet, it may attain its goals provided growing numbers of people everywhere become committed to cooperative, constructive, direct action toward self-empowerment, and create massive networks of new and healthy cells within the decaying institutions of the old order, capable of replacing that order from within.

Dilemmas of Violence

The discussion of nonconventional political practice raises difficult dilemmas concerning the role of violence and armed struggle in revolutionary processes toward democratic socialism. To deal adequately with this issue would require a separate essay. Hence, I can offer here only tentative comments.

Violence is, in my view, acts or conditions which obstruct the spontaneous unfolding of innate human potential, the inherent human drive toward development and self-actualization.[21] Erich Fromm reached similar conclusions when he interpreted violence as "unlived life."[22] Violent acts by individuals are not a primary human tendency, but reactions to blockings of spontaneous, constructive life energy. Throughout history, major sources of blocking of constructive human energy have been social, economic, and political structures involving inequalities in status, power and rights among individuals, sexes, age groups, social classes, peoples, races, etc. All social formations which involve inequalities as a basis for domination and exploitation, from patriarchy and slavery through feudalism, capitalism and authoritarianism, are therefore intrinsically violent societies. They violate human beings and their individual development, and they bring forth, inevitably, violent reactions from oppressed individuals and groups.

Like all social systems involving structural inequalities, capitalism originated in and is maintained by overt and covert coercive force. Capitalist states, in spite of formal political democracy, are considered by many critical scholars to be in fact subtle dictatorships of propertied minorities over majorities of expropriated and continuously exploited working classes. For the majorities would never choose voluntarily conditions of oppression, exploitation, deprivation, and poverty unless the minorities were able to maintain and defend established unjust orders through ideological hegemony and socialization, and as a last resort, through overt and covert force and coercion by the military, police, and secret services.[23]

Democratic socialism as conceived here is based on comprehensive equality in every domain of existence—social, economic, political, and civil. Hence, it is free of coercion and structural blocks to individual development. It is the ultimate antithesis to capitalism and to every other form of structural social inequality, domination, and exploitation. It is the negation of all violence in human relations—a thoroughly nonviolent social order.

The analysis of the violent dynamics of capitalist states and the nonviolent essence of a possible, future, global system of democratic socialism suggests that the complete transformation of the former into the latter may be unattainable by violent, coercive measures which, by their very nature, involve inequalities between agents and victims of violence. Though this abstract conclusion seems valid theoretically and philosophically, it does conflict with prevailing concrete realities. Intense levels of structural violence, exploitation and oppression in societies, such as the white-supremacy regimes in Africa and military dictatorships in Latin America, and also subtle oppressive dynamics of capitalist democracies, have provoked in the past and will provoke in the future, organized armed liberation struggles. The more intense the oppression, the greater the level of frustration and despair, and the greater the likelihood of organized counterviolence.

There is a further reason why liberation movements may be lured into violent interactions with defenders of the status quo. This is the fact that their consciousness has been shaped largely in the context of a dominant mentality according to which "might is right" and "power originates in the barrel of a gun." This one-dimensional view of struggle and power is taught through daily experiences to people living under capitalist and authoritarian systems. It is not surprising, therefore, that liberation movements get this message, believe in it, and act on it. Few people only, under conditions prevailing in contemporary nation-states, become familiar with alternative conceptions of struggle and power, conceptions of nonviolent struggle and self-empowerment as developed and practiced by Gandhi, Martin Luther King, and others.[24]

It seems that as long as legitimate violence, monopolized by states, will maintain oppression and exploitation as law and order, liberation movements will react with counterviolence in efforts to eliminate the sources of their oppression, especially in situations in which they do not perceive opportunities for non-armed liberation struggles. Revolutionary strategies involving armed struggle, and postrevolutionary coercive and defensive force, seem therefore understandable. They may even be inevitable in situations such as the bourgeois revolutions against absolute monarchies and aristocrats from the seventeenth to the twentieth centuries, and the proletarian revolutions and colonial liberation struggles of the twentieth century.

But, while these past armed struggles may have been inevitable, one needs, nevertheless, to confront critically the consequences of the use of force and coercion in revolutionary processes and in postrevolutionary situations. Such examinations reveal that past revolutions, for internal and external reasons, have not resulted in genuinely democratic socialism, nor is it likely that armed revolutions in the future can achieve such an outcome. For it does not seem possible to bring about an egalitarian way of life through inherently inegalitarian measures such as coercive force. Revolutions achieved by armed struggle, however justified they may be, are therefore likely to be incomplete in terms of democratic socialism, and would have to be continued into a nonviolent phase toward that goal.

These observations suggest that democratic-socialist movements need to explore during prerevolutionary stages whether in their particular social situation armed struggle is indeed inevitable, or whether opportunities exist for the immediate use of nonviolent, direct action and self-empowerment strategies, so as not to postpone the nonviolent stage of transformation until after an armed conquest of state power. In my judgment, the prevailing situation in the United States does not now preclude possibilities to engage in nonviolent revolutionary practice toward democratic socialism.

Further Dilemmas of Political Practice

The world in the twentieth century is an interdependent social system. Democratic socialism can, therefore, not be realized fully in any one part of the globe but only on a global scale. Lenin and Trotsky were aware of the difficulties socialism would encounter in a single country because of intense resistance from global capitalism. China, Cuba, and Chile, each in a different way, have also encountered external resistance on their way toward socialism. Many deviations from socialist principles following the revolutions in Russia and other countries resulted in part from antagonistic interactions with nonsocialist states.

While it is necessary, therefore, to pursue the long-range goal of democratic socialism on a global scale, political practice is inevitably focused on limited geographic areas. One concrete way to deal with this contradiction seems to be to strengthen global consciousness and to advance revolutionary possibilities elsewhere by adjusting locally evolved political practice and programs to the developmental needs and requirements of people in other parts of the world. An illustration of this approach is programs for reducing the use of global resources by the United States to levels roughly corresponding to the size of its population relative to the world population. When democratic socialists, wherever they operate, develop political and economic programs compatible with the needs and requirements of people elsewhere, these programs can gradually aggregate into integrated global designs without direction from a central authority. This process should be enhanced through continuous horizontal communications among affiliated groups of a global movement and through common efforts to develop a shared social-political ideology to guide local practice and program development.

The revolution toward global, decentralized, democratic socialism is a lengthy process rather than a brief event. People in different parts of the world are at different stages of this process. Some may be relatively advanced while many have not yet joined the struggle. A decentralized process makes it possible to move at different rates and to use different approaches compatible with different conditions and different stages of consciousness. This seems a realistic model for a global movement and process. Efforts to achieve a single "correct" strategy tend to result in wasteful internal conflicts which weaken the movement. Since no one can be sure in advance of the correctness of strategic approaches, and since different circumstances demand different strategies, a global movement should support and respect multidimensional, occasionally contradictory strategies toward the common goal of democratic social- ism in accordance with Mao Tse-tung's thought: "Let hundred schools of thought contend and let hundred flowers blossom."

NOTES

1. Barry Commoner, *The Closing Circle* (New York Bantam Books, 1972); Robert L. Heilbroner, *An Inquiry Into the Human Prospect* (New York: Norton & Co., 1974); Mihajlo Mesarovic and Edward Pestel, *Mankind at the Turning Point* (New York: E.P. Dutton & Co., 1974).

2. *The New York Times*, December 2, 1976.

3. Wassily Leontief et al., *The Future of the World Economy* (New York: Oxford University Press, 1977).

4. John Dewey, *Liberalism and Social Action* (New York: G.P. Putnam's Sons, 1935); Erich Fromm, *The Sane Society* (Greenwich, CT: Fawcett Publications, 1955); Abraham H. Maslow, *Motivation and Personality* (New York: Harper & Row, 1970).

5. See chapter 2 in this book.

6. R.H.Tawney, *The Acquisitive Society* (New York: Harcourt, Brace & World, Inc., 1920); Karl Polanyi, *The Great Transformation* (Boston Beacon Press, 1957, [1944]).

7. Barry Braverman, *Labor and Monopoly Capital: The Degradation of Work in the Twentieth Century* (New York: Monthly Review Press, 1974).

8. David G. Gil, "The Hidden Success of Schooling in the United States," *The Humanist*, Vol. 39, No. 6 (November/December 1979). See chapter seven in this book.

9. Gabriel Kolko, *Wealth and Power in America* (New York: Praeger Publishers, 1962); Richard M. Titmuss, *Income Distribution and Social Change* (London: George Allen & Unwin, 1962); Letitia Upton and Nancy Lyons, *Basic Facts: Distribution of Personal Income and Wealth in the United States* (Cambridge, MA: Cambridge Institute, 1972); *Statistical Abstract of the United States*, published annually, Bureau of the Census.

10. *The New York Times*, October 19, 1980, p. 24. ("Near-poverty" corresponds to 125 percent of the poverty index.)

11. Karl Marx, *Capital* (New York: International Publishers, 1967); J.A. Hobson, *Imperialism: A Study* (London: Allen & Unwin, 1902); V.I. Lenin, *Imperialism, The Highest Stage of Capitalism* (Petrograd, 1917); Paul M. Sweezy, *The Theory of Capitalist Development* (New York: Monthly Review Press, 1968 [1942]) Paul A. Baran and Paul M. Sweezy, *Monopoly Capital* (New York: Monthly Review Press, 1966); Harry Magdoff, *The Age of Imperalism* (New York: Monthly Review Press, 1969); George Lichtheim, *Imperialism* (New York: Praeger Publishers, 1971); Joseph Schumpeter, *Imperialism* (New York: Meridian Books, 1955).

12. Andre Gunder Frank, *World Accumulation, 1492-1789* (New York:Monthly Review Press, 1977); Harry Magdoff, *Imperialism: from the Colonial Age to the Present* (New York: Monthly Review Press, 1977).

13. Gunnar Myrdal, *The Challenge of World Poverty* (New York: Pantheon Books, 1970).

14. Aaron L. Danzig, "After 7 Years It's Unjust to Monday-Morning-Quarterback the Sea Law," *The New York Times*, March 27, 1981.

15. Albert Einstein, "Why Socialism?", in *Out of My Later Years* (New York: Philosophical Library, Inc., 1950).

16. R.H. Tawney, *Equality* (London: Allen & Unwin, 1931, 1964).

17. Peter Berger and Thomas Luckmann, *The Social Construction of Reality* (Garden City: Doubleday, 1966).

18. Paulo Freire, *Pedagogy of the Oppressed* (New York: Herder & Herder, 1970): Paulo Freire, *Education for Critical Consciousness* (New York: Seabury, 1973); Antonio Gramsci, *Selections from the Prison Notebooks* (New York: International Publishers, 1971).

19. Andre Gorz, *Strategy for Labor* (Boston: Beacon Press, 1967).

20. David G. Gil, "Workplace Collectives as a Strategy Toward Decentralized Democratic Socialism," in *Beyond the Jungle* (Cambridge, MA: Schenkman Publishing Co., 1979).

21. David G. Gil, *Beyond the Jungle* (Cambridge, MA: Schenkman Publishing Co., 1979).

22. Erich Fromm, *Escape From Freedom* (New York: Rinehart & Co., 1941).

23. Ralph Miliband, *The State in Capitalist Society* (New York: Basic Books, 1969).

24. Severyn T. Bruyn and Paul M. Rayman, eds,. *Nonviolent Action and Social Change* (New York: Irvington Publishers, Inc., 1979).

10

*Toward Constitutional Guarantees for Employment and Income**

In October 1985, the Massachusetts legislature passed a resolution (S 139) urging the Congress of the United States

> ...to enact legislation presenting to the states a proposed constitutional amendment wherein the right to employment shall be guaranteed to every person in the United States in accordance with his (sic) capacity, at a rate of compensation sufficient to support such individual and his (sic) family in dignity and self-respect...

While this resolution has no immediate concrete consequences, it is nevertheless an early step in a process which could eventually lead to the enactment of an Economic Bill of Rights as a complement to civil and political rights guaranteed by the U.S. Constitution and its amendments. An Economic Bill of Rights would assure to all the means necessary for "life, liberty, and the pursuit of happiness," which the Declaration of Independence asserts to be everyone's inalienable right, but which many people are unable to exercise under prevailing social, economic, and political conditions.

FULL EMPLOYMENT AS TRANSITION POLICY AND "NON-REFORMIST REFORM"

Employment refers to an economic relationship in which employees are hired at the discretion and in the interest of employers as "factors"

**Humanity and Society*, vol. 10, no. 2 (May 1986); *Changing Work* (Winter/Spring, 1987); Gil, David G., & Gil, Eva A., editors, *The Future of Work* (Cambridge, MA: Schenkman, 1987).

rather than "masters" of production. In this sense, employment is the archetype of capitalist relations. Accordingly, "employment" cannot be a long-range goal of democratic-socialist strategy, for it is the antithesis of democratic control of economic activity and of self direction by workers.

However, the qualifier "full," when added to the term employment, transforms an implicit validation of capitalist relations into a subtle challenge. For full employment implies abolishing the "reserve army of labor," a necessary and nearly constant condition of capitalist production. Full employment means also shifting power from employers to employees by reducing internal competition and divisions, and by reversing gradually the objective conditions which now underlie the discriminatory dynamics of racism and sexism. Full employment would also reduce the pervasive sense of insecurity which now affects nearly everyone who depends on wages for a living. Employers are well aware of challenges to their status and their material interests implicit in full employment, and they have fairly consistently resisted efforts to incorporate this concept into public policy. When, after World War II, a Full Employment Act was introduced in Congress, it emerged in a watered-down version as an Employment Act, which declared it to be public policy to aim for maximum employment compatible with free enterprise, rather than full employment. Some thirty years later when unemployment once again reached disastrous levels, the Humphrey-Hawkins Equal Opportunity and Full Employment Act, though using the term full employment, made no provisions for attaining it.

The concept of full employment subtly combines affirmation of, and challenge to, the social and economic status quo. Were it to be guaranteed by the U.S. Constitution, it would test and strain the limits of liberal capitalism. It would be a "non-reformist reform" as defined and advocated by Andre Gorz in his writings on transition from western-style, advanced capitalism toward democratic socialism.

Full employment has a further potential meaning: the egalitarian principle that all members of society should have rights and responsibilities to participate in socially necessary production in accordance with their capacities, and corresponding rights to meet their human needs out of the aggregate social product. Marx's pithy phrase, "from each according to capacity, to each according to need," is a classic formulation of this principle.

In humanist-socialist thought, self-directed, creative, and productive work is a fundamental human necessity and right: for people become fully human only when able to act creatively and productively in the world. This is how they establish their identity, how they gain a place in their community, and how they find and give meaning to their relations to other people and nature. In this sense, work connects people to life since it bridges the gaps between their intrinsic needs and the material and cultural sources from which their needs can be met. Since creative and meaningful work is so essential to the life process, being excluded from participation in society's aggregate work means being negated as a member of society.

"Full employment" is certainly not the same as liberated, creative, productive, and self-directed work. We are far from such a mode of production and cannot bring it into being by a single policy reform. Yet the deeper meanings and implications of full employment contain the seeds of a future liberated mode of work. Constitutional guarantees of full employment seem thus an essential step toward the long-range goal of a liberated work context.

ARGUMENTS AGAINST FULL EMPLOYMENT RE-EXAMINED

It seems necessary to comment here on arguments which suggest that the high-tech revolution and global market dynamics will result in continuous decline of necessary human work; that full employment is therefore no longer a viable socialist goal; and that priority should be assigned to demands for guaranteed shares of the social product ... i.e. "social wages," rather than to demands for guaranteed shares in determining, designing, creating, and enjoying that product. The last of these arguments has merit in the prevailing context of growing deprivation among large segments of society, especially women and racial minorities, when advanced as a short-range strategy to deal with an emergency. The former arguments, however, reflect uncritical acceptance of a view of reality shaped mainly by the interests and ideologies of entrepreneurial classes. Implicit in these arguments is also a readiness to surrender decisions on the design and organization of production to propertied and managerial classes in exchange for guaranteed welfare state provisions and services.

Western and Northern European social-democratic and labor parties have pursued similar strategies over many decades. Yet, while they were relatively successful in expanding the welfare state, they have failed to overcome the hegemony of capitalist ideologies and institutions. In the United States, the New Deal and similar strategies pursued by liberal and progressive forces have also secured important concessions in the form of welfare provisions and services, though far less adequate in scope and philosophy than in Europe. Also, while some welfare state programs, such as Social Security, are by now widely accepted, the political struggles to establish and expand these programs have in no way weakened the capitalist mentality in the United States. The opposite is true: these programs have actually reinforced the dominant ideology and institutions, since liberal and progressive coalitions which fought for them have usually avoided any challenge to capitalist ideology.

The assumption of continuous decline in socially necessary work due to technological developments and global market dynamics requires critical reexamination. The predictions seem less valid when one refuses to consider capitalism, chauvinism, and imperialism as constants and when one introduces into the analysis egalitarian, democratic, and global-humanistic considerations and values. Demographic projections indicate that within sixty-five years the global population will double to about ten billion. The composition, size, quality, and distribution of the current global product does not satisfy the most basic needs of large segments of the present global population of five billion humans. Even in wealthy, advanced capitalist societies, many millions suffer now from poverty, hunger, homelessness, disease, ignorance, and despair. We will need much more work to produce and distribute the goods and services necessary for adequately meeting current human needs and the needs of twice the current global population within a few decades, especially when one takes into account the progressive depletion and ultimate limits of nonrenewable sources of energy, and the slow development of reliable substitute sources. The assumption that the needs of humankind will soon be met mainly by energy-intensive, high-tech production processes seems unsupportable by currently available evidence. The scope of necessary production and human work can and should be reduced significantly by phasing out defense industries and wasteful practices such as constant fashion and model changes, built-in obsolescence, manipulative advertising, useless packaging, etc. However, as societies all over the globe adjust the composition, scope, and quality of production to actual human needs, rather than to "effective demand" as determined by inequalities of purchasing power, the aggregate of objectively necessary human labor is likely to increase, rather than decrease, along with increases in population, at least for the next several decades.

Since the objective need for human work in the global context is not likely to decline in the foreseeable future, democratic-socialist strategy should focus on assuring to all a just share in controlling and implementing production and in enjoying its fruits. It should focus also on reconceptualizing work as a fundamental human activity geared to meeting human needs rather than to generating profits, and on transforming and redesigning work from an alienating experience into a source of human development and well-being. Science and technology are necessary components of this transformation, but their blessings should accrue not just to owners and managers but to all people. While democratic-socialist strategy should emphasize full employment with adequate income, and transformation of work processes in ways compatible with human development, it should also include, as an immediate demand, adequate levels of provisions and services for all people, whether or not they are now participating in the existing, irrational, profit-oriented work and production system. However, in struggling for "social wages" within the existing antisocial mode of life, democratic-socialist analysis should challenge, rather than validate, capitalist dynamics which reproduce class divisions, unemployment, and poverty, and which yield inadequate social wages.

CONSTITUTIONAL AMENDMENT PROCESS
AS DEMOCRATIC-SOCIALIST STRATEGY

Political and educational efforts to pass and ratify a constitutional amendment guaranteeing rights to employment and income would fit into a democratic-socialist strategy whose long-range goals include participation by everyone in shaping, controlling, creating and enjoying the aggregate social product.

The U.S. Constitution and its amendments codify the fundamental structures of the social order and the inalienable rights of the people, reflect the dominant values and ideology of society, and define the possibilities and limits of social, economic, and political patterns. These possibilities and limits can be transcended when the Constitution is amended or reinterpreted by the courts. Amending the Constitution or securing judicial reinterpretations means formalizing elements of social transformation. Depending on their substance, scope, and significance, constitutional amendments and reinterpretations may be "reformist," or "non-reformist" in Gorz's terms. In other words, the amendment process could be used as a vehicle toward a nonviolent, democratic revolution.

Because of the conservative bias of the Constitution and its function to maintain the societal status quo, it is more difficult to pass and ratify amendments to it, than to enact simple legislation. Conversely, constitutional amendments are also more effective than simple legislation in assuring and protecting rights. Furthermore, rights specified by constitutional amendment can be enforced by the courts, and all prior and subsequent legislation must conform to the spirit and letter of constitutional amendments once they are ratified. Legislation, on the other hand, is often vague in terms of rights granted. The ineffectiveness of vague legislation is illustrated by the failure of the Employment Act of 1946 and the Humphrey-Hawkins Act of 1978 to eliminate unemployment.

One further aspect of the constitutional amendment and ratification process relevant to democratic-socialist strategy is that it provides opportunities to expand people's critical consciousness of the reality of the prevailing way of life, and to challenge the hegemony of capitalist ideology. The amendment and ratification process usually requires several years and must be carried into every state and community. It is therefore necessary to organize a social movement to interpret a proposed amendment and mobilize political support for it. Such a movement would insist on inclusion of the proposed amendment in public political discourse, and would use the public arena to present its critique of established institutions.

RIGHTS TO EMPLOYMENT, CULTURAL TENDENCIES, AND POLITICAL STRATEGY

When designing democratic-socialist strategy, policy proposals should be compatible as far as possible with value tendencies in the culture and consciousness of the people. When such links exist, policies will not be perceived as rooted in alien ideologies, and there will be less resistance and hostility directed at them. Constitutional guarantees of rights to employment and income are certainly compatible with values which have deep roots in the history and culture of this country.

Early European settlers brought with them a "work ethic" which originated in the biblical injunction "to earn bread by the sweat of one's brow." They believed that everyone had obligations and rights to be self-reliant through hard work. They also thought people were entitled to use natural resources to satisfy their needs by working with these resources. These ideas originated in ancient Judeo-Christian traditions according to which the earth was given to humans to derive their livelihood; no one was to be excluded from using God-given resources for self-support; and people who lost their shares due to adversity were to regain them during the jubilee year. The vastness of the American continent enabled people for centuries to move beyond settled regions in pursuit of a self-reliant existence. These experiences reinforced the notion that anyone could and should make an adequate living by working, and that all should have rights and means to do so.

Recent developments in Catholic theology concerning work and workers' rights may prefigure potential shifts in values and consciousness toward the early cultural layers. Pope John Paul II's Encyclical, "On Human Work," asserts the "priority of labor over capital," and stresses the worth, dignity, and inalienable rights of every worker as a human person. The pope's arguments are based on the same Judeo-Christian premises which underlie the early ideological themes of this country, and lead to the conclusion that unemployment is incompatible with human dignity, needs, rights, and responsibilities. The Catholic bishops of the United States applied the same premises to an analysis of our economic system in a recent pastoral letter. They, too, declare unemployment and poverty unacceptable on moral grounds and recommend policies that would guarantee dignified work and adequate income to all. Many Protestant and Jewish clergy have voiced similar positions.

A further requirement of effective strategy is to advance policies which are compatible with the objective interests of most people and which do not divide workers against each other. Policies which by implication sanction unemployment are inevitably divisive and tend to intensify discriminatory practices. "Affirmative action" to compensate for past discrimination against women and racial minorities resulted in antagonisms and divisions among workers since it aimed to redistribute scarce employment opportunities, rather than to provide such opportunities for everyone. A constitutional guarantee of rights to employment and income, on the other hand, aims to eliminate the divisive, socially constructed scarcity of work opportunities. Hence it is a genuinely unifying policy compatible with the objective interests of everyone who depends on employment—about ninety percent of the population.

IMPLEMENTING FULL EMPLOYMENT IN A CAPITALISTIC ECONOMY

Employment and income guarantees can be implemented without major transformations of the prevailing economic system, though some constraints on existing rights of owners and management would be necessary.

There are several approaches to assure full employment. One is to include everyone in the aggregate of work by adjusting the average length of the work day, week, or year to assure a match between the size of the work force and the number of work positions. Thus, for instance, if the economy employs about 100 million workers working eight hours per day, the same output can be produced by 114 million workers working seven hours per day. By reducing the workday by one hour, 14 million unemployed workers can be absorbed without modifying the scope and substance of production. However, many workers would require preparation to take on positions created by reducing the average work time of those now employed.

Would the real income of individual workers be reduced when working fewer hours? Not necessarily, since wages are negotiated in a power context, and the power of workers would increase when the threat of unemployment is removed. As long as the aggregate economic output is not changed the surplus available for wages and profits remains about the same. However, when the relative power of workers is increased, the share of the surplus going to wages could increase. Also, shares of the surplus that are now channeled into unemployment funds and some welfare programs would be available for wages. Thus, while individual wages may change, the aggregate of wages could increase, and the conditions of life of workers as a class would therefore improve.

A second approach is to change the scope and substance of aggregate production by publicly sponsoring projects focused on unmet human needs. Such projects could be implemented directly by public authorities or delegated to worker cooperatives. The scope of publicly sponsored projects could be adjusted periodically to correspond to the size of the work force not employed by private enterprises. Wages in the public sector would have to meet the test of adequacy as measured by actual costs of living.

A third approach is based on the fact that many people are actually working but do not receive social recognition and economic rewards for their labor. Parents caring for children and people caring for sick relatives belong in this category of workers. Were child care by parents and similar care-giving situations defined as work, decent wages would have to be paid out of government revenues obtained through appropriate modifications of the tax system. A "parents' wages" policy would not only reduce unemployment, but would also eliminate the AFDC component of the public welfare system, a very desirable reform in terms of human dignity.

The approaches sketched here would require simple acts of Congress, such as periodic adjustments of work time and minimum wages, authorization and funding of publicly financed projects, creation and funding of parents' wages and tax reforms, none of which involve transformations of the legal structures of capitalism. However, these policies would test and strain the limits of the status quo which is, after all, what "nonreformist reforms" are supposed to do.

EPILOGUE: BEYOND CONSTITUTIONAL GUARANTEES
OF EMPLOYMENT AND INCOME

Once employment and income are assured to all by the Constitution, and once Congress has enacted legislation to implement these new rights, the United States will enter a new phase in its history. A sense of mutualism and security will gradually replace the current sense of competition and insecurity, and everyone will have more opportunities than now to develop innate capacities and talents. The quality of life will be enriched, and society as a whole will benefit.

At that new stage, it will be possible to put on the political agenda issues concerning redefinition, reorganization, redesign of work and production, and recomposition of the social product. It will also be possible at that stage to tackle issues of human relations, including sexism, racism, ageism, class antagonism, and global peace and justice, which defy fundamental solutions while threats of unemployment and poverty are an ever-present experience.

These issues cannot be addressed effectively now, because in the absence of employment and income security, people tend to protect whatever employment they have, whether or not their work is compatible with their needs and development, and satisfying and meaningful in personal, social, ethical and ecological terms. Nor will people now be genuinely committed to the protection of the needs, rights, and interests of disadvantaged groups, when such protection poses threats to their own employment and income security.

Under prevailing conditions of insecurity, workers and their unions resist changes in the organization and design of work and production which could threaten their positions and way of life, even when such changes would enrich the quality of production processes and products. Similarly, workers will defend employment opportunities which result in products that are poor in quality, useless, or even damaging to people and to the environment. The list of contradictions, irrationalities, and waste and corruption in production in which people now participate, readily or reluctantly, for want of appropriate and meaningful alternative work and income opportunities, is long indeed—the huge defense industry is only the most obvious and visible illustration.

The issues noted above as items for the political agenda, following the establishment of universal rights to employment and income, are crucial for human survival and the enrichment of the quality of life. Social movements have emerged in recent decades around many of these issues. These movements are important since they enhance critical consciousness in the population and since they can reduce the intensity of suffering, oppression and alienation. Yet these movements are unlikely to achieve their separate objectives because the continued existence of socially structured and sanctioned unemployment, poverty, and insecurity prevents large segments of the population from concerning themselves now with issues beyond their economic survival and security needs. For most people, these will take precedence over any other issue, including the threat of nuclear holocaust.

There are no shortcuts in the transformation of the United States toward a democratic-socialist society. The essential next step is to enact employment and income guarantees so that people will feel secure enough to risk subsequent necessary steps. Movements such as those for the rights of women and minorities, for peace, food, health, housing, and ecology, should broaden their agenda and join in a political coalition to promote a constitutional amendment guaranteeing the right to employment and income. If several states follow the lead of Massachusetts, and if there is broad enough popular support, Congress may be persuaded to act. The United States Constitution will have its two hundredth anniversary in 1987. We should celebrate this event by adding a new Bill of Economic Rights which assures everyone's rights to participate actively in building and enjoying life.

REFERENCES

Gorz, Andre, *Strategy for Labor* (Boston Beacon Press, 1967).
Pope John Paul, II, On Human Work (Boston: Daughters of St. Paul, 1981).
National Conference of Catholic Bishops, *Economic Justice for All* (Washington, D.C.: United States Catholic Conference, 1986).

11

Social Sciences, Human Survival, Development and Liberation*

In this essay, I will develop a tentative set of principles and an agenda for the social sciences from a humanist perspective. Such a perspective implies unconditional respect for every human being, rooted in egalitarian, libertarian, and democratic values, and a corresponding political philosophy according to which humans are, in spite of their individual differences, equals in intrinsic worth and entitled to equal rights and responsibilities in every domain of social life. Humanism involves an unequivocal commitment to human survival, development, and liberation, the underlying themes of this essay.

Principles for social sciences will be derived here from certain fundamental aspects of the human condition in nature and from the related proposition that every moment of human existence, social relations, and interactions involves, inevitably, political and value dimensions. As a societal process, the practice of social sciences involves, therefore, political and value dimensions and is thus a political act—whether or not social scientists intend it to be that way.

The notion that social sciences could and should be practiced in a value-free manner has by now been rejected by many scholars. The related notion, however, that social scientists could and should be politically neutral when practicing their scholarly disciplines is often taken for granted even now. This notion requires critical scrutiny.

---

*Humanity and Society, vol. 11, no. 2 (May 1987); Kenneth Westhues, ed. Basic Principles for Social Science in Our Time (Waterloo, Ontario: The University of St. Jerome College Press, 1987).

THE MEANING OF "POLITICAL"

Before discussing aspects of the human condition relevant to the formulation of social science principles, it seems necessary to clarify the meaning of the term "political" as used here. I am using this term not in the conventional narrow sense of electoral, party, and interest group politics, but in a comprehensive, dynamic sense. In this sense, *political* refers to *conscious and intentional, as well as unconscious and unintentional acts or inactions by individuals and groups, which affect established patterns and conditions of life in society either by reproducing and perpetuating these patterns or by challenging them and promoting transformations in them.*

When the term *political* is used in this comprehensive, dynamic sense, political neutrality turns out to be an impossibility for people living and acting in an established society—this includes scholars who study it. Every human action and thought in such an established context will either conform to, reproduce, reinforce, and validate the status quo of preexisting patterns and conditions of life, or will confront, challenge, and subvert prevailing social organization and consciousness. Political neutrality is possible only in a hypothetical situation of total absence of societal patterns, such as Rawls' "veil of ignorance" context.[1]

THE POLITICAL NATURE OF VALUES AND MORALS

Once the term *political* is understood comprehensively and dynamically, the essentially political nature of societal values and morals becomes evident. For values and morals are products of social processes rather than politically neutral absolutes derived from extra-human sources. They are guides for socially expected, "valued" consciousness, behavior, and social relations. Their usual consequence or "function" is to induce consciousness, actions, and relations compatible with the reproduction of established patterns of social life, and to prevent consciousness, actions, and relations which threaten, subvert, and transform established patterns. Analogously, "alternative" values and morals are advocated and practiced by individuals and social groups whose aim is to bring about changes in consciousness, behavior, and relations conducive to transformations of established patterns of life. Values and morals are always rooted in and reflective of important needs and interests either of all members of a society or of certain social groups or classes. Thus the value of the sanctity of life expressed by the ancient commandment, "Thou shalt not kill," clearly represents a universal human need and interest. On the other hand, patriarchal values and morals which prescribe preferential status and treatment for boys and men represent the interests of a privileged, dominant segment of society. Similarly, racist values promote differential rights, responsibilities, and treatment for different racial and ethnic groups, and thus represent divided and factional rather than universal interests. Values and morals concerning the sanctity of property derive from the interests of propertied segments of societies. Whenever property is distributed unequally and unfairly, these values and morals serve mainly the interests of privileged classes.

The political importance of values and morals is largely due to the fact that, in the course of socialization, values which serve the interests of dominant and privileged classes tend to be internalized into the consciousness not only of these classes, but also of dominated and deprived classes. Consequently, the consciousness, behaviors, and relations of all societal groups tend to conform more or less to patterns of life which reproduce the status quo, and which serve the interests of dominant and privileged groups while hurting, in direct and subtle ways, the interests of other groups in society.

The essentially political nature and consequences of values and morals indicated by this analysis mean that implicit in a rejection of the possibility of value-free practice of social sciences is also a rejection of the possibility of politically neutral practice. Hence, social scientists who reject only the possibility of value-free practice, but not of politically neutral practice, may be enacting a new variation on the conventional theme of avoiding explicit political challenges to the social status quo. Such scholars may actually protect and preserve their academic standing and respectability when asserting commitments to values as abstractions rather than as political acts.

ASPECTS OF THE HUMAN CONDITION UNDERLYING THE POLITICAL NATURE OF LIFE IN SOCIETY AND OF THE SOCIAL SCIENCES

Humans share with other species biological tendencies to survive and propagate and to unfold spontaneously their innate potential when living in environments in which they can realize their basic needs. Basic needs of humans include, however, not only biological, but also psychological, social, security, spiritual, and creative-productive needs.[2] As to the environment, it consists for humans not only of the natural setting, but also of a human-originated and evolved sociocultural context. It follows that, while humans share major biological tendencies with other species, their basic needs and environmental requirements seem more complex.

In biological terms, humans seem less adequately prepared for survival than other species since, genetically, they may be the "least programmed" species. Also, as with many species, human offspring are immature at birth and totally dependent on care and support from adults for an extended period. Being genetically less programmed does not mean that human existence is not genetically circumscribed. It means merely that human genes determine only ranges and limits for behavior, within which humans must make choices when developing patterns for their lives and social relations. Their genes do not determine and transmit specifications for patterns of life and behavior as the genes of other species seem to do to a far larger extent.

As a consequence of the relative absence of genetic specifications and the immaturity of their offspring at birth, *humans survive as individuals and a species only when they create for themselves relatively stable patterns of existence within genetically evolved limits, including systems of care and socialization for their young, conducive to maturation and to integration into established existential designs.* Human existential patterns and social organizations are, therefore, ordained by neither biology nor extra-human forces. Rather they are historical products of interactions among individuals, social groups, and natural environments. Societal processes evolved thus into substitutes for genetically specified patterns of life. This circumstance of the human condition—*the existential imperative to create patterns of social life*—is the source of the inevitability of political processes in human societies, aimed at recreating, maintaining, or transforming human-evolved patterns of social life.

As genetic specifications declined in the course of biological evolution, the capacity for mental processes and consciousness of the nervous system and the brain seems to have increased, making possible the eventual substitution of sociocultural programming for genetic programming. Mental capacities and processes are thus a product of biological evolution, as well as the medium for and ongoing product of sociocultural evolution.

The evolutionary shift from genetic specificity toward genetic openness has had important consequences for the political dimension of human life. On the positive side, the human species became relatively flexible to adapt to diverse and changing environmental contexts all over the globe. On the other hand, lacking a pattern of life tested and finely tuned by biological evolution, the human species is constantly faced with the risk of creating, transmitting, and perpetuating patterns of life which are less than optimal in terms of survival, development and meeting basic needs of all members of societies. This risk was certainly not negligible in the context in which human groups took their early steps toward creating patterns of social organization. This early context involved pervasive ignorance of life, nature, human nature, and the universe; limited technological capacity and skills; and a deep sense of insecurity due to precarious conditions of life. It is not surprising, therefore, that existential patterns, once evolved by trial and error, tended to be preserved and reproduced, provided they proved to be minimally adequate.

Human societies seem to have developed strong conservative tendencies to hold on to established ways of life since early stages of social evolution. Several social-psychological factors may account for this tendency: a sense of security derived from familiar patterns which seem somehow to work and to satisfy perceived needs and interests of people; intense fear of the unknown and of untried alternative approaches to existential problems; comprehensive ignorance and limited experience and skills; habit and inertia; and an apparent tendency to deal with perceived problems as isolated fragments, by small, incremental steps, rather than reexamining the entire societal context from which the problems arise and readjusting that context in order to prevent the problems at their sources.

The conservative tendencies of human societies seem also to emerge from interactions of biological, social, and psychological factors inherent in the physical and mental immaturity, the economic and emotional dependence, and the limited capacity for critical reflection and consciousness of children during stages of life when they are socialized into and absorb the established ways of life and the dominant values and ideologies of their societies.

Yet in spite of strong conservative tendencies in human societies, societal patterns, values, and ideologies have never been static, but have always undergone changes, usually gradually, but often also at accelerated rates. While these changes result from various internal and external societal forces and also from environmental factors, the role played in social change by critical reflection and consciousness on the part of individuals and groups within societies is of special importance in this discussion of political and value dimensions of social life and of the social sciences.

A UNITARY CONCEPT OF SCIENCE DERIVED FROM THE HUMAN CONDITION

As a human function, science originated in the just described aspects of the human condition which underlie the existential imperative to create viable patterns for social organization. Science appears thus to be a "twin" of the political dimension of human life which, as noted above, also derives from that existential imperative.

In a fundamental sense, science is an ongoing multidimensional process—the entire array of explorations, discoveries and inventions by which humans strive to orient themselves to the world and to gain some control over their existence and environment, as they create, maintain or transform the patterns of their societies. The products of the diverse processes of science include consciousness of self, others, society and the human species; of social relations and relations to the environment; of nature, the supernatural and the universe; of life and death; of time, space and history; and of origins and destination. This generic concept of science includes not only the natural and social sciences but also mythology, religion, ideology, philosophy, art and literature. Implicit in this broad concept is the notion that there are no precise, qualitative boundaries between these different human approaches to gaining consciousness of and comprehending the world. For these approaches are overlapping and complementary stages, dimensions, and media of a unitary process which is intrinsic to, and shaped by, the aspects of the human condition sketched above: the drive to survive, the dynamics of meeting basic human needs, the relative lack of genetic specifications for human existence, the compensatory biological capacity for mental activity and consciousness, and the inescapable necessity to create patterns for social life.

While science is a process and product of consciousness-generating mental activity originated in the human condition, and is shaped and reshaped by the intrinsic imperatives of that condition and the human interest in satisfying real and perceived needs, it has gradually evolved into a substantial force toward creating, maintaining, interpreting and justifying patterns of social existence. However, science can also become a source and means for critical consciousness and transformative practice concerning established patterns of life when these patterns fail to satisfy basic human needs.

STAGES OF THE POLITICAL ORIENTATION OF SCIENCE

Throughout history, the goals and practice of science were shaped, directly or indirectly, by experienced and perceived needs, the satisfaction of which has always been a key human interest. Implicit in the relationship of science to needs and interests is a fundamental political question: Whose needs and interests are being served by scientific activity in different societies during different times?

During early stages of social evolution, humans tended to live in small, relatively egalitarian communities of hunters and gatherers which were organized to meet everyone's basic needs as far as was possible in the context of limited knowledge and technology. People in such communities, therefore, had shared interests and their "scientific practices" were consequently conducive to meeting everyone's needs and interests. Clearly, to the extent to which, and as long as, such "classless" and relatively conflict-free communities existed, scientific achievements benefited everyone fairly equally. The political dimension of science at that stage of social evolution may be considered egalitarian and humanistic since it facilitated and justified the maintenance and perpetuation of ways of life which satisfied the needs and interests of everyone.

As population growth led, some ten to twenty thousand years ago, to gradual transformations of small communities into larger societies, to the discovery and development of agriculture and early technologies, and to social differentiations based on age, sex, origin, occupation, and residence, inegalitarian societal patterns were introduced coercively into earlier egalitarian settings. These new societal patterns had to be maintained by physical force and ideological indoctrination. They involved domination, exploitation and oppression of various groups and classes within societies, and often also wars with and conquests of other societies.

Once societies were no longer organized to satisfy the basic human needs and interests of all their members, and large population segments were forced to serve the needs and interests of dominant, privileged elites, the practice of science also came to be dominated largely by those same elites and was adapted to serve their interests. The political dimension of science in this new context had shifted toward an inegalitarian and elitist orientation geared to the perpetuation of exploitative patterns of life.

The transformation of egalitarian, cooperative, small communities into inegalitarian, exploitative, larger societies (and the related transformation of humanistic, egalitarian science which served everyone's interest into oppressive, inegalitarian science which served mainly the interests of dominant, oppressive elites) has also resulted in the gradual emergence of a counterestablishment, emancipatory science. This alternative tendency in science evolved from efforts of oppressed and exploited individuals and groups (and their allies from other social groups) to reflect on their conditions and make sense out of their lives; to orient themselves to their world and comprehend it in order to regain control over their lives; and to develop critical consciousness concerning the dynamics of their situation and the requirements of liberation.

PRINCIPLES AND AGENDA FOR HUMANIST SOCIAL SCIENCES

Now that policies, values, and sciences have been traced to their sources in fundamental aspects of the human condition, a tentative set of principles and a related, general agenda for humanist social sciences can be suggested.

1. A key principle derives from the realization that social sciences involve, inevitably, political and value positions favoring either preservation or change of established ways of life and social relations. Social scientists should, therefore, choose consciously and reexamine continuously, political and value positions for their practice and theory. In doing so, it seems preferable to specify positions not as abstract concepts and labels but in terms of desired human conditions and outcomes.

2. It is not enough merely to choose and reexamine political and value positions. Rather, chosen positions ought to be integrated consciously into every aspect and stage of scholarly practice: agenda, methods and designs, human relations, teaching, communications, and publications. Furthermore, it is necessary to resist involvement in projects which conflict with one's politics and values.

3. From a humanist political perspective, *the social sciences should facilitate changes of social orders which inhibit the realization of basic human needs and thus obstruct development toward alternative orders whose institutions, values, and dynamics would be conducive to the full development or self-actualization of every human being.* This humanist political perspective derives from the above analysis of the human condition, according to which people tend to develop and to unfold their innate potential spontaneously when living in natural and socially evolved environments in which they can realize their basic needs. *To facilitate transformations of development-inhibiting into development-conducive environments should be the central mission of humanist social sciences.*

4. The humanist political perspective sketched here implies the following themes as key components of a social science agenda:

   (a) roots, dynamics, history, past and present context of development-obstructing patterns of social life, in any culture and any part of the world;
   (b) actual patterns of social life, past and present, in any culture and country, and theoretical models of possible future patterns of social life, conducive to realization of basic human needs and to unobstructed human developments;
   (c) forces and processes which inhibit consciousness and understanding of the essence of social reality, with attention to the role of conventional, mainstream social sciences;
   (d) models of education and communication oriented toward overcoming forces and processes which inhibit consciousness and understanding of the essence of social reality, and toward facilitating the emergence of critical consciousness;
   (e) political strategies and social movements oriented toward transforming development-obstructing institutions, values, and consciousness into development-conducive alternatives. This theme should involve not only theoretical study but also active involvement by humanist scholars in political practice oriented toward human liberation, social justice, and equality.

5. The relationship of scholars to people involved in study projects should be free of all forms of domination, manipulation, and exploitation. People should be considered and treated as autonomous subjects rather than as objects and "guinea pigs." This principle derives from the humanistic premise that all people are to be regarded as equals in intrinsic worth and dignity. In concrete terms, this attitude towards people requires that decisions on the goals, foci, questions, methods, designs, and reports of a study should not be made by scholars alone, but by all people involved in the study or their representatives, in cooperation and consultation with the investigators. This requirement goes far beyond the conventional "informed consent" concept. Such participation in shaping and controlling social science investigations is likely to

enhance the interest and motivation of people involved in them, and should therefore strengthen the quality of studies. It also seems appropriate to compensate people involved in studies for time and effort contributed by them, rather than expect them to volunteer their contributions. As long as scholars are paid for their work in a scientific project, the work of other participants ought to be acknowledged in the same currency.

6. Methods and designs ought to follow logically from the nature of the studies and the question to be explored. As there are no universally valid methodologies and designs for the study of social issues, every study, question, and context is likely to require specific combinations of research approaches. Controversies concerning quantitative vs. qualitative approaches, large sample surveys vs. intensive case studies, empirical-positivist vs. alternative epistemologies, etc., seem therefore to raise false issues, as any of these modes of inquiry may be appropriate for different studies, contexts, and purposes.

7. Considerations of validity, reliability, precision, and the overall level of scholarly competence are not less important for humanist than for conventional, mainstream social sciences. These considerations are necessary to assure the integrity of social science projects, and integrity is certainly a key requirement of a humanist approach.

8. Integrity is, however, not merely a matter of research technology, but is intimately related to political and value dimensions. Consequently, a study could not pass the test of integrity when its substance and/or procedures are in conflict with or irrelevant to the humanist perspective even though the method and design of the study are valid, reliable, precise, of high quality, and in general reflective of scholarly sophistication and competence. Thus, for instance, studies of the effects of hunger, homelessness, poverty, and discrimination on human development seem to lack integrity, for these conditions are unacceptable on moral and political grounds, and ought to be abolished through political practice,

irrespective of their scientifically measured consequences. Such studies are often conducted not to guide policy, but to delay and avoid action on what is already well known. Such studies are also often undertaken to further the economic interests of research institutes, universities, and scholars. From a humanist perspective, studies of this type should be shunned because of their amoral, or even immoral, quality.

9. When writing and publishing their scholarly work and findings, humanist social scientists should avoid the use of professional jargon with which only select groups are familiar. Instead they should write in as clear, concise, and simple a style and language as possible. This does not mean that scholars should not present and explain the complex nature of social phenomena they have studied. It only means that substantive complexity should not be made more difficult to comprehend by the use of unnecessarily complicated language and style.

   The historic roots of professional jargons and scholarly style reach back to early processes of social differentiations and elite formation. The purpose of limiting the spread of literacy and of developing separate forms of language and communications for priesthoods, scholars, and dominant social classes, has been to exclude dominated classes from access to knowledge and information which they might use in efforts to liberate themselves from domination and exploitation. Humanist scholars should not participate in perpetuating this tradition through their modes of communication and publication.

10. Teaching is usually a process by which established ways of life, and the values and ideologies underlying them, are transmitted to successive generations of students. It is thus a medium for shaping the consciousness of students, but also a potential medium for challenging that consciousness—political acts *par excellence*. The messages of teaching are conveyed cognitively as well as experientially, through substantive content, teaching style, human relations and expressed attitudes.

For social scientists who have come to acknowledge the political and value dimensions of scholarly work, and who have chosen a humanist political philosophy, the classroom and teaching context can become major arenas for political practice toward human liberation. Here they can help students, through a dialogical process free of elements of indoctrination, to develop innate capacities for critical thought and consciousness, to gain penetrating insights into the sources, history and present dynamics of social life, and to develop personal commitment to human liberation and social justice. By practicing the humanist pedagogy of ancient and contemporary philosophers from Socrates to Martin Buber and Paulo Freire,[3] teachers can consciously transform their classrooms and the entire educational experience into a "liberated space," that is, a counter-reality to institutional domination and control, in which students can taste in the here and now prefigurations of possible future patterns of social life and human relations, involving self-direction and freedom in the context of justice and participatory democracy. Teachers choosing this educational philosophy should act as guides, facilitators, and resource persons who respond sensitively and caringly to the evolving motivations and capacities of students, and who refrain consistently from controlling and dominating them through requirements, examinations, and grades.

As to substance, education in humanist social science should involve exploration of the many related dimensions of natural and culturally shaped realities; of what is, what was, and what can be; how all this facilitates and inhibits human development; and how a better fit can be attained between developmental needs of people all over the globe and emerging, human-shaped social realities. The ultimate purpose of humanist education is to facilitate discovery by students of themselves as potentially creative and productive subjects in relation to other individuals, communities, society, nature, and the universe.

Humanist approaches to the social sciences in general and to teaching in particular are likely to conflict with dominant approaches in many contemporary schools and universities, which for many reasons are intimately tied to, and committed to the preservation of the social status quo. Humanist scholars will, therefore, experience tensions, rejection, alienation, and isolation in their places of work, in relations with individual colleagues and with academic departments and institutions. These experiences, which may range from mild to intense levels in different institutions at different times, cannot be avoided when scholars insist on their academic freedom to pursue their chosen political-philosophical course. Constructive responses are possible for dealing with this dilemma, stressing mutual respect, openness, and tolerance. One should, however, also realize and acknowledge openly that perfect solutions are not possible. For the conflict is real and serious between majorities who support established ways of life, actively or by implication, and small minorities who are not only committed philosophically to fundamental systemic changes, but also work constantly for transformations of the established social order in line with their philosophy.

11. This dilemma underlies the final principle to be suggested here. Humanist social scientists should be involved actively in social-political liberation movements on local and trans-local levels. Such involvement is necessary and appropriate in personal and political terms, and also to assure scholarly integrity. In a personal sense, involvement in humanist caucuses in workplaces and in scholarly and occupational societies, and also in chapters of political movements is important for mutual support and confirmation of individuals whose alienation is, at least partly, related to their political and philosophical minority status. In a political sense, involvement in organizations and movements is necessary since social change cannot be accomplished without organized, collective practice. Individual efforts in everyday life are, of course, important to promote critical consciousness—a precondition for social transformations. However, individual efforts can only be a necessary complement to collective action, never a substitute for it. Finally, personal integrity of humanist scholars seems to require their active involvement in political practice for

fundamental social change. This necessity was stressed, some 150 years ago, by an important humanist social scientist, Karl Marx, in his apt critique of academic philosophy: "The philosophers have only interpreted the world in various ways; the point, however, is to change it."[4] Marx's pithy observation on philosophers is equally applicable to social scientists, and in a way summarizes the conclusions of this essay concerning principles for humanist practice conducive to human survival, development and liberation.

NOTES

1. John Rawls, *A Theory of Justice* (Cambridge: Harvard University Press, 1971).

2. Abraham Maslow, *Motivation and Personality* (New York: Harper and Row, 1954, 1971).

3. Paulo Freire, *Pedagogy of the Oppressed* (New York: Herder & Herder, 1970).

4. Karl Marx, "Theses on Feuerbach, 1845," in Robert C. Tucker, ed., *The Marx-Engels Reader* (New York: Norton, 1978).

12
Implications of Conservative Tendencies for Practice and Education in Social Welfare*

Political discourse, public opinion, and public policy in the United States have undoubtedly shifted in conservative directions since the early seventies, and especially so during the Reagan administration. Illustrative of the conservative mentality is the widespread, uncritical acceptance of such notions as fiscal constraints and their limiting impact in human services; misguidedness of "active government" in the interest of human well-being, and of the welfare state philosophy and programs; balanced budgets without corresponding progressive taxation, economic growth and competitiveness as self-evident public goods; equating democracy with formal elections, freedom with capitalist economics, and "national interest" with the business interests of multinational corporations; defining "national security" in terms of military superiority without clarifying the threats to security and the identity of "the enemy"; and, selfish pursuit of material wealth in the midst of growing poverty, and disregard for a sense of community.

It would be an oversimplification to blame prevailing social ills and waste of human potential and natural resources on the conservative philosophy and domestic and foreign policies of President Reagan and some of his predecessors, although these dehumanizing conditions have certainly intensified since the Nixon years. Rather, it seems that these social, economic, and ecological ills are the inevitable results of perva-

---

*This essay was presented at the invitation of the Council on Social Work Education at its Annual Program Meeting in Atlanta, Georgia on March 7, 1988.

243

sive conservative tendencies which have shaped the institutional order and the public consciousness of this country since colonial times. These tendencies, which were brought to the "New World" by European colonizers, have become the shared ideology, with minor variations, of all major political parties. Evidence of this underlying consensus concerning fundamental economic, political, and philosophical premises can be gleaned from the relative continuity of domestic and foreign policies throughout U.S. history, and from the absence of strong opposition movements promoting alternative visions of social and economic life. More specific evidence of the influence and durability of conservative tendencies, of special concern to the social welfare field, is the continuity of welfare policies and programs focused on changing individuals rather than changing social and economic institutions, and the de-facto acceptance of the alleged inevitability of unemployment, poverty, homelessness and hunger in the midst of affluence.

The conservative tendencies, which are shared in varying degrees by the major political parties, are also shared by many practitioners, educators, and professional organizations in the social welfare field, although they tend to identify themselves as "liberals." Hence, rather than merely challenging extreme conservative philosophies and policies of the current and of future administrations, we should explore our personal and collective entrapment in the pervasive conservative mentality of this society and culture, and we ought to search for ways to liberate ourselves from these dynamics and to assist students and people we serve through practice to do likewise.

MEANINGS AND SOURCES OF CONSERVATIVE TENDENCIES

Webster's dictionary defines conservatism as "a disposition in politics to preserve what is established; a political philosophy based on tradition and social stability, stressing established institutions and preferring gradual development to abrupt change." This definition is a good starting point for this exploration, though it does not unravel the roots and dynamics of conservative tendencies. According to anthropological and historical studies, these tendencies involve mutually reinforcing biological, psychological, social, economic, political and ideological dimensions.

Humans developed social orders by interacting with one another and with their natural environments in pursuit of survival and security, usually in the face of relative scarcities of life-sustaining resources and other life-threatening conditions. As human groups discovered solutions to survival and security problems and established ways of life which somehow satisfied survival needs, they simultaneously evolved a tendency to "conserve" what seemed to work, more or less, because it served their needs and perceived interests. They also came to regard changes in traditional patterns as threats to their very existence, developed taboos against them, and made sure that established ways of life were transmitted without deviations from generation to generation. The slow rate of social change and development in small, isolated, preagricultural, communal societies seems largely due to the complementary tendencies of conserving established patterns of existence and of resisting changes and innovation. An important function of religious institutions in these societies has usually been to reinforce these tendencies.

The conservative bias which seems inherent in societal evolution is reinforced on the individual level by the biological and psychological conditions of the socialization experience of infants and children. This experience takes place in imbalanced, inegalitarian relationships involving physical, emotional, mental, economic and social dependence. Though infants and children are active participants in socialization relationships, adults are in control of power, resources, rewards, and sanctions. Children are exposed to a preexisting way of life as "objective reality" and as "good and valued," and they absorb the ideas which sustain and justify that way of life, under conditions conducive to uncritical acceptance rather than to critical reflection and informed choice. Children's faculties for critical consciousness emerge only gradually over several years. By the time these faculties eventually mature, children have already internalized their society's institutional order along with the interpretations and justifications which legitimate and validate it, and they are no longer inclined to ask critical questions about it. They have come to take it for granted and are ready, in turn, to pass it on unchallenged to their children. In the relatively few instances in which "primary" socialization fails to bring about conformity and adaptation to established patterns of behavior, relations, and beliefs, societies tend to respond with concrete and symbolic sanctions, i.e., "secondary" socialization, to promote and enforce social adaptation.

When human societies were not divided into dominant and dominated social groups, and their ways of life were designed to satisfy everyone's needs in accordance with egalitarian, cooperative, and communal values, conserving the status-quo was in everyone's perceived interest. Conformity and adaptation on the part of individuals to the established social order led to a sense of belonging, security, and well-being in physical-material, emotional-spiritual, and social-political terms. Motivation for social change was, therefore, limited, as long as population increases did not upset the balance between natural, life-sustaining resources and the existential needs of people, and encounters with other human groups did not result in tensions, conflicts, and crises.

Following increases of population and the subsequent development of agriculture, crafts, and trade some 10,000 years ago, societies began to produce an economic surplus. This new societal context and capacity made possible the gradual emergence, within and between societies, of differentiations into dominant and dominated, exploiting and exploited, and privileged and deprived classes, races, and peoples. These social, economic, and political differentiations gave also rise to corresponding differentiations in life styles and consciousness of different social groups and peoples.

Social differentiation began in nomadic, preagricultural, hunting and gathering societies as a relatively nonexploitative division of work and roles, mainly by age and sex. In sedentary, agricultural societies, social differentiation evolved, however, into essentially exploitative divisions of labor, social status and prestige, economic control and rewards, and political roles and power. Differentiations in agricultural societies did not come about voluntarily, but as a result of coercive processes involving organized physical violence and ideological hegemony by emerging secular ruling classes and their priestly associates. Ideological domination brought about internalization into popular consciousness of ex-post-facto validation and legitimation of coercively established inegalitarian, unjust, and exploitative social orders. People came to believe that institutionalized inequalities along occupational, social, economic, political and civil dimensions were "natural," inevitable and unchangeable aspects of social organization. Usually these inequalities were explained and perceived as ordained by super-human sources, rather than as originated and maintained by humans. Having but limited insight into the coercive origins and dynamics of their exploitation and oppression, and lacking awareness of past and possible future, nonoppressive, egalitarian ways of life, people tended to submit to established social arrangements with varying degrees of overt acceptance and adaptation and covert rejection and resistance. Yet frequently throughout history, covert rejection and resistance flared up as overt insurrection, revolt, and revolution.

Once systemic inequalities in human relations and material exchanges have been established within and among different societies, intra- and intersocietal conflicts become inevitable. Inequalities are not readily accepted and maintained in spite of ongoing physical and ideological coercion. Hence, inegalitarian social and global systems tend to be unstable. They are usually in a stage of temporary equilibrium resulting from antagonistic and competitive interactions among individuals, social classes and peoples, aimed at conserving or expanding relative advantages, or at transforming the entire system. Over time, antagonistic and competitive dynamics tend to intensify.

The transformation of early, egalitarian-cooperative-communal societies into later, exploitative, competitive and internally divided ones is reflected also in the emergence of new versions and functions of conservatism. While in early societies conservatism conserved ways of life which served everyone's needs and interests, in antagonistically divided social and global orders, conservatism came to protect primarily the interests of privileged social classes by conserving the structures and dynamics of domination and exploitation, and by resisting efforts to bring about fundamental social transformations. Contemporary "liberalism" is merely a "soft" version of political conservatism as it aims to conserve "lesser-degrees" of exploitation and privilege. However, just as other versions of conservatism, liberalism is opposed to unconditional elimination of all forms of structural inequalities, exploitation, domination and privilege, though it favors assuring a floor of social, economic, and political rights to everyone.

IDEOLOGICAL THEMES OF CONSERVATISM

Advantageous conditions of living and privileged social status in stratified societies are usually accepted uncritically by individuals and groups benefiting from them. They tend to take advantages for granted and to perceive them as "natural," valid, and just, as long as they conform to "law and order." Privileged conditions have been explained and justified as due to the "grace of god," to "innate superiority," or to merit by virtue of exceptional capacities and unusual efforts. These interpretations are conducive to "victim-blaming" attitudes which place responsibility for the conditions of disadvantaged individuals and classes on them rather than on oppressive social dynamics. Victim-blaming attitudes, in turn, tend to relieve the guilt and conscience of individuals from privileged classes, and also to protect unjust social orders against fundamental structural changes.

Conservative ideology tends to stress negative views concerning human nature, according to which people are selfish, greedy, lazy and power-hungry. Hence, they ought to be closely watched and controlled. Most people are thought to lack capacity for self-direction.

The negative characteristics of human nature are projected in conservative ideology mainly on dominated and exploited social classes, races and peoples while dominant classes, races and peoples are supposedly endowed with positive characteristics. Negative characteristics of oppressed groups are considered biologically determined rather than reactions and adaptations to oppressive conditions, and defenses against these conditions.

A related theme of conservative ideology is that certain individuals, races, and peoples are by nature superior to others. The superior ones should dominate and control and should be entitled to privileged conditions, since they are intrinsically worthier and more important. Domination and control by naturally superior individuals and groups is said to be for the benefit of inferior ones who, allegedly, lack capacities to assure their own well-being through productive activity.

DOMINANCE OF CONSERVATIVE THEMES AND TENDENCIES IN SOCIAL WELFARE

Overt and covert support for inegalitarian social orders, divided into dominant and privileged, and dominated and deprived classes, can be discerned as major themes and tendencies of institutionalized social welfare throughout history and on the contemporary scene. Of course, other themes and tendencies, including ethical and religious imperatives, and struggles for social justice and human equality and liberation, can also be traced throughout social welfare history; however, these themes were never dominant but merely provided a counterpoint.

In the course of several millennia, community-sponsored assistance to people in need was usually not intended to overcome the sources of poverty and assorted social ills, but only to alleviate their symptoms, case by case, and often in a dehumanizing and stigmatizing manner. Public assistance posed, therefore, no threat to established social orders. Instead, it actually contributed in subtle ways to their preservation by administering limited concessions to the claims of dominated and deprived classes, and by acting thus as a balancing and stabilizing force against potentially insurrectionary tendencies. Along with this conservative function, institutionalized social welfare has also been motivated by genuine humane tendencies, by a vague sense of guilt on the part of privileged, dominant classes, and by religious and ethical values.

On the contemporary social welfare scene, conservative themes and tendencies are evident in theory and practice, and in policies, language, and politics. Dominant theories tend to interpret human problems mainly as rooted in shortcomings and deviance of individuals, and they tend to de-emphasize social structural sources of these problems. These theoretical premises are reflected in practice focused on personal solutions through individual change and adaptation to prevailing unjust and alienating social conditions, rather than on collective solutions through social change and adaptation of existing social conditions to human needs and development.

Dominant theories also tend to fragmentize human problems into separate fields of practice, each concerned with different sets of symptoms and different population groups. Fragmented conceptions of human problems suggest, analogous to medical models, that experts can devise specific technical-professional solutions and treatments for every problem, and that, therefore, fundamental social change is not necessary for dealing with them. Alternative social welfare theories reject fragmentation and view all human problems as linked and rooted in underlying, common social dynamics. This view suggests interventions analogous to public health models, involving long-range political efforts toward fundamental social change along with services aimed at immediate and short-range relief of human suffering.

As to policy development, conservative tendencies of social welfare are reflected in support for incremental, "liberal" reforms which accept, rather than challenge, the continuation of injustice and privilege, albeit with minor modifications. An apt illustration of this is support for "welfare reforms," rather than political action aimed at eliminating poverty and the welfare system and welfare mentality through policies such as constitutional guarantees of suitable, meaningful work and adequate income.

The language of spokespeople for social welfare in policy and political discourse also reveals conservative tendencies. They will often advocate "more justice and more equality," rather than "unqualified justice and equality." What they are actually advocating are merely different levels of injustice and inequality from levels now prevailing. Qualifying the concepts "justice and equality" with the term "more" is also illogical, since there are no degrees of justice and equality. A social order is either just and egalitarian, or it is not so designed. There are, to be sure, degrees of injustice and inequality. Another semantic reflection of conservative tendencies in social welfare is the use of the adjective "poor" as a noun in the phrase, "the poor," when referring to poor people. When used as a noun to designate a class of people, other, no less important, attributes of the same people are ignored, and the condition of poverty is treated as their main characteristic, as if it were intrinsic to them. Once poverty is perceived as intrinsic to a class of people, rather than the result of human-created, changeable social conditions, it assumes an aura of permanence. This is a deeply conservative position, an implicit confirmation of the ancient myth that poverty is inevitable.

Involvement in politics by social welfare organizations conforms usually to conventional "realpolitik," an approach used by most participants in the political arena in the United States. Realpolitik can be effective for short-range, limited objectives within the established social and economic order. However, it is not suited at all for a long-range political struggle and strategy toward an alternative social order shaped by values of social justice, equality and liberty. It follows that the political style of social welfare organizations, with very few exceptions such as radical caucuses and the Bertha Reynolds Society, is thoroughly compatible with their conservative, incremental policy agenda.

The earlier noted fragmentation of social welfare into fields of practice concerned with different problems and populations tends to reinforce the political pragmatism, as different fields are usually forced to compete against each other for the limited resources available for human well-being under prevailing political conditions. This destructive competition tends to reinforce the status quo. It is unlikely to be overcome as long as social welfare organizations are trapped in the conservative mentality of fiscal constraints and scarcity of resources for human needs. Some day they may come to realize that this scarcity is a fiction, that it is not real in an economic sense but only in a political sense. The simple evidence of the fictional nature of scarcity in the midst of plenty is the vast aggregate material wealth available in this country and a trillion dollar annual federal budget of which some 300 billion are invested in the illusion of national security, and about 150 billion are used to pay interest on the national debt—a euphemism for a "guaranteed income" to privileged classes from whom the government borrows to cover the budgetary deficit, instead of taxing their wealth.

BEYOND CONSERVATIVE TENDENCIES

Conservative tendencies which have dominated societal institutions and consciousness for centuries in the United States and many other countries have led to conflicts and wars within and among nations, as well as to worldwide deterioration of the quality of life in social, psychological, economic and ecologic terms, in spite of advances in science and technology, and increases in material production. By now, these trends pose threats to the survival of the human species and necessitate a search for alternative societal paradigms geared to free and full development for all people, anywhere on earth. These paradigms should incorporate values and principles such as these: that all people be considered equals in intrinsic worth, rights and responsibilities; that no individual and no social group be exploited and dominated by others; and that the concrete and abstract resources discovered and developed by people throughout history be considered the shared inheritance of the species, to be used and preserved rationally in the interest of present and future generations.

Paradigmatic shifts of social institutions and values, from dominant conservative tendencies toward egalitarian, cooperative, communal, and liberating alternatives will take much time to accomplish, as there are no known short-cuts to such comprehensive fundamental transformations. Widespread assumptions notwithstanding, such changes are unlikely to be achieved coercively through violent revolutionary events aimed at the seizure of state power. Rather, they seem to require extended, nonviolent, democratic-revolutionary processes, designed to facilitate large-scale transformations of consciousness, involving new insights into history, present realities, and future human possibilities, and redefinitions of individual and social interests. Such transformations of consciousness seem to be essential precursors of fundamental institutional transformations, and social movements are therefore needed to act as catalysts for these transformations.

Practitioners and educators in social welfare, because of their work with people victimized by existing social conditions, and with students of these conditions, could contribute to the development of social movements toward fundamental social change. They could do so by consciously integrating a liberating political perspective into practice and education in human service settings. More specifically, they could develop and advocate equitable transition policies to replace the prevailing conservative social policy system, and they could experiment with innovative approaches to political action, practice, and teaching, designed to be consistent with the goals and values of liberating societal paradigms.

An important step in challenging the prevailing conservative mentality is to put on the political agenda a coherent set of social policies derived from values of social and economic justice, yet feasible within the legal framework of the established social order. Such policies are intended to eliminate unemployment, poverty, and related conditions, and to obviate thus existing, demeaning welfare programs, rather than merely "reform" them. The elimination of unemployment and poverty are feasible, first-aid measures, attainable even before overcoming their sources in capitalist dynamics.

The policies suggested below are based on an economic and political analysis which rejects many assumptions of neo-classical economics, including the notion of fiscal constraints with respect to human needs. Assumptions implicit in these policies are that the real wealth of a society, as differentiated from symbolic wealth, i.e., money, consists of the physical, intellectual, and emotional capacities of all its members, the aggregate of natural resources, and the aggregate of human generated material products, knowledge, and technology; that these "factors of wealth and well-being" be used and allocated rationally, so as to meet the needs of the entire population, rather than the profit interests of dominant individuals and classes; that these factors of wealth and well-being be developed and preserved wisely, rather than wasted; and finally, that decisions concerning the use and investment of societal resources be made democratically rather than by economic elites.

Here are a set of policies suggested for a transition program.

(a) Constitutional guarantees of employment suited to individual capacities and compensated at wage levels corresponding, at least, to the actual cost of a decent standard of living. Full employment can be achieved through adjusting the legal length of the workday or workweek in order to match the number of positions in the economy to the number of individuals requiring work, or by publicly sponsoring projects designed to meet human needs not filled by private enterprise (e.g., housing, highways and bridges, hospitals, schools, parks, etc.)

(b) Constitutional guarantees of adequate income, out of tax revenues, for people unable to work due to age, illness, and handicapping conditions. Income guarantees can be implemented through universal systems of children's allowances, retirement pensions, and sickness and disability benefits, and paid at levels corresponding to the actual costs of a decent standard of living.

(c) Legal redefinition of the care of one's children and of disabled relatives in the home as socially necessary work; inclusion of such work in the G.N.P., and payment of adequate wages out of federal revenues to individuals engaging in this type of work rather than working outside their homes.

(d) Federally financed high-quality, public child care as an option for parents.

(e) Paid parental leave of 12 weeks; paid annual leave of 4 weeks; and eventually a universal system of paid sabbatical leave.

(f) Federally financed, preventive and curative health care, administered in a decentralized manner.

(g) Federally financed, life-long education, administered in a de centralized manner.

(h) Federally financed construction and maintenance of housing stock, infrastructure, and public transportation within and between cities and towns, administered in a decentralized manner.

(i) Federally financed environmental protection and conservation programs.

(j) Comprehensive tax reform to assure adequate financing, without requiring government borrowing, for the policies listed above. Tax-reform should establish a tax-exempt basic income corresponding to the actual cost of living. Income beyond this level, regardless of source, would be subject to progressive taxation.

(k) Elimination of existing, stigmatizing welfare programs, AFDC, SSI, food stamps, Medicaid, etc., and phasing out of the regressive social security system.

(i) Moratorium on interest payments on the public debt.

Implicit in this policy agenda is an unequivocal rejection of the notion that the people of the United States cannot afford the programs to be authorized under these policies. Contrary to widely taken-for-granted assumptions, these programs do not involve real economic cost, but only political costs. Rather, they are likely to revitalize economic activity and human resources, and to enrich the quality of life and human relations. They involve full use and development of available productive and creative human capacities, and reallocation of existing factors of wealth and well-being. They also imply equitable redistribution of rights to use available resources and wealth.

Implementation of the proposed transition policies would make possible further stages of social and economic development which are unrealizable under present conditions. Full employment and elimination of poverty would reduce the dynamics of individual and intergroup competition, and would thus remove economic sources of discrimination by race, sex, age and other factors. Once economic sources of discrimination are overcome, it should be possible to deal with its psychological and social dimensions.

Next, it will be possible to focus on reorganizing and redesigning work in order to minimize stress and alienation and overcome obstacles to individual development inherent in the present mode of work and production. And, it will also be possible to focus on transforming the quality of goods and services in order to eliminate built-in obsolescence and waste of resources and to assure long-term use of high-quality products.

The foregoing changes would be conducive to a global justice focus which necessitates voluntary reductions of resource use by "over-developed," countries to fair levels in terms of population size, and cooperative, nonexploitative economic relations between developed and developing countries. Fairness and justice in economic relations among the regions and countries of the world are preconditions for real peace. In turn, elimination of economic sources of wars should make possible signficant reductions of massive, irrational and wasteful investments of resources for "defense," thus freeing these resources for programs focused on the real needs of people.

Implementation of a nonconservative policy agenda requires readiness to reintroduce the notion of social and economic planning to the public agenda. Planning for people's needs through democratic processes would have to become a public priority, replacing the prevailing laissez-faire ideology, since fulfillment of human needs cannot be left to selfish interactions of profit-motivated actors in the market place. History has proved convincingly, that reliance on automatic, self-regulation by the "invisible hand" to promote the public good, is a hopeless fallacy.

SOCIAL CHANGE-ORIENTED POLITICS

Working toward a just society requires a style of politics compatible with the goals and values of such a society, rather than with those of prevailing unjust social orders. This means that pragmatic interest-group politics concerned with short-range solutions for separate policy issues and with winning limited concessions which do not challenge the status quo of power and privilege would have to be replaced with principled, nonmanipulative politics aimed at promoting critical consciousness and redefinitions of interests, and at organizing social movements committed to long-range efforts toward social and economic justice. Realpolitik, the dominant mode of conventional politics, and the assumptions underlying it, are shaped by the dynamics and mentality of the established way of life and tend, therefore, to reproduce it more or less intact. This approach can achieve incremental changes which may ameliorate suffering and problems. Such gains are meaningful as first-aid measures, but they are unlikely to add up to fundamental social changes.

Electoral politics in the United States and in many capitalist democracies are usually not conducive to alternative approaches to politics. Electoral politics are geared primarily to winning by manipulating the voting of ill-informed electorates. This involves dichotomizing issues into over-simplified alternatives, reinforcing unexamined assumptions and stereotypes, and generating distorting images through media-technologies. Fundamental social change which requires profound transformations of consciousness and actions, is therefore unlikely to be accomplished through electoral politics. In spite of these dynamics and limitations, the arena of electoral politics should not be abandoned by social change activists. Rather, participation in this arena seems necessary for the following reasons, provided such participation is free from illusions concerning the social change potential of elections:

(a) damage control or containment and reduction of the degree of destructive consequences of conservative politics for exploited and oppressed classes;

(b) protection of civil and political rights by resisting tendencies to inhibit expression of system-challenging political positions, and to repress social movements promoting fundamental social change;

(c) Using the electoral arena for political education by presenting critiques of capitalist democracy and its fallacious assumptions, and visions of feasible, alternative social orders based on social and economic justice, and doing this in an open, honest, nonmanipulative dialogical manner.

From a social change perspective, electoral politics seem thus suited mainly for defense against severe exploitation, oppression, and repression, but less suited to advancing long-range social change goals. Those goals require strategies that reach beyond the electoral arena. Under present conditions in the United States, these strategies should include the following components:

(a) promoting critical consciousness through communications and interactions in everyday life, in places of work and education, and in social situations;

(b) building networks of liberation movements, starting through organizing on local levels and linking up with similar efforts elsewhere, within and beyond national boundaries;

(c) organizing active, nonviolent resistance to, and nonparticipation in, unjust practices and institutions;

(d) developing horizontally linked and coordinated networks of voluntary, egalitarian-cooperative-democratic institutions for production, exchange, and consumption of goods and services in available spaces within, or parallel to, existing institutions and organizations.

Should conditions become more repressive, strategies may have to be modified, since every social situation requires different approaches toward social transformation.

SOCIAL CHANGE-ORIENTED PRACTICE

To overcome conservative tendencies in practice and to function as agents for fundamental social change, practitioners require different theoretical frameworks from those now dominant, as well as attitudes of experimentation and critical consciousness toward their practice experience. They also need to help one another to study and evaluate evolving alternative approaches to practice, and to deal with resistance from administrators and supervisors in organizations practicing along conventional, status quo reinforcing lines. An effective means for such help are support groups of practitioners from different organizations who feel isolated and alienated in their respective places of work.

The following are suggested as elements of a framework for social change-oriented practice:

(a) Human problems with which social welfare practice deals are usually rooted in societal institutions and values, rather than in people's attributes and shortcomings. Resolution and prevention of these problems require therefore, not merely individual adjustments, but transformations of established societal patterns in ways conducive to fulfillment of human needs and to individual and social development for all.

(b) People, through their interactions, shape and maintain societal institutions and values. Hence, they are also able to transform established institutions and values through collective action, and to adjust them in ways compatible with their needs and with requirements of healthy development.

(c) Practice cannot be politically neutral. It always involves explicit or implicit political dimensions; it either confronts and challenges established societal institutions or it conforms to them openly or tacitly. Practitioners should avoid the illusion of neutrality and should consciously choose and acknowledge their political philosophy.

(d) Practice can also not be value-neutral; it either reflects or rejects the dominant values of the established social order. Social change-oriented practice should reflect values opposed to those underlying the status quo: equality, cooperation, freedom from domination and exploitation, and affirmation of community.

(e) Practice should transcend technical-professional approaches, fragmented by fields, and concerned with relieving symptoms, reducing suffering, and facilitating adaptation and coping under prevailing social conditions. While these are valid and important short-range objectives, they are not sufficient to overcome problems which are essentially social, economic, and political. Furthermore, human problems are usually not isolated fragments which can be solved by specific technical fixes, but symptoms of a way of life which needs to be transformed so that the problems may be overcome and prevented.

(f) A major medium for social change-oriented practice is a dialogical process, which begins with a sensitive exploration of problems experienced and perceived by people and moves on to help them discover links between their problems and societal dynamics. The process should facilitate insights into people's capacities to shape and change societal institutions, and should help them to assert their worth, dignity, and rights. Finally, it should encourage and support people to work on solutions to their problems through involvement in collective action for necessary social change. The dialogical process must never involve indoctrination and manipulation: its aim is to facilitate the development of critical consciousness through a supportive, liberating, nonauthoritarian, sensitive relationship.

(g) Practice should involve advocacy to assure for people the rights and services available under prevailing conditions. However, the maximum available at present is unlikely to be just and adequate. Hence, advocacy should transcend demands for fulfillment of already existing rights, present demands for equal rights and responsibilities, and reject policies which are merely variations on the ancient theme of inequality.

(h) Practice should encourage development of everyone's innate capacities as the goal of just and free societies. It should unravel obstacles to such development in institutional and interpersonal violence—consequences of coercively established and maintained exploiting and alienating modes of work and exchange. And it should facilitate insights into the need for reorganizing and redesigning work as a condition for unobstructed human development.

(i) Practitioners should explore, individually and in support groups, whether, in prevailing social realities, they too are unable to actualize their innate potential; whether their individual development is also inhibited; and whether they too are victimized by exploiting and oppressive social and economic dynamics, though in different forms and to a lesser extent than the people they serve. They may realize through such explorations that they too have a personal stake in human liberation and equality, and that they should cease to identify with dominant classes and their agencies and policies, and should instead identify with, and join the struggles and movements of oppressed people. They may also conclude that they should transcend divisions between themselves and the people they serve, divisions reflective of conservative concepts of professionalism, according to which education and professional skills entitle people to privilege, higher status and authority.

(j) As far as possible, social change-oriented practitioners should aim to transform the style and quality of practice-relations and of administration from vertical, authoritarian, inegalitarian toward horizontal, democratic, egalitarian patterns. Every space over which practitioners have influence should be so transformed to reflect alternative possible human relations. In this way, counter-realities or prefigurations of future possibilities can be imagined and experimented with within existing human services settings, by and for the providers and users of the services. Unions and support groups of workers and service users could incorporate such prefigurations. Undoubtedly, such experiments are difficult. They do involve risks, resistance and conflicts since they test and strain the limits of what is possible within the prevailing social order. Such testing and straining of limits are, however, necessary elements of liberation processes.

(k) Finally, social change-oriented practitioners should initiate dialogues with colleagues concerning practice and work place issues, in order to spread critical consciousness concerning these matters. They should also try to organize unions, support groups, and units of social movements at places of work, and they should participate in social and political action.

SOCIAL CHANGE-ORIENTED EDUCATION

Universities, and especially professional schools, tend to prepare students for "successful" adaptation to established ways of life and for assumption of appropriate roles and positions, rather than for critical consciousness concerning societal dynamics and their consequences.

Because of these conservative tendencies of schools, teachers pursuing a social-change perspective through education are often isolated and may encounter resistance from colleagues and administrators. Philosophically, these teachers inhabit a different universe of discourse than most of their colleagues, and they have to link up with similarly oriented teachers and practitioners from other schools and work places to develop mutually supportive and affirming relationships and help one another to develop and evaluate their educational practice.

Style and substance of social-change oriented teaching are discussed below separately. It should be noted, however, that these are but two related dimensions of a unified process. For style is also substance: it either complements and reflects social change-oriented substance, or it contradicts it.

Education can be a liberating experience when students are expected to be responsible for, and self-directing in, their studies, and when teachers serve as advisors, facilitators, resources, and nonauthoritarian assistants. This does not mean abandoning responsibility, initiative and leadership by teachers. It does mean, however, clarity concerning the limits of responsibilities of students and teachers, and fulfillment of one's part of a shared undertaking.

Major aims of liberating education are development of critical consciousness concerning socially shaped realities, alleged facts, and personal opinions, and discovery of one's self as a potentially creative, productive, and self-directing subject in relation to community, society, and nature. Such critical consciousness and self-awareness tend to emerge within cooperative, nonhierarchical settings in which teachers act as colleagues in pursuit of knowledge rather than as "experts" and authorities. In such settings, learning can be mutual and dialogical rather than competitive and one-directional. Also, in such a context, learning goals, requirements, and evaluations can be worked out cooperatively by students and teachers.

Teachers should map and recommend domains for study, facilitate the dialogical learning process, suggest appropriate sources and projects, consult with students on individual learning goals, respond critically and constructively to student projects, and facilitate student evaluations of their own learning. Implicit in this teaching style is the assumption that education toward self-actualization in a just and democratic society of the future requires creation, in the present, of liberated spaces, i.e., counter-realities to domination and control, in which students can experience in the here and now of a classroom, prefigurations of self-direction and freedom.

The teaching style suggested here involves, however, dilemmas concerning the reactions of students to the absence of structures and controls and to the expectations that they assume responsibility for self-direction of their studies. For most students this is a new experience, different from previous schooling as well as from experiences in other classes in which they are concurrently enrolled. Reactions tend to range from uncertainty and helplessness to creative and enriching learning and personal growth. A constructive response to this is using reactions of students as opportunities for exploring the meanings, costs, and benefits of self-direction and freedom.

Other dilemmas result from conflicts with colleagues concerning the introduction of a radically different educational style and philosophy into a school. An appropriate focus for coping with this is everyone's commitment, in principle, to academic freedom. Experience suggests that being open about what one does, asserting one's right to teach in accordance with one's educational philosophy and values, while respecting different philosophies, styles, and values of colleagues, does eventually bring about a modus vivendi and a measure of mutual tolerance.

As to substance, the following social change-oriented curriculum has been derived from the practice framework suggested above. It reflects efforts to help students overcome misconceptions concerning societal realities which result from the hegemony of conservative ideology over all stages of education and consciousness formation:

(a) human nature, human needs, and the natural environment of human life: the human condition;
(b) requirements and dynamics of human development;
(c) natural and human-created obstacles to human development;

(d) sources, evolution, and dynamics of social life and of different cultures;
(e) consequences of variations in social institutions and ideologies, and in the organization of work, production, and exchange for human development and well-being;
(f) critical-historical analysis of social, economic, political, cultural, and ideological dimensions of life in the United States with special attention to race, gender, and social class dynamics;
(g) sources, evolution, and functions of value systems in social life;
(h) exploration of personal values and interests in relation to personal history, experiences and goals;
(i) social change-oriented practice in direct service to individuals and social units, service design and administration, analysis and development of social policy, and social and political action toward short- and long-range objectives;
(j) psychological insights for working sensitively and constructively with people of diverse backgrounds, in different situations, focused on different human concerns;
(k) critical approaches to social research, transcending empirical, descriptive, positivist approaches.

The study foci listed here are organized by issues rather than by academic disciplines. Studying these issues may require different combinations of sources and methods from social and natural sciences. The various sciences should be viewed and used as complementary perspectives on aspects of human life in nature and in society.

The social change-oriented curriculum suggested here involves dilemmas. It is obvious that there is more to study than students are able to in a conventional graduate program in social welfare which usually leaves little time for elective studies. The reason there is so much is that preparation for alternative practice does require an entire "alternative" curriculum, including studies of theoretical foundations and practice, as well as analysis and critique of conventional foundations, assumptions, and service approaches. There is no solution to this dilemma other than acknowledging it, introducing students to the many domains they ought to explore, and motivating them to continue the process of study and critical experimentation as an integral aspect of responsible practice throughout their lives. A related dilemma is that teachers may lack competence in some substantive domains to which students should be exposed. There, too, the solution is to acknowledge this reality and to guide students to appropriate study sources. Of course, teachers are also students, and they should, over time, broaden and deepen their own knowledge, experience, and competence.

EPILOGUE

I have argued throughout this essay that people can overcome conservative tendencies which now threaten human development on local and global scales. I have also suggested approaches through which social change-oriented practitioners and educators in social welfare can contribute to the struggle for human survival and liberation. The suggestions sketched here are tentative and incomplete, for the search for practice and teaching approaches consistent with an egalitarian-democratic philosophy is only in its early stages. This search has been going on for several years in the United States and elsewhere. Gradually, organizations and a literature have been emerging through which people are sharing and examining relevant experiences and ideas. Also, in many places, practitioners and teachers are meeting regularly to support one another and learn from one another, in order to advance the liberation process and to transcend firmly entrenched conservative tendencies. The more people will get involved in these efforts, the greater the likelihood that we will succeed, and that the human species will survive and actualize its rich potential.

13

Children and Work: Rights to Become Creative and Productive*

This essay reviews adverse consequences of contemporary modes of work, child rearing, and schooling for human development and the quality of life, and, more specifically, for the unfolding of the creative and productive capacities of children. It suggests that these consequences could be ameliorated, but not overcome at their roots, when the recently adopted *United Nations Convention on the Rights of the Child* enters into force. The essay also discusses changes in work and education conducive to human development, and indicates ways in which educators could advance such changes. The concluding section, "Emancipatory Pedagogy," derives implications from the preceding analysis for the practice of educators who intend to facilitate the unfolding of their students' innate capacities, in spite of institutional and cultural obstacles.

This article is concerned primarily with the rights of children to optimal development and to realization of their innate creativity and productivity, through satisfaction of their biological, social, and psychological needs, and through harmonious integration into the work life of their communities.[1] It addresses these issues, however, in the context of pursuing the same rights for all people, regardless of age. Doing so seems ethically valid because social justice should include everyone. It is also sound social policy, because the living conditions and rights of children, and their consciousness, aspirations, and motivation, are inextricably interwoven with the living conditions, consciousness, and rights of adults in their homes, communities, and society. Pursuing children's rights apart from the rights of all individuals and groups in society, as is often done, seems ethically questionable and politically counterproductive.

School Psychology Review, Vol. 20, No.3, 1991

UNIVERSAL ASPECTS OF WORK

In a biological and social sense, work may be defined as *activities geared toward individual and collective survival and development of people, fulfillment of their intrinsic and perceived needs, and enhancement of the quality of life.* From this perspective, activities which obstruct survival, development, and fulfillment of needs, and which depress the quality of life should be considered "counterwork," rather than work. The drive to sustain life and to enhance its quality by meeting biological, social, and psychological needs seems the motivating source of work; and work may be understood as a bridge between people's needs and means for meeting them. Based on this conception of work, a fitting criterion for, and measure of, the effectiveness and productivity of the mode of work of any society, at different times and places, would be the extent to which it meets people's needs and sustains and enhances their lives. [2]

Work requires systematic interactions among people (on local and trans-local levels) and between people and their environments. It involves the use of their mental, physical, and emotional capacities. When working, people combine these capacities with natural resources, with products of prior human work and with discoveries, inventions, knowledge, and skills evolved throughout history and transmitted between generations and different regions of the world. The effectiveness, efficiency, and productivity of different modes of work therefore depends on the extent to which the policies and values of particular societies facilitate

1. uninhibited development of people's innate capacities;
2. unobstructed access to and use of discoveries, inventions, knowledge, and skills, products of earlier work, and natural resources; and
3. use of the products of people's work, directly or indirectly (through fair exchange), toward meeting their needs and enhancing the quality of their lives.

Human work has biological sources and functions, but is always shaped, maintained, or transformed through social, political, and cultural processes; it is influenced by scientific and technological developments; and it has psychological, social, economic, and ecological dimensions and consequences. Changes in the social organization of work and in education for it, and in the terms of exchange and distribution of products of work, tend to result in corresponding changes in individual and social development; in the circumstances and quality of life of individuals, groups, and classes; in their relative social power; and in their relations to one another. It follows that desired changes in the circumstances and quality of people's lives, their power, relations, and development can be attained only by way of appropriate changes in work and education for it, and in the terms of exchange and distribution of products of work.[3]

CONTEMPORARY MODES OF WORK

Contemporary modes of work, in many societies all over the world, appear to have many adverse consequences for people in general, and more specifically for the development of children in homes, schools, workplaces, and communities. They are, nevertheless, widely regarded as effective, efficient, and productive in terms of conventional economic and political criteria and measures. Consequently, they tend to be taken for granted, and their assumptions and basic principles are only rarely questioned.[4]

Prevailing modes of work have evolved over thousands of years, mainly following the discovery and spread of agriculture. Their development accelerated significantly during the 19th and 20th centuries, following the industrial, cybernetic, and "high-tech" revolutions. The emergence and maintenance of these modes of work involved, and continues to involve, overt and covert coercion and violence, social domination and economic exploitation, and little real freedom and democracy.

Perhaps the most dehumanizing aspect of established modes of work is that workers tend to be perceived and treated as means to the ends of employers, or in the revealing jargon of conventional economics, as "hired hands" and "factors of production," rather than as free, self-directing individuals and "masters of production." Related, destructive aspects of these modes of work are the nearly total separation of mental from physical dimensions of production, of design and management functions from actual production tasks, and the fragmentation of production processes into meaningless routines.[5] As a result, most workers make little use of their mental faculties and creative capacities at work, and these faculties and capacities tend to atrophy from non-use. Moreover, since everyday life, child care, and socialization in homes, schools, and neighborhoods are influenced by the realities and requirements of adult work life, many children tend to lose motivation to develop their innate intellectual and creative capacities long before they enter the world of work.

The fragmentation and divisions of work, and matching practices of socialization, tend to result in pervasive underdevelopment of innate human capacities.[6] These aspects of work and socialization fit, however, into the internal logic of social orders divided into dominant, propertied minorities and dominated, expropriated majorities. In such divided societies, most people do not have rights of access to, and use of productive resources in accordance with their needs, as these resources are controlled by propertied and managerial classes and used by them in accordance with their perceived interests. Propertyless people are not able to work at their own initiative and direction, nor in their own interests, but only in the interests and under the direction of owners and/or managers of productive resources. Under such conditions, work and production are not designed to meet the real needs of all people, but primarily to maximize material gains of those who own and control productive resources. Fragmentation and divisions of work seem compatible with exploitation and profit-maximizing dynamics, because they supposedly enhance efficiency of production. Moreover, they lower the wages of workers (and the income and standard of living of their families) as a result of reductions in skill levels and in the time and cost of preparation for work.

Wages of workers tend to decline, and profits tend to increase accordingly, when the numbers of workers seeking work exceeds significantly the number of positions to be filled. Profit-motivated entrepreneurs tend, therefore, to favor policies which cause an oversupply of workers relative to available positions. For workers and their families, such policies involve the threat, and the frequent reality, of temporary or even permanent underemployment, unemployment, and poverty. Scarcity of employment, especially with respect to fulfilling jobs, tends to result in competition among individual workers and different groups in society, for entry into the work force and for promotions within workplaces. Competition inhibits unity among working people and is a major source of discrimination by race, ethnicity, religion, sex, sexual orientation, age, and physical conditions. Discriminatory practices have acquired seemingly independent dynamics in the course of human history, and their source in economic competition is often disregarded. However, they are unlikely to be overcome as long as workers are dependent on propertied and managerial classes for their livelihood, can be dismissed at the discretion and in the interest of employers, and are not assured unconditional rights to participate in socially meaningful and economically rewarding work.

The competitive dynamics and the exploitative economic relations of contemporary modes of work on local, national, and global levels result in relatively stable, interrelated, and mutually reinforcing systems of social, economic, and occupational classes. These class structures did not evolve voluntarily, but have been forced upon people and entire nations by economic, social, political, and cultural-ideological realities. To escape class dynamics is difficult at any age, but especially during childhood, when one interacts intensely with the realities of one's class at home and in schools, in workplaces and at worship, in neighborhoods and in the mass media; and when one's capacity for critical consciousness has not matured sufficiently to question the realities of everyday life. Hence, most children, like the adults around them, end up trapped in their class positions and share a sense of powerlessness in confronting these constraining aspects of their existence.

The class structures of everyday life are reproduced primarily by the reality of established, "legitimate" controls over productive resources and places of work, as well as by the public consciousness, values, and ideology reflective of these institutional realities. These realities and corresponding public consciousness exert a strong influence on the consciousness and behavior of most individuals and groups, causing them to conform to the signals of class dynamics. Hence, people tend to persist in efforts to "defend their turf," and to hold on to and enhance their positions on the slippery slopes of social, economic, and occupational pyramids.

The realities of class dynamics are unlikely to change significantly unless its victims can overcome their multiple divisions and act cooperatively to transform their consciousness and the social, economic, and political institutions of established ways of life. Such organizing is difficult for objective and subjective reasons. It has usually encountered overt and covert resistance from dominant classes in divided societies, and from governments beholden to them, as well as from segments of "middle classes" and dominated classes who identify with the perceptions and interests of dominant classes in hopes of being able to achieve privileged positions and conditions.

The class dynamics of societies permeate most workplaces by means of hierarchical occupational and authority structures, and bureaucratic domination and controls. [7] As a result, human relations and experiences at work are often unfulfilling, dehumanizing, and alienating; and people's development and health are adversely affected. The frustrating quality of work life is often reflected in physical, emotional, and social ills, and in destructive and self-destructive behaviors in workplaces, communities, and homes. Destructive and self-destructive behaviors such as domestic violence, alcoholism, drug addiction, mental illness, suicide, and crime are usually not traced to their likely sources in the social dynamics of work life, but tend to be interpreted as personal shortcomings of individual workers. [8]

Prevailing patterns of exchange and distribution of the aggregate global product leave about one-third of the world's five billion people in severe poverty, while a mere one-fifth of humankind, mainly in industrialized countries, absorb consistently about four-fifths of global resources, goods, and services. As a result, hunger, homelessness, ill health, lack of education, and underdevelopment are widespread, not only in developing countries, but also among poverty-stricken segments of as wealthy and technically developed a country as the United States. Clearly, contemporary modes of work and distribution fail to use natural and human-created resources effectively and efficiently to assure the development and well-being of the human species. These destructive consequences are, however, not due to objective scarcities of resources, knowledge, and technology. Rather, they are inevitable results of waste and inappropriate allocations of these resources—intrinsic tendencies of competitive, profit-driven modes of work, exchange, and distribution all over the globe. [9]

CONTEMPORARY MODES OF WORK AND EDUCATION

Throughout history, the mission of education has been not only to facilitate development of children, but also to assure the continuity of established ways of life and work, along with their caste and class systems. This latter, frequently overlooked, and even denied mission requires that successive generations of children be socialized to fit into the positions they will have to fill as adults. Accordingly, educational settings and processes tend to be shaped by the realities and dynamics of work life. [10]

The individual and societal dimensions and mission of education are incompatible when societies are divided internally into social, economic, and occupational classes. In accordance with the attributes of contemporary modes of work, a majority of high school "graduates" and/ or "dropouts" must be ready and willing to fill positions which involve thoughtless and uncritical subordination to authority, along with a sense of inadequacy and powerlessness. Since most children are born endowed richly with capacities for critical thinking, creativity, and self-direction, these innate capacities must be stunted in the course of formal and informal socialization in order to bring about an approximate fit between people's attitudes and attributes and the types of work they will be hired to do. Somehow, child rearing and education in homes, neighborhoods, and schools accomplish this sad and oppressive result, although many parents and teachers are deeply committed to promoting the optimum development of individual children. What seems to undermine the conscious efforts of parents and teachers are subtle influences and messages emanating from the realities and dynamics of prevailing ways of life and work which children encounter since birth. For many children, these encounters result in hopelessness, lack of ambition and aspirations, and, eventually, loss of motivation. Once motivation for development and creativity are lost, efforts of parents and teachers may be doomed to fail, and children's growth energy will be blocked and transformed into destructive energy, and be reflected in destructive and self-destructive attitudes and behaviors.

In preparing children for adult roles in the established work system, schools contribute to the underdevelopment of large segments of the population. Work experiences during adolescence also are usually destructive. Most workplaces which hire youths tend to exploit them economically in largely meaningless jobs. Employers are no more concerned with the development and education of young workers than they are with the development and well-being of adult employees. Also, workplaces are usually worlds apart from schools and homes, and they reinforce through their dynamics the destructive influences and messages concerning the realities of work life which people absorb throughout childhood and adolescence.

CONVENTION ON THE RIGHTS OF THE CHILD: OPPORTUNITIES AND LIMITATIONS

Adoption of the *Convention on the Rights of the Child* by the United Nations in 1989 was an important symbolic event. *The Convention* promulgates standards and goals for equal rights of all children to life, liberty, dignity, and personal and cultural identity; to optimum development, health, education, care, and protection; to social and economic security; to freedom from exploitation, abuse, and neglect; and to civil and political rights. It also affirms the rights of parents with respect to children, and of children with respect to parents, in the context of the "best interest of the child." *The Convention* obligates states, who become parties to it, to provide all children opportunities to exercise these rights. Finally, the *Convention* acknowledges the role of international cooperation with regard to economic, social, and cultural rights.

Conditions for comprehensive development of children everywhere would improve significantly, and their creativity and productivity would no longer be stunted, were the United Nations Convention on the Rights of the Child implemented. However, implementation of this convention beyond token efforts is unlikely in the foreseeable future, since global economic and political dynamics and underlying modes of work, exchange, and distribution contradict the values and goals of United Nations human rights declarations and conventions, including the one on the rights of children. Well-intentioned, humane rhetoric notwithstanding, the actual policies and practices of the United Nations will continue to reflect global economic and political realities, rather than principles of liberty, equality, and solidarity.

The United Nations is not a parliament of free and equal citizens of the world, but an organization of nation-states who differ in size, wealth, and power. Since its founding at the end of World War II, it has validated and legitimated by implication the status quo of economic and political inequalities among its member nations and the regions of the globe. Neither the Charter of the United Nations nor its declarations and conventions on human rights question or challenge the established global order of massive inequalities of wealth and power within and between nations. These inequalities are the results of violent conquests, genocide, enslavement, domination, and economic exploitation throughout history, and they continue to be reflected in contemporary exploitative economic relations on local, national, and international scales.

The plight of children everywhere, but especially in poor and powerless developing countries, is an inevitable consequence of past and ongoing processes of political domination and economic exploitation. This plight could be reduced and ameliorated by efforts to implement the *Convention on the Rights of the Child,* but cannot be eliminated and prevented because the Convention *fails to identify sources of the destructive conditions of the world's children in prevailing economic and political inequalities within and among member states of the United Nations, and in prevailing modes of work, exchange, and distribution which inevitably reproduce these inequalities; and fails to insist on transforming contemporary, exploitative modes of work, exchange, and distribution into alternatives, conducive to optimum human development, everywhere.* It is simply not enough to assert the rights of children. To realize these rights, it seems necessary to confront and overcome the fact that the world order is inherently exploitative, and that many countries who are obligated by the Convention to assure children freedom from exploitation along with other fundamental rights are themselves agents and beneficiaries of historical and contemporary processes and relationships involving massive economic exploitation.

TOWARD MODES OF WORK CONDUCIVE TO OPTIMUM HUMAN DEVELOPMENT

Children, work, and education cannot be discussed effectively without reference to the political, economic, and cultural context, and to the social values which permeate that context. It seems impossible to overcome existing, massive underdevelopment of children and adults, and to change schools and the ways in which children are prepared for adulthood and work, *unless established modes of work, exchange, and distribution are thoroughly democratized and oriented toward meeting the real human needs of people everywhere.* These necessary changes are not mere technical and professional issues, but deeply philosophical and political ones. They cannot be accomplished speedily by way of quick fixes, but require extended, nonviolent, political, and educational processes, involving thorough transformations of consciousness and the emergence of new perceptions of individual and collective interests.

Transition from prevailing development-inhibiting, global modes of work, exchange, and distribution toward development-conducive democratic alternatives seems to require conceptual redefinitions and corresponding structural reorganization and redesign of work and education.[11] Elements of such transformations are sketched below.

Conceptual redefinition would involve a shift from a purely economic concept of work, which refers mainly to profit-motivated-and-linked activities, undertaken by people in control of productive resources with little regard for consequences for workers, their families, communities, society, and the natural environment, toward a humane concept of work, which integrates biological, social, psychological, political, economic, and ecological dimensions. According to such a concept, work would mean activities concerned with survival and development of people by meeting needs and enhancing the quality of life, with due regard for the needs of people everywhere, and in harmony with the natural environment. Also, workers would be considered "masters" of production, rather than "factors" to be used and abused, and hired and fired, in the interest of employers.

Structural reorganization of work in line with the above definition would require transfer of control over natural and human-evolved productive resources from propertied and managerial elites to democratically administered "public trusts," for use by all people, on equal terms, and in harmony with nature. This shift in control over resources would gradually equalize social power and eliminate economic exploitation. Knowledge and skills would be accessible to all through schools, universities, libraries, and occupational practice centers, and all people could claim materials, energy, and tools from the public trust for work they did, either by themselves or in cooperation with others. Everyone would have *rights and responsibilities to work.* Unemployment and underemployment and the economic sources of discrimination would thus be eliminated. The work people would do would be related to their capacities, physical and mental conditions, and other attributes. Along with rights and responsibilities to work, people would also be entitled to fair shares of goods and services in accordance with their needs, which also vary among individuals and over time.

Decisions concerning the types and qualities of goods and services to be produced and production priorities would be made democratically on local and trans-local levels with due regard for the needs of people all over the world. Related to production decisions and to considerations of needs of people elsewhere are the terms of exchange or trade. Guiding principles for trade should be that all the world's people should have equal rights to meet their needs out of the aggregate of global resources and products, and that exchanges of goods and services among producers in different locations ought to be balanced, with each party contributing about as much energy and materials as they receive.

Further guiding principles should be that goods should be produced for long-term use, should be of high quality, and should be made of renewable rather than nonrenewable, raw materials. The purpose of these provisions is to minimize waste and to conserve resources.

Another essential structural change would be the phasing out of social, economic, and occupational class systems. To accomplish this, preparation for and entry into an occupation would have to be open to everyone on equal terms. Also, all work and all workers would have to be accorded equal social recognition and dignity, as well as equal economic rights to share in the aggregate of goods and services throughout life in accordance with individual needs.

A further structural change related to the elimination of class systems concerns the manner in which people would enter, and change positions in, the work system: they should be entitled to freely choose their work. Should voluntary self-assignment fail to fill all essential positions, vacant positions should be filled by rotating them among all people, for a limited time, similar to the principles of assignment to jury duty.

Redesigning of work would involve the transformation of meaningless, fragmented, and alienating activities into their opposites, so as to be conducive to human development. Work can be meaningful and humane when workers use their intellectual, physical, and emotional capacities in an integrated manner, when they are involved in choosing and designing their products and in managing production; when they comprehend the products, the materials and the tools; when production is in harmony with the environment, and when the products are something to be proud of, something of meaning to people and communities; and when there is a connection between work efforts and the well-being of workers and their families. It seems possible to redesign many production processes along these lines when mass production of low-quality, short-lived goods is transformed into production of high-quality, durable goods. Once work is thus redesigned, people would be more likely to chose voluntarily a much wider range of occupations, and fewer tasks would have to be assigned by rotation.[12]

Redesign of work would also involve reductions and refocusing of the use of automation. Automation would be applied mainly to production which cannot be redesigned in meaningful ways, and which is inherently unpleasant, unhealthy, and dangerous. Production which can be made more meaningful with less automation should be redesigned accordingly. This would also reduce energy use to sustainable levels and would increase opportunities for people to participate in production by shifting from energy-and-capital-intensive processes to worker-intensive alternatives.

IMPLICATIONS FOR EDUCATION AND SOCIAL ACTION

The creative and productive potential of children is a rich resource for humankind. Yet, the ways of life in different societies have obstructed the unfolding and realization of this potential. As a result, widespread underdevelopment of individuals and societies seems now to threaten human survival and life on earth.

The elements of alternative modes of work sketched above might overcome systemic obstructions of children's creativity and productivity. They are not a definitive blueprint, however, but a contribution to a necessary public discourse and search for paradigmatic shifts, without which humankind seems unable to extricate itself from its present destructive course. A sine qua non of such shifts are modes of work which would assure meaningful options for everyone to build a fulfilling life in community with others. For only such modes of work can rekindle hope, aspiration, and motivation, and can channel innate developmental energies into constructive directions.

Such alternative modes of work would gradually induce transformations of prevailing, development-inhibiting processes of socialization, once the message and consequences of meaningful work begin to permeate homes, schools, communities, and society. Work would cease to be regarded as a separate, necessary, yet dehumanizing domain, when it is experienced as a life-enhancing, integral dimension of other existential domains. Children would be expected and encouraged to work alongside adults, to unfold and discover their creative and productive capacities as an important, harmonious aspect of their education and preparation for adulthood. They would not have to be legally excluded and protected from work once work would no longer be a medium of exploitation. Adults could become lifelong students to sustain their creativity and enhance their productivity. People would reap the fruits of their work directly or through fair and nonexploitative exchanges. Unemployment, poverty, ignorance, and preventable disease would be gradually eliminated and would be remembered as inevitable symptoms of past paradigms of social life rather than as inherent aspects of human existence.

These ideas may be regarded as "utopian," as they imply fundamental changes in taken-for-granted patterns of social life. Yet, today's actual utopia may not be visions of life-enhancing changes, but the illusion that the future of humankind can be assured by continuing along courses suggested by conventional wisdom. The unspeakable plight of children and people everywhere demonstrates the fallacy of this latter position. It follows that we ought to pursue social, economic, political, and value transformations, even though they may seem "utopian." Mere technical modifications within the existing social, economic, political, and value paradigm seem hopelessly inadequate to realize the goals of the *United Nations Convention on the Rights of the Child*. Rather, implementing these goals and overcoming the prevailing tragic conditions of children and people requires nonviolent social movements committed to the transformation of today's utopian visions into tomorrow's social realities.

EMANCIPATORY PEDAGOGY

It seems appropriate to conclude this discussion by shifting the focus from the macro-social, global level to the everyday reality of practice of individual educators.

Teachers could contribute to movements for human liberation and transformation of work by facilitating critical consciousness, optimum development, and creativity of children. Respected educators and philosophers from Socrates in ancient times to Paulo Freire in our time have pursued these goals and have urged others to do likewise.[13] However, many teachers who realize the necessity of paradigmatic social transformations may feel overwhelmed and powerless in view of the enormity of this task. They may conclude that whatever they did in schools and how they related to students and others was of little consequence in terms of macro-social changes. Such a defeatist perspective inhibits a social change-oriented pedagogy and reinforces, by implication, conventional educational approaches.

Moreover, history seems to refute the notion that actions by individuals are inconsequential for social change. Major social transformations have been initiated by persistent efforts of committed individuals who persuaded others to join their cause. Christianity spread through the missionary zeal of 12 men recruited by Christ. Capitalism emerged in the Middle Ages from efforts of merchants and artisans bent on transcending the constraints of feudalism and absolute royal power. The modern women's movement originated in small "consciousness-raising" groups which enabled individuals to examine and challenge male-dominated social institutions. One black woman's insistence to sit in the front of a bus became an important stimulus for a social movement struggling for rights for black and other oppressed minorities. These illustrations reveal the crucial role individuals and small groups can play in promoting critical consciousness and personal commitment to a cause — essential aspects of effective movements for social change. Social change-committed educators need not feel powerless. Fundamental social change is not a brief, dramatic event, but a lengthy process. It requires changes in consciousness, values, perceptions of interests, and motivation for action by many people. Education seems, therefore, an appropriate medium for promoting social transformations, but individual educators should not expect quick results. They should pursue social change goals, regardless of uncertainties. This is admittedly difficult and requires trust in one's social and educational philosophy. History, incidentally, reveals that shortcuts toward fundamental social change, involving authoritarian coercion rather than democratic education, result in destructive outcomes, as demonstrated by violent revolutions during this and earlier centuries.

While conventional schooling prepares students, experientially and cognitively, to fit into established ways of life and work, emancipatory pedagogy aims to prepare them, through an alternative style and substance, to transcend and transform the status quo of social life and work. Accordingly, liberation-oriented educators help students (in ways geared to different developmental stages) to think critically about the prevailing "socially constructed reality," which most people, including most teachers, take for granted as inevitable and unchangeable. They especially help them explore dehumanizing, oppressive, and exploitative social dynamics and values beneath the "law-and-order" surface of current ways of life and work, and their internal, "common-sense" logic.

These explorations should reveal social evolution, from local to global levels, as the emerging product of human actions, choices, thoughts, and relations. Students would thus realize that people can become masters of their lives, and that by acting together, they can reconstruct their world and make it compatible with their " . . . inalienable rights . . . to life, liberty, and the pursuit of happiness . . ." This is, of course, the essential message of the 1776 Declaration of Independence that emancipatory pedagogy is meant to resurrect.

To advance the cause of human liberation, educators would have to yield responsibility for learning to students and would have to redefine their own roles and responsibilities as facilitators, assistants, and resources, rather than as experts who dispense and allocate knowledge and skills, and make sure students absorb what teachers dispense in the prescribed manner. This does not mean abandoning responsibility, initiative, and leadership by teachers. It merely means clarity concerning the respective responsibilities of students and teachers, and fulfillment of the teacher's appropriate part in a shared undertaking.

The inherent developmental energies of students and their natural curiosity and motivation—the really effective media for study—tend to be realized spontaneously when educators refrain consistently from using coercion and manipulative techniques. Admittedly, many students come now to schools damaged in capacities and motivation as a result of growing up under dehumanizing, development-inhibiting and coercive conditions. However, such students require especially sensitive assistance to overcome prior educational harm and deficits, rather than punitive coercion and "conditioning."

"The medium is the message" in emancipatory pedagogy, and style, milieu, and context become substance. The teacher-student relationship ought to prefigure caring, nonhierarchical, egalitarian-democratic patterns of human relations of future ways of life and work free from coercion, domination, and exploitation. Individual classrooms and eventually entire schools ought to become "liberated spaces" in the midst of a conventional world, where students can experience and explore the meaning and consequences of self-directed work and study in cooperation and community with self-directing peers.

Teachers should, however, anticipate ambivalent reactions from students to the absence of structures and controls, and to the expectation that they assume responsibility for self-direction of their studies. For most students, a noncoercive context is a new experience, different from previous schooling and their upbringing at home, as well as from experiences in other classes in which they may be enrolled. Reactions may vary from frustration, uncertainty, and helplessness, to constructive and enriching learning and growth. Once teachers overcome their own fears and pursue the emancipatory approach consistently, students' responses tend to be constructive. A helpful way to handle this dilemma is to use expected and actual reactions of students as opportunities for learning about the meanings, costs, and benefits of self-direction and freedom, by facilitating open discussion about reactions and feelings aroused by this educational style.

Teachers can facilitate an emancipatory education milieu by developing a searching dialogue focused on issues relevant to the life, development, and learning of students. Dialogue must, of course, never deteriorate into indoctrination. Its aims include helping students discover and affirm their worth, dignity, capacities, and possibilities, and their rights and responsibilities as members of communities and of the global human family. Dialogue should also enhance critical consciousness through supportive, nonauthoritarian and caring interaction among students and teachers.

Studying is an important dimension of all creative and productive work. Moreover, studying *is* work as this term has been used in this discussion. The transformation of studying into self-directed work should prepare and empower students for taking part in the liberation and transformation of all work into creative, integrated processes, managed democratically by workers knowledgeable about the nature of their products and the design and processes of production.

Emancipatory pedagogy should aim also to overcome conventional, destructive, and dehumanizing divisions and fragmentations of work into mental and physical labor, and along gender, race, and social class dimensions. Students and teachers should engage not only in intellectual, abstract pursuits, but also in concrete, humanized production projects in their communities when such projects can be organized, as well as in student-designed, individual, and cooperative work projects in schools. In this way, students and teachers can experience and study innovative modes of integrated, productive, and creative, democratized work, while making valuable economic contributions to their communities.

Pursuing emancipatory pedagogy within conventional schools involves inevitable dilemmas and conflicts because such pedagogy derives from social values, political goals, assumptions, and principles at odds with the "common sense" view of the world reflected in established ways of life, work and schools, and in the consciousness of most teachers. Educators pursuing emancipatory pedagogy currently are a minority, and they may encounter resistance from colleagues, administrators, school boards, and parents, in spite of public commitments to "academic freedom."

In dealing with such conflicts, it is important to be open about one's educational philosophy, values, goals, and assumptions, and to convey understanding and respect for the different philosophies, styles, and values of colleagues. One should avoid turning differences in educational philosophies into personal animosity, while asserting the right to teach in accordance with one's conscience and consciousness. Such an approach tends to bring about a measure of mutual tolerance, especially when students respond favorably to alternative ways of teaching, and progress in their studies.

Despite efforts to deal constructively with ideological conflicts in conventional schools, individuals pursuing the cause of liberation through educational practice may often feel lonely. One potentially effective way for dealing with this is to organize support groups for social change-oriented educators from different schools, and networks of such groups from different localities. The purpose of these groups and networks is to create mutually supportive, democratic milieus and relationships for educators who are isolated in conventional schools; to engage in cooperative study of the theory and practice of emancipatory pedagogy; and to help individual teachers to deal constructively with ideological and personal conflicts in their respective schools. Support groups could also link the educational practice of their members with the liberation struggles of social and political movements from local to global levels.

Emancipatory pedagogy could make important contributions to nonviolent struggles toward real democracy and social justice, in spite of the status quo maintaining mission of conventional schools. But more teachers must become involved in alternative educational practice. The vicious circle of dehumanizing work and development-stunting schools can be challenged and reversed at any point—in workplaces, schools, homes, and public life. Educators have opportunities to interfere with this circle in their schools, and the more teachers can be recruited to seize these opportunities, the greater the chance for meaningfully social change and for the eventual liberation of the creativity and productivity of children and all people.

NOTES

1. Maslow, A H., *Motivation and Personality*. (New York: Harper and Row, 1970).

2. See also chapters 6, 10, and 14 in this book; Pope John Paul II, *On Human Work—Laborem Exercens*. (Boston: Daughters of St. Paul).

3. Magdoff, H., "The Meaning of Work," *Monthly Review*, 34(5), 1982, pp.1-15; Marx, K., "Economic and Philosophic Manuscripts of 1844" in Q. Hoare (Ed.), *Early Writings* (New York: Vintage Books. pp. 279-400).

4. Fromm, E., *The Sane Society* (Greenwich, CT: Fawcett, 1955).

5. Braverman, H., *Labor and Monopoly Capital* (New York: Monthly Review Press, 1970).

6. Bowles, S., & Gintis, H. *Schooling in Capitalist America* (New York: Basic Books, 1976); See also chapter 7 in this book.

7. Salaman, G., *Work Organization and Class Structure* (Armonk, NY: M. E. Sharpe, 1984).

8. Lerner, M., *Surplus Powerlessness* (Oakland, CA: The Institute for Labor and Mental Health,1986); Senett, R., & Cobb, J. *The Hidden Injuries of Class* (New York: Knopf, 1972); Terkel, S., *Working* (New York: Pantheon,1974); Ollman, B., *Alienation, 2nd ed.* (New York: Cambridge University Press, 1976).

9. Leontief, W., Carter, A. P., Petri, P., Stern, J. J. & Drost, R. *The Future of the World Economy* (New York: Oxford University Press, 1977); Magdoff, H., *Imperialism: From the Colonial Age to the Present* (New York: Monthly Review Press, 1977).

10. Bernfeld, S., *Sisyphus* (Wien: Internationaler Psychoanalitischer Verlag, 1926).

11. See chapter 9 in this book.

12 Illich, I., *Tools for Conviviality*. (New York: Harper and Row, 1973).

13. Freire, P., *Pedagogy of the Oppressed* (New York: Herder and Herder, 1970).

14

Work, Violence, Injustice, and War: Have We Really Overcome Hitler?*

INTRODUCTION

I was almost 14 years old when Austria was invaded and annexed by Germany on March 12, 1938, and when Vienna, the beautiful city of my childhood, celebrated Hitler's arrival. I dimly remember a huge crowd on the Ringstrasse, in front of the Hotel Imperial, shouting ecstatically, "ein Volk, ein Reich, ein Fuhrer," (one people, one empire, one leader) when Hitler appeared on a balcony decked with swastika flags to address the people. The night before, our family had listened in shock to the sad farewell message over the radio of the then Austrian Chancellor, Kurt von Schuschnig, who had yielded to Hitler's ultimatum.

These events meant a sudden, traumatic end to a "normal" childhood, if Vienna between the world wars can be considered a normal situation, in spite of a civil war between socialists and an indigenous Austrian fascist movement, and the assassination of Chancellor Dolfus during an early Nazi putsch in 1934. My parents sheltered my brother and me from these upheavals around us by hardly talking about them in our presence, or by subtly denying their reality.

Ours was a stable, Jewish, "middle-class" family. My parents and paternal grandparents, with whom we shared an apartment, owned a retail dry-goods business, in which they all worked regularly. We lived in comfortable economic circumstances and we children felt loved, cared about, and secure. Our parents had high aspirations for our education and

---

*Keynote address at the International Congress on Child Abuse and Neglect, Hamburg, West Germany, September 4, 1990.

future careers. We took our way of life for granted, as "natural" and valid, and did not ask why the lives of many people were very different from ours, why, for instance, many people were unemployed, and many children and their families were poor. One could not avoid noticing unemployment and poverty in the streets of Vienna during the twenties and thirties, but this was of no real concern to us. We also did not talk much about anti-Semitism which was then widespread in Vienna, nor about events in neighboring Germany since 1933, although we had a vague sense that these matters affected us. Neither our parents, nor our schools, nor the books we read, opened our eyes to actual social dynamics beneath the smooth surface of "normal" everyday life.

Our "normal" world vanished abruptly within days of Hitler's entry into Vienna. I was dismissed from the prestigious "Akademische Gymnasium" and assigned to a segregated school for Jewish children where, in spite of the scary events around us, I began to develop a positive "Jewish" identity in a historic and cultural sense. Our family's business and source of livelihood was forcefully expropriated and "aryanized," and my father was jailed in a concentration camp. From that terrible moment on, my mother assumed the unaccustomed role of managing all our affairs. She mounted frantic efforts to locate my father, to gain his release, and to secure opportunities for the family to emigrate, which, at that time, was a condition for the release of concentration camp inmates. When she failed to find a country where we all could go together, she decided reluctantly to break up our family and to send me to Sweden early in 1939 with a group of refugee children, and my older brother to Palestine. In 1940, during the war, she succeeded eventually to secure space on an illegal transport to Palestine for herself and my father who was then released from the camp. Their ship was caught by the British coast guard off Palestine and subsequently sunk by the Haganah (Jewish underground) in the port of Haifa. My parents survived the sinking, but were arrested by the British and ended up in an internment camp for illegal immigrants where my mother died of typhoid in 1941. The only time I saw her after I had left home in 1939 was across barbed wire fences in the internment camp, shortly before she died. I had meanwhile immigrated to Palestine from Sweden in 1940, but our family never reestablished a home, although my father was eventually released from the British internment camp and began to reconstruct his own life in Palestine.* Why, you may ask do I burden you with my painful childhood experiences, which I survived somehow while many millions perished. Because the violence inflicted by Nazi Germany upon one child symbolizes what has been happening for several millennia, and tragically continues to happen to this very day to many millions of children and adults whose lives were and are being destroyed by violence, domination, exploitation, conflicts and wars among peoples and social classes. Usually, these children and adults are as ignorant as I was, at the time of my victimization, of the social dynamics which threaten and often destroy them.

A further reason for sharing my and my family's experiences under Hitler is that the traumatic separation from my family became the impetus for my involvement in intellectual efforts to make sense out of incomprehensible happenings and to gain insights into the sources and dynamics of human violence, as well as insights into strategies aimed at overcoming violent interactions in human relations, of which the events of the Nazi era were merely an extreme manifestation. One tentative conclusion I have reached in this search is that, although every event in history is unique, it also reflects common human dynamics. Accordingly, Nazi Germany was unique as well as a symptom of widespread societal dynamics. To understand these dynamics of domination, exploitation, violence, and dehumanization, and to overcome them at their roots, we must identify and confront these tendencies in ourselves and in our ways of life and social institutions, and not only in the ways of life and social institutions of those who oppress us.

Another insight which I developed soon after leaving home was that violence against German children, mothers, and fathers would be as senseless and tragic as the violence perpetrated by the Nazis against Jewish children and their families. To revenge Hitler's evils would

---

*My mother's tragic efforts to save her family are described, blow by blow, in letters she wrote to me almost every week after I left home until shortly before her death. The letters were published in 1988 by the City of Vienna in a series of books, *Die Wahrheit 38-45* (*The Truth 38-45*), Vienna, Austria: J & V Edition Wien, 1988. (ISBN 3-8508-020-2)

accomplish nothing and would merely continue the vicious cycle of violence and destruction. Some other response seemed called for, but what that response ought to be, I did not know then. These ideas, which differed from the views of most people around me, evolved initially on an intuitive-emotional level. They eventually became intellectually grounded when I chanced to read Romain Rolland's biography of *Mahatma Gandhi* and Petr Kropotkin's scholarly study, *Mutual Aid.* [1]

The following thoughts on the dynamics and prevention of violence evolved gradually out of insights gained during my adolescence as a refugee from the Nazi empire. They are the tentative results of an analysis which I felt driven to pursue from the moment my "normal" world fell apart in 1938.

THE VICIOUS CIRCLE OF SOCIETAL VIOLENCE, COUNTERVIOLENCE AND REPRESSIVE VIOLENCE

Germany under Nazi rule, as other societies before and after it, was but an extreme instance of a way of life shaped by societal violence, counterviolence, and repressive violence. The concept of societal violence refers to systemic obstructions to human development and self-actualization inherent in a society's institutional order; its policies, practices, and human relations; its circumstances of living and quality of life; and its values and ideology. Societal violence inhibits the unfolding of people's innate potential, their spontaneous drive to become what they are capable of becoming, by interfering with the fulfillment of their biological, psychological, and social needs. Illustrations of societal violence are such aspects of "normal" social life, past and present, as slavery, unemployment, poverty, hunger, and discrimination by race, sex, age, and social class.

Implicit in the concept of societal violence is the assumption that humans, like seeds, are born with a tendency towards spontaneous growth and development of innate capacities. Seeds will grow into healthy plants only when imbedded in nutritious soil and when exposed to adequate amounts of sunshine and rain. Analogously, human development will proceed healthily only when people live in natural and social environments compatible with their developmental needs. Consistent frustration of these needs "violates" human development, blocks constructive, developmental energy, and transforms it into destructive energy. Fromm, who witnessed Hitler's rise to power in Germany, described these dynamics insightfully: "...The more the drive toward life is thwarted, the stronger is the drive toward destruction; the more life is realized, the less is the strength of destructiveness. Destructiveness is the outcome of unlived life." [2]

Societal violence tends to set in motion chain reactions of counterviolence from its victims. However, counterviolence will usually not be aimed at the sources of societal violence in the institutional order of society, but will be displaced onto helpless and powerless victims. Domestic violence and violent crime, as well as suicide, addictions, and mental ills are direct and indirect expressions of counterviolence. Violent, destructive, and self-destructive attitudes and behaviors of individuals and groups will often seem senseless and irrational to observers of isolated episodes. However, when such episodes are viewed in the context of individual and social history, they seem no longer senseless and irrational, but reveal their inner logic as "counterviolence" to violent societal practices and conditions.

Journalistic treatment and public debate of violence, as well as many scholarly studies, tend to obscure rather than unravel the underlying dynamics of violence when they focus exclusively on the counterviolence of violated individuals and groups, while disregarding the socially structured violation of the developmental needs of these individuals and groups. Such fragmented studies of moments in the cycle of violence tend, however, to serve the interests of privileged, dominant social classes, for they deny by implication the causal dynamics of societal violence. Society is thus absolved of guilt, and the need for fundamental structural changes toward nonviolent institutions is discounted while individuals and oppressed groups are scapegoated.

Societies whose violent policies and practices give rise to counterviolence on the part of violated individuals and groups tend to respond by disregarding the actual causes, "blaming the victims," and steadily increasing repressive violence. The tragic, vicious circle of societal violence, counterviolence, and repressive violence will continue as long as its roots—systemic societal obstacles to human development as an aspect of the normal workings of everyday life—are not acknowledged and transcended within and among societies and nations.

SOURCES OF VIOLENCE: NATURE VS. CULTURE

There is a widely held assumption that violent interactions among individuals and human groups are biologically determined and, therefore, inevitable. Advocates of social justice and nonviolence need to confront this position. It is undoubtedly true that the human species does manifest physical, psychological and social capacities for violent attitudes and behaviors. In this sense, violent interactions are, indeed, an element of human nature. However, these natural capacities are not actualized continuously in human behavior, but only at certain times and under certain conditions. There is also ample evidence that the human species has physical, psychological, and social capacities for nonviolent, caring, loving, and nurturing attitudes and behaviors. These capacities too are not actualized continuously but only at certain times and under certain conditions. They too are elements of human nature in the same way as the capacities for violence. Which of the species' natural capacities are actualized by individuals and groups at different times and places, and in different social relationships and circumstances, seems to depend on the prior experiences of those involved and on the historic and contemporary contexts of these experiences. It seems therefore valid to assume that while both violent and nonviolent attitudes and behaviors are definitely part of human nature, their expression is never an inevitable biological function but is always socially and culturally conditioned.

WORK AND EXCHANGE AND DISTRIBUTION
OF PRODUCTS OF WORK

History reveals that societal violence which has obstructed human development over several thousand years, and which has caused violent interactions and wars from local to global levels, can be traced to the use of coercive measures concerning the organization of work and the exchange and distribution of products of work.

Humans must work to secure life-sustaining and enhancing resources from their natural and social environments. The organization of work and the exchange of work products, as well as ideas concerning these processes, are therefore key elements of human cultures. The extent to which human needs can be satisfied, the scope of individual and social development, and the quality of life in a society depend always on its organization of work and the terms of exchange and distribution of work products.

Work is an essential ingredient of all the goods and services, and all the ideas, knowledge, and skills, which the human species has developed throughout its history. Work is not a series of individual acts, but an inter- and cross-generational process, involving ever-new combinations of physical, mental, emotional, and spiritual capacities of people with nonhuman elements of nature and with concrete and abstract products of earlier human work. The aggregate of human creativity and productivity is therefore contained in every newly created concrete or abstract product.

In psychological and social terms, people's work could be a means for discovering their capacities, and a source of their social and individual identity. Furthermore, work could be an important medium for individual development and self-actualization as well as for mutually enriching social relations and societal development. Humans seem to have an innate need to be active in the world, i.e., to work, and they seem self-motivated to engage in work when it meets their perceived needs and furthers their well-being. In this sense, work is a rational human activity. On the other hand, the frequently observed tendency to avoid work does not seem to be an innate human tendency but a defensive reaction to socially evolved, oppressive and alienating conditions of work and to exploitative terms of exchange. Under such conditions, work avoidance makes sense.[3]

WORK AND PEACE OR WAR

Whether or not the organization of work and the exchange of work products involve coercion, domination, and exploitation has been throughout history a major determinant of conflict and harmony within societies, and of war and peace among them. During long stages of preagricultural societal evolution, exchanges among members of small, communal societies tended to be essentially balanced, i.e., nonexploitative. In the course of their lives, most people contributed to, and received from aggregate social production about as much as others. Also, occupational differentiation was linked mainly to age and sex, but not to caste and class. These essentially egalitarian modes of work, exchange, and distribution may not have required coercion. For under these conditions, people were likely to have been self-motivated to work, as their work was linked directly to their perceived interests, the satisfaction of their basic needs.

Imbalanced, i.e., exploitative, modes of work and exchange in which most people routinely contribute more than they receive, while social elites routinely receive more than they contribute, were established by many, but not all, human societies during the last ten thousand years as a result of the following interacting processes: population increase and resulting scarcities of land, food, and other needed resources; discovery and development of agriculture, crafts, science, and technology; production of economic surplus and struggles over its distribution, use and control; spatial and social differentiation into rural and urban communities; social division of labor between manual and mental work and establishment of social and occupational castes and classes including peasants, craftsmen, traders, priests and scholars, soldiers, civilian administrators, and ruling elites.

Transitions from early, egalitarian, communal, cooperative, and relatively harmonious cultures to later inegalitarian, selfish and competitive ways of life, modes of work, exchange of products and distribution of rights are unlikely to have been accomplished through voluntary, harmonious processes. Rather, these transitions seem to have involved coercive and violent processes and relations within and between societies. Moreover, once inegalitarian structures and principles were established coercively concerning work, the division of labor, the exchange of products, and the distribution of statuses, prestige and rights, they required continuous coercive measures, i.e., societal violence, for their maintenance and reproduction. For under conditions of injustice, self-motivation to work seems to have declined in proportion to the increase in domination, oppression and exploitation, and work discipline had, therefore, to be maintained by overt and covert force. Coercive measures became institutionalized as regular, overt and subtle aspects of socialization and of religions and ideologies which interpreted and justified established, inegalitarian conditions of life and work. Socialization and indoctrination were backed by elaborate systems of conformity-inducing rewards and sanctions, and by secret and open police and military forces, the instruments of "legitimate violence" within inegalitarian societies and among nations of inegalitarian global systems.

Human history over the past ten thousand years is essentially a series of variations on the themes of imbalanced, inegalitarian, grossly unjust, coercively instituted and maintained modes of work, division of labor, exchange of products and distribution of rights. This history of social-structural violence is a tragic one, indeed. The mere mention of inegalitarian work systems such as ancient and recent slavery, feudal serfdom, and early and contemporary industrial and agricultural wage labor brings to mind images of toiling people transformed (not by their own choices) into dehumanized "factors of production" dominated and exploited by masters, lords, and individual and corporate employers. Such work systems could never have been established and perpetuated without the massive coercion of societal violence in the form of war, genocide, murder, torture, imprisonment, starvation, destitution, discrimination, unemployment, and the ever-present threat of these and other violent measures.

Yet human history is also a record of resistance and counterviolence by oppressed and exploited peoples, social groups, and individuals against domination and injustice, and of struggles for human liberation and a renaissance of social orders based on egalitarian, nonexploitative modes of work and just and balanced terms of exchange and distribution of the products of human work. Accordingly, conflicts within societies and wars among tribes and nations can usually be understood when viewed in the historic context of societal violence and counterviolence concerning the organization of work and the exchange and distribution of the products of human work.

INSTITUTIONAL JUSTICE

Since societal violence has been used throughout history to establish and maintain different types of unjust social orders, the establishment of just social orders depends on the eradication of societal violence and the vicious circle of counter and repressive violence. Institutional justice means, therefore, transcendence of societal violence and attainment of nonviolent social orders free from coercive practices and conditions.

Societies are just when institutional practices concerning the organization of work and the exchange and distribution of work products facilitate satisfaction of people's basic material, psychological, and social needs and the development of everyone's innate capacities. This conception of institutional justice applies to every level of social relations and organization, from local to global. Institutional justice is assumed to result in gradual termination of counterviolence, as people's innate developmental energy would no longer be blocked by societal violence and transformed into violent attitudes and behaviors, but could be actualized freely in constructive directions. This means that such intractable social problems as intergroup, interpersonal, and domestic violence, and violent crimes are likely to decline and eventually cease under conditions of institutional justice.

Implicit in this conception of institutional justice is a value position according to which all humans are intrinsically of equal worth in spite of their differences, and ought, therefore, to be entitled to equal consideration, rights, and responsibilities. As used here, social equality is not a mathematical notion implying monotonous sameness and enforced conformity. Rather, as suggested by Tawney, it is a philosophical notion implying equal rights for all to develop their individuality. Freedom is likely to increase rather than decrease when socially structured inequalities are reduced, and genuine freedom for all, rather than freedom for ruling classes to dominate and exploit, will become possible only when institutional justice and equality are attained by a society.[4]

TOWARD GENUINE PEACE THROUGH INSTITUTIONAL JUSTICE

Genuine peace, as distinguished from coercively maintained "pacification" such as the ancient "pax Romana," can be attained only by transcending societal violence and establishing in its place institutional justice, from local to global levels, within and among all human societies. This means that attainment of real peace necessitates comprehensive institutional changes in the organization of work and in the terms of exchange and distribution of goods and services, as well as corresponding changes in the consciousness, values, perceptions of interests, and motivations of people everywhere. Achieving such major institutional and ideological changes requires organization, on local and global levels, of social movements committed to intense nonviolent, political action over many decades. Long-term commitment seems necessary because the movements would have to overcome violent institutional dynamics and ideologies which have evolved over many centuries and are now permeating most established social orders. Obviously, the institutional and ideological products of centuries of social evolution cannot be reversed easily and quickly. Intense activism seems necessary because working for fundamental social changes against tremendous odds would require the secular equivalent of missionary work. And nonviolent approaches seem necessary because the vicious circle of societal violence and counterviolence cannot be broken and transcended by participating in it and thus actually reinforcing it.

Yet, while promoting genuine peace requires the building of movements for fundamental transformations of existing social orders and human relations all over the globe, it is also necessary to work simultaneously for immediate reductions of injustice and suffering and for prevention of "hot wars," provided such relief is not mistaken for the necessary fundamental social transformations and presented as a real solution to current human dilemmas. Limited amelioration of destructive social conditions and peace based on a balance of terror among armed, institutionally violent and unjust societies make possible a modicum of survival and provide time for building movements committed to fundamental social transformations. Hence, they are preferable to more intense levels of oppression and to open warfare.

Peace movements in the United States have usually worked for peace and nuclear disarmament but have been reluctant to work for fundamental social change which alone can reverse the dynamics of societal violence, injustice, counterviolence and war. They have done so in order to mobilize the broadest possible support for their immediate goals and to avoid alienating potential constituencies who support the established social order. As a result, these movements are trapped in a tragic contradiction of struggling for peace while not opposing the causes of wars. By failing to link their work for peace to comprehensive struggles against societal violence and injustice at home and abroad, peace movements actually support the maintenance of practices and conditions which result inevitably in more conflicts and wars.

LIBERATING WORK LIFE: ESSENTIAL STEPS TOWARD GENUINE PEACE

If indeed, the usual function of societal violence and wars, at home and abroad, has been to establish and maintain exploitative systems of work and unjust terms of exchange and distribution of goods and services, then violence and wars will continue as long as dominant social classes strive to ensure for themselves privileged positions in the organization of work and privileged shares in the distribution of goods and services. To be effective, peace movements should therefore confront the historic, causal links between exploitative, imbalanced modes of work and distribution, and societal violence and wars. For there can be no magic shortcuts to genuine peace while domination and exploitation at work and privilege in the distribution of goods, services, and social rights are preserved.

What then are the main features of nonviolent, liberated systems of work, exchange, and distribution which peace and social justice movements should promote in order to be effective beyond short-range goals? Such systems should facilitate optimum individual and social development all over the globe and should therefore be designed to meet the biological, psychological, and social needs of all people through humane reorganization and redesign of work and through equitable distribution of the aggregate global product. These systems would have to be shaped by values of social equality, freedom and self-direction, cooperation and mutualism, community orientation and human solidarity rather than social inequality, domination and control, competition, selfishness and rugged individualism. Workers would have to be in control of their work as "masters of production" rather than as "factors of production" used and exploited by individual and corporate employers. They would have to determine, design, and implement the goals and processes of work and receive fair shares of the products.

Nonviolent modes of work would also have to be in harmony with nature and adapted to the reality of population increases involving a doubling of the globe's population to about ten billion by the middle of the next century.[5] Such ecological and demographic considerations suggest avoidance of waste in relation to the environment and to natural resources, commitment to high-quality, durable products, and rejection of practices such as built-in obsolescence and wasteful, marginal product changes promoted through advertising, all of which tend to be widespread in capitalist economic systems.

To sum up, nonviolent systems of work and distribution would be democratically controlled; nonhierarchical, decentralized, and horizontally coordinated; egalitarian, cooperative, humanistic, universalistic, and ecological; and oriented to serve the interest of everyone living now and in the future.

THE TRANSITION PROCESS

Established modes of work, exchange, and distribution are very distant from the nonviolent approach sketched here. An extended process of reexamination of consciousness and political action is therefore necessary to bring about the desired transformations. During this process, visions of, and experimentation with, alternative models of work and distribution can serve as a frame of reference for peace and social justice movements as they develop strategies and policy proposals for the transition from structurally violent ways of life and work toward structurally just, nonviolent alternatives.

An important theoretical requirement for the transition process is a conceptual redefinition of work. If the purposes of human work are to be the maintenance of life, the enrichment of its quality and the furthering of individual and social development, then work should be defined as activities designed to meet biological, psychological, and social-cultural needs of people. A corollary of this definition is that activities which threaten or endanger life, reduce its quality, and inhibit individual and social development should not be considered work but "counterwork," a concept akin to the notion of violence as developed in this essay.

Implicit in the definitions of work and counterwork are criteria for the design and evaluation of human-development-oriented systems of work and production, as well as criteria for including and excluding activities into and from a revised concept of "Gross National Product" (GNP). Activities necessary for and conducive to human development and well-being should be included in the GNP and should be recognized socially and rewarded materially, while activities which obstruct or are harmful to human development and well-being should be excluded from the GNP, should not be recognized and rewarded, and should eventually be terminated.

An essential first step in the transition to a nonviolent, human-development-oriented system of work is the elimination of the societally violent and wasteful practice of excluding people from socially necessary employment through "unemployment" and "underemployment," at the discretion and in the self-defined interest of owners and managers of means of production. The elimination of unemployment could be achieved by an amendment to the United States Constitution guaranteeing to every individual rights to suitable employment and adequate income. Congress could implement an employment guarantee by modifying periodically the legal length of the workday (week, month, or year) in order to match the number of workers with the number of positions in the nation's work-system and with changes in the volume of aggregate production. A mandated reduction of the average work day by just one or two hours, and mandated prohibition of overtime, would make possible the absorption of nearly all currently unemployed and underemployed workers, assuming the scope of current production were not changed. Congress could also establish appropriate and meaningful work programs to provide additional work when needed and to meet major gaps in real needs of the population, not supplied by the market, in housing, health, education, transportation, conservation, etc. Such publicly financed work programs could be carried out by workers' cooperatives and sponsored by communities and regions, as well as by more conventional enterprises.[6]

Establishing unconditional rights to work for all is an essential, though not sufficient, measure toward eventually solving many social problems such as poverty and discrimination by sex, age, race, social class, handicaps, etc. It is also a precondition toward phasing out socially useless and harmful "counterwork," such as military production, built-in obsolescence, "feather-bedding," etc., which workers, understandably, are reluctant to forego in the absence of assured, alternative, meaningful work. In short, guaranteeing work to everyone is necessary in order to develop a rational, equitable, efficient, and effective economic system, conducive to human development and well-being for all, at home and abroad.

The redefinition of work would lead to a further important transition policy, the inclusion in the GNP of parental child care and similar caretaker tasks in people's homes as socially necessary components of the work system. Such an approach was endorsed in 1985 by the United Nations World Conference on Women in Nairobi and ratified subsequently by the U.N. General Assembly which asked the governments of all countries "to include women's unwaged work in the GNP." Were the Congress to enact such a policy, women and men preferring this kind of work to employment outside their homes, would be entitled to receive adequate wages out of federal revenues raised through appropriate modifications of income tax rates.[7]

Redefining parental child care and other caretaker tasks as work, and paying for it adequate wages out of public revenues, would enhance the physical and mental health, the social prestige, and the political power of people performing this work. One further benefit of such a policy would be the phasing out of the dehumanizing Aid to Families with Dependent Children (AFDC) program. Altogether, the proposed transition policies of employment guarantees and parent and caretaker wages would, when fully implemented, eliminate nearly all poverty and its multiple correlates in our society, no small feat, indeed, considering the limited success, on this score, of the New Deal, the War on Poverty, Model Cities, and several other well-intended, yet inadequate efforts. A residual group of the population who are unable to work because of age or handicaps would have to be protected against poverty through a guaranteed adequate income policy. Also, all people would have to be entitled to comprehensive, preventive and curative health care, child care and education, and suitable housing, all provided through federally funded and locally administered programs.

The transition policies sketched here are compatible with values rooted in the history and culture of the United States. Early European settlers brought with them a work ethic which originated in the biblical injunction "to earn bread by the sweat of one's brow." They believed that everyone had obligations and rights to be self-reliant through hard work. They also thought that people were entitled to use natural resources to satisfy their needs by working on and with these resources. These ideas originated in ancient Judeo-Christian traditions according to which the earth belongs to God, is available to humans to derive their livelihood, and no one was to be excluded from using God-given resources for self-support. This ancient ethic of European immigrants is similar to the ethic and practices of Native American tribes as well as of African tribes, the roots of black Americans.

Catholic theology concerning work and workers' rights contains similar themes. Pope John Paul II's Encyclical "On Human Work" asserts the "priority of labor over capital," stresses the worth, dignity and inalienable rights of workers, and concludes that unemployment is incompatible with human dignity, needs, rights and responsibilities.[8] The Catholic bishops of the United States applied the same premises to an analysis of the established economic system in a recent pastoral letter. They, too, declare unemployment and poverty unacceptable on moral grounds and recommend policies that would guarantee dignified work and adequate income to all, similar to the transition policies suggested here.[9] Many Protestant and Jewish clergy have voiced similar positions.

In view of correspondence between values upheld by some people and groups in the United States and the transition policies suggested here, it may be possible to mobilize political support for these policies in spite of likely opposition from propertied and managerial classes and their privilege-pursuing allies. The proposed policies could actually be enacted and implemented without structural transformations of prevailing capitalist institutions. The limits of these institutions would, however, be tested and strained, for these policies involve major challenges to the customary rights of owners and managers, as well as constraints on "free enterprise" similar to ones prevailing in capitalist democracies such as Sweden. In Gorz's terms, these policies involve "nonreformist reforms" since they are conceived "not in terms of what is possible within the framework of a given system and administration, but in view of what should be made possible in terms of human needs and demands."[10]

Shifts in power from propertied and managerial elites to majorities of working people, and corresponding shifts in the distribution of social, psychological, and economic goods which would result were the proposed transition policies implemented, could gradually open up opportunities for expanding democratic control by workers, consumers and communities over society's productive resources and capacities. Of course, such social transformations would not happen automatically. Rather, they would require the emergence of broadly based liberation movements which transcended conventional interest-group politics and promoted instead a unifying, humanistic consciousness and a corresponding nonviolent political practice.

The gradual unfolding of a comprehensive democratic renaissance initiated by such liberation movements could eventually lead to efforts to redesign work processes and products in accordance with humanistic values, enhancing their quality and bringing them into harmony with the intrinsic needs of people and the natural environment. At that stage, it would also be possible to tackle deep-seated conflicts in human relations, including sexism, ageism, racism, and class antagonism at home, and economic injustice and wars abroad. These issues, i.e., the organization and design of work, the nature of products, and relations of humans to one another and to the environment defy fundamental solutions as long as unemployment and poverty are ever-present possibilities. For in the absence of employment and income security, people tend to protect whatever employment they have, whether or not their work is compatible with their intrinsic needs and development, and is satisfying and meaningful in personal, social, ethical, ecological, and international terms. Nor will people be committed to the protection of the needs, rights, and interest of oppressed and deprived individuals, classes, and nations, when such protection could threaten their own employment and income security.

If peace and social justice movements could achieve implementation of the transition policies sketched here, and if they then focused their efforts on qualitative transformations of work, products, and human relations, they would set in motion countercycles of institutional justice in place of the prevailing cycles of societal violence which for millennia have coercively maintained domination and exploitation at work and polarities of privilege and deprivation from local to global levels. This approach would seem to be a feasible, long-range strategy toward real peace and human liberation, as it aims to overcome institutional obstacles to individual and social development—the ultimate sources of oppression and wars.

EPILOGUE

In concluding the analysis of the sources and dynamics of societal violence and of feasible strategies toward overcoming it, the tragic truth needs to be confronted, that humankind has barely begun to extricate itself from the vicious circle of violence which periodically reaches monstrous proportions as it did in Germany under Hitler's rule. Children and adults continue to be wasted and destroyed by the millions, every year, on every continent, as a consequence of societal violence on local and global scales. Waste and destruction occur during civil and regional conflicts and wars which have not ceased following the slaughters of the World Wars of this century. More frequently, waste and destruction of human life result from the "normal" workings of established social, economic, political, educational, and cultural institutions which involve domination, exploitation, underdevelopment, poverty, disease, and ignorance, as well as irreversible degradation of the biosphere. Sadly, one must conclude that what Hitler has come to symbolize is very much alive today and is far from being overcome.

Societal violence will not cease, and may even result in the gradual self-destruction of humankind, unless prevailing tendencies are reversed through paradigmatic transformations of development-negating, violent, exploitative and competitive modes of work, exchange, and distribution into development-affirming, non-violent, humanistic-democratic, and cooperative alternatives. Such paradigmatic shifts toward universal, institutional justice were expressed symbolically by the German poet Schiller in his "Ode to Joy," and immortalized in Beethoven's Choral Symphony: "Alle Menschen werden Bruder,'' (All people become brothers)—the ultimate antithesis of Hitler's "Mein Kampf."

NOTES

1. Kropotkin, P., *Mutual Aid* (Boston: Porter Sargent; 1956).

2. Fromm, Erich, *Escape From Freedom* (New York: Reinhart and Company, 1941).

3. Marx, Karl, *Economic and Philosophical Manuscripts* (1844) (New York: Vintage Books, 1975); Pope John Paul, II, *On Human Work* (Boston: Daughters of St. Paul, 1981).

4. Tawney, R.H., *Equality* (London: Allen and Unwin, 1931 and 1964).

5. The World Bank, *World Development Report,* 1984 (Washington, D.C.: The World Bank, 1984).

6. Gil, David G, "Toward Constitutional Guarantees for Employment and Income," *Changing Work*, Winter/Spring, 1987, see chapter 10 in this book.

7. See appendix in this book.

8. Pope John Paul, II, *On Human Work.*

9. National Conference of Catholic Bishops, *Economic Justice for All* (Washington, D.C.: United States Catholic Conference, 1986).

10. Gorz, Andre, *Strategy for Labor* (Boston: Beacon Press, 1967).

TECHNICAL APPENDIX

An Illustration of Social Policy
Analysis and Development

Mothers' Wages, Children's Allowances, Parents' Wages—Analysis and Development of a Social Policy Cluster

The use of the framework for social policy analysis and development is illustrated in a discussion of a social policy proposal involving mothers' wages and children's allowances referred to hereafter for brevity as "Mothers' Wages Policy." This proposal was developed and published years ago as a contribution to the public debate on eliminating, or at least reducing the scope of poverty in the United States.[1] The proposal is outlined below and is then subjected to analysis in accordance with the framework. The analysis was carried out during 1971 and is based on data and information available at that time. The fact that many changes have occurred since then does not invalidate the illustrative aim of this analysis.

THE PROPOSAL

The policy proposal of "Mothers' Wages" derives from the following premises. Childbearing and child rearing are not merely private and familial functions but are also societal functions since they assure the continuity and survival of a society. These functions are usually performed by families as "agents" of society. But society as a whole, having, supposedly, a very real interest in the optimal development of all newly born citizens, should share responsibility for their rearing and socialization. Efforts and energy invested, and work performed, toward these objectives should be considered components of the Gross National Product. Society should, therefore, compensate mothers who choose, or are obliged to stay out of, or to disengage themselves partly or completely from the labor market in order to engage in child care.

Society in the United States tends to be ambiguous in defining the scope of parental and societal roles and responsibilities for the rearing of children. It would seem, however, quite consistent with nineteenth- and twentieth-century social and legal developments concerning children to accept the rearing of the next generation as a societal function and responsibility, and to recognize the rights of mothers—and of fathers under certain circumstances—to be compensated adequately for their efforts. Indeed, the unpleasant truth needs to be faced that unless society compensates mothers for their partly voluntary, partly forced withdrawal from the labor market and for the assumption of the complex tasks of childbearing and rearing, it is actually exploiting the biological role of women as a basis for the recruitment of "child care slave labor."

Society has gradually come to accept responsibility for the child rearing tasks and for the socialization function whenever children enter institutionalized settings. No one would any longer question the appropriateness and legitimacy of compensating teachers, child care workers, and foster parents for efforts on behalf of children assigned to their care, although, especially with regard to foster parents, the compensation is sometimes provided reluctantly and is often minimal or merely symbolic.

In view of these considerations, the proposed policy provides for society to pay wages to every mother and to every expectant mother for as long as childbearing and child rearing tasks keep her outside the labor market by choice or by necessity. Such wages should be fixed by federal law, should correspond at least to the prevailing minimum wage established by the Fair Labor Standards Act, and should be paid for eight hours a day, seven days a week, and fifty-two weeks a year to mothers engaged in no other gainful work. A mother's wage should vary in relation to the extent to which she chooses to participate in the labor market. Thus, mothers who undertook part-time employment or self-employment should receive wages on a prorated basis. Mothers who engaged in full-time employment should, however, receive 25 percent of full mother's wages to compensate for the fact that maternal child rearing involves around-the-clock, 365-days-a-year, stand-by responsibilities.

A mother's wage should not vary with the number of her children since it is paid as compensation for staying outside the labor market and for investment of effort in a societal function. However, in accordance with this policy proposal, mothers' wages should be linked to a system of adequate children's allowances payable on behalf of all minors to assure larger incomes for larger family groups.

The sole criteria for receiving mothers' wages and for determining their amount are motherhood or expectant motherhood and the extent of a mother's participation in the labor force. Accordingly, marital status, ownership of property, support from husbands, or income from other sources would be disregarded in determining a mother's right to the wage. However, since mothers' wages constitute income, the income tax system would assure recoupment of progressively larger portions of mothers' wages from families with other sources of income, and thus the net amount of mothers' wages would decrease as the total resources of a family increased. Children's allowances, too, would be subject to income tax for the same reasons as mothers' wages.

Mothers' wages would also be subject to social security deductions in order to assure to mothers the same social security benefits for which other workers are eligible, such as old age, survivors, disability, and health insurance (OASDHI).

Mothers' wages as conceived by the proposal are a compensation related to a specified societal event and context, namely, disengagement from the labor market because of motherhood or maternity. This conceptualization places mothers' wages within the social security model, and the program should therefore be administered by the Social Security Administration. To obtain her wages, a mother or expectant mother would register her claim at the nearest Social Security office giving the necessary information concerning herself, her children, and her employment. Wages would be paid to her as long as she remained eligible and provided the Social Security office with the required relevant information. Such limited data as would be required could be provided routinely on the back of signed paychecks. Information furnished by a mother would be considered valid, subject merely to random checks, and no special eligibility investigations would be necessary. Provisions would also be made for due process review and appeal procedures concerning administrative eligibility decisions. Children's allowances would also be administered in the same simple manner. Both mothers' wages and children's allowances would be financed entirely from general revenue derived from appropriate, progressive reform of the federal tax system.

Fathers could receive "mothers' wages" on the same terms as mothers during a temporary absence or disability of a mother, or in single parent homes headed by fathers.

ANALYSIS

A.ISSUES DEALT WITH BY THE POLICY

1. Nature, scope, and distribution of the issues: The "Mothers' Wages" policy deals with the following related issues:
a. rights of women
b. rights of children
c. definition of work
d. redistribution of rights through transfer of purchasing power

Throughout the evolution of human societies, the work of women and their share of concrete and symbolic rights has been influenced by their biological role in childbearing. This influence is reflected in socially structured inequalities between males and females which usually took the form of narrowing the scope of work and rights open to women, and of assigning them to roles involving limited rights. These institutional limitations on the options of women have led frequently to overt and covert exploitation and discrimination. The work and rights of women as women tend to be independent of other criteria of social stratification such as age, ethnicity, intellectual potential, educational and occupational achievement, wealth, etc. Because of this, inequality of roles and rights between the sexes can usually be discerned within any social group or class, although there are variations in these inequalities among the different social groups and during different stages of social, cultural, economic, and technological development.

Women in the United States at the present time continue to be subjected to rather widespread exploitation and discrimination, in spite of recent trends toward equality between the sexes with respect to roles and rights, especially among more privileged social classes. One important source of discriminatory practices against women is the traditional expectation for mothers to assume primary responsibility for the care of their own children. This expectation tends to limit considerably the freedom of women to choose and enter other occupations. Moreover, it also tends to deprive them of equal access to goods and services since the tasks of caring for one's own children are excluded from the societal and economic definition of "work," and mothers are consequently not entitled to rewards for their child-caring responsibilities. Mothers who own no personal wealth from savings, gifts, or inheritance, and who lack occupational skills and opportunities for "gainful" employment or self-employment in which they engage in addition to caring for their children, have thus to depend on their husbands for their rights and those of their children. Within the existing social order, such mothers have few options indeed when the income of their husbands is inadequate, when husbands fail to support them, or when they have no husbands. In such circumstances they are forced to work in unskilled, poorly paid jobs, frequently under alienating working conditions, to seek aid from relatives and friends, or, as a last resort, to subsist on grossly inadequate public assistance grants. None of these options is satisfactory as each tends to result in adverse consequences for the mothers and their children.

In the United States, the rights of children are linked closely to the work and rights of their parents. However, the scope of rights to which children are entitled as children and which society is ready to guarantee (e.g., public education) has been increasing steadily since earlier times when the circumstances and authority of parents determined the rights of their children with hardly a challenge by society. Recent years have seen important legal and judicial developments toward strengthening the social and civil rights of children. Implied in this issue are such conceptual questions as whether children are the "property" of their parents or whether they "belong" to society; whether they have specifiable civil and social rights and, hence, whether society has specific obligations to assure these rights; and, if so, what are the rights of children, and what is the extent of societal obligations toward them.

The way a society defines the concept "work" has important consequences for the circumstances of living of individuals and their relative power and relations to each other, especially when rewards for the performance of work roles constitute a major mechanism for distributing rights to individuals. By excluding certain functions and contexts from the social and economic definition of work, persons assigned to these functions are deprived of economic rewards. Also, by defining certain functions and contexts as "voluntary work," symbolic and psychological rewards are substituted for economic ones, which is merely another mechanism for economic exploitation. It should be noted in this context that women are constantly urged to engage in "voluntary work." Business executives who entertain prospective customers are "working," and so are professional ball players who are throwing balls, but volunteers who "entertain" patients in a hospital or tutor "slow learning" children in schools, and women who clean their family's home, prepare meals, and care for children are "not working." These brief comments on the issue of defining the concept of "work" illustrate the essentially social nature and dynamics of this definitional process and, hence, the relevance of this issue for social policy analysis and development.

The final issue identified above as being dealt with by the mothers' wages policy is the redistribution of rights through transfer of purchasing power. In a capitalistic economy, individual purchasing power is an important means for securing one's rights to goods and services since many essential and other goods and services must be purchased in the market. Consequently, one obvious approach toward redistributing and reducing inequalities of rights in such an economy is to transfer purchasing power from groups in the population whose purchasing power is above the mean to groups whose purchasing power is below the mean. Different techniques are available to carry out such transfers, each having their own strengths, weaknesses, and side effects. It should be noted that the specific transfer technique selected may be less important than the aggregate amounts of purchasing power involved in the transfer, the resulting shape of the distribution of purchasing power in the population, and the characteristics of the population segments affected by the transfers.

The four issues reviewed above with which the mothers' wages policy is expected to deal are reflected in many aspects of life throughout all strata of society. All women at some points in their lives experience the sex-linked tendencies of the processes of work and rights distribution. Similarly, all children are affected by the manner in which their rights are determined, be it on the basis of the rights of their parents, on the basis of universal societal arrangements, or, as is the present situation, on the basis of some combination of these factors. The societal definition of the concept of work concerns every individual in a society in which work constitutes a major source of personal rights. Of equal relevance and importance is the shape of the distribution of rights throughout society, and modifications of that distribution by way of transfers of purchasing power. While these four issues affect directly or indirectly the lives of nearly every individual in society, the problematic aspects inherent in them are especially detrimental for groups in the population who are subjected to severe, absolute or relative deprivation as a result of other criteria of social stratification such as age, race, education, etc. Thus the discriminatory and exploitative tendencies toward women, the lack of adequate societal provisions for children, the societal definition of work, and the unequal distribution of rights have relatively minor adverse effects on women and children in privileged social strata, while their effects are extremely destructive for families and individuals in the lowest fifth of the income distribution, and nearly as destructive for those in the next to the lowest fifth.

2. Causal theories or hypotheses concerning the dynamics of the issues: Sex-linked differences and inequalities concerning work and the distribution of rights seem to be a result of societal dynamics similar to other socially structured inequalities among individuals and groups. Their specific origin was, obviously, the biological difference between the sexes, which was utilized during early stages of societal evolution as an important criterion for the division of work. As these early, nature-linked arrangements were elaborated socially into stable cultural patterns and taboos, male dominance and its corollary, subjugation and exploitation of females, became institutionalized in human societies. Socialization over countless generations resulted in widespread identification of men and women with the socially determined range of sex roles, and hence, fairly general acceptance of constraints in the allocation of work and the distribution of rights. It should not be overlooked, however, that throughout history many women and some men have questioned, and occasionally revolted against, traditional patterns of sex-linked limitations on work and rights, and as a result traditional constraints were gradually reduced, especially during the twentieth century.

Socially structured limitations of the rights of children are another social pattern derived from biological conditions. The rights of children are usually linked closely to the rights of their parents. Human infants are utterly dependent on their mothers and, indirectly, their fathers. Children, at least during their early years, lack physical strength, social skills, and awareness, and their ability to survive unaided is consequently limited. This bio-psycho-social imbalance between adults and children constitutes the source of various forms of protection, domination, and exploitation of children by their parents, who are the adults closest to them in biological, psychological, and social terms. In many societies, especially those who adopted private property as one major principle of social organization, children came to be viewed as the "property" as well as the responsibility of their parents. They were, in fact, an economic asset and a means toward enhancing family power. It is only in recent centuries that Western societies began to view children as "citizens" in their own rights who are entitled to a growing measure of protection by society against excessive parental power and exploitation, and against economic exploitation by agricultural, commercial, and industrial enterprises. The notion that children were individuals in their own rights, rather than merely possessions of their parents, gradually led to the concept of a societal obligation to assure the rights of all children and to limit the extent to which their rights are determined by the rights and authority of their parents.

The societal definition of work seems rooted in the principles and values which underlie a society's overall organization and, more specifically, the organization of its economy. In a general "socioeconomic" sense, "work" includes all activities presumed to contribute to a society's existence and survival, that is, activities involved in the production and distribution of all life-sustaining and life-enhancing goods and services, as well as ritualistic activities. Participation in "work" at appropriate stages during the life cycle is the usual basis for an individual's claim to a share in his society's manifold resources. The foregoing generic definition of work tends to undergo modifications in relation to the social contexts in which activities are performed. Thus, for instance, services performed within a family group by wives for husbands and vice versa, by parents for minor children, by adult children for aged parents, by any individual for a sick or handicapped relative, etc., are usually excluded from the generic socioeconomic definition of work and are defined instead as "duties" intrinsic to specific social relationships. Such familial duties do not entitle the individuals performing them to specific economic rewards but to certain "reciprocal duties" and societal recognition. Failure to perform such duties tends to result in severe social sanctions. Socially structured relationships often involve inequalities of rights and power, and in such situations the definition of work as "reciprocal duty" may be merely a rationalization for covert exploitation of individuals who are less powerful by those who are more powerful. While the redefinition of "work" as "duty" may result in exploitation even in situations when reciprocity functions well, severe exploitation is usually unavoidable when individuals are expected to perform "duties" in spite of breakdowns of reciprocity systems. Child care performed by mothers in fatherless families is one illustration of this type of situation. The mother's activity continues to be defined as "duty" which entitles her to certain reciprocal duties from an absent or nonexistent man, but not to specific economic rewards as would be the case if society defined child care as work. The societal context of "reciprocal duty" as well as the earlier mentioned context of "voluntary work," both of which are used to obtain "free labor," support the hypothesis that societal definitions of work serve to bias the distribution of rights in society in favor of more powerful individuals, groups, and classes by depriving less powerful ones of economic rewards for their work.

Significant inequalities in the distribution of income, wealth, and all other forms of rights among individuals and groups seem to result from several principles which were institutionalized by many societies during early stages of their development, and from a set of values which emerged simultaneously with these principles, interacted with them, and reinforced them. Foremost among these principles are: provision of unequal rewards for performance of different roles; accumulation of private property of land and of other forms of durable wealth; intergenerational transmission of privately controlled property as inheritance, and, hence, amassing of family wealth and economic and political power. These principles and the corresponding values of individualism, competition, and inequality have shaped, and continue to maintain, the social order and the economic system of many societies. In modern times these principles and values led to the development of "capitalism," an economic system in which production is organized primarily to maximize profit for capital owned and controlled by individual entrepreneurs or corporations, rather than to maximize the common good of all individuals and groups in society. Major inequalities in the distribution of income and wealth, and of all other life-sustaining and life-enhancing concrete and symbolic goods and services, seem to be intrinsic consequences of the principles and values mentioned above, and of social orders and economic systems derived from them. In spite of the inevitability of such inequalities, it is possible to obtain minor shifts in the distribution of rights and in the dimensions of inequality without thoroughly changing these principles and values, and the social orders and economic systems which they sustain. Such marginal, incremental changes do, in fact, occur constantly as a result of conflicts and negotiations among interest groups who compete with each other in the political arena. However, major reductions of inequalities in the distribution of rights through significant transfers of purchasing power, and through other appropriate structural measures, cannot materialize unless a society constrains the uninhibited operation of the foregoing principles and values, and develops a social order and economic system based on alternative principles and on alternative values of collectivism, cooperation, and equality.

B. OBJECTIVES, VALUE PREMISES, THEORETICAL POSITIONS, TARGET SEGMENTS, AND SUBSTANTIVE EFFECTS OF THE POLICY

1. Policy objectives:

a. to assure women who choose to care for their children a minimum level of rights and economic independence in the form of purchasing power transferred to them as wages out of the national income; hence, to assure women the right to obtain goods and services in the market without having to engage in "gainful employment or self-employment" other than caring for their children. This objective also involves widening the options of mothers by eliminating the threat of economic sanctions which under existing social policies force them to accept employment on unfavorable terms even when they prefer to care for their children. Finally, this objective involves freeing mothers from economic dependency on husbands or on other related and unrelated individuals

b. to assure minor children the opportunity to be cared for by their mothers with society assuming the cost of such care whenever mothers choose to provide it, and, further, to assure children a minimum level of economic rights in the form of purchasing power—children's allowances—transferred on their behalf from the national income

c. to redefine child care provided by mothers to their own children as "work" which entitles women performing it to social and economic rewards in the same manner as other work

d. to redistribute rights in society by reducing inequalities of purchasing power affecting families with children

e. to assure fathers the same rights as are assured mothers under this policy, whenever special circumstances in a family require fathers to assume the care of their children

2. Value premises and ideological orientation underlying the policy objectives: The objectives pursued by the mothers' wages policy involve a weakening of the primacy of values upholding individualism and inequality, and a corresponding shift toward values stressing collective responsibility and equality of rights. These changes in value premises are reflected in societal assumption of a larger share of responsibility for the care of children, in a lessening of opportunities for economic exploitation of women, and in significant reductions in the dimensions of inequality of purchasing power. These shifts in value premises constitute a major departure from dominant beliefs, values, customs, and traditions with respect to child care, motherhood, parental rights and responsibilities, and economic relations. Because of this, the mothers' wages policy is likely to encounter resistance prior to adoption and, if adopted, in the course of its implementation.

While, then, the mothers' wages policy involves important shifts in overt value premises, it involves also continuity with regard to covert values of discrimination against women in the allocation of work. This is reflected in the fact that the policy strengthens the rights of women who care for their own children without, at the same time, opening access of women to all work. Also, the fact that the policy is directed primarily at mothers, and only marginally at fathers, reveals the underlying bias against equality of rights for both sexes.

3. Theories or hypotheses underlying the strategies and substantive provisions of the policy: The strategies and substantive provisions of the mothers' wages policy are derived mainly from theoretical premises similar to those discussed above in connection with the dynamics of the issues dealt with by this policy. It was shown there that socioeconomic deprivation of mothers and children was largely a result of discriminatory and exploitative societal practices patterned around biological phenomena. The strategies and provisions of the mothers' wages policy are designed to counteract these practices. Thus, defining child care as a joint responsibility of parents and society would reduce the extent to which the rights of children are determined primarily by the rights and authority of their parents. And assumption by society of the cost of maternal child care and provisions of children's allowances would be concrete expressions of increased societal commitment to assure the rights of all children. Similarly, defining child care performed by mothers as "work," paying wages for it out of national income, and including mothers in the Social Security system would significantly reduce the scope of established patterns of social discrimination against, and economic exploitation of, women. Furthermore, transferring sizable amounts of purchasing power from high income segments of the population to segments whose income is below the median, through mothers' wages, social security benefits, and children's allowances, as well as through appropriate corresponding modifications of the income tax system, would effectively reduce major inequalities in the shape of the rights distribution.

One further theoretical premise implicit in the strategies and provisions of this policy is that income transfers such as children's allowances which utilize the principle of "universal entitlement" are preferable to income transfers such as "Negative Income Taxes" which utilize the principle of "selectivity based on need." Universal entitlement is assumed to be more conducive to societal cohesiveness and solidarity than selectivity since all individuals within a specified social category, such as children, are treated equally with respect to the transfer process, irrespective of their economic circumstances. Universal entitlements avoid also the controversial issue of "work incentives" since they are paid independently of other income. Selectivity on the other hand is often considered to be more efficient in economic terms since income transfers are channeled only to individuals within categories defined by economic need. It should be noted, however, that the net economic effect of income transfers can be designed to be roughly equal in both approaches by means of suitable adjustments of income tax provisions.[2]

Finally, theoretical premises underlying the proposed levels of mothers' wages and children's allowances need to be made explicit. The federally established minimum wage has been suggested as standard rate for mothers' wages, and $50 per month (in 1970 dollars) as the standard children's allowance for the following reasons. Firstly, the proposed rate for mothers' wages reflects a societal position that the social and economic value of child care performed by mothers is not less than that of other tasks for which the government established a minimum wage floor. Secondly, as shown by the following calculations, these rates for mothers' wages and children's allowances would bring about significant reductions of income inequalities between men and women, and among families with children, and would greatly reduce social and economic deprivation among these families. The minimum wage at the 1970 level of $1.60 per hour paid for eight hours a day, 365 days a year would give mothers a personal annual income of $4,672. This is nearly half the 1970 median family income of $9,870, more than twice the 1970 median income of women of $2,240, yet only 70 percent of the 1970 median income of men of $6,670.[3] Such a wage combined with a children's allowance of $50 per month would provide a fatherless family of four with an annual income of $6,472, which is nearly two-thirds of the 1970 median family income of $9,870, or 92 percent of $6,960, the lower level budget for an urban family of four as measured by the Bureau of Labor Statistics in the spring of 1970.[4] The United States economy seems capable of sustaining income transfers at the suggested levels since the redistributive potential of an economy is reflected in the mean income which tends to be higher than the median, the statistic used in the foregoing argument. Since the suggested transfer rate would not bring the income of all families up to the median, the redistributive potential within the economy would not be exceeded. Increases over time in minimum wages, GNP, mean and median income, and inflation have not changed substantially the conclusions of the 1971 analysis.

The foregoing arguments are relevant also to a related aspect of the mothers' wages policy. This is the choice of a uniform rate of mothers' wages rather than of a differential wage scale based on different levels of opportunity costs, or potential earnings, which mothers forego when engaging in child care instead of in employment outside their homes. A uniform rate of mothers' wages is considered conducive to the reduction of inequalities of rights among families with children, whereas a differential wage scale would counteract this policy objective. Furthermore, a uniform rate of mothers' wages symbolizes a societal position according to which the value of child care is deemed equal for all children, irrespective of variations in the occupational skills and earning potential of mothers who provide the care.

4. Target segments of society: Since the mothers' wages policy deals with the rights of women and children through redistribution of purchasing power both vertically between income strata and horizontally within income strata, it is bound to affect the circumstances of living of all individuals and segments of society. Its specific targets, however, are mothers and children or families with children, especially those whose annual income falls within the lower half of the income distribution. The following figures derived from publications of the United States Bureau of the Census indicate the numerical size of the target segments of the policy. In 1969 the United States population included 70.8 million children under age eighteen in 29.8 million families. About one-half of these families with children under age eighteen had annual incomes under $10,000. This latter segment of slightly over fifteen million families constitutes the primary target of the mothers' wages policy. This group of families is classified by income steps in Table A.1.

To grasp the full meaning of the income distribution shown in this

TABLE A.1
TOTAL MONEY INCOME OF FAMILIES WITH
CHILDREN UNDER AGE EIGHTEEN—1969*

INCOME	NUMBER OF FAMILIES	NUMBER OF FAMILIES CUMULATIVE
under $3,000	2,040,000	2,040,000
$3,000-$4,999	2,560,000	4,600,000
$5,000-$6,999	3,600,000	8,200,000
$7,000-$9,999	6,957,000	15,157,000
$10,000 and over	14,664,000	29,821,000

Source: U.S. Department of Commerce, Bureau of the Census, *Consumer Income, Current Population Reports*, Series P-60, No. 75, December 14, 1970, Table 14, p. 29.

table, it should be realized that nearly 3.5 million families, including 10.5 million children under age eighteen, were classified in 1970 as "poor" in accordance with poverty criteria established by the United States government. For a nonfarm family of four, the official poverty threshold was $3,968 in 1970.[5] Of these 3.5 million poor families with children under age eighteen, about 1.7 million were headed by women and about 1.8 million were headed by men. Nearly 2.6 million families among those in "poverty" were by the end of 1970 on the rolls of the "Aid to Families with Dependent Children" program. These AFDC families had a total of 9.7 million individuals, 7.1 million of whom were children.[6] Furthermore, the number of children under age eighteen in families whose income in 1970 was below the "near-poverty" level was 14.6 million, over one-fifth of all children under age eighteen in the United States.[7] The "near-poverty" level is defined as 125 percent of the official poverty level. Thus the near-poverty threshold for a nonfarm family of four was $4,960 in 1970.

The foregoing discussion of family income indicates that the target segments of the mothers' wages policy include poor, marginally poor, and working or lower middle class families with children under age eighteen. It is important to note that the target segments of this policy do not include families without children under age eighteen, and "unrelated individuals." Consequently, nearly 1.8 million families without children under age eighteen and over 5 million unrelated individuals who together constituted 33.7 percent of all persons classified as poor in 1970 are not included in the target segments.[8] These poor families and individuals who are outside the scope of the mothers' wages policy are mainly retired older men and women, as well as unemployed, underemployed, or marginally employed individuals of all ages. Families without children under age eighteen and unrelated individuals among the near-poor and the working or lower middle class are also not included in the target segments of the mothers' wages policy and would therefore not derive direct benefits from it.

The income criterion used here to identify the target segments of the mothers' wages policy reveals also several other characteristics of the target population which tend to be associated with poverty and low income. The target population, though distributed all over the nation in rural and urban areas, is more highly concentrated in inner cities and in economically depressed and less developed regions of the country. Families belonging to the target segments tend to be subject to higher rates of physical and emotional illness, social and psychological deviance, and family breakdown than families with children under age eighteen in the upper half of the income distribution. Also among target segment families, educational achievement and occupational levels tend to be lower, unemployment rates tend to be higher, quality of housing and neighborhoods tends to be lower, and levels of social involvement and participation tend to be lower.

Families belonging to racial minorities are significantly overrepresented among the target segments of the mothers' wages policy. While less than 12 percent of all families with children under age eighteen in the United States are black, one-third of all poor families with children under age eighteen are black. Also, while about 8 percent of white families with children under age eighteen were officially classified as poor in 1970, about 34 percent of black families with children under age eighteen were so classified. Furthermore, 10 percent of white children under age eighteen as against 40 percent of black children under age eighteen were poor.[9] And finally, 74 percent of black families as against 48 percent of white families had incomes under $10,000 in 1970.[10]

Families headed by women are also significantly overrepresented among the target segments of the mothers' wages policy. While 10 percent of all families with children under age eighteen were headed by women in 1969,[11] 47 percent of all poor families with children under age eighteen and 61 percent of black poor families with children under age eighteen were headed by women.[12] Families among the target segments, especially among poor people and even more so among black poor people, also tend to have more children under age eighteen than all families with children in the United States. Thus, while in 1969 about 18 percent of all families with children under age eighteen in the nation had four or more children, 35 percent of poor families with children under age eighteen and 46 percent of poor black families with children under age eighteen had that many children. Conversely, while 63 percent of all families with children under age eighteen had one or two children, 47 percent of all poor, and 38 percent of poor black families with children under age eighteen had one or two children.[13]

The numerical size and major characteristics of the above sketched target segments of the mothers' wages policy have remained fairly constant relative to the entire United States population over the past twenty five years. This stability of relative size is not likely to change unless social policies are developed and implemented which will bring about significant redistribution of purchasing power among the entire population. The foregoing conclusion concerning the magnitude of the target segments seems inescapable since the target segments are defined primarily in terms of family income strata and characteristics associated with these strata, and since the general shape of the income distribution of the United States population has remained essentially unchanged since the end of World War II.[14] The only long-term changes to be expected in the future in the absolute size of the target segments, assuming no real changes in social policy, are, therefore, changes due to the natural increase of the population. In addition to this, certain short-run variations should be expected in the relative magnitude of target segments as a result of fluctuations in aggregate economic activity and the impact of this activity on employment rates, wage levels, and the cost of goods and services as well as a result of constantly occurring marginal, incremental modifications of the social policy system.[15]

5. Short- and long-range effects: When implemented, the mothers' wages policy would result in the attainment of the several objectives specified above, provided federal tax and other economic measures will be amended so as not to counteract the overall redistributive purposes of this policy. The transfer income of mothers from full-time mothers' wages would be $4,672 per year in accordance with the 1971 minimum wage level. This amount is more than twice the 1970 nonfarm poverty threshold for unrelated women of $1,935, and even slightly more than the 1970 nonfarm poverty threshold for female-headed, five-person households of $4,639.[16] When, as specified in the policy, mothers' wages are linked with a $600 a year children's allowance per child in 1970 constant dollars, the total transfer income of families with children under age eighteen would exceed the 1970 nonfarm poverty and near-poverty thresholds for female-headed families with any number of children. Table A.2 demonstrates these circumstances by showing the excess of transfer income for different family sizes over corresponding poverty and near-poverty thresholds.

Table A.2 suggests several important observations. Firstly, no female-headed family consisting of mothers and children under age eighteen would have to live on an income below the near-poverty threshold once the mothers' wages policy is implemented. However, the combined transfer income of mothers' wages and children's allowances would be less than the 1970 median family income of $9,870 as long as a mother had fewer than nine children under age eighteen. Clearly, also, the federally financed program of Aid to Families with Dependent Children, or the expanded yet inadequate Family Assistance Program, if enacted, as well as supplementary state-financed programs of general assistance for families and children would no longer be needed. The table also reveals that mothers and children would not be lifted merely out of conditions of severe poverty, but they would have sizable amounts of purchasing power beyond the official near-poverty levels. While this margin of purchasing power beyond the near-poverty threshold would

TABLE A.2 MOTHERS' WAGES AND CHILDREN'S ALLOWANCES COMPARED WITH 1970 NONFARM POVERTY AND NEAR-POVERTY THRESHOLDS FOR FEMALE-HEADED HOUSEHOLDS

SIZE OF FAMILY UNIT	MOTHERS' WAGES	CHIL- DREN'S ALLOW- ANCE	TOTAL TRANSFER INCOME	POVERTY THRESH- OLD*	EXCESS OVER POVERTY THRESH- OLD	NEAR POVERTY THRESH- OLD*	EXCESS OVER NEAR- POV- ERTY THRESH- OLD
Mother, 1 child	4,672	600	5,272	2,522	2,750	3,153	2,119
Mother, 2 children	4,672	1,200	5,872	3,003	2,869	3,754	2,118
Mother, 3 children	4,672	1,800	6,472	3,948	2,524	4,935	1,537
Mother, 4 children	4,672	2,400	7,072	4,639	2,433	5,799	1,273
Mother, 5 children	4,672	3,000	7,672	5,220	2,452	6,525	1,147
Mother, 6 children	4,672	3,600	8,272	6,317	1,955	7,896	376

*Source: U.S. Department of Commerce, Bureau of the Census, Consumer Income, Current Population Reports, Series P 60, No. 77, May 7, 1971, Table No. 6, p. 6.

decrease gradually with family size, economics of scale can be expected to compensate to a certain extent for this gradual decrease of purchasing power.

Mothers in female-headed or male-headed families with children under age eighteen are not likely to engage in part- or full-time employment outside their homes unless such employment would markedly improve the overall economic and psycho-social situation of a family. It seems consequently safe to assume that families with children under age eighteen would be assured at least the level of purchasing power resulting from the combined full-time mothers' wages and children's allowances to which they would be entitled. Any income earned by fathers and/or husbands, as well as by children, would of course improve the overall economic circumstances of families with children under age eighteen beyond the levels guaranteed by mothers' wages and children's allowances.

Before continuing the exploration of the multiple effects of the mothers' wages policy, it seems necessary at this point to present an estimate of the magnitude and incidence of the aggregate transfer of purchasing power pursuant to this policy. Yet prior to considering such an estimate, a caveat seems in order which is that a transfer of purchasing power among consumption units and segments of a society is not to be equated with a real economic cost in a societal sense, although such transfers may involve considerable "costs" in the form of taxes paid by various individuals, business firms, and segments of society. A transfer of purchasing power merely means that claims to the totality of goods and services produced by a society are being reshuffled or redistributed. As a result of this redistribution, the rates at which different individuals and segments of society can participate in the consumption of goods and services are readjusted, and pre-transfer consumption patterns are transformed into new post-transfer patterns. Ultimately redistribution of purchasing power may lead to modifications of aggregate production, consumption, savings, and investment of capital and work effort, and in this way real economic costs and/or gains may result from the transfers. The extent to which such costs and gains will actually materialize following the transfer of purchasing power depends on many other policies pursued by a society including fiscal, monetary, wage, price, interest, and foreign trade measures. The important thing to keep in mind, however, is that the magnitude of the transfer of purchasing power is not, in itself, a direct measure of real economic costs or gains.

In 1970 the United States population included about twenty-nine million mothers with children under age eighteen and about seventy-one million children. If all these mothers were to collect mothers' wages, the aggregate wage at minimum wage rates prevailing in 1970 would be $135.5 billion. The aggregate transfer amount for children's allowances for the same year would be $42.6 billion, and the combined amount for both these transfer programs would be $178.1 billion.

About ten million mothers participated in the work force during 1970 and would have been entitled only to fractions of full mothers' wages in proportion to their work force participation. Some mothers—and no one knows how many—would, of course, withdraw from employment outside their homes once a mothers' wages policy is implemented. It seems safe to assume that mothers whose purchasing power would not increase noticeably as a result of employment outside their homes would withdraw from such employment. Few mothers work year-round in full-time employment, and most working mothers are employed in low-level jobs which offer low wages and limited job satisfaction. Less than 10 percent of working mothers earn more than $5,000 per year,[17] and it thus seems that nine out of ten, or about nine million mothers, are likely to withdraw from the work force once a mothers' wages policy is introduced. These considerations suggest that the aggregate transfer amount for mothers' wages be reduced by about $3.5 billion as a consequence of work force participation by mothers, and the total amount needed to carry out the transfer programs of mothers' wages and children's allowances in 1970 would thus have been close to $175 billion.

Since mothers' wages and children's allowances would be paid on a universal basis to all mothers and children irrespective of economic position, nearly half the aggregate transfer, or $85 billion, would be paid to mothers and children in families whose annual income is above the median of the national income distribution. These "horizontal" transfers among income units in the upper half of the distribution would involve mainly transfers from childless households to families with children under age eighteen, and would reduce existing inequalities in per capita purchasing power within the more affluent segments of the population.

About $90 billion of the total transfer amount would go to mothers and children in families whose income is below the median of the income distribution. This amount, which is less than 10 percent of current GNP, represents the extent of real "vertical" transfers from the affluent segments of society to currently poor, near-poor, and working or lower middle class families with children under age eighteen. Some horizontal transfers would also occur within the lower half of the income distribution from childless households to families with children under age eighteen, and would reduce inequalities within that segment of the population.

In connection with the estimate of the magnitude of vertical transfers of purchasing power, consideration should be given to fiscal implications of phasing out existing vertical transfer programs and of using amounts budgeted for these programs for the mothers' wages policy. Between $5 and $6 billion would be available from the AFDC program, federal food programs, and state-operated general assistance programs. Should the federal Family Assistance Program be enacted, another $5 billion would be available. Furthermore, a broad range of programs aimed at aiding poor and near-poor families which are now operated by the Office of Economic Opportunity and by the United States Departments of Health, Education, and Welfare; Housing and Urban Development; Labor; and Agriculture could also be gradually phased out, and funds appropriated for these programs could then be used to offset new appropriations for the mothers' wages policy. The scope of new revenue for vertical transfers pursuant to the mothers' wages policy could thus be reduced to under $80 billion.

Financing the total income transfers of the mothers' wages policy would require major adjustments and reforms of the nation's tax system. Several comments seem indicated in this context. First of all, mothers' wages and children's allowances would be subject to income tax in order to reduce progressively the transfer amounts retained by families with other sources, and varying amounts, of income. Secondly, existing income tax deductions for children, wives, and husbands would have to be eliminated since their effects on after-tax purchasing power are regressive and thus in conflict with the redistributive objectives of mothers' wages and children's allowances. Thirdly, many special provisions in the tax laws which now favor selected interest groups such as oil companies, real estate enterprises, and individual home owners would have to be eliminated, and in this way the annual tax yield under present tax rates could be increased by about $50 billion.[18] Finally, the entire federal tax system would have to be overhauled, amended, and reformed in order to generate the revenue flow necessary for the vertical and horizontal transfers involved in the mothers' wages policy, and in order to eliminate from the existing provisions all regressive tendencies which counteract the principles and values of the new policy.

Transfer payments of the magnitude indicated here, if financed through a consistently progressive tax system, would result in significant changes in the existing shape of the income or rights distribution in society. The socioeconomic distance between high-income groups and low-income families with children under age eighteen would be narrowed considerably, and the proposed policy would thus have a decisive impact, over time, not only on absolute poverty, but also on relative poverty and bio-psycho-social deprivation. It may thus be expected that various biological, psychological, social, and cultural correlates of poverty and low-income life in the United States would gradually decrease in scope and intensity. It is not suggested here that such destructive phenomena as delinquency, crime, family breakdown, mental illness and retardation, psycho-social alienation, drug addiction, deterioration of neighborhoods, and a variety of physical ailments would disappear as soon as the economic roots of poverty are eradicated. It is submitted, though, that progress in overcoming these phenomena is possible only when economic deprivation is no longer permitted to exist in an affluent society, and that, therefore, social policies involving significant reductions in income inequalities constitute essential, though not sufficient, measures for controlling and eventually preventing these dysfunctional phenomena.

Having reviewed effects of the mothers' wages policy in general terms, several more specific observations seem now indicated. The work force participation response of mothers is one important aspect which has already been referred to. It was suggested that most working mothers, nine out of ten, would probably withdraw from employment outside their homes since such employment provides them presently with fewer benefits than mothers' wages would. This response of mothers could lead to wage increases and general improvements of working conditions in service occupations and in many industrial jobs now filled by women. It could also lead to reduced unemployment and better working conditions for men and for women who are not engaged in rearing their children, and in reduction of poverty among unrelated individuals and couples without children whose poverty would not be directly ameliorated by the income transfers of the mothers' wages policy. A further consequence could be accelerated development of automation which is now often held back because of the availability of cheap labor. Gradual price increases for certain goods and services could result from the foregoing changes in the work force and the price of labor, but increased efficiency in methods of production due to increases in automation would counteract the pressures from higher cost of labor. Furthermore, overall economic activity would be stimulated considerably as the consumption potential of the population for basic goods and services would expand. This increase in economic activity would in turn yield additional taxes for local, state, and federal governments which could lead to overall improvements in public services.

Critics of children's allowances and also of mothers' wages expect an increase in the birthrate to follow the introduction of such programs. Evidence from many countries, including Canada, England, and France, who have had similar programs on a smaller scale for many years, does not support this assumption.[19] Human behavior concerning fertility is the resultant of a complex set of forces. Economic factors are certainly important elements of this set of forces. However, the relationship between economics and fertility is not a linear one. While it is probably true that some families are more likely to have children as their ability to provide for them adequately increases with income, it is also true that escape from poverty has usually been followed by decreases in fertility of formerly poverty-stricken social strata along with overall changes in attitudes and life style of these strata. The assumption that mothers and families are going to have more children simply in order to obtain additional mothers' wages and children's allowances seems to derive from an oversimplification of complex psycho-social processes, especially in view of the fact that wages and allowances per child do not cover the cost of supporting an additional child. It may be of interest in this context to point to a significant decrease in birthrates among recipients of AFDC in New York City following the legalization of abortions in New York State and increased availability of family planning services to participants of the AFDC program.[20]

The mothers' wages policy is also expected to affect the self-image of mothers and fathers, the relations of women and men, and, consequently, family life and all aspects of child development. Freeing mothers from total economic dependence on their husbands is apt to result in more meaningful intrafamilial relations. Mothers would be more equal as partners in a marriage and more equally respected as members of society once their work would be remunerative economically and rewarded with social prestige, both in their homes and in the labor market where they could no longer be severely exploited. While fewer marriages may be contracted, and fewer marriages would continue merely for economic reasons, once mothers' wages are instituted, couples who married and remained together would probably lead a more harmonious family life than many families do now. With economic elements receding in importance as far as family relations are concerned, human relations would become the dominant force for maintaining family life and keeping families together. Increased harmony in intrafamilial relations should have positive effects on the overall functioning of family members in and outside the home.

Along with changes in the role of mothers, the roles of husbands and fathers would also undergo changes. Fathers and husbands would be valued in their families for their human qualities and not primarily as economic providers. Such a change may not be easy for many men who were socialized into a specific pattern of the male and father role. Some men are likely to resent the change and so may also some women. These negative reactions by men as well as by women would seem to be understandable consequences of attitudes which evolved over countless generations. These reactions may lead to conflicts and separations in some families during early stages of the implementation of the mothers' wages policy. In the long run though, positive reactions are likely to outweigh by far such negative ones, and family relations are expected to improve over time to a considerable degree.

Economic security and gradual improvements in the quality of family life will in turn enhance physical, intellectual, educational, social, and emotional aspects of child life and child development among the main target segments of the mothers' wages policy. In this sense the policy can be viewed as a long-range "societal investment in human capital."

Some individuals, families, and business firms whose wealth and earnings would be subject to higher taxes following introduction of the mothers' wages policy might view this policy as damaging to their interests, and might reduce their work efforts, savings, and investments when additional income would, in their judgment, yield too little additional benefits. Some persons might even choose to emigrate while some might attempt to reduce their tax liabilities in various ways. Other members of higher income strata may, however, be more favorably disposed toward the mothers' wages policy and may cooperate in its implementation upon realizing the dynamics of human interdependence in society and the likelihood that direct and immediate benefits which their higher taxes provided for low income families with children would eventually lead to indirect, comprehensive, and long-range benefits for all members and segments of society. It would seem that chances for cooperation of upper income strata could be enhanced by emphasizing, in promoting the mothers' wages policy, its long-range potential for serving the interests of all groups in society, rather than merely the important short-run benefits for the policy's target segments.

The overall benefits and costs of the mothers' wages policy can now be summarized:

Benefits

—Elimination of poverty and near-poverty for families with children under age eighteen, a total of about 17 million individuals out of 25.5 million poor persons in 1970

—Increase in purchasing power of all families with children under age eighteen whose income is now below the median family income as a result of a $90 billion vertical transfer of purchasing power from the upper half of the national income distribution

—Reduction of inequalities in per capita purchasing power of families with children under age eighteen throughout the population by way of horizontal transfers from households without children under age eighteen

—Overall stimulation of economic activity to meet increased demand for basic goods and services. Related to this, reduction of unemployment and of poverty among able-bodied unrelated persons and couples without children under age eighteen who would not benefit directly from mothers' wages and children's allowances. Unemployment among men and women without children under age eighteen would also decrease as a result of reduced work force participation of mothers

—Increase in tax revenue of local, state, and federal governments derived from transfer income and increased economic activity. These additional taxes could support more and better public services

—Wage increases and improvements in working conditions in unskilled and marginal jobs formerly filled by poor mothers

—Acceleration in the development of automation to counteract shortages of cheap labor

—Development of a more equitable and more consistently progressive system of taxation without special benefits for powerful interest groups

—Improvement in self-image and social prestige of mothers along with marked improvement in their social rights and economic circumstances

—Shifts in the role of fathers and husbands in the family from economic control toward sharing as equals in a more meaningful relationship

—Improvement in the human quality of family life, and in relations between men and women

—Improvement in economic, biological, emotional, intellectual, social, and cultural aspects of child life and child development throughout all social strata but especially among poor, near-poor, and working class families

—Increased societal responsibility for the economic security and general well-being of children

—Over time, reduction of incidence and prevalence of physical and mental illness, mental retardation, and of various forms of deviance in social and psychological functioning

—Over time, improvement in the quality of housing, neighborhoods, and public services

—Entitlement to social security benefits for women on the basis of maternal child care work

—Phasing out of AFDC and several other public welfare programs resulting in savings of over $10 billion

Costs

—An annual transfer flow of $175 billion of purchasing power generated through marked increases in progressive taxation on individuals and groups in the upper half of the income distribution. Nearly half of this transfer would be circulated horizontally among households in the upper half of the income distribution, while the

rest would be transferred vertically to poor, near-poor, and working or "lower middle class" families with children under age eighteen
—Loss of cheap labor of about nine million mothers
—Increases in the price of labor and the cost of production and, related to this, increases in the price of some goods and services
—Loss of economic control of wives by husbands
—Increases in taxation and corresponding reductions in consumption and profits of individuals and business enterprises. Related to this, possible decreases in work effort, savings, and investments
—Significant reductions of economic inequalities and, related to this, gradual reductions in social prestige and privileges of upper income strata

A review of these benefits and costs suggests that anticipated benefits of the mothers' wages policy outweigh by far its perceived costs when humanistic, public interest, and egalitarian criteria are applied. Clearly, this is a value judgment and different conclusions could be reached by applying different criteria. It should also be noted that many elements (e.g., the increase of wages for marginal jobs) can be viewed as a benefit as well as a cost, depending on one's value premises. However, even within the humanistic, public interest, and egalitarian value premises, one could question whether the mothers' wages policy represents the most effective and efficient use of this sizable amount of transfer funds. In other words, since even an affluent society is faced with limitations of resources, questions of opportunity costs must be considered. It thus could be asked whether the same amount of transfer funds should be used to yield an adequate income for all poor persons rather than primarily for families with children under age eighteen. Or whether, perhaps, some of these transfer funds should preferably be channeled into ecological rehabilitation programs, aid to poor and developing nations, or some other, not less critical, societal need. These essentially evaluative questions belong, however, to the final section of an analysis. They are mentioned at this point merely to illustrate the proposition that social policies cannot be evaluated properly in terms of their intrinsic benefits and costs, but need to be examined in relation to the entire policy system of a society.

C. *IMPLICATIONS OF THE POLICY FOR THE OPERATING AND OUTCOME VARIABLES OF SOCIAL POLICIES*

1. Changes in the development, management, and conservation of resources, goods, and services: The mothers' wages policy is not intended to cause changes in the development, management, and conservation of resources, goods, and services. However, vertical transfers of significant amounts of purchasing power from higher to lower income groups of the population, and consequent stimulation of economic activity and comprehensive changes in the consumption patterns of former low income households, would result nevertheless in marked qualitative and quantitative changes in the development of goods and services by private and public sources.

In general, the direction of these changes would be away from the production of less essential and luxury-type goods and services which are consumed primarily by upper income households, toward the production of more basic necessities including homes, home-furnishings, durable goods, clothing, and health care services. Improvements in economic circumstances and life styles of former low income groups, and related increases in tax payments to local and state governments, would result in increased pressures for equalization of the quality and quantity of public services. These demands and newly available revenue would in time bring about the development of better schools, transportation, sanitation, fire and police services, and ecological and neighborhood rehabilitation.

Priority decisions affecting development of these new patterns of resources would be mediated, as in the past, through the operation of the market and the political system. The difference with respect to these decision mechanisms following the introduction of the mothers' wages policy would be that formerly poor and low income households would now share more equally in economic and political power, and would thus have a better chance to register their preferences and to influence the eventual outcome of decisions.

Implementation of the mothers' wages policy may slow down the development of one important, yet controversial, service resource which for a variety of reasons has attracted in recent years considerable interest from many different groups. This service resource encompasses various types of child care services such as group and family day care facilities, nursery schools, early childhood education programs, etc.[21] A wide range of benefits and costs are assumed to be associated with these services, depending on variations in quality and objectives. The common element intrinsic to all these services is a shift of child care functions away from mothers. It seems that demand for such services by mothers and by the public would decrease, and motivation to promote their development would lessen, when mothers could care for their own children without being penalized economically, socially, and psychologically.

2. *Changes in the organization of work and production:* The mothers' wages policy is also not aimed directly at bringing about major changes in the access of individuals and groups to work. However, while the direct impact of the policy on access to work would not be very significant, the indirect, long-term impact could be considerable.

One direct consequence of the mothers' wages policy for the work system would be the redefinition of maternal child care as socially recognized work for which mothers would receive concrete and symbolic rewards in the form of purchasing power, social security benefits, and a measure of social prestige. This redefinition would strengthen the social position of mothers and would afford them increased protection against forced allocation to undesirable work in service and industrial occupations which tend to offer low rewards in purchasing power, prestige, and job satisfaction.

Another direct consequence of the policy would be the strengthening and protection of the social position of children by increasing societal responsibility for their economic security and by assuring them the right to be cared for by their own parents whenever mothers or fathers wish to provide such care, with society assuming the cost of the work.

The mothers' wages policy would also eliminate certain existing social roles, namely, those of clients and administrators of AFDC and other public assistance programs. Over time, as various programs for aiding poor families would be phased out, the roles of clients and administrators of these programs would also be eliminated.

The policy would also modify the roles of fathers and husbands. The power and control inherent in these roles at present because of economic dynamics would be reduced, and social and psychological aspects in relation to other family members which are also inherent in these roles would be enhanced. Also, under certain circumstances, such as the absence of mothers from a family, the role of father would be broadened to encompass child care and prerogatives intrinsic to that redefined role.

The mothers' wages policy would not bring about significant changes in criteria and procedures by which women gain access to the wide range of work in society. In a certain sense, the policy may even strengthen the traditional linkage between child care and biological motherhood, and may thus decelerate progress toward equal access for women to all work in society.

Indirect, long-term effects of the mothers' wages policy on access to work would be mediated through the reductions it would bring about in inequalities of economic circumstances, educational opportunities, and life styles. Access to many valued roles in society tends to depend on extended educational preparations, yet educational opportunities are at present not available to all children on an equal basis. Economic circumstances of families appear to be important determinants of the educational opportunities of their children and, hence, of the occupational options and eventual social conditions of adults. Reductions of major economic inequalities through social policies such as the mothers' wages would, therefore, over time reduce inequalities of educational opportunities and would in this way gradually reduce existing obstacles to equal access to all work and roles for individuals from former low income families.

3. Changes concerning exchange and distribution of goods, services, rights, and responsibilities: The major, direct thrust of the mothers' wages policy is obviously aimed at changing the distribution of rights as it affects mothers and children in general, and, more specifically, currently poor, near-poor, and lower income families with children under age eighteen. The policy would also directly modify the shape of the distribution of rights throughout society.

The most important change due to the policy would be a task-and role-specific reward for mothers who choose to care for their children. While at present such mothers may receive no direct economic rewards from society other than public assistance in the form of means-tested relief, they would receive socially financed wages and social security benefits once the mothers' wages policy is implemented. Children under age eighteen, too, would be recipients of a new specific entitlement, a children's allowance, which in itself would guarantee them minimal economic security and which, in combination with their mothers' societal wages, would assure them the right to an adequate standard of living. Besides, as indicated above, children would also gain the right to be cared for by their mothers or fathers, depending on family choices and circumstances.

Along with the new rights for mothers and children, the policy involves a set of corresponding new constraints through progressive tax reforms, affecting primarily segments in the population whose income is above the median. In aggregate terms, about 10 percent of total national income would be shifted from the 50 percent of the population who now obtain about 75 percent of all income, to the other half of the population who now obtain merely 25 percent of all income. The policy would therefore result in a new income ratio between the two halves of the population, and a related new pattern of rights and responsibilities. The new ratio would be approximately 65 to 35 percent of national income instead of 75 to 25 percent.

The mothers' wages policy would result also in a minor shift among the two distributive mechanisms of task-specific rewards and general or specific entitlements. As a result of the children's allowance, about $43 billion, or approximately 4 percent of 1970 GNP, would be distributed as a universal entitlement to all members of society under age eighteen, independent of any work performed by the recipients. Mothers' wages themselves, it should be noted, are not a universal entitlement, but a task- and role-specific reward for work performed by mothers, and thus would fit more closely the more conventional pattern of rights distribution in the United States, namely, rewards for work.

The new rights pursuant to the mothers' wages policy would be distributed entirely in the form of purchasing power, that is as "rights-equivalents." However, to the extent that a portion of this purchasing power will be absorbed by local and state taxation, it will be transformed into, and distributed "in kind" as, public services primarily for groups in the population who receive at present inferior and inadequate public services.

The mothers' wages policy would establish new definitions of minimal economic rights for mothers and fathers caring for their children as well as for all children. These minimal levels of rights would be set sufficiently high so as to assure an adequate standard of living for all families with children under age eighteen. The minimal level of mothers' wages would be linked to the minimum federal wage, and the level of children's allowances would be linked to the value of the 1970 dollar. In this way, the new minimum levels would have to be adjusted automatically as minimum wages are adjusted throughout the economy and as the value of the dollar would change with inflation or, perhaps, deflation. The relative position of families with children under age eighteen would thus be assured within the overall rights distribution of society. Coverage of the designated new minimal economic rights would be provided for in law through authorization of annual open-ended appropriations and through corresponding, progressive modifications of the federal tax system.

In summarizing the various changes in the distribution of rights, it is evident that the mothers' wages policy would result in significant shifts in the relative distribution of purchasing power from affluent to low income segments of the population, and hence in marked reduction of inequalities of many rights which are associated with purchasing power. It should be reemphasized, however, that the redistribution of purchasing power and of related rights under this policy would not directly benefit low income families without children under age eighteen and low income unrelated individuals. Some of these families and individuals, namely those of working age, would probably benefit from the indirect effects of the redistribution of purchasing power, the growth in economic activity, and shortages of workers for unskilled and semiskilled work. However, others, and this includes mainly poor and near-poor aged and disabled couples and individuals, would receive neither direct nor indirect benefits. On the contrary, the inequalities of purchasing power and of related rights suffered now by these segments of the population would probably increase in relative terms unless special, vertical transfer programs are developed and enacted which would eliminate poverty and near-poverty for aging and disabled members of society who would otherwise constitute a "new underclass."

Finally, in discussing the effects of the mothers' wages policy on the overall distribution of rights, it needs to be reemphasized that, while strengthening considerably the economic security of mothers, it would have only limited effects on the more complex issues of equalizing the rights of women to those of men in terms of access to work and roles in society.

4. Changes in Governance and Legitimation: The mothers' wages policy is not intended to change the established system and structure of governance and legitimation, but to initiate new governmental functions. These functions are assurance of a minimum level of economic rights to all children up to age eighteen through a universal children's allowance and the inclusion of child care work undertaken by mothers (by choice or necessity) in the aggregate of socially necessary work, entitling them to a fair share of the GNP. Related to these functions would be new governmental responsibility for the design and implementation of the children's allowance and mother's wages.

The new functions of government do not include new supervisory responsibilities concerning the child care work of mothers receiving wages from public funds, or the manner in which households choose to use children's allowances. The purpose of the policy is reduction of economic and social injustices, but not interference with established civil rights to privacy of mothers and children. Mothers receiving wages and children receiving allowances would be subject to the same child care and child protection policies, services, and provisions as all children and households. But there would definitely be no special provisions for public supervision and control of child care practices by mothers receiving mothers' wages.

Over time, there are likely to be indirect effects on governance and legitimation as a result of gradual changes in the objective conditions and subjective sense of self and power of previously poor and socially marginalized households, many of whom might be motivated to exercise their civil and political rights more actively. In this way, previously excluded groups and classes should become effective forces in the political arena and in processes of governance. This should strengthen intrasocietal solidarity, reduce social alienation, and have a positive impact on the dynamics of legitimation.

5. *Changes Concerning Reproduction, Socialization and Social Control:* The mothers' wages policy is intended to have a major impact on child care and socialization. Effects of the policy on reproduction and social control are likely to be indirect, but not less significant, over time, than the consequences for child care and socialization.

Eliminating poverty and social and economic deprivation for households with children, and providing mothers with real and meaningful options concerning work and child care, would undoubtedly enrich, over time, the quality of child care, home life, and socialization. As these changes took hold and gradually stabilized, they would affect the attitudes and practices of people concerning responsibility for sexual relations and the birth of children, and concerning the objectively appropriate and subjectively desired size of their households. These economic, social, emotional, and attitudinal shifts should be reflected in increases in domestic harmony and in physical and mental health, corresponding further improvements in child care and socialization, and decreases in emotional disturbance and social deviance. Accordingly, the prevalence of conditions requiring secondary socialization and measures of social control should decline over time.

6. *Consequences of changes concerning resources, work and production, rights, governance and legitimation, and reproduction, socialization, and social control for the circumstances of living and the power of individuals, groups and classes, the nature and quality of intrasocietal human relations, and the overall quality of life:* Precise answers to questions implied in this focus of the analysis are not possible since sufficient knowledge concerning many relevant variables is not available. Yet in spite of this, it seems possible to anticipate certain likely societal developments should the mothers' wages policy be adopted.

In examining consequences of the mothers' wages policy for the outcome variables of social policies in all relevant spheres, three major segments of society need to be considered. These are (1) the primary target segment of the policy, namely, families with children under age eighteen, especially those whose income is below the national median; (2) low income households without children under age eighteen consisting mainly of aged persons and individuals with handicaps and disabilities; and (3) upper income families and unrelated individuals.

Economic: The most important change in circumstances of living from which many other constructive changes would gradually emanate would be a major improvement in the economic situation of several million families with children under age eighteen who are now living in conditions of poverty, near-poverty, and low income, and who tend to experience feelings of insecurity, frustration, and alienation. The assurance of economic security at an adequate level for these families would set in motion a process of social rehabilitation and reconstruction, the effects of which would reach into many spheres of their lives, as well as the lives of other groups in society.

No seriously adverse economic consequences are likely to result for population segments who would pay higher taxes than now to generate the transfer funds needed for implementation of the mothers' wages policy since the estimated tax increase would be less than 10 percent of their aggregate income. Their wealth and after-tax income would still exceed by far the wealth and income of the recipients of the transfers, and no major decline in their standard of living is likely to occur. While then the financial costs borne by the more affluent segments of the population would not cause them real economic damage and serious disadvantage, they would benefit from the subtle consequences of the mothers' wages policy for the overall quality of life in society in the various spheres of societal existence discussed below. The aggregate effect over time of these various benefits would be a less divided, less alienated, less pathological, and a more humane and better integrated society.

Households without children, consisting mainly of aged persons and people with handicaps and disabilities, would derive no immediate direct economic benefits from the mothers' wages policy and would initially even experience a decline in their circumstances of living in relative terms since they would be the only population segment left without adequate income. These households include less than 10 percent of the entire population. Their being left behind when all other low income groups would achieve considerable progress would pose serious questions of equity, would lead to intensive political pressures, and would probably before long result in the development of income transfer policies geared to their special circumstances. It should be noted in this context that public attitudes toward elderly people with handicaps and disabilities tend to be less rejecting than toward younger, able-bodied poor persons. It thus seems that while this segment of the population would derive no immediate economic benefits from the mothers' wages policy, and while it would even experience initially more severe relative social deprivation, its chances to benefit over time from the far-reaching social changes stimulated by this policy seem considerable.

Biological: Early consequences of the new economic strength of formerly deprived families would probably occur in spheres of concrete primary human needs such as nutrition and physical health. Qualitative and quantitative deficiencies in nutrition are now an important source of morbidity and mortality among low income segments of the population. An adequate diet made possible by an adequate income would soon be reflected in improvements in the health of expectant mothers and newborn infants, in lower rates of infant mortality and of physical and mental deficiencies, in heightened resistance to a variety of pathogenic influences throughout the life cycle, and, hence, in an all-around healthier population. Along with adequate nutrition, former low income families would also be able to secure a more equitable share of health care and medical services even if no progress were made toward a long overdue, comprehensive reorganization of the health care system of the United States.

Improvements in the diet of present low income segments of the population would have no adverse effects on upper income groups since proper food is certainly available in sufficient quantity in the United States. Increased food consumption might even improve the conditions of the farming sector of the economy. Improvements in the general state of health of poor families is also an improvement in the overall quality of life in society and would thus indirectly benefit all members of society.

Increasing the share of low income families in medical care may result in reductions of the quantity and quality of these services for other population segments unless the entire health care system is reorganized.

Chances are good that movement toward such a reorganization would accelerate once demands for health care, and political pressures supporting these demands, are broadened throughout society. It should be noted that because of the existence of "Medicare" within the Social Security system, the elderly segment of the population would not be affected adversely to a significant extent by improvements in medical services for families with children.

Demographic: Demographic consequences are linked closely to biological and economic ones. Improvements in the physical health of mothers and infants, and of poor families in general, would over time affect survival rates and thus population size and the age distribution of the population. "Economic incentives" may initially cause increases in the birthrate, yet, since economic improvements would also lead to improvements in education, and through it to shifts in attitudes concerning life styles and the number of children women desire to raise, such initial increases would soon be compensated by subsequent decreases. The net effect of the mothers' wages policy, over time, on population size and age distribution seems therefore to be negligible.

Ecological: Substantial improvements of economic conditions of low income families would gradually be reflected in improvements in the quality and quantity of housing; the patterns of settlement and land use; the quality of neighborhoods; and the quality, quantity, and distribution of public services, including public education. In view of the current depressed state of housing and neighborhoods, and of all public services in low income areas, improvements in this complex sphere of human needs would take considerable time. Furthermore, if the supply of housing and land and the rehabilitation of neighborhoods were left to "self regulation" by the "market" without adequate public initiative, controls, and planning, progress would be spotty, and large amounts of newly transferred purchasing power would be transformed into profits of private real estate, construction, and other enterprises, rather than into ecological improvements. These comments illustrate the interdependence of social policies and, hence, the importance of striving for coordinated and consistent changes throughout the social policy system, rather than for piecemeal changes of single, narrowly circumscribed policies. For without coordination and consistency among separate social policies, objectives achieved by one policy could be nullified by contrasting tendencies of other policies.

It is obvious that ecological changes would benefit entire communities and regions and not just former low income families who would be the primary beneficiaries. For changes of ecological dimensions certainly involve changes in the overall quality of life in society.

Psychological and social: Improvements spurred by economic gains of low income families in such concrete spheres as nutrition, health, housing, neighborhoods, and public services would eventually lead to improvements in psychological and social functioning. The now prevailing sense of insecurity, powerlessness, and alienation would gradually give way to a sense of security, power, trust, and solidarity. The self-image of inadequacy of many low income individuals which is shaped by a reality of frustrating experiences and failures would be replaced by one of adequacy, shaped by a different reality of more positive experiences and successes. Over time, these psychosocial changes would be reflected in lower prevalence of mental illness and emotional stress, in more constructive and satisfying intra- and extrafamilial relations, in more effective social functioning in primary groups and in other social contexts, and in a gradual decrease of juvenile delinquency and adult crime to the extent that these socially deviant acts are rooted in hostility against, and alienation from, a frustrating social order. Similarly, there would also be a decrease in alcoholism and drug addiction, as there would be less individual need, and less peer group pressure, to escape from reality.

Here again it should be noted that these psychological and social consequences for the circumstances of living of former low income families would stimulate far-reaching improvements in the overall quality of life and would thus greatly benefit all segments of society.

Cultural and political: Economic, ecological, psychological, social, and educational changes would over time result also in marked changes in life styles, in attitudes, in family and personal aspirations, in cultural orientations, and in recreational interests of former low income families. Simultaneously, as a result of increasing consciousness of their changing circumstances of living, of their generally increased rights and especially of their newly gained economic strength and related political power potential, these families would become more involved in community affairs, in voluntary associations, and in informal political processes on the local level and beyond. The content and direction of these new family and personal aspirations, attitudes, cultural orientations, and political activities would, of course, be influenced by the total societal context prevailing at the time the mothers' wages policy would be implemented, and especially by developments concerning society's system of beliefs and values.

From a social-structural perspective it would seem that changes in the several spheres of the circumstances of living discussed so far would result in significant transformations of society. Existing multidimensional divisions in life experiences and life styles among segments of the population who differ in income, education, occupation, neighborhoods, and ethnicity would be reduced along with the flattening of the shape of the income distribution. This process would be reflected in a gradual bridging of existing gaps between the various ethnic groups, especially between the white majority and the several nonwhite minorities, between inner city dwellers and suburbanites, between rural and urban populations, between the several geographic regions, between blue and white collar workers, etc.

Intrasocietal human relations: While a wide range of intrasocietal human relations would be affected by the changes in the processes of social policies implicit in the mothers' wage policy, several specific sets of relations would undergo significant modifications. These specific sets are relations between men and women in general and, more specifically, between husbands and wives; relations between parents and children; and relations between women and their actual or prospective employers.

Changes in relations between men and women in general and, more specifically, between husbands and wives would derive from the new social and economic rights of women which would free them from economic control and exploitation by men. At present, only a minority of women can expect to be economically independent throughout their adult lives. They are now especially disadvantaged when they have children. Awareness of these circumstances by both sexes tends to affect in subtle and, at times, not so subtle ways, relations between men and women prior to, and subsequent to, marriage.

While with the implementation of the mothers' wages policy women would not gain full equality in terms of access to occupations and social roles, they could, nevertheless, expect a fairly adequate personal income throughout life: from employment when not bearing and rearing children, from mothers' wages during periods of pregnancy and child rearing, and from earned social security benefits during periods of unemployment and retirement. Women would thus no longer have to fear economic dependency and would be in a better position to relate to men on a freer and less unequal basis. Men, too, would be well aware of this changed context and would gradually learn to relate to women in a more egalitarian and humane manner. Male-female relations would more likely be based on mutual attraction and respect, rooted in personal qualities, as they would be overshadowed by economic considerations to a far lesser extent than they are now. The quality of relations between the sexes is thus likely to become more balanced, more secure, more satisfying, and relatively free from elements of coercion.

Not only women and mothers would be economically more secure than they are now once the mother's wages policy would be implemented, but also all families with children under age eighteen would be assured sufficient income and would no longer be threatened by the depressing consequences, or prospects, of actual or potential poverty. Awareness of these changed circumstances would be reflected in a new sense of economic security which, in turn, would enhance the quality of all intrafamilial relations, between husbands and wives, as well as between parents and children. It hardly needs to be pointed out that strains and worries of life in poverty and near-poverty, and its multifaceted destructive correlates, tend to be important factors of family breakdowns. Elimination of these strains and prevention of related feelings of insecurity and self-doubt would contribute to the development of stronger and healthier mutual relations among family members.

The relations of children to parents would also be affected by changes in the sources from which families obtain their economic support and by changes in the relative shares of fathers, mothers, and children in providing a family's economic support. At present fathers are considered in most families as the dominant source of economic support, although many mothers and children participate in earning their families' livelihood. The dominant position of fathers in this respect affects the father and mother images in the perception of family members and determines qualitative and quantitative aspects of the children's interaction with their parents, and the parents' interaction with each other. Fathers are considered in many families the final authority with regard to major decisions. Also, because of their economic and occupational responsibilities, fathers tend to be away from their home for much of the day, and they are thus experienced as less familiar and more distant and powerful in social and psychological terms.

Under the mothers' wages policy the work of mothers would become a steady and secure source of family income, and children too would be recipients of regular, unconditional allowances from society. These important shifts in the economic resources of families would lead to corresponding shifts in structural and psychological elements of intrafamilial relations. The role of fathers would no longer be as dominant as now. Parents in many families would carry a fairly equal share as economic providers and, consequently, as decision makers concerning family affairs. The images of fathers and mothers would undergo corresponding changes in their own and in their children's perceptions, and these changes, in turn, would be reflected in modifications in the relations and interactions of parents and children.

Since children, too, would be a source of income for families, it may be assumed that they would gain a larger measure of independence than they now enjoy, and a larger share in decisions affecting them directly. These economic and structural changes would also be reflected in intrafamilial relations and in patterns of family interaction.

The trends discussed here concerning family economics and family relations could also lead to an increase in the number, the rate, and the general societal acceptance of single parent families since mothers, and also fathers, would be able to support and care for children without a second parent. The development of the single parent family into a socially sanctioned alternative family type would have important consequences for child development and for parent-child relations in such families.

Finally, with the assumption by society of increased responsibility for the support and the care of children, the relations of children and families to society as a whole would undergo subtle modifications since society would over time develop a growing interest in protecting the quality of care children receive in their families.

One further specific set of human relations to be considered are relations between women, especially mothers, and actual or prospective employers. Under existing circumstances the bargaining position and power of most women and mothers in the labor market is weak, and they are consequently frequently subjected to severe exploitation. Women are often forced to choose either to undertake poorly paid, undesirable, and unsatisfying work, while neglecting the care of their children, or to exist with their children on an utterly inadequate and demeaning public assistance grant. With such limited options open to them, many women and mothers are likely to feel powerless and alienated in the employment relationship.

The economic rights mothers would be assured under the mothers' wages policy would significantly change the bargaining position of women in the labor market and, hence, their relations to actual and prospective employers. Employment relationships would no longer have as coercive and alienating a quality as now, because women would have a more genuine choice to accept or reject a position and, therefore, a real opportunity to negotiate the terms of their employment. Women could no longer be subjected to rude exploitation by employers who would have to relate to them in a humane manner if they wanted to keep them on the job. Employers would have to respect the rights of women, to consider their personal needs and interests, and to improve their working conditions and wages if they wanted to induce them to accept, and to stay with, offered positions. While the mothers' wages policy would protect primarily mothers by offering them an alternative to employment in the market, the effects of the policy would reach all working women since the withdrawal of many mothers from work would result in labor shortages, and the bargaining position and power of all women who were ready to fill vacant jobs would consequently be considerably strengthened.

In concluding the discussion of consequences of the mothers' wages policy for intrasocietal human relations it should be noted that the gradual bridging of divisions and gaps among many diverse subsegments of society which was mentioned above would be reflected in significant changes in relations among members of these subsegments. These changes in relations would parallel a series of developments beginning with income transfers from higher to lower income segments of the population, involving reduction in economic distance between these segments; reductions in major differences of life styles, attitudes, and aspirations; and, ultimately, reduction in social distance. Throughout the stages of this process the self-image and the consciousness of members of social segments affected by it would undergo changes. Along with these changes would occur corresponding changes in the relations of individuals and groups to other individuals and groups in their own, and in other, social segments, as well as in the relations of the several social segments to each other and to society as a whole. In general, these changes in the quality of human relations among individuals and subsegments of society would involve a gradual decrease in hierarchical, and a corresponding increase in egalitarian elements.

D. INTERACTIONS OF THE POLICY WITH FORCES AFFECTING SOCIAL EVOLUTION

1. History of the policy: The mothers' wages policy, except for the children's allowance component, is an innovative social policy which, so far, has received little attention in the public policy arena in the United States. The proposal was circulated to political leaders and organizations during the 1968 presidential campaign. The press reported the proposal after it was published in a professional journal in 1968 and presented at the National Conference on Social Welfare in 1969.[22] The policy was not adopted by any social action group, and since neither its author nor any one else engaged in further attempts to publicize and promote it, it faded from public attention shortly after its initial publication.

While the mothers' wages proposal aroused little interest in the United States, several European countries have for some time implemented policies involving similar principles. In France, mothers who care for their children and who are not employed outside their homes receive special supplements to family allowances.[23] And in Hungary, mothers of children under age three are entitled to special allowances in order to encourage them to care for their own children.[24]

In spite of the European experience, mothers' wages are still a new and essentially untried social policy. Children's allowances, on the other hand, have an extended history in Europe, as well as in Canada, Australia, and New Zealand, and in several African, Asian, and South American countries. They have been widely used in both capitalist and socialist societies.[25] The United States is actually the only modern industrial society which has never utilized a "direct," universal children's allowance.

The purpose of children's allowances has remained unchanged since they were introduced in Europe early in this century. This purpose is to promote the well-being of children by publicly subsidizing the cost of rearing them. The purpose is achieved through governmental payments of allowances to families on behalf of every eligible child. These transfer payments are designed to reduce vertical inequalities of income among families with children belonging to different income strata, as well as horizontal inequalities of per capita purchasing power among families of different sizes belonging to the same income strata. The amounts of children's allowances are the same for all children of a specified age, in families of a specified size, irrespective of total family income. However, after-tax amounts of allowances are adjusted through progressive tax rates of graduated income taxes, so that allowances decrease as the size of total family income increases.

A review of the history of children's allowances reveals considerable differences among societies using this policy concerning such variables as size of allowances relative to per capita income and to total family income; number of children per family for whom allowances are payable; age range of children included in the program; administrative procedures; financing; etc. Although there has been controversy in many societies concerning various aspects of children's allowances, few countries abolished this policy after having established it. In general, the overall experience with children's allowances has not been favorable. Fears, respectively hopes, that children's allowances would stimulate increases in the birthrate did not materialize to any significant extent. In many instances, however, children's allowances failed to attain their objectives since the size of allowances tended to be relatively small, and since allowances frequently did not keep up with increases in the cost of living.

While the United States never adopted a children's allowance policy in the usual meaning of this term, it instituted, nevertheless, a similar policy involving tax-free exemptions for dependent children through the income tax system. One usually unnoticed aspect of this "indirect children's allowance" is that its cash value increases, rather than decreases, as total family income increases.

During the 1960s, several individuals and organizations attempted to promote adoption of a "direct" children's allowance in the United States.[26] These efforts coincided with mounting public interest in eliminating poverty and reforming the welfare system which was generally viewed as utterly unsatisfactory. Interest in the children's allowance concept was shared for some time by several government departments, and in 1968 the Office of Economic Opportunity and the Department of Health, Education, and Welfare were about to sponsor a large scale experiment to explore the effects of children's allowances.[27] This experiment was designed to parallel an earlier initiated study which explored the effects of "negative income taxes." Implementation of the children's allowance experiment was, however, cancelled when the government adopted in 1969 the Family Assistance Plan, a derivative of the negative income tax, as its answer to poverty and to the welfare crisis. The government thereupon decided against launching experiments designed to test alternative approaches to the income maintenance policy it had selected.[28] These developments seem to have led to the shelving of efforts to test a children's allowance policy in the United States, at least for the time being.

2. Political forces in society promoting or resisting the policy: Since the mothers' wages policy has never been actively promoted in the political arena in the United States, potential support for or resistance to it can only be estimated roughly on the basis of theoretical considerations. In general one may expect that population segments who would benefit if the policy were implemented would tend to support it, while segments whose perceived interests would be adversely affected would be more likely to oppose it. Segments whose circumstances remained essentially unchanged would tend to be neutral, or, depending on their value premises, would sympathize with supporters or opponents of the policy.

The foregoing general assumptions involve, however, several difficulties if one wants to estimate expected political responses to a policy. One major difficulty is that determining what constitutes "benefits" or "disbenefits," and what is one's "interest," is not a simple, objective process, but depends on the criteria one uses and on such complex factors as "objective facts," subjective perceptions, nature and scope of available information and interpretation concerning a policy, and one's values and beliefs. The manner in which, and by whom, a policy is promoted and interpreted is likely to affect perceptions of, and attitudes and reactions toward it, on the part of individuals and social groups. These variables would therefore have to be considered along with factual aspects concerning a policy.

Another difficulty in anticipating support for, or resistance to, a policy is that such political decisions involve strategic and tactical considerations which go beyond the mere evaluation of a policy on its merits. A policy involving a set of benefits may, when enacted into law, prevent enactment of another policy involving more extensive benefits. Because of this, potential beneficiaries of the former policy may choose to oppose it and may hold out for enactment of an alternative policy. Similarly, groups whose interests would be adversely affected by a policy may decide to support it nevertheless, so as to forestall enactment of policies they consider even less desirable.

Finally to be mentioned in the context of estimating likely responses to a policy is the fact that some individuals and groups may support or resist a policy on the basis of abstract principles and long-range benefits or "dis-benefits." Such criteria for choosing among policies could be viewed, however, as extensions of the "benefits" and "interest" criteria since correspondence between a policy and one's principles, as well as anticipated long-range benefits irrespective of short-run costs constitute, nevertheless, "benefits."

The foregoing considerations suggest that political alignments for or against the mothers' wages policy would depend to a considerable extent on the societal context prevailing at the time some political action group decided to promote this policy, and on the manner in which it would go about it. With these caveats in mind, the following estimates may be ventured.

When promoted by a humanistic movement and interpreted constructively as serving the underlying interests of society as a whole, support for the mothers' wages policy can be expected from many diverse segments of society. However, in spite of such an emphasis, considerable opposition to the policy should also be expected. Strong support for the policy would come from families with children whose total income is below the national median, be they poor or near-poor, headed by men or by women, white or nonwhite, urban, suburban, or rural, and whether the family-head is working, unemployed, or unable to work. These families would, of course, be the primary beneficiaries of the policy, and most of them would receive considerable amounts of transfer funds, were it enacted. Unless alternative income transfer policies offering higher benefits or more satisfactory terms were promoted simultaneously, these families would have few substantive, strategic, or tactical reasons for opposing the mothers' wages policy.

One important political asset of the policy should be noted here. This is the fact that the mothers' wages policy could unite poor, near-poor, and working or lower middle-class families with children into one unified political force sharing a common interest since all these families would benefit directly and immediately from the implementation of this policy. Working or lower middle-class families would, therefore, not be forced into conflict and competition with poor and near-poor families, the typical context surrounding "selective" welfare and antipoverty policies which involve means tests.

It should not be assumed, however, that there would be no opposition at all to the mothers' wages policy from individuals and groups among the policy's primary target segments. Some opposition can be expected on "moral," "philosophical" or "religious" principles to such aspects of the policy as "paying for motherhood," "paying for sex-relations" and for "having out-of-wedlock children," and "giving rights to women." Chances are that some groups in the population who would oppose the policy, as it would not serve their perceived interests, would mask their materialistically motivated opposition in moral, philosophical, and religious arguments in order to stimulate resistance to the policy among its potential beneficiaries.

Furthermore, many individuals and groups among the low income population who would not benefit directly and immediately from implementation of the mothers' wages policy, such as aged persons and people with handicaps and disabilities living in households without children under age eighteen, are likely to object to the policy on substantive grounds, unless it were amended to assure appropriate transfer benefits for them as well.

Women's rights groups, and especially the intellectual, middle-class leaders of that movement, are likely to respond to the mothers' wages policy in an ambivalent manner. They might favor some aspects of the policy such as children's allowances and enhanced economic rights for women. However, they are likely to be critical of the fact that the policy fails to assure women equality of access to all occupations and roles, and that it may strengthen the ties between women and child care and homemaking roles.

Major opposition to the mothers' wages policy is likely to come from individuals and organized economic interest groups among upper income segments and among owners of great wealth. Their main objections would focus on the relatively large scope of income transfers involved in the policy; large, that is, in terms of conventional social policies concerning income transfers to poor, near-poor, and other low income groups. A shift of about 10 percent of national income from the upper to the lower half of the income distribution would seem to many of this group as a radical and unwise measure which could threaten the very "stability" of the national economy, and the survival of society and the social order to which they have become accustomed.

It may be expected that some economists, and political and other social scientists, would supply technical arguments to opponents of the mothers' wages policy from among upper income and wealth strata since these scientists, too, might consider the scope of the transfers as excessively large, unconventional, untested, and a serious threat to the existing economic and social system. They might advocate experiments to study the effects of the policy before implementing it. It may be of interest that experimentation to study effects of a policy prior to its implementation has never been recommended by social scientists when government transfers and subsidies to upper income groups are involved, such as oil depletion allowances, major tax cuts for industry, loan guarantees to failing corporations, and subsidies to shipping, air transport, and other powerful interest groups.

Some economists would be opposed to the mothers' wages policy also because it utilizes the principle of "universality" rather than "selectivity" with regard to transfers of purchasing power. The principle of universality, it will be recalled, is considered by many economists as an inefficient approach to filling income gaps of low income segments of the population.

Other economists and social scientists may take a more positive, though not uncritical, stance toward the mothers' wages policy as they would recognize the overall, long-range, social, and economic benefits inherent in it, and as they might not be committed to the preservation of the social status quo and the usual principles of "free enterprise."

Not all individuals and groups among upper income and wealthy segments of the population would oppose the mothers' wages policy. Some might favor it because they endorsed the children's allowance concept and the horizontal transfers involved in it. Others might support the policy because they identified with its principles and philosophy. In this connection it should not be overlooked that many middle and upper class persons tend to support liberal, progressive, and even radical political causes and movements, and are thus likely to support policies which would promote social justice and the general human welfare even if in the short run these policies would result in material losses for them. Still others among these upper income groups would recognize the long-range, economic, and social benefits which would result from the mothers' wages policy for all groups in society and would support it on this basis.

It does not seem possible to estimate the size, organizational structure, resources, overall strength, level of interest, values, and ideologies of the various groups whose orientations toward the mothers' wages policy were sketched above. These aspects would depend on the nature of the social movement that would spearhead a political thrust advocating the mothers' wages policy; the substantive content, quality, and scope of political and educational activities undertaken by that movement; the general societal context and value orientations at the time these efforts are launched; and finally, the existence or generation (in the political arena) of alternative social policies addressed to the same policy issues.

3. Attributes of the natural environment: Implementation of the mothers' wages policy would encounter no limits or constraints from the natural environment and would hardly be affected by it since the policy involves no procedures which would be in conflict with natural forces and processes. It also requires no significant increases in resources drawn from the environment, but merely redistribution of claims to these resources.

As for reverse effects resulting from implementation of the mothers' wages policy for the natural environment, no immediate and direct consequences are likely to ensue. Yet to the extent that this policy could, over time, contribute toward more thoughtful attitudes concerning resource development and utilization and ecological issues (as neighborhoods and housing stock are rehabilitated under the policy's direct impact), it may also contribute, indirectly, to the evolution of less exploitative and more protective approaches toward the natural environment and may thus enhance chances for its preservation.

4. Intrinsic attributes and tendencies of people and their socially shaped elaborations: No limits or constraints would be encountered by (and no marked effects would result for) the policy from biological and intrinsic psychological properties of the population. However, certain deeply ingrained psychological orientations which were acquired through processes of socialization over countless generations, and which involve relatively fixed images concerning parental roles and parent-child relations, could constitute severe blocks to the notion of payment for maternal child care. This deep-seated, powerful, psychologically determined resistance to the acceptance of the mothers' wages policy does not, however, seem insurmountable since it is not rooted in human-biological processes, but is acquired through learning in social experience.

Effects of the mothers' wages policy on biological and psychological properties of the population are likely to be significant over time. Expected improvements, due to the policy, in physical and mental health and, hence, in overall bio-psycho-social functioning of individuals would increase the ratio of stronger and healthier persons in lower income segments and throughout the population. Such improvements in health and functioning of the population would eventually be transmitted between generations through biological, psychological, and social processes.

Were the mothers' wages policy implemented, learned perceptions of parental roles and parent-child relations would also undergo gradual changes, and the modified perceptions would be internalized through early social learning and would also be transmitted between generations. In this way, acquired psychological characteristics which would constitute sources of early resistance to acceptance of the mothers' wages policy would themselves be modified, over time, under that policy's influence.

5. *Basic and Perceived Needs of People:* The mothers' wages policy is designed to eliminate conditions of poverty and near-poverty among families with children under age eighteen and is thus focused specifically on overcoming obstacles to the fulfillment of material, psychological, social, and security needs of about one third of the population. Were the policy implemented, it would lead to improvements in the overall quality of life and human relations, and would expand opportunities for people to pursue personal development, self-actualization, and spiritual needs. Changes in people's sense of worth, power, community, and security may, in turn, lead to changes in perceptions and definitions of needs, from an emphasis on material goods toward an emphasis on meaningful human relations and activities.

In spite of the constructive possibilities inherent in the mothers' wages policy concerning the satisfaction of human needs, many people who do not belong to its target segment are likely to view this policy as a threat to the fulfillment of their perceived needs and would, therefore, oppose its enactment and implementation, unless their perceptions of needs and interests changed.

6. *Demographic Developments and Changes in the Ratio of Population Size to Available Resources:* The mothers' wages policy is not expected to have significant, long-range effects on the size of the population, although there could be a temporary increase in the birthrate among former poor and low income families soon after the policy's enactment, in reaction to a marked increase in their financial resources. Over time,

however, as the new policy became a regular feature of society's distributive mechanisms, and as increased economic resources were gradually transformed into education and other life-style elements, the initial increase in the birthrate would be likely to drop again, and fertility would be likely to stabilize at a somewhat lower level than it had been prior to implementation of the mothers' wages policy. Increases in life expectancy related to the elimination of poverty among a large segment of the population are likely to be offset by gradual declines in fertility. This may affect the age distribution of the population and may change the ratio of productive to retired workers. However, the ratio of the population to available resources is unlikely to change significantly, and demographic developments are therefore, unlikely to interfere with the implementation of the mothers' wages policy.

7. Economic Surplus and Its Disposition: Economic surplus (i.e., goods and services in excess of levels necessary for daily consumption and survival) has been an important source for individual and social development throughout the evolution of the human species. The mothers' wages policy is one feasible approach to reducing coercively instituted imbalances in the allocation of economic surplus. These imbalances have led to the exclusion of large segments of the population from sharing in the developmental opportunities inherent in the surplus. Implementation of the policy would significantly reduce prevailing inequalities in the distribution and utilization of the economic surplus and would, therefore, broaden its constructive impact by including previously excluded classes. In turn, this should result in qualitative and quantitative improvements in the ongoing generation of economic surplus. Social classes who, in their perception, benefit from the prevailing distribution of the economic surplus are likely, however, to resist changes in its disposition as long as their perceptions remain unchanged.

8. Social, Occupational, and Spatial Differentiations, and Differentiations of Rights and Perceptions of Interests; Class Structure and Class Consciousness; Conflicts Concerning Work, Rights, and Disposition of the Economic Surplus: Prevailing intrasocietal differentiations in the United States do not pose objective obstacles to the implementation of the mothers' wages policy. However, differentiations in perceptions of rights and interests, and conflicts concerning definition and access to work and roles, the distribution of rights, and the allocation of economic surplus, are likely to result in strong opposition to the policy. Implementation of the policy would reduce the rigidities of prevailing intrasocietal differentiations as it would facilitate social, occupational, and spatial mobility of groups and classes now trapped in poverty and excluded from access to quality education, desirable work, and corresponding rights. This constructive impact of the policy would be most noticeable in relation to the rights of mothers in single parent households. These women, especially when they belong to nonwhite minority groups, now face a very high risk of experiencing social, cultural, and economic deprivation.

9. Development of Ideas, Knowledge, Science, Technology and Skills: The current stage of development of knowledge, science, and technology in the United States would not obstruct the implementation of the mothers' wages policy, nor would this policy adversely affect ongoing developments in these domains. On the contrary, the fact that large segments of the population now excluded from access to quality education and meaningful work would no longer be excluded (they would be able to develop in social, cultural, and occupational spheres following implementation of the mothers' wages policy) should result in significant increases in human resources for the generation of knowledge, science, and technology. Moreover, increase in purchasing power of currently poor people and shortages of "cheap labor" would cause qualitative and quantitative changes in production, which should spur technological innovations and expanded use of automation.

Obstacles to the implementation of the mothers' wages policy would result from dominant ideas concerning the roles and rights of women and children, and societal responsibilities with regard to these matters. The redefinition of maternal child care as work entitling mothers to wages out of public revenues and the notion of children's allowances paid by society are strange and controversial ideas in terms of the dominant system of ideas. However, development and change of ideas is a continuous process, and complex and pluralistic cultures can integrate innovative, and seemingly strange, elements, especially when these elements do not represent total discontinuity with respect to the existing culture. Since the new and unconventional elements of the mothers' wages policy involve conceptual continuities with some elements and ideas already accepted in the United States, their integration should proceed in spite of ongoing resistance, once sufficient political support could be generated to secure that policy's enactment. Once integrated, the new elements could stimulate further developments in the direction of humanistic and egalitarian sociocultural patterns.

10. Prevailing symbolic universe and consciousness including images of established ways of life; customs and traditions; ideas, beliefs, and meanings; conventional wisdom; perceptions of needs and interests; value positions; and ideology: The value premises and ideological orientation implicit in the objectives of the mothers' wages policy are, in many ways, incompatible with the dominant mentality, beliefs, values, ideologies, customs, and traditions of people in the United States. While this incompatibility is not absolute, and while many linkages and continuities exist between the values implicit in the policy and those dominant in society, the value conflict seems serious enough to generate strong resistance to the acceptance of the mothers' wages policy in the foreseeable future unless, of course, significant shifts were to take place in dominant value premises and ideological orientation.

In terms of major policy-relevant value dimensions, the mothers' wages policy reflects different positions from the dominant positions of the social policy system of the United States. Thus, while the policy system stresses individualism and competitiveness in pursuit of self-interest and self-support, the mothers' wages policy reflects a mutualistic, communal, and cooperative ideology through societal wages for maternal child care and universal children's allowances. By custom and tradition, parents, and especially fathers, are now responsible for the livelihood of families, and mothers are expected to care for their children. The circumstances of living of children depend, consequently, on the circumstances and opportunities of their parents. The mothers' wages policy would cause significant departures from these firmly established traditions by requiring society to compensate mothers for their work in caring for children, as well as to subsidize the costs of child support. Were such a policy implemented, the circumstances of living of families would no longer depend nearly exclusively on the circumstances, efforts, and opportunities of parents but, at least in part, on measures taken collectively by society as a whole.

The provisions of the mothers' wages policy would conflict not only with long established values and traditions concerning primary parental responsibilities for child care and support, but would also interfere with principles of "free enterprise" by protecting mothers against exploitation in low-paying, undesirable service and industrial jobs which many women are now forced to fill in order to escape starvation or its only alternative, inadequate and dehumanizing public assistance.

The most significant deviation, however, of the mothers' wages policy from the dominant value premises and ideology of the established social policy system concerns the dimension of equality vs. inequality. While the dominant values and ideology uphold and defend social and economic inequalities as an organizing principle of circumstances of living and of all spheres of societal existence, the mothers' wages policy would result in marked reductions of inequalities of rights through redistribution of purchasing power and also through redistribution and readjustments of general public and social services. These egalitarian trends of the policy would seem objectionable to important segments of society who are ideologically opposed to the notion that the state should take measures to reduce inequalities in circumstances of living, social power, and economic opportunities of members of society. Yet at the same time, the notion of equality of rights and opportunities for all is not really a foreign idea, at least not on a philosophical level. For this notion has been expressed as a goal in important public documents and declarations, though it has never been translated into social reality, nor has much use been made of it as a guiding principle for development (and as a yardstick for evaluation) of social policies. The egalitarian ideology of the mothers' wages policy represents, therefore, continuity in terms of early ideology in the United States, and supporters of the policy could rightfully claim that they promote values which this society has always enunciated and believed in, but so far has failed to live up to.

The value of collective interest in, and responsibility for, the well-being of all members of a community, as well as the value of cooperation among members of a community in pursuit of common interest are by no means new ideas. However, the fate of these values has tended to be similar to that of the value of equality of rights and opportunities. They are considered to be impractical ideals and, as such, their influence on social and political reality has tended to be limited. The mothers' wages policy would require that these "impractical ideals" be translated into organizing principles of the social order and, because of this, it would meet resistance from powerful segments of society whose perceived interests benefit from adherence to the dominant values of pursuit of self-interest, competition, and inequality.

While, then, the mothers' wages policy would deviate in major ways from dominant values, ideologies, and traditions of the policy system, it conforms to them with respect to two important issues, namely, the linkage between motherhood, child care, and homemaking functions, and the emphasis on work as a principal mechanism for the distribution of rights. The policy is expected to increase the proportion of mothers who choose to care for their own children and to reduce the participation of women in the work force. This reduction would affect primarily less desirable, unskilled occupations, and would probably have minor effects on technical and professional occupations which offer women real career opportunities, more desirable working conditions, and higher compensation than mothers' wages. The policy would, therefore, not discourage women from pursuing meaningful careers, but would give them an opportunity for a real choice between caring for their children and engaging in less meaningful, less gratifying and economically less rewarding occupations. Yet in spite (or perhaps because) of these features, the mothers' wages policy would slow the movement of women away from child care and homemaking functions into occupations and careers outside their homes.

As for the traditional emphasis on work as the major mechanism for the distribution of rights, the mothers' wages policy would use this value premise to legitimate new economic rights for mothers by redefining their traditional roles as "work." This redefinition is not a mere tactical step or political trick. Rather, it is a correction of earlier political processes which resulted in the denial of the reality of mothers' work, and which thus constructed a "new reality," one that was more suited to the exploitation of mothers, wives, and women.

In concluding this discussion of the value premises and of the ideological orientation of the mothers' wages policy, it should be noted that the values and ideology implicit in the objectives of this policy are not internally consistent. The overall ideological thrust of this policy is in the direction of social and economic equality. However, this egalitarian thrust is not followed through with respect to equality of opportunities for women and men concerning work and social roles. As noted above, the mothers' wages policy conforms to the traditional societal bias of steering women into child rearing and homemaking roles. While the policy provides for the possibility that men would occasionally undertake child care roles and be eligible for "mothers' wages," this is considered an exceptional, temporary occurrence. The policy does not encourage parents to develop their own, unique, egalitarian patterns for sharing child care responsibilities so that both husbands and wives could also pursue occupational and career interests. Instead, there is a built-in assumption that, in the case of two-parent families, the wife would care for the children and receive mothers' wages, while the husband would pursue a gainful occupation away from home. There are corresponding assumptions that in a female-headed, one-parent family the mother would stay home, care for her children, and draw mothers' wages throughout the years of their childhood, while in a male-headed, one-parent family the father would care for his children and receive mothers' wages on a temporary basis only until he could make alternative arrangements for their care and return to his occupation away from home.

There is one further aspect of the mothers' wages policy which reflects inconsistency with respect to its egalitarian thrust. This is the fact that the policy aims to improve the circumstances of living of specified population segments only, albeit very large and important ones, rather than of all low income segments. Consequently, in spite of the relatively large scope of aggregate income transfers provided for in this policy, several million households without children under age eighteen, consisting mainly of aged individuals and people with handicaps and disabilities, would still continue to live in poverty and deprivation after the policy were implemented.

Finally, it should be noted that the mothers' wages policy does not aim to establish equality of social and economic rights for all members of society, but merely to reduce certain existing inequalities. It is thus a reform policy which would, if enacted, significantly modify social conditions in a humanistic, egalitarian direction, but it is not a radical policy which would restructure the social order and the economic system by eliminating the structural roots and dynamics of inequality so as to assure equal social and economic rights and opportunities to all.

11. Critical Consciousness and Alternative Visions: The mothers' wages policy is based on critical consciousness concerning prevailing notions of work, child care, the rights of mothers and children, and the responsibility of society concerning these issues. The policy reflects alternative visions concerning the values and organizing principles of social life. Were it implemented in spite of political resistance rooted in conventional consciousness and dominant views of social life, experience related to its provisions would facilitate the spreading of critical consciousness and alternative social visions.

12. Interactions with Other Societies and Exposure to Alternative Ways of Life and Consciousness: While the mothers' wages policy derives from critical consciousness concerning aspects of social life in the United States and alternative visions of social life, it is also influenced by the ways of life and social policies of other countries (including Sweden, France, England, Canada, Hungary, Israel, etc.) and through interaction with people from these countries. All these societies have implemented versions of children's allowances and mothers' wages, and have organized their way of life in accordance with different values and visions. Were the United States to implement its own version of a mothers' wages policy, people in this country are likely to become more open to ways and visions of social life as realized elsewhere without apparent adverse effects.

13. Social and Foreign Policies Relevant to the Focal Issues of the Policy: The most significant effects of the mothers' wages policy are expected in the area of rights distribution throughout society and, more specifically, the distribution of purchasing power. However, if the objectives of the policy in this area are to be achieved rather than counteracted, other policies dealing with the distribution of rights and purchasing power would have to be coordinated with the mothers' wages policy. Included among these policies would be policies dealing with taxation, the government's chief tool for constraining individual purchasing power and for generating transfer funds; and policies dealing with social security, public assistance, and general public and social welfare services, tools the government uses for distributing rights through purchasing power and in kind.

Of crucial importance for the "real" size and effects of mothers' wages and children's allowances would be the incidence of new taxes which would have to be enacted in order to raise the revenue needed for implementing the new policy. The more progressive the incidence of these new taxes would be, the more "on target" would be the effects of the new policy, and the more adequate would be the net amounts of mothers' wages and children's allowance. It would seem appropriate if these new taxes were raised from households with incomes above the median, and if tax rates would rise in an increasingly steeper progression for households in the upper half of the income distribution. It seems indicated also to repeal currently existing tax-free exemptions for children and several other special provisions, the effects of which on tax incidence are regressive. In addition to reforming individual federal income taxes, policies concerning federal taxes on capital gains, corporate income, various forms of wealth, gifts and inheritances, as well as corresponding state and local taxes, would have to be gradually adjusted so as to conform to the redistributive objectives of the mothers' wages policy. Obviously, these multiple adjustments in tax policies on all levels of government would not be enacted automatically once the mothers' wages policy is accepted, as each adjustment would involve separate political contests. However, these controversial issues are likely to surface and would have to be dealt with over time if, and when, the mothers' wages policy is introduced into the political arena.

The existing social security system would also have to undergo modifications in order to conform to the mothers' wages policy, especially as a result of the redefinition of maternal child care as "work." This change in social and political philosophy would bestow on mothers the right to be included in the social security system as contributors and beneficiaries. To finance the new benefits, the government, as "employer" of mothers, would have to transfer its share of "payroll deductions" into the social security trust fund, and it may also be necessary to raise the wage base which would have to be subjected to social security deductions in order to assure the solvency of the trust fund over time. These comments involve the assumption that the existing social security system would continue to operate. It would, of course, be possible to substitute in its place a more equitable system financed through progressively raised general revenue, rather than through regressive payroll deductions.

While effects of the mothers' wages policy on tax policies, and vice versa, would involve intensive political contests, its effects on existing cash and, in kind, public assistance transfer policies and programs would be largely automatic. Increases in income of families with children under age eighteen from mothers' wages and children's allowances would usually exceed public assistance eligibility standards and would, therefore, cause the phasing out of the following programs, as far as such families are concerned: AFDC or its proposed, more far-reaching, yet inadequate substitutes, the "Family Assistance Program" (FAP) and the Opportunities for Families Program (OFF); state general assistance; food stamps and commodity distribution; and Medicaid. Considerable savings in transfer funds and administrative costs could be realized from termination of these programs. However, at the same time, large numbers of federal and state civil service employees now engaged in their administration would be displaced from their jobs. This could cause bureaucratic resistance and political controversy unless compensatory measures were designed.

Policies concerning housing, zoning, neighborhood development, urban renewal, and urban, suburban and rural settlement and land use would also be affected by (and would in turn affect) the mothers' wages policy. Existing public housing policies involve eligibility standards similar to the ones used in public assistance, food, and medical assistance programs, and families with children under age eighteen would thus no longer be eligible for public housing. One consequence of this would be that poor and near-poor households without children under age eighteen would encounter shorter waiting periods for public housing accommodations. However, this would also mean an increase in residential segregation of aged persons and people with handicaps and disabilities from the rest of the population.

Another consequence would be that demand for housing by families whose improved economic circumstances would result in loss of eligibility for public housing would cause strong pressures on the housing situation. Merely raising eligibility standards for existing public housing projects would not be an adequate answer to these pressures since many former low income families with children would no longer be satisfied with the type and quality of housing which is now available to them in housing projects, and would be likely to demand better homes without the connotations and stigma of existing public housing projects. Increased economic and political strength of these families would make it more likely that their demands would be heard, and responded to, in the political arena. This could lead to the phasing out of existing public housing and urban renewal policies, and their gradual replacement by an integrated set of policies concerning housing, zoning, neighborhood development, urban renewal, and urban, suburban, and rural settlement and land use, which would be more in line with newly emergent social, economic, and political realities, and ecological insights.

It needs hardly be mentioned that resolution of the complex housing and settlement issues which would be raised by enactment of the mothers' wages policy would involve political strife, the outcome of which may not be as constructive as suggested above. It is not unlikely that solutions of housing and related problems would be left to a large extent to the vagaries of free enterprise. Adequately integrated policies and programs would not be likely to emerge in this way, and some potential benefits of the mothers' wages policy for target segments of the population and for society as a whole would be unlikely to materialize since resources needed for their realization would be transformed into profits for private enterprises. In view of the complexity of the issues involved, planning and guidance by public authorities seems essential, so as to enhance chances for a constructive outcome with maximum benefits for all segments of society.

One further cluster of social policies which would be affected by the mothers' wages policy and would, in turn, affect its implementation includes policies concerning general public and social welfare services such as public health, sanitation, and safety; public education; employment services; and special social services operated by antipoverty programs. At present, all these services tend to be administered with a built-in, official or unofficial means test—that is, they are segregated by socioeconomic position of consumers.

Some of these services, especially those sponsored by the Office of Economic Opportunity, the Model Cities Administration of the Department of Housing and Urban Development, and the Department of Health, Education, and Welfare, tend to be earmarked for utilization by poor segments of the population, and this special context is reflected in the qualitative aspects of the services. They tend to reflect a "poor house" mentality and milieu, and, though they are supposedly rehabilitative, antipoverty measures, most consumers continue to be poor while, and after, experiencing these services, official claims to the contrary notwithstanding.

Other services such as public health, sanitation and safety, employment, work training, education, and personal social services are administered without a formal, official means test. However, as a result of residential segregation by socioeconomic position, members of different socioeconomic strata tend to receive segregated public services. Not infrequently, these public services are not only segregated by socioeconomic strata, but services in lower income neighborhoods tend to be of lesser quality than those available in areas inhabited by middle and upper income strata.

Improvements in socioeconomic conditions of families with children due to mothers' wages and children's allowances would probably result in the phasing out of policies and special programs administered now for poor families only. It may, however, be more appropriate, instead of terminating such special services as "Headstart," child development and day care programs, work training programs, and special educational programs, etc., to continue them within non-stigmatizing contexts, in settings not segregated by socioeconomic positions of consumers. For many special social services are now doomed to failure, not necessarily because of intrinsic philosophical and methodological shortcomings, but since their consumers are left in a state of severe economic deprivation without realistic escape routes. The services simply cannot overcome the structural causes of poverty, as they have not been designed to do so.

Once these structural aspects were dealt with successfully through adequate transfers of purchasing power, as would be the case were the mothers' wages policy implemented, some of the special social services could probably contribute in important ways to the enhancement of human potentialities and the enrichment of life.

Demand for certain social services such as child welfare, child protection, child placement (including adoptive placements), and day care services would probably decrease were the mothers' wages policy implemented. Presently, many families with children require these services as a direct or indirect consequence of poverty and low income. It seems logical to expect a significant reduction in the need for these child welfare services, as well as for other social services which deal with poverty-related problems of families with children, once poverty is successfully eliminated for such families.

With respect to policies governing the administration of general public and social welfare services, implementation of the mothers' wages policy would ensue in intensified political pressures for elimination of all "de facto" means tests, or segregation by socioeconomic position of consumers, and of the discriminatory differences in the quality of these services which are now associated with residential patterns. The thrust of the mothers' wages policy for overall reductions in social inequalities would certainly be severely inhibited, or even defeated, unless these political pressures for elimination of discriminatory administration of general public services were successful.

Health maintenance and medical care policies are likely to be affected by implementation of the mothers' wages policy in a similar way as policies concerning general public services. It seems even likely that the increase in economic strength and political power of families with children could become an important factor in a political thrust for adoption of a universal, comprehensive national health maintenance system financed through general revenue and available to all on an equal basis.

In concluding this review of interactions between the mothers' wages policy and other social policies, some comments are also indicated concerning the broad policy issues of the rights of women and children. The mothers' wages policy would strengthen social and economic rights of mothers and would protect them, and other women, against coercion concerning work. However, it would not assure women free choice and equal access to work and social roles. One unintended consequence of enactment of the mothers' wages policy could therefore be a delay in obtaining acceptance of a more comprehensive social policy which would not merely strengthen social and economic rights of mothers but would assure full equality of rights to all women.

The mothers' wages policy would also strengthen the social and economic rights of all children by establishing a societal subsidy for their support. However, here, too, an unintended consequence could ensue, as agencies of the state, charged with administering mothers' wages and children's allowances to families with children, could move beyond this original objective toward attempts to influence the quality of child rearing. This could, under certain circumstances, lead to inappropriate and undesirable interventions in parent-child relations, especially among less powerful segments of the population.

While the mothers' wages policy would have no direct effects on United States foreign policies, and while its implementation would also not be influenced directly by foreign policies and by extrasocietal forces, important indirect interactions are likely to occur.

The primary context of these interactions would be competition for societal resources through appropriations in the federal budget. Implementing the mothers' wages policy would require allocation of significant portions of the budget for income transfers. Such allocations for a major, innovative social policy seem, however, unlikely as long as the United States would continue to commit sizable portions of its national resources to the conduct of overt and covert foreign wars, and to the preparation for, or prevention of, possible future wars through the maintenance of a powerful military establishment. This assumption derives from political rather than from economic realities, as in theory there would be no "real" economic obstacles to implementing income transfers such as those involved in the mothers' wages policy simultaneously with large-scale defense appropriations. For, as has already been pointed out, income transfers do not constitute real economic costs to society, although they tend to be perceived in this way by groups in society who are required to finance the transfers through higher taxes.

Political consequences of these subjective perceptions of economic realities would present nearly insurmountable obstacles to the acceptance of the mothers' wages policy prior to termination of a major foreign war and prior to significant cuts in defense appropriations .

Major reductions of the United States defense budget would lessen resistance to the mothers' wages policy not only by freeing necessary economic resources but also as a result of possible shifts in this nation's dominant values which could underlie such reductions in the defense budget. The existing defense budget reflects a certain national stance concerning the United States' relations to the rest of the world. One important factor shaping these relations in recent decades has been efforts to maintain and defend an economically advantageous position of this country vis-a-vis other nations. The United States controls about 40 percent of the world's resources and consumes annually a similar portion of worldwide production, while its population constitutes less than 6 percent of humankind. The United States foreign and defense policies protect and perpetuate this glaring inequality of worldwide resource distribution. In order to do so, the United States defends not merely its own territory and its worldwide perceived economic interests, but also the values and ideology of capitalism, a major source of its privileged position, whenever and wherever these values and ideology, and societies supporting them, are threatened. Many past and present international conflicts in which the United States has become involved were related to this complex, ideological struggle, as well as to the concrete issue of defending a powerful and advantageous position. Defense budgets of the United States are operational expressions of these dual tendencies of its foreign policies, namely, to protect the benefits derived from the unequal distribution of world resources and to contain societies committed to political and economic value premises which challenge this privileged position and the value premises sustaining it.

To the extent that reductions of the United States defense budget would derive from a lessening of the tendency to resist with force the spreading of an ideology different from its own, and to the extent that the lessening of such a tendency would derive from increasingly tolerant attitudes toward egalitarian and collectivistic philosophies and values in other societies, the United States may gradually become more tolerant, also, toward such philosophies and values among its own citizens and would thus be more likely to implement policies such as mothers' wages, which aim to reduce social and economic inequalities within society, and to strengthen egalitarian and collectivistic values in the social order.

In the not too likely case that the mothers' wages policy would gain sufficient support and be adopted in the United States prior to major changes in foreign and defense policies, this policy would be likely to contribute toward eventual changes in the foreign sphere as well. For implementation of the mothers' wages policy would constitute a considerable departure from prevailing social policies. Such a change would involve major shifts in the dominant value premises of society, which could not fail to be reflected eventually also in the foreign and defense policies of the United States and in the quality of its relations to other nations. If significant reduction of inequalities within its own country can become a working principle of social policies in the United States, similar efforts in other societies would no longer have to be perceived as a serious threat, and the United States might even adopt a more positive attitude toward the complex issue of redistributing the world's resources more equitably among all nations.

Implementation of the mothers' wages policy would enhance the image of the United States abroad. This society is respected for its scientific and technological achievements, but its failure to solve social problems and human conflicts in spite of immense natural wealth and scientific strength is a cause for contempt. Adoption of an innovative social policy which could contribute to the reduction of many serious social ills would be noticed abroad and would change the existing image of failure in the social domain. The United States could thus regain the moral leadership it earned during its early years when it committed itself to humanistic principles through its Declaration of Independence and its Bill of Rights.

14. Summary and conclusions: The review of political interactions between the mothers' wages policy and forces within and beyond the United States revealed that this policy proposal has never had a political constituency committed to its promotion, nor has it had a political history in this country. Therefore, "predictions" ought to deal with the questions whether such a constituency is likely to emerge in the political arena in the forseeable future, what the composition of such a constituency might be, and what chances, if any, it would have for gaining acceptance for the mothers' wages policy.

Before suggesting answers to these questions, it seems important to note that analysis of the mothers' wages policy did not reveal contradictions or obstacles to its implementation in terms of "real" economic, ecological, biological, demographic, technological, and social-structural factors. The feasibility of implementing this policy is consequently a function of political, ideological, cultural, and psychological factors. In terms of these latter factors, the analysis seems to lead to the conclusion that existing political parties and social action organizations would not be eager to adopt the mothers' wages policy in its proposed comprehensive form, and that, also, no new organization would be likely to emerge in the political arena in the near future that would be committed to the promotion of this policy.

The foregoing conclusions seem warranted in spite of the fact that considerable political support could be generated for the mothers' wages policy among low income and other segments of the population, in view of the policy's immediate, concrete benefits for low income families with children under age eighteen, and its potential, long-range, constructive consequences for society as a whole. Yet, the relatively liberal income transfer provisions of this policy and the value premises implicit in it seem to constitute too marked a deviation from (and too obvious a challenge to) the existing social and economic order of the United States and its underlying political balance; the perceived interests of powerful economic forces; and the firmly established beliefs, values, ideologies, and traditions of the prevailing culture. Hence, the policy would trigger intensive resistance from a broad spectrum of political forces, were any party or organization bold, idealistic, or perhaps naive enough to inject the mothers' wages policy into the political process of the nation.

The political opposition would be likely to derive considerable support from "expert" opinions of civil servants and professionals, many of whom would be critical of selected technical and economic aspects of the mothers' wages policy, such as the principle of "universality" and resulting "inefficiencies" concerning income transfers, as well as the aggregate scope of the transfers which they would interpret as a threat to the stability of the existing economic system. Such expert opinions would carry considerable weight in political contests surrounding the mothers' wages policy since they would be viewed as "objective and neutral facts" rather than merely as opinions based on fallible assumptions concerning human behavior and the workings of the economy, assumptions which in turn are derived from the dynamics and the ideology of the established social order and its economic system

Opposition to the mothers' wages policy would thus be formidable, were a coalition of low income interest groups and liberal and progressive upper and middle class sympathizers to sponsor it on the political scene. This policy would also evoke little enthusiasm and support from radical social and political action groups who reject the existing social order, its economic system, and its underlying dominant beliefs, values, ideology, and traditions. For these groups would object to the intrinsic value inconsistencies of the mothers' wages policy and to shortcomings in its substantive provisions. They would, therefore, tend not to lend support to a political coalition sponsoring the policy and would be likely to promote instead alternative policies concerning the issues dealt with by the mothers' wages policy. Such alternative policies would be internally consistent in terms of value premises and ideological orientation, and would aim to reduce, or perhaps even to eliminate, social and economic inequalities for all segments of society rather than for specific population segments only, and would also avoid the built-in, traditional sex bias of the mothers' wages policy.

In summing up these considerations, it seems that, while the mothers' wages policy could constitute one feasible reform for the social policy system of the United States, it is not likely to attract, within the existing political milieu, a pragmatically minded social action coalition willing to sponsor its adoption, and willing also to invest considerable human and economic resources in a political struggle with a limited chance of success. Yet, in case such a political coalition were to come into being, and succeeded in overcoming its opposition and to gain enactment of the mothers' wages policy, the policy, once it was the law of the land, would generate its own dynamics and would gradually gain acceptance as a result of its direct and indirect benefits. The mothers' wages policy would thus become an integral component of the social policy system and culture in the same way in which earlier significant social reform policies, such as "Social Security" and "Medicare," were integrated relatively quickly and easily after overcoming intensive political opposition prior to their enactment.

E. DEVELOPMENT OF ALTERNATIVE SOCIAL POLICIES; COMPARISON AND EVALUATION

Alternative policies to a specific social policy may be designed to achieve the same, or nearly the same, objectives as the ones pursued by the original policy, or to achieve markedly different objectives concerning the same policy issues. Alternative policies of the former type utilize different measures from the ones employed by the original policy, measures which are expected to be more effective, and/or efficient, in attaining the original objectives, but which may, at times, also modify these original objectives. The different measures are often also likely to reflect differences in underlying value premises and ideological orientations. Alternative policies of the second type substitute, by design, different objectives for the objectives of the original policy. These different objectives are usually derived from different value premises and ideological orientations. Obviously, alternative policies of the second type involve also different policy measures geared to the attainment of their different objectives. Two alternative social policies to the mothers' wages policy are presented below, one illustrating an alternative policy of the first type, the other an alternative policy of the second type.

1. Alternative social policies:

a. aimed at the same policy objectives, but involving alternative policy measures: The first alternative policy aims to attain, or to approximate, the objectives of the mothers' wages policy more efficiently by substituting the principle of "selectivity" for that of "universality" concerning the payment of mothers' wages and children's allowances. This change would involve (1) limiting eligibility for income transfers, under both provisions, to families with children under age eighteen, with total current income below the median family income, adjusted for family size, and (2) modifying the amounts of mothers' wages and children's allowances so that the combined income of families, including transfer payments, would in no case exceed the adjusted median income. Other aspects of the original policy would remain on the whole unchanged, with the exception of horizontal income transfers among households with incomes above the median. This specific provision would be eliminated automatically since no income transfers would be made to families with incomes above the adjusted median, irrespective of their size.

This alternative policy also establishes procedures for implementing the means test implicit in its provisions. The procedures would require potentially eligible families to file a claim for transfer payments and a declaration of income with appropriate local government offices. Claims and declarations would be accepted as valid subject only to random checks, rather than to case-by-case investigations. The transfer programs would be administered in conjunction with the Internal Revenue Service. Annual income tax returns could thus be used as supplementary checks on claims and on declarations of income, and as a basis for annual adjustments of accounts for all households whether or not they had filed claims during the year.

The administrative purpose implicit in this alternative policy is to avoid transferring income to families from whom it would have to be recouped eventually through income taxes, as would be the case were the original policy implemented. In this way, efficiency is expected to increase and administrative costs to decrease while the net aggregate amount of vertical income transfers from population segments with incomes above the adjusted median to families with children under age eighteen with total incomes below the adjusted median would be the same as under the original policy. The net amounts of transfer payments received by individual families would also remain essentially unchanged.

b. aimed at different policy objectives concerning the same policy issues: The second alternative policy is designed to modify the objectives of the original mothers' wages policy so as to overcome the built-in sex bias of that policy, which tends to strengthen the traditional ties between motherhood and child care and homemaking roles. This alternative policy would reduce, but not eliminate, the inconsistencies in value premises noted in the analysis of the original mothers' wages policy by instituting additional modifications in the policy processes of work organization and rights distribution. The policy would remove conventional obstacles for women in access to work by enhancing options concerning intra- and extrafamilial child care modalities and by providing in this way real opportunities for mothers to pursue careers outside their homes. With respect to rights distribution, this policy would go beyond the original mothers' wages policy by broadening the nature and scope of provisions designed to reduce inequalities of social and economic rights.

To attain these wider objectives, the following substantive changes in, and additions to, the provisions of the original mothers' wages policy would be instituted:

—Mothers' wages would be redefined as "parents' wages" or "child care wages." These wages would be payable to mothers and/or fathers on equal terms in relation to the time they would devote to child care work or to gainful employment, respectively. Families with children would thus be encouraged to design their individual division of work within and outside the home. The combined parents' wages of families would in no case exceed the equivalent of one full-time wage.

—Publicly financed, comprehensive child care and child development services would be established throughout the country by the federal government in cooperation with state and local governments. The quality of child care and the equality of standards in these public facilities would be ensured through supervision by the federal government. Parents, irrespective of their economic circumstances, would be able to use these facilities at their discretion in accordance with their employment and/or educational schedules. It would, therefore, be necessary to operate some facilities on a twenty-four hour basis. Special facilities would have to be established for children with exceptional needs, be these needs physical, mental or emotional. Parents would have the right to participate on a decision-making level in the operation of these child care and child development facilities. Provisions would be made for reduction of children's allowances in proportion to the time children would be cared for in public child care facilities. Parents' wages, too, would be reduced when all children of a family would be cared for in child care facilities.

2. *Comparison and evaluation*

The two alternative policies developed above will now be analyzed in accordance with the standard framework and will be compared with the mothers' wages policy throughout this analysis. Since the major purpose of this chapter has been to illustrate an approach to social policy analysis and development rather than to explore the mothers' wages policy and alternative policies, and since this purpose seems to have been accomplished already, the analysis and comparison will be conducted in an abbreviated, instead of in a comprehensive manner. Similarities to, and differences from, the mothers' wages policy will be indicated. Material reported in the analysis of the original policy will not be repeated as it can be reviewed under the corresponding items in that analysis. The first alternative policy will be referred to as "selective mothers' wages" policy and the second alternative policy as "parents' wages" policy. Capital letters and Arabic numerals refer to corresponding sections and foci of the standard framework for policy analysis and development.

A— Both alternative policies are designed to deal with the same issues and problems as the original policy.

B-1— Objectives of the selective mothers' wages policy are nearly identical to those of the original policy though modified by the "selectivity" principle which would eliminate direct benefits for families with children under age eighteen with incomes above the adjusted median.

In addition to the objectives of the original policy, the parents' wages policy would aim to eliminate inequalities between wives and husbands, and mothers and fathers, concerning child care responsibilities and concerning educational, occupational, career, and economic opportunities. This policy would also strengthen societal responsibilities and provisions for child development through the establishment of universal, comprehensive child care services.

B-2— The underlying value and ideological orientation of the selective mothers' wages policy are similar to those of the original policy. However, the egalitarian and collective thrust of the original policy would be blunted under this policy since the entire population would be divided more sharply into recipients and nonrecipients of transfer payments. Internal value inconsistencies as well as continuities with the dominant value premises of the United States which are reflected in the objectives of the original policy would thus be even more evident in this alternative policy.

The egalitarian and collective value premises of the original policy would be strengthened in the parents' wages policy. This policy would facilitate equality of rights and of access to intra- and extrafamilial roles for husbands and wives, and would strengthen societal responsibilities and provisions to assure more equal opportunities for men, women and children. It would thus overcome some, though not all, of the value inconsistencies of the original policy and would therefore involve less continuity with the dominant value premises than the mothers' wages policy.

B-3— The theories and hypotheses underlying the strategies and provisions of the selective mothers' wages policy are essentially identical to those of the original policy except for several additional hypotheses concerning the principle of selectivity. This principle is assumed to maximize the preservation of societal resources, to be equitable and straightforward, and to have no divisive effects on the population. These hypotheses are untested, and their validity would seem to depend on many aspects of the total societal context.

The parents' wages policy also involves additional hypotheses to those of the original policy. One further hypothesis is that defining mothers' wages as parents' wages and making the wages available on equal terms to fathers and mothers would result in a more egalitarian division of work within the family, and in more equal opportunities for women in access to work and roles outside the family. Another hypothesis is that child development would not be adversely affected, but would be enhanced by shifting many child rearing functions away from the family to public child care facilities. These hypotheses, too, have not been tested sufficiently, and their validity would also seem to depend on many variables of the societal context.

B-4— The target segment of the selective mothers' wages policy would be smaller than that of the original policy since mothers and children in families with incomes above the adjusted median would be excluded from direct benefits.

The target segment of the parents' wages policy would be larger than that of the original policy since children from all families, irrespective of social and economic circumstances, would be eligible for services from public child care facilities, and also because parents' wages and child care services would gradually affect the division of work in nearly all families with children under age eighteen.

B-5—Substantive short- and long- range effects of the selective mothers' wages policy are expected to match the specified objectives of this policy. These effects would be similar, in all relevant spheres, to the effects of the original policy, with respect to the more limited target segment. However, the general societal context surrounding the implementation of this policy, and especially psychological and political dimensions, would differ from the context of the original policy since families with children with incomes above the adjusted median would not receive direct benefits, irrespective of family size. This fact could adversely influence attitudes toward this policy and its beneficiaries. Costs of the selective mothers' wages policy would seem to be less than those of the original policy since the aggregate amount of transfer payments would be $85 billion less than the amount required for the original policy. This reduction would be reflected in lower tax rates for individuals and business firms and in a smaller scope of new tax measures which would have to be instituted. This reduced need for new taxes would, however, be more apparent than real since the scope of vertical transfer payments would remain unchanged. The reduction in taxes would merely reflect elimination of that portion of the transfer payments which, under the original policy, would be largely recouped through taxes, and elimination of horizontal transfers from smaller to larger families with incomes above the adjusted median.

Substantive short- and long- range effects of the parents' wages policy are also expected to match the objectives of that policy. These effects are expected to exceed those of the original policy in terms of significant changes in intrafamilial roles, relations, and life styles; patterns of child care and child development; the composition of the work force and the occupational distribution of women, etc. These changes would spread throughout the population and would not be limited to one or another population segment. The parents' wages policy would involve a significant increase in real economic costs compared to the original policy, to finance the establishment and operation of public child care services. Assuming full utilization by eligible children, this increase in real costs could eventually exceed $50 billion per year. The scope of transfer payments for parents' wages and children's allowances would, however, decrease as utilization of child care services would gradually increase. It should be noted, however, that the establishment and operation of these costly facilities is likely to have constructive effects for the economy, the occupational structure of the work force, and for the rights of mothers, fathers and children. Moreover, children are assumed to derive comprehensive developmental benefits from these services.

C-1—The selective mothers' wages policy would have similar implications to the original policy for the development, management, and conservation of resources, goods, and services.

The parents' wages policy would also have similar implications to the original policy for resource development except for the area of child care services. Whereas the original policy would be likely to reduce demand for the development of child care facilities since government funds would be available for mothers' wages and children's allowances but not for child care services, the parents' wages policy would probably accelerate the establishment of child care services as it would allocate new government resources for this purpose, in addition to making provisions for parents' wages and children's allowances. Demand for these services would be likely to increase once they became available since the parents' wages policy would encourage parents to develop their own patterns of combinations of child care and occupational careers.

C-2—Effects of the selective mothers' wages policy on the organization of work would be similar to those of the original policy but would be concentrated mainly on families with children in the lower half of the income distribution.

The parents' wages policy would have important, direct effects on the organization of work in addition to the indirect effects it would have in common with the original policy. These direct effects would be reductions in inequalities of intra- and extrafamilial work and roles between husbands and wives in families with children.

C-3— Effects of the selective mothers' wages policy on the distribution of rights would be similar to the effects of the mothers' wages policy but concentrated on families with children with incomes below the median. Effects of the parents' wages policy on the distribution of rights would go beyond the effects of the original policy. Conventional intrafamilial inequalities of rights between husbands and wives tend to be rooted in their differential access to work and roles. To the extent, therefore, that the parents' wages policy would significantly reduce the inequalities of intra- and extrafamilial access to work and roles for women and men, it would result also in corresponding reductions in inequalities of rights between husbands and wives. As for children, this policy would enhance their rights significantly beyond the mothers' wages policy through the establishment of public, comprehensive child care services, which would especially strengthen the rights of children from low income families. Shortcomings in the original policy concerning the distribution of rights to poor and low income households without children under age eighteen would not be overcome by the parents' wages policy in spite of its stronger egalitarian thrust.

C-4— Consequences of the selective mothers' wages policy for circumstances of living, power, and the overall quality of life would be nearly the same as the consequences of the original policy. Yet while the original policy is expected to facilitate societal integration and a sense of solidarity through the distributive principle of universality, the alternative policy, by substituting the distributive principle of selectivity, could adversely affect tendencies toward integration and solidarity. Effects of the selective mothers' wages policy on intrafamilial and on employment relations would be the same as the effects of the original policy but would be limited primarily to the lower half of the income distribution.

Consequences of the parents' wages policy for circumstances of living, power, and the overall quality of life would exceed the consequences of the original policy. Parents, especially in lower, but also in middle income strata, would be likely to experience new freedoms and new opportunities as conventional patterns concerning access to work, roles, and rights would gradually change. These new opportunities could generate, also, some stress and anxiety during early stages of adjustment, but are expected to result over time in constructive changes in patterns of family life, characterized by equality, freedom, independence, and mutual respect. The foregoing changes in family milieu, as well as the universal availability of comprehensive child care and child development services are, in turn, expected to provide children with enriching and growth-enhancing experiences. Progress in this sphere would also not be smooth since establishment and operation of a new, nationwide service system would encounter many administrative and substantive difficulties. However, the overall trend would be in a positive direction as far as child development is concerned. The many constructive changes expected to result from the parents' wages policy, especially for women and children, and hence for the patterns and quality of family life, would be reflected, eventually, in psychological, social, cultural, and political aspects of local community life and, in time, throughout the entire social structure of the nation. Effects of the parents' wages policy on specific sets of intrasocietal human relations between men and women, husbands and wives, parents and children, and women and men and their employers would also exceed the effects of the original policy because of more thorough changes under the parents' wages policy in the work roles and rights of men, women, and children. The general trend of these changes would be reflected in further reductions of inequalities and hierarchical elements in all these relations.

D-1— The history of the selective mothers' wages policy is identical to that of the original policy—it has no history except for the children's allowance component, and it has no political support in the United States.

The history of the parents' wages policy is similar to that of the original policy except for the child care services component which has had an extended history and which currently has strong political support in the United States.

D-2— Political reactions to the selective mothers' wages policy would be similar to reactions to the original policy. However, there is likely to be less resistance from upper income segments of the population because of the reduced scope of total transfer payments, and from government and academic economists because of the shift to the "selectivity" principle. On the other hand, some potential supporters of the original policy among middle income groups may be less ready to support this alternative policy because of its potentially divisive effects, and because of the elimination of horizontal income transfers which, under the original policy, would reduce inequalities of per capita purchasing power among families with children in the upper half of the income distribution.

Reactions to the parents' wages policy would also be similar to reactions to the original policy. However, many opponents of the original policy would be likely to oppose this policy even more intensely because of its increased costs and stronger egalitarian tendencies. On the other hand, women's rights groups, groups interested in the promotion of public child care services, and groups committed to egalitarian ideologies would be more inclined to support this policy than the original policy.

D-3 and D-4— Effects of interactions between the selective mothers' wages policy and physical and biological properties of the natural environment, and biological and psychological properties of people, would be nearly the same as effects of such interactions with the original policy.

Effects of interactions between the parents' wages policy and physical and biological properties of the natural environment, and biological and psychological properties of people, would also be similar to effects of such interactions with the original policy. However, psychologically and culturally conditioned resistance to the notions of parents' wages, and equality of access to work and roles for women, could be more intense than to the notions of mothers' wages and of stronger economic rights for mothers and children. Should the parents' wages policy be adopted in spite of such resistance, experiences of children in public child care facilities could become, over time, important factors in changing psychologically and culturally conditioned attitudes concerning the roles, work, and rights of women and men.

D-5— Effects of the selective mothers' wages on the satisfaction of material and security needs would be similar to the effects of the mothers' wages policy. However, because of the means test implicit in the selective mothers' wages policy, its effects on social and psychological needs are likely to be less adequate. On the other hand, the selective mothers' wages policy would be a lesser threat to the perceived needs of nontarget segments of the population, and resistance to it is, therefore, likely to be less than to the mothers' wages policy.

Effects of the parents' wages policy on the satisfaction of basic and perceived needs would be broader than the effects of the mothers' wages policy. This policy would enable mothers to satisfy their needs for equality with fathers concerning work, social roles, and self-actualization. And it would enable fathers to satisfy their usually unmet needs for caring and nurturing relations with their children. The needs of children for harmonious relations with, and between, their parents are also more likely to be met in truly egalitarian families in which both parents have equal opportunities to develop their capacities. The broader scope for needs fulfillment of the parents' wages policy is likely to result in increased resistance on the part of people who consider egalitarian tendencies as a threat to their values and their perceived needs and interests.

D-6— Interactions of demographic developments with the selective mothers' wages policy and the parents' wages policy are likely to have about the same effects as interactions of demographic developments with the mothers' wages policy.

D-7— Actual effects of the selective mothers' wages policy on the disposition of the economic surplus would be about the same as the effects of the mothers' wages policy. However, the apparent effects will seem to be significantly lower since households with incomes above the median would not be entitled to receive child care wages and children's allowances. Because of the apparent difference in effects on the economic surplus, resistance to the selective mothers' wages policy by privileged classes is likely to be less intense. However, there is likely to be less support for the selective mothers' wages policy from middle income households who might be more inclined to support the mothers' wages policy because of perceived benefits for them from that policy.

Effects of the parents' wages policy on the disposition of the economic surplus would be significantly broader than the effects of the mothers' wages policy because of the real economic costs and the related opportunity costs of universal public child care. Resistance to this policy would therefore be more intense than to the mothers' wages policy by groups and classes whose perceived interests are served well by prevailing allocations of the economic surplus. On the other hand, groups who favor universal provision of child care and equal opportunities for women are likely to be more supportive of the parents' wages policy, in spite of its effects on the disposition of the economic surplus.

D-8— Effects of the selective mothers' wages policy on intrasocietal differentiations and conflicts concerning work and rights would be similar to the effects of the mothers' wages policy. However, effects of the parents' wages policy on differentiations and conflicts would be significantly broader due to the equalization of rights and opportunities of mothers. Their entry into previously male-dominated occupations and roles would greatly expand intrasocietal differentiations. It could also cause conflicts concerning work and rights. Eventually, these processes could result in major changes in work organization and rights distribution for women as well as for men.

D-9— Effects of the selective mothers' wages policy on development of ideas, knowledge, science, and technology would not differ significantly from the effects of the mothers' wages policy. Also, resistance to the ideas underlying both policies would be similar in scope, as these ideas do not differ in substance, but only with regard to the size and economic situation of the target groups of the policies.

The effects of the parents' wages policy on development of ideas, knowledge, science, and technology would be more profound than the effects of the mothers' wages policy because of the equalization of opportunities for mothers to enter social and occupational roles. Active involvement of women in development of ideas, knowledge, science, and technology would expand the human resources available for these functions and would bring new perspectives to them.

The ideas underlying the parents' wages policy are more "radical" than the ideas underlying the mothers' wages and selective mothers' wages policies.

D-10— The value premises and ideological orientation of the selective mothers' wages policy are similar to those of the original policy, but involve more continuity with the dominant value premises and ideological orientation of the United States. Effects of interactions between this policy and dominant beliefs, values, ideologies, customs, and traditions would, however, not differ markedly from effects of such interactions with the original policy.

The parents' wages policy reflects more egalitarian and collective, and less traditional, values concerning the roles and rights of women and children than the original policy, and involves less continuity with dominant values and ideologies. Interactions between this policy and dominant beliefs, values, ideologies, and traditions of the United States would, therefore, generate more intense conflicts and resistance than would result from such interactions with the original policy. While the parents' wages policy would eliminate one major value inconsistency of the mothers' wages policy, namely, the built-in bias favoring a close linkage between motherhood and child care and homemaking roles, it would not overcome another value inconsistency of the original policy, namely, its failure to eliminate poverty and to reduce social and economic inequalities for families and individuals in households without children under age eighteen.

D-11— The selective mothers' wages policy derives from a similar level of critical consciousness, and reflects similar alternative visions of social life, as the mothers' wages policy although it does not pursue consistently the implications of that consciousness and vision. Its effects on the spreading of critical consciousness and social vision would, therefore, not differ much from the effects of the mothers' wages policy.

The parents' wages policy derives from a more radical level of critical consciousness and a more comprehensive egalitarian social vision than the mothers' wages policy. This would cause more intense resistance as well as more enthusiastic support from political forces supporting the status quo and equality, respectively. Were the parents' wages policy implemented, its effects on spreading critical consciousness and an egalitarian social vision would exceed the effects of the mothers' wages policy.

D-12— All three policies reflect similar influences from social policies and social visions of other societies.

D-13— Effects of interactions between the selective mothers' wages policy and relevant other social policies would be similar to effects of such interactions with the original policy. However, because of the reduced scope of transfer payments under the selective mothers' wages policy, effects on tax policies would be more limited. Also, since this policy incorporates the principle of selectivity, it would be less likely than the original policy to further the elimination of formal and informal means tests and other divisive features in the administration of public and social services.

Effects of interactions between the parents' wage policy and relevant other social policies would also be similar to effects of such interactions with the original policy. However, because of the cost of child care services, the impact of this policy on tax policies would be more extensive. Because of its stronger egalitarian thrust, this policy would also be more likely than the original policy to further the elimination of formal and informal means tests and other divisive features in the administration of public and social services. Another difference of the interaction effects of this policy from those of the original policy would be acceleration rather than deceleration in the development of child care services. Furthermore, contrary to probably unintended effects of the original policy of slowing progress toward equality of rights, work, and roles for women, this policy would accelerate progress toward such equalities. Finally, establishment of public child care services under this policy may increase the risk, noted in the analysis of the original policy, of excessive intervention by public authorities in parent-child relations and in child care provided by parents.

Effects of interactions between the selective mothers' wages policy and relevant foreign and defense policies of the United States would be similar to effects of such interactions with the original policy. However, since the amounts of transfer funds required for the implementation of this policy are smaller than the amounts required for implementation of the original policy, chances for implementation of this policy prior to major reductions in defense appropriations seem better than for implementation of the original policy.

Effects of interactions between the parents' wages policy and relevant foreign and defense policies of the United States would also be similar to effects of such interactions with the original policy. However, because of the significantly higher costs of this policy, chances for its implementation prior to major reductions in defense appropriations would be even less than chances for implementation of the original policy. In the unlikely case that this policy would, nevertheless, be implemented prior to major reductions in defense appropriations, and prior to major changes in the underlying premises and thrust of the foreign policies of the United States, this policy would be likely to exert a stronger influence than the original policy toward reductions in defense spending and changes in foreign policies because of its stronger humanistic and egalitarian thrust.

D-14—Nearly all conclusions and predictions concerning interaction effects between the original policy and societal forces are relevant also to the selective mothers' wages policy. Chances for promotion and adoption of this policy within the existing political milieu of the United States are only slightly better than chances for adoption of the original policy. The slight difference is due to significantly lower perceived costs of the selective mothers' wages policy and to its presumably higher efficiency. It should be noted, however, that, while opposition to the selective mothers' wages policy is likely to be less intense than to the original policy, potential support for it does not seem to be any stronger.

Conclusions and predictions concerning the likely fate of the parents' wages policy within the extant context of the political arena in the United

States would have to be even less optimistic than conclusions and predictions concerning the original policy. The stronger, less ambiguous, egalitarian and collective thrust of this policy, its innovative, comprehensive provisions for child care services, and its relatively high costs would generate even more intense political resistance than the original policy. Yet those very same aspects of the parents' wages policy could result in stronger support for it, than for the original policy, from diverse political forces, including women's rights groups, proponents of child care services, and groups committed to egalitarian and collective ideologies. However, such additional potential support would hardly suffice to overcome the strong resistance this policy would be likely to trigger among political forces committed to the preservation of the existing social order and its value premises and ideology, were it promoted in the currently prevailing political milieu of the United States.

SUMMARY

The abbreviated, comparative analysis of the selective mothers' wages and parents' wages policies and the preceding comprehensive analysis of the mothers' wages policy suggest the following summary.

1. All three policies reflect egalitarian and collective values and are thus at variance with dominant beliefs, values, ideologies, and traditions of the social policy system of the United States which stresses individualism, competition, and social and economic inequalities.

While all three policies aim to significantly reduce extant social and economic inequalities and to strengthen collective responsibility for the well-being of members of society, they vary in the degree of consistency with which they pursue these objectives. The parents' wages policy is most consistent by these criteria, the mothers' wages policy involves several ambiguities and inconsistencies, and the selective mothers' wages policy is the least consistent of the three policies. Conversely, the selective mothers' wages policy is closest to dominant value premises of the established social policy system, the mothers' wages policy involves several linkages to dominant value premises but is less close to them than the selective mothers' wages policy, and the parents' wages policy seems farthest removed from the dominant values and ideology of the prevailing social policy system.

2. The three policies share a common set of objectives concerning the policy issues of the roles, work, and rights of women; the rights of children; the definition of mothers' work; and the redistribution of social and economic rights through the transfer of purchasing power. In addition to the common objectives, each policy pursues also separate objectives. All three policies would assure a minimum level of rights and economic independence to mothers in low income families by recognizing and rewarding their contributions to society. All three policies would also protect mothers from serious exploitation in the labor market. Furthermore, the three policies would assure children minimal economic rights as well as the right to maternal care when mothers wish to offer such care. To assure the foregoing rights, the three policies would effect a vertical transfer of purchasing power from the upper to the lower half of the income distribution. This transfer of roughly 10 percent of national income would eliminate poverty for all families with children under age eighteen, reduce social and economic inequalities throughout society, and stimulate the national economy. The mothers' wages and parents' wages policies would involve, also, horizontal income transfers from smaller to larger families throughout the population and would thus also reduce per capita inequalities of purchasing power within socioeconomic strata. The parents' wages policy would achieve the additional objectives of reducing inequalities of roles and rights between wives and husbands within the family, and of reducing inequalities in access to occupations and education for women throughout society. Furthermore, the parents' wages policy would provide comprehensive public child care and child development services and facilities and would stimulate the evolution of new patterns of family life and child care. The selective mothers' wages policy would emphasize fiscal efficiency and would limit direct benefits to families with children under age eighteen with incomes below the median. The mothers' wages and parents' wages policies are likely to strengthen trends toward societal integration and solidarity while the selective mothers' wages policy could have divisive effects on society as a whole. All three policies are likely to achieve their

specified objectives if implemented as proposed. Finally, it should be noted that all three policies would fail to deal directly with poverty and inequalities of families and individuals in households without children under age eighteen, households which consist primarily of aged individuals and individuals with handicaps and disabilities.

3. The mothers' wages and selective mothers' wages policy could have the unintended effect of slowing progress toward equal rights for women concerning access to occupations and education as these policies would tend to strengthen the traditional linkage between motherhood and child care and homemaking roles. All three policies, but especially the parents' wages policy, could have the further unintended effect of excessive public intervention in parent-child relations because of growing societal responsibilities for economic support and direct care of children.

4. All three policies would have a minor impact on the social structure and on the entire system of social policies. They would cause constructive shifts in the quality and quantity of resources developed in response to changes in demands for goods and services resulting from the sizeable transfers of purchasing power to lower income groups. The parents' wages policy would stimulate nationwide development of a new resource—public child care facilities and services. As for the organization of work, all three policies would result in modifications of intrafamilial roles and would also improve the access to education and occupations for children from currently poor and low income segments of the population. The parents' wages policy would also remove intrafamilial obstacles to equality of roles especially for women and would enhance their chances for occupational and educational equality beyond the family setting. The major impact of the three policies would, however, be in the area of rights distribution as a result of relatively large-scale vertical and, in the case of the mothers' and parents' wages policies, horizontal transfers of purchasing power. In a highly developed money economy such as the United States, purchasing power is perhaps the most valid indicator of an individual's rights and of his command over resources, goods and services. In these terms, the three policies would involve considerable shifts in the existing rights distribution toward less inequalities. About 10

percent of national income would be shifted to the lower half of the income distribution and all families with children would be assured a minimally adequate income. Under the parents' wages policy, children would be assured additional new rights through "in-kind" public child care services. All three policies would also enhance the "entitlement" approach to rights distribution through children's allowances. The selective mothers' wages policy would, however, exclude children in families with incomes above the median from receiving children's allowances.

The several major modifications in resource development, work organization, and rights distribution would be reflected in marked changes in the overall quality of life and in the circumstances of living and power. These changes would involve improvements in ecological, biological, psychological, economic, social, and cultural aspects of living. Finally, human relations within and beyond the family would undergo changes toward more egalitarian and less hierarchical patterns. These changes would be especially marked under the parents' wages policy, less so under the mother's wages policy, and least under the selective mothers' wages policy.

5. The amounts of transfer payments involved in the three policies would be considerable, but "real" economic costs are likely to be limited. The annual income transfers for the selective mothers' wages policy (based on calculations in 1971) would be approximately $90 billion, and for the mothers' and parents' wages policies approximately $175 billion. The parents' wages policy may require, eventually, up to $50 billion per year for the establishment of child care services. However, as the utilization of child care facilities would increase, parents' wages and children's allowances would decrease. The amounts required for child care services would involve real economic costs. Another economic cost of the three policies would be the loss of cheap labor supplied now by poor mothers, and resulting increases in the prices of some goods and services.

As for "benefits," the three policies would eliminate poverty and near-poverty for families with children under age eighteen. This, in turn, would result in considerable stimulation of the economy, in constructive, qualitative and quantitative changes in production, and in reduction of unemployment. The direct benefits to families with children would thus spread through wider groups of society. The tax structure would become more equitable, the overall yield of tax revenue on local, state, and federal levels would increase, and general public and social services would be improved considerably and distributed more equitably. The development of automation in industry and in public services would be accelerated to counteract shortages of cheap labor, and general working conditions would improve.

Benefits of the three policies for family life would include improvements in the self-image, power, and social prestige of mothers along with improvements in their social and economic rights; shifts in the role of fathers and husbands from economic control toward sharing as equals in meaningful human relations; general improvements in the quality of family life, and in relations between women and men; and improvements in economic, biological, emotional, intellectual, social, and cultural aspects of child development, especially in poor, near-poor, and working or lower middle class families. Over time, a gradual reduction could be expected in the incidence of physical and mental illness, mental retardation, and various forms of deviance in social and psychological functioning, and a corresponding increase in overall societal integration. Furthermore, there would be gradual improvements in the quality of housing and neighborhoods and in the patterns of land use and settlement. The foregoing benefits would tend to be more limited in nearly every sphere under the selective mothers' wages policy. On the other hand, under the parents' wages policy there would be additional benefits, namely, accelerated progress toward intra- and extrafamilial equality of social and economic rights and equal access to occupations and education for women and men, and universal availability of comprehensive child care and child development services.

Summarizing these multifaceted societal costs and benefits, it seems that the benefits of any one of the three policies would exceed real and perceived costs if humanistic, egalitarian, and collective interest criteria are used in the evaluation. The benefits-to-costs ratio, by these criteria, would be most favorable under the parents' wages policy, intermediate under the mothers' wages policy, and least favorable under the selective mothers' wages policy. One hidden opportunity cost item of all three policies, however, would be their failure to include among the recipients of direct income transfers poor and low income families and individuals in households without children under age eighteen. This shortcoming of the three policies could be corrected by adding to the parents' wages policy a special income transfer feature geared to the needs of this population segment and assuring all its members an adequate annual income.

6. Finally, it should be noted that implementation of any one of the three policies would be feasible in the United States in terms of physical and biological properties of the natural environment, biological and psychological properties of the population, the current stage of economic and technological development, and the size and institutional differentiation of society. However, in spite of objective feasibility, all three policies would be opposed intensely were they promoted in the political arena by a coalition of potential beneficiaries and sympathizers committed to the objectives, value premises, and ideological orientations implicit in these policies. Opposition would derive from the perceived interests of powerful economic forces and from dominant beliefs, values, ideologies, and traditions prevailing in the extant culture, and reflected throughout the existing system of social policies of the United States. Because of this, it does not seem likely that any one of these three policies will be sponsored on the political scene in the near future, nor that sufficient political support could be generated, were some social action group willing to undertake such sponsorship.

The foregoing summary completes the illustration of the use of the conceptual model and the standard framework in the analysis, development, and comparison of social policies.

NOTES

1. David G. Gil, "Mothers' Wages—One Way to Attack Poverty," *Children*, Vol. 15, No 1. 6 (November-December 1968) Reprinted in *Social Service Outlook*, Vol 4, No. 4, (April 1969).
   "Mothers Wages—An Alternative Attack on Poverty," in *Social Work Practice*, 1969 (New York: Columbia University Press, 1969), published for the National Conference on Social Welfare.

2. Mike Reddin, "Universality versus Selectivity" in William A. Robson and Bernard Crick, *The Future of the Social Services* (Harmondsworth, England: Penguin Books, 1970).
   Eveline M. Burns, ed., *Children's Allowances and the Economic Welfare of Children* (New York: Citizens' Committee for Children of New York, Inc., 1968).
   Christopher Green, *Negative Taxes and the Poverty Program* (Washington, D.C.: The Brookings Institution, 1967).
   Note: To avoid misunderstandings it needs to be pointed out, parenthetically, that the assumptions concerning the advantages and disadvantages of universal and selective income transfer mechanisms oversimplify a complex technical issue. First of all, the differentiation between the two approaches is not absolute since each approach contains elements of the other. Thus, universal entitlement programs such as the Children's Allowance involve a "delayed" means test and also "indirect" work incentive features through the income tax mechanism. Negative income taxes, on the other hand, involve "universal entitlement" since all individuals within a category defined by income are entitled to benefits. Secondly, as far as the economic efficiency argument is concerned, negative income taxes lose efficiency because of the direct work incentive feature. Because of the indirect work incentive feature of Children's Allowances, this approach may, in fact, result in higher economic efficiency than is generally realized. This would depend on the provisions of the income tax. Thirdly, the arguments concerning societal cohesiveness and solidarity are also inconclusive since these social phenomena depend less on technical aspects of an income transfer system than on the general value orientations of a society. Given an overall egalitarian and humanistic value system, either transfer mechanism would be conducive to social cohesiveness and solidarity. On the other hand, an individualistic, nonegalitarian value system is likely to result in tension and conflict between recipients of transfer payments and taxpayers, irrespective of the transfer techniques employed. In summary then, important as the technical aspects of income transfers are, the more significant issues seem

to be the size of the transfers, the extent to which they are intended to eliminate inequalities, and the value premises underlying the transfer policy.

3. U.S. Department of Commerce, Bureau of the Census, *Consumer Income, Current Population Reports*, Series P-60, No. 78 (May 20, 1971), p 1.

4. U. S. Department of Labor, News Release USDL-ll-606 (December 21, 1970), p. 1.

5. U.S. Department of Commerce, Bureau of the Census, *Consumer Income, Current Population Reports*, Series P-60, No. 77 (May 7, 1971), Tables No. 1, p. 2; No. 4, p. 5; No. 6, p.6.

6. U.S. Department of Health, Education and Welfare, Social Security Administration, Social Security Bulletin, Vol. 34, No. 6 (June 1971), Table M-24, p. 46.
   The apparent discrepancy between the number of poor families headed by women in 1970, namely 1.7 million, and the number of families participating in the AFDC program at the end of 1970, namely 2.6 million, seems due to the following circumstances: AFDC payments are available in many states not only to female-headed families but also to male-headed families when fathers are unemployed and have exhausted unemployment benefits. Furthermore, poverty figures are estimates based on annual sample surveys and are subject to sampling errors, whereas figures of AFDC recipients are based on actual counts. There has been a steep increase in the number of AFDC recipients during 1970 from 1,875,000 families at the beginning of the year to 2,553,000 families at the end of that year. Finally, eligibility for AFDC is determined on the basis of circumstances prevailing at the point of application while poverty is measured on the basis of income in the course of an entire year. Hence, families whose total income during 1970 exceeded the poverty level may, nevertheless, be entitled to AFDC payments at any time during the year when they may be without sufficient income.

7. U.S. Department of Commerce, Bureau of the Census, *Consumer Income, Current Population Reports*, Series P-60, No. 77 (May 7, 1971), Table No. 9, p. 8.

8. U.S. Department of Commerce, Bureau of the Census, *Consumer Income, Current Population Reports,* Series P-60, No. 77 (May 7, 1971), Table No. 1, p. 2 and Table No. 4 p. 5.

9. U.S. Department of Commerce, Bureau of the Census, *Consumer Income, Current Population Reports*, Series P-60, No. 77 (May 7,1971), Table No. 1, p. 3 and Table No. 4, p. 5.

10. U.S. Department of Commerce, Bureau of the Census, *Consumer Income, Current Population Reports*, Series P-60, No. 78 (May 20, 1971), Table No. 2, p. 3.

11. U.S. Department of Commerce, Bureau of the Census, *Statistical Abstract of the United States*, 1970, Table No. 44, p. 38.

12. U.S. Department of Commerce, Bureau of the Census, *Consumer Income, Current Population Reports*, Series P-60, No. 76 (December 16, 1970), Table No. 8, p. 51.

13. U.S. Department of Commerce, Bureau of the Census, *Consumer Income, Current Population Reports*, Series P-60, No. 76 (December 16, 1970), Table No. 8, p. 51.

14. U.S. Department of Commerce, Bureau of the Census, *Consumer Income, Current Population Reports*, Series P-60, No. 75 (December 14, 1970), Table No. 11, p. 26.
This table reveals that since 1947, the lowest fifth of families received consistently about 5 percent of aggregate income, the second lowest fifth about 12 percent, the third fifth about 18 percent, the fourth fifth about 23 percent and the highest fifth about 41 percent. The top 5 percent of families received consistently about 15 percent of aggregate income. The income distribution for black families is even more skewed, and so is the distribution for unrelated individuals.

15. To shorten this illustrative analysis, actual projections of the numerical size of target segments have been omitted. The technique for obtaining these estimates is quite simple. It involves applying general population projections of the U.S. Bureau of the Census to portions of the population included in the target segments, e.g., children under age eighteen, mothers, families with children, percentiles of the income distribution, racial minorities, etc.

16. U.S. Department of Commerce, Bureau of the Census, *Consumer Income*, Current Population Reports, Series P-60, No. 77 (May 7, 1971), Table 6, p. 6.

17. Florence A. Ruderman, *Child Care and Working Mothers,* (New York: Child Welfare League of America, Inc., 1968), p. 153.

18. "Treasury Secretary Warns of Taxpayers' Revolt," *New York Times,* January 18, 1969.

19. Eveline M. Burns, ed., *Children's Allowances and the Economic Welfare of Children* (New York: Citizens' Committee for Children of New York, Inc., 1968).

20. Editorial, "Reversing a Welfare Trend," *New York Times,* July 10, 1971.

21. Florence A. Ruderman, *Child Care and Working Mothers,* (New York: Child Welfare League of America, Inc., 1968). *The Changing Dimensions of Day Care: Highlights from Child Welfare* (New York: Child Welfare League of America, 1970).
    Seth Low and Pearl G. Spindler, *Child Care Arrangements of Working Mothers in the United States,* Washington, D.C.: Superintendent of Documents, 1968 (Children's Bureau Publication No. 461, 1968).
    Marvin Bloom and Frank J. Hodges, "Day Care Centers?," *The Humanist,* Vol. 31, No. 4 (July/August, 1971), p 33.

22. David G. Gil, "Mothers' Wages—One Way to Attack Poverty," *Children,* Vol 15, No. 6 (November-December, 1968), 229-230; reprinted in *Social Service Outlook,* Vol. 4, No. 4 (April 1969), p. 1-2.
    David G. Gil, "Mothers' Wages—An Alternative Attack on Poverty," in *Social Work Practice,* 1969 (New York: Columbia University Press, 1969) p. 187-197. For a sampling of press reactions to the Mothers' Wages policy proposal see: *The Christian Science Monitor,* July 29, 1968; *The Evening Star,* Washington, D.C., May 27, 1969; *Daily News,* New York City, June 2, 1969; *The Times,* London, England, June 3, 1969; *Daily News,* Philadelphia, Pa., August 1, 1969; *Family Weekly,* February 1, 1970; *Sunday Express and News,* San Antonio, Texas, October 3, 1971. For a similar proposal see: William V. Shannon, "A Radical, Direct, Simple, Utopian Alternative to Day Care Centers," The New York Times Magazine, April 30, 1972.

23. Pierre Larogue, ed., *Les Institutions Sociales de la France* (Paris: La Documentation Francaise, 1963). English translation: M. M. Philip Gaunt and Noel Lindsay, *Social Welfare in France.* See especially: *Part II:* French

Family Policy and its Achievements; *Section B*: The Equalization of Family Liabilities; *II Family Benefits*: The Single Wage Allowance, pp. 455-456, Mother in the Home Allowance, p. 457.

24. Susan Ferge, *Social Policy in Connection with Maternity and Children in Hungary after 1945*. (Paper presented at an International Conference on Family Poverty and Social Policy, University of Manchester, Manchester, England, September 1969).

25. James C. Vadakin, *Children, Poverty, and Family Allowances* with a Foreword by Daniel P. Moynihan (New York and London: Basic Books, Inc., 1968).

26. The following publications during the late 1960s reflect these efforts: Alvin L. Schorr, *Poor Kids* (New York and London: Basic Books, Inc., 1966). James C. Vadakin, *Children, Poverty, and Family Allowances* with a Foreword by Daniel P. Moynihan (New York and London: Basic Books, Inc., 1968).
Eveline M. Burns, ed., *Children's Allowances and the Economic Welfare of Children* (New York: Citizens' Committee for Children of New York, Inc., 1968).
Children's Allowance Project, *Why We Need Children's Allowances in the United States—A Proposal* (New York: Citizen Committee for Children of New York, Inc., 1969).
Vera Shlakman, *Children's Allowances* (New York: Citizens' Committee for Children of New York, Inc.; A publication of the Children's Allowance Project, 1969).

27. Evidence for the government's interest in the children's allowance concept is reflected in the following excerpt from the *Fiscal Year 1969 Plan*, Research and Demonstrations, Community Action Program, Office of Economic Opportunity. This document is dated October 14, 1968, and was approved by Mr. Bertrand M. Harding, Acting Director of OEO on November 25, 1968. The excerpt is from pages 47 and 48:

> FY 1968 $1,279,886
> FY 1969 $1,950,000

V. Income Maintenance—Nearly half of those in poverty are children. In the consideration of strategies for income maintenance, children's allowances similar to those in effect in Canada and European countries have been much discussed. There is as yet, however, no operational children's allowance model in the United States on which to base a comparison with alternate income maintenance systems. R&D will fund a children's allowance demonstration in an urban model cities neighborhood together with related research to provide a model for comparison with other systems, and to answer the numerous speculative questions which have so far been unanswered by individual prejudices and conjecture. The question of particular relevance is the effect, if any, on birth rates associated with a system of children's allowances, and particular attention will be placed upon this question in the research design of the project. Other research questions would be the effects of such an allowance on consumer behavior; effects on patterns of child rearing; whether it might vary patterns of labor force participation differently than under income maintenance programs (such as the Graduated Work Incentive Experiment); and the effects of a direct transfer of money to families in the poverty environment. This project will be developed with other Federal agencies, with each sharing resources and talent in order to develop a well-designed children's allowance model, and to participate in financing transfer payments and related research and evaluation. The groundwork for such an effort is already being laid. (1. Model Children's Allowance $500,000)

Additional funding of our graduated work incentives experiment will be required in Fiscal Year 1969. (2. Graduated Work Incentives Experiment $1,400,000)

Income Maintenance Priority List

1. Model Children's Allowance	500,000
2. Graduated Work Incentive Experiment	1,400,000
TOTAL:	1,950,000
REFUNDING TOTAL:	1,400,000

As further evidence of the government's interest in experimenting with the children's allowance policy, see the following news story:

Martin F. Nolan, "U.S., Brandeis Eye Family Allowance Trial," in *The Boston Globe,* May 1, 1969.

28. Richard L. Strout, "Nixon Aides Argue Merits of Family Aid Plans," *The Christian Science Monitor*, New England Edition, Weekend Edition, June 21-23, 1969.

LEGAL APPENDIX

The Unremunerated Work Act of 1991 (H.R. 3625)

*Continuation of House Proceedings of October 23, 1991,
Issue No. 153; and Proceedings of October 24, 1991, Issue No. 154*

Vol. 137   WASHINGTON, THURSDAY, OCTOBER 24, 1991   No. 154

Congressional Record

THE UNREMUNERATED WORK ACT OF 1991

(Mrs. COLLINS of Michigan asked and was given permission to address the House for 1 minute and to revise and extend her remarks.)

Mrs. COLLINS of Michigan: Mr. Speaker, today I am pleased to introduce a very vital and valuable bill that would require the Bureau of Labor Statistics to conduct time use surveys to measure the unwaged work women and men do inside and outside the home and to include these measures into the gross national product (GNP) and in other national statistics.

For many women, unpaid work in the home is their full time, life time occupation. For other women and men engaged in paid market work, household work absorbs many hours a week. Yet, remarkably little is known about the value of household work. There is only one major national survey for the entire adult population. A 1975-76 study conducted by the Survey Research Center at the University of Michigan. This circumstance certainly reflects the fact that official government statistics ignore household work.

If the value of housework were included in the GNP, the significance of these tasks would not be continuously debated and bills like the family and medical leave act, which help families survive, would be quickly enacted.

Please join me and cosponsor this important piece of legislation.

PROCEEDINGS AND DEBATES OF THE 102d CONGRESS, FIRST SESSION

102D CONGRESS
1ST SESSION

H.R. 3625

To require the Commissioner of the Bureau of Labor Statistics to conduct time use surveys of unremunerated work performed in the United States and to calculate the monetary value of such work.

IN THE HOUSE OF REPRESENTATIVES
OCTOBER 24, 1991

Mrs. COLLINS of Michigan (for herself, Mr. DYMALLY, Mr. HAYES of Illinois, Mr. STOKES, Mr. DELLUMS, Mr. RANGEL, Mrs. COLLINS of Illinois, Mr. FORD of Tennessee, Mr. DIXON, Mr. SAVAGE, Mr. OWENS of New York, Mr. TOWNS, Mr. WHEAT, Mr. CONYERS, Mr. ESPY, Mr. FLAKE, Mr. LEWIS of Georgia, Mr. MFUME, Mr. PAYNE of New Jersey, Mr. WASHINGTON, Ms. NORTON, Mr. JERFFERSON, Ms. WATERS, and Mr. CLAY) introduced the following bill; which was referred to the Committee on Educaton and Labor.

A BILL

To require the Commissioner of the Bureau of Labor Statistics to conduct time use surveys of unremunerated work performed in the United States and to calculate the monetary value of such work.

Be it enacted by the Senate and House of Representatives of the United States of America in Congress assembled,

SECTION 1. SHORT TITLE

This Act may be cited as the "Unremunerated Work Act of 1991."

SEC. 2. FINDINGS.

The Congress finds that—

(1) women perform 2/3 of the work in the world relating to the production of goods and services;

(2) in 1985 the United Nations General Assembly adopted a resolution which included part of the Forward Looking Strategies for the Advancementof Women, which states that "the remunerated and, in particular, the unremunerated contributions of women to all aspects and sectors of development should be recognized, and appropriate efforts should be made to measure and reflect these contributions in national accounts and economic statistics and in the gross national product";

(3) such resolution also states that "concrete steps should be taken to quantify the unremunerated contribution of women to agriculture, food production, reproduction, and household activities"; and

(4) the unremunerated contribution by women to the economy of the United States should be recognized.

SEC. 3. CALCULATION OF MONETARY VALUE OF UNREMUNERATED WORK

(a) In GENERAL—The Commissioner of the Bureau of Labor Statistics shall—

(1) conduct time use surveys of unremunerated work performed in the United States, including household work, work related to child care and other care services, agricultural work, work related to food production, work related to family business, and volunteer work; and

(2) calculate the monetary value of such unremunerated work.

(b) SEPARATE MONETARY VALUES BASED ON GENDER—Separate monetary values shall be calculated pursuant to subsection (a) for men and women.

(c) INCLUSION IN GROSS NATIONAL PRODUCT—The monetary value of the unremunerated work calculated pursuant to subsection (a) shall be included in statistics used to determine the gross national product.

*HR 3625

Index

*All charts are italicized

409

and political action, 111-122, 139
Social groups or classes, 58, 91-92,
    106, 234
  conflicts between, 57, 73, 106-111,
    155, 247
  deprived, 110, 112, 114, 116, 117
  dominant vs. dominated, 48, 49-50,
    52, 53, 56, 61, 66, 134-135, 188,
    193, 197-198, 229, 234, 238, 246,
    248, 249, 268
  middle and upper class, 116
  organization of, 58, 61, 106, 187-
    188
  and policy issues, 73, 106-107
  privileged, 52, 53, 57, 83, 92, 107,
    108, 109-110, 112, 113, 114, 116-
    117, 135, 153, 154, 158, 170, 174,
    193, 198, 229, 234, 238, 246, 247,
    248, 249, 251, 260, 296
  relations between, 73, 350
Social ideology, 55-57, 107, 114-115,
    193-194
  alternative, 111-120, 360-361
Social institutions, 22-23, 26, 27, 186
  See also Institutional systems
Socialization, 18, 23, 32, 45-46, 73,
    115, 119, 156, 188, 190, 195, 229,
    245-246, 268, 271, 277, 293, 308,
    313, 341
  and education, 137, 166, 170-175,
    176-177
  policy issues of, 32-33, 87
Social justice, 120, 123, 249, 250,
    256, 265, 282
Social life, changes in, 59-64
Social orders, 105, 131-132, 144, 152,
    186, 245, 250
  alternative, fear of, 122-123
  changes in, 139, 144-145, 158, 179,

    181, 189, 207-208, 228-229, 235,
    293, 295-302
  egalitarian and humanistic, 66, 105,
    111-123, 130, 133-134, 137, 152,
    156, 160-161, 176-177, 199-202,
    203-205, 209, 256-257, 294
  maintenance of, 143-144, 188, 203,
    220, 228, 230, 231-232, 244-246,
    248, 249, 273, 294, 296
  prevailing, 118, 130, 134-140, 154,
    170, 187-188, 204-205
Social policies
  alternative, 19, 20, 22, 70, 74, 76,
    82, 95-98, 112-120, 252-255, 376
  analysis of, xviii-xix, 36, 69-100
  analysts of, xviii-xix, xxii, 3-10, 77,
    98
  benefits of, 71, 82, 353
  changes in, 16, 22, 35-37, 51, 108
    109, 111, 112, 119, 123, 144
  and collective interests, 107
  common domain or focus of, x, 20,
    22-23, 70, 74-75, 75-76, 106
  conceptual model of, xviii, xix, xx,
    9-10, 20-24, 26, 82
  costs of, 71, 82, 109
  definition of, 3-10, 13, 21-22, 24-
    25, 62, 143
  development of, 69-100, 106-111
  and economic policies, 9-10, 38-39
  effects of, 69, 71, 80-82
  evaluation of, 19, 26, 112
  evolution of, 13-16, 19, 22, 58-64,
    144, 149
  forces affecting, 58-64, *63*, 89-95
  and foreign influence, 93-94
  and foreign policies, 94, 120-122,
    123
  framework for analysis and devel-